Teaching in the Early Years

Teaching in the Early Years

BERNARD SPODEK

Professor of Early Childhood Education
University of Illinois

PRENTICE-HALL, INC., Englewood Cliffs, New Jersey

PRENTICE-HALL SERIES IN EARLY CHILDHOOD
Bernard Spodek, Editor

© Copyright 1972 by Prentice-Hall, Inc.,
Englewood Cliffs, New Jersey

Library of Congress Catalog Card Number: 72–075000

PRINTED IN THE UNITED STATES OF AMERICA

ISBN: 0–13–892463–5

10 9 8 7 6 5 4 3 2 1

Acknowledgments for chapter-opening photos

Chapter 3: John Pitkin; chapters 5, 7, 9, 10, 11, 13, 15: Joseph DiDio for National
Education Association; chapter 6: Hank Kranzler; chapter 14: Irene B. Bayer for
Monkmeyer Press Photo Service; chapters 2, 4, 8, 12 were taken by the author, 12
with the kind permission of Mrs. Mary Boston, teacher, and the Columbus School
of Champaign, Ill.

PRENTICE-HALL INTERNATIONAL, INC., *London*
PRENTICE-HALL OF AUSTRALIA, PTY. LTD., *Sydney*
PRENTICE-HALL OF CANADA, LTD., *Toronto*
PRENTICE-HALL OF INDIA PRIVATE LIMITED, *New Delhi*
PRENTICE-HALL OF JAPAN, INC., *Tokyo*

To Esther Yin-ling and Jonathan Chou
and to their teachers,
past, present, and future.

Contents

Preface

This book is addressed to teachers and to those who are preparing to be teachers of young children. Although eclectic in its foundation, the approach suggested here is not a conglomerate of all the approaches available in early childhood education today. Rather it is based upon a judgment of what can be done with children, selecting from educational points of view that fit within a consistent framework.

Early childhood education is a unified field, encompassing the nursery, kindergarten, and primary years. While levels may be separated out administratively, children do not change from year to year to fit the expectations of educational grade levels. Change that does occur is gradual and developmental, with differences among individual children. This change is one of the assumptions upon which this volume is based. Other assumptions relate to the nature of early childhood curriculum and the role of the teacher.

Curriculum comes from many sources. Values are an important base of curriculum, as is understanding of how children grow and learn. The various subject areas provide yet another source. The state of the art of education must also be recognized as an important source, determining both possibilities for and limitations of education for young children. Finally, the tradition of the field becomes an important source of classroom practice. The teacher is viewed here as more than just a participant in classroom activities. She is a decision maker whose actions even prior to her entrance into the classroom help determine what will be learned by children.

This book is divided into three parts. The first three chapters provide the foundation for a look at curriculum and teaching in the early years. The second section, Chapters 4 through 10, deals with the specific subject areas that make up the school program. Each chapter is divided into two sections, one reviewing what we know about the particular area of the curriculum and one suggesting the content for school programs and the ways in which this content might be approached. Play is treated as a legitimate part of the school program.

The final portion of the book deals with other educational concerns of the teacher: classroom organization, techniques of working with parents and children, and the evaluation of education. Because the concern for the education of "disadvantaged" children has been given such attention during the past decade and because issues in early childhood education are so wrapped up with issues of the "disadvantaged," no matter how the latter are defined, a separate chapter is devoted to this topic.

An apology is in order to all my male colleagues in the field. Throughout the text, the pronoun *she* is used when referring to the teacher. The decision to use this pronoun is based upon the observation that most teachers of young children are women. No slight is meant to the increasing number of men who, like myself, have found their way into the field of early childhood education.

A number of acknowledgments are also in order. I should like to thank the editors of *Young Children, Phi Delta Kappan*, and the *Peabody Journal of Education* for permission to use, in modified form, material that previously appeared in those journals. I also wish to acknowledge my debt to the many teachers and children with whom I have worked over the past two decades. The ideas expressed here have grown out of many interactions with many people. I should especially like to thank a number of my colleagues for reading and reacting to all or part of this manuscript. They include J. Myron Atkin, Karl Koenke, Harold Lerch, Theodore Manolakes, John McGill, and Mary Weir. Judy Hancock and Jean Patterson helped with the final preparation of the manuscript.

Finally, and most important, I should like to acknowledge the encouragement, love, and support I have received and continue to receive from my wife Prudence.

BERNARD SPODEK

Teaching in the Early Years

Teaching

A roomful of children in the early years of school presents an exciting picture. Children may be involved in a number of activities that are all available at the same time. Many different instructional materials may be in use and there will be a continual shifting of activities as children move through the daily program. Groups of children will form and reform and individuals may continually vie for the attention of the teacher.

Whether standing in front of the classroom commanding the attention of all the children or sitting quietly in a corner working with a small group, the teacher is the center of all activity. Directly or indirectly, she controls much of the activity of the classroom and is responsible for all that occurs to these children during school. She must respond to their many needs as they become manifest during the day. She must assure that there is purpose to the activities that occur and that there is educational benefit received by the children as a result of school activity.

The teacher's role requires her to perform many different tasks. She functions as lecturer, story teller, group discussion leader, traffic director, mediator of conflicts, psychological diagnostician, custodian, assigner of academic work, and file clerk as she operates in her multifaceted role. Most important of these occasions are the times when she must directly interact with children. The interactions may be verbal, as in a discussion, or they may be behavioral, as when she places her arm around a child's shoulders or puts a child on her knee. The interactions may be gross, such as moving a child from one part of the room to another, or subtle, such as giving a child a "knowing look."

Teacher-child interactions serve many purposes. They are used to further instruction and to provide information about the child as well as to communicate emotional support and assurance. Because the interactions of teacher and child are so easily observable, they have been the focus of a number of studies of the nature of teaching. Many educational evaluators have suggested that a teacher's performance should be judged using criteria based upon observable behavior, which is primarily within the range of teacher-child interaction.

The classroom behavior of teachers, however, is not all there is to teaching, and, as a matter of fact, may represent its least rational aspects. Much of the activity of teaching occurs away from children. This activity includes the determination of what to teach, the selection, procurement, and organization of materials and equipment for teaching, the evaluation of learning, and the recording and reporting of children's progress.

Jackson has differentiated between two modes of teaching behavior —*preactive* teaching and *interactive* teaching:

> Preactive behavior is more or less deliberate. Teachers, when grading exams, planning a lesson, or deciding what to do about a particularly difficult student, tend to ponder the matter, to weigh evidence, to hypothesize about the possible outcomes of a certain action. During these moments teachers often resemble, albeit crudely, the stereotype of the problem solver, the decision maker, the hypothesis tester, the inquirer. At such times teaching looks like a highly rational process.
>
> . . . In the interactive setting the teacher's behavior is more or less spontaneous. When students are in front of him, and the fat is in the fire, so to speak, the teacher tends to do what he *feels*, or *knows*, rather than what he *thinks*, is right.[1]

Jackson suggests that the differences in teachers' cognitive styles that are evident in preactive and interactive teaching behavior stem from two conditions of the interactive phase of teaching: the fact that the students place controls on what the teacher does, and the rapidity of events that occur in the classroom. The teacher is to a great extent reacting to the children in her class. The children control the behavior of the teacher by forcing certain responses which are necessitated by their initial action. The control is not necessarily conscious. Jackson suggests that there are approximately one thousand changes in the teacher's focus of concern that take place during the day—far too many to be able to handle individually in a rational, problem-solving manner. The teacher is responding to rapid occurrence all during the school day, and the style of behavior required is more often intuitive than analytic.

Understanding the intuitive nature of interactive teaching helps to explain why this form of teaching is so resistant to change, especially

[1]Philip W. Jackson, "The Way Teaching Is," in *The Way Teaching Is* (Washington, D.C.: Association for Supervision and Curriculum Development, 1966), p. 13.

through the tactics used in most teacher education programs. Courses, conferences, and workshops are verbally oriented activities that focus primarily on the language of teaching. These activities can help set the rational basis for the profession. It is the more practice-oriented teacher education activities such as classroom participation, microteaching, or student teaching that seem to have a better chance of changing the interactive behavior of teaching.

The behavior of teachers, however, does have a rational basis. How one behaves is a function of how one feels he ought to behave, and what one feels is right cannot be fully separated from what one thinks is right. Perhaps the process of teacher education needs to include, to some extent, the training of intuition based upon rational thought.

A volume such as this must address itself to the more rational aspects of teaching behavior, assuming that discourse about teaching will ultimately affect not only the thoughts of teachers but their behavior as well. It is based upon the assumption that the professional actions of teachers are primarily manifest in the decision-making process during the time children are in the presence of teachers as well as when teachers are operating alone. It is, as a matter of fact, the decision-making process that is at the heart of the professional behavior of teachers.

TEACHING AS INSTRUCTION

When we think of teaching, we usually conceive of the instructional role of the teacher.

If a number of laymen were asked to describe what a teacher does, they would probably paint a verbal picture of a person in front of a group of children in a classroom, talking to the children. The conventional view of the teacher is that of a person who transmits knowledge to others through some form of verbalization. The use of books, displays, or audio-visual devices becomes another way of telling something to pupils.

Such a view of teaching is based upon a set of assumptions about knowledge and about schools that often remains unexamined. One assumption is that knowledge consists of a body of facts and information; this knowledge can be assimilated by an individual who has read or heard the facts and information. The teacher has the role of determining what knowledge is important for the children in her class. (That decision may have been made for her already.) Then the teacher "tells" the children what they must know through some forms of lectures, storytelling, or demonstrations, as well as through the use of more sophisticated forms of telling such as films, sound recordings, or television. Over the years the child attends school he accumulates more facts and more information and therefore becomes more knowledgeable.

This represents a rather simplistic view of education and the development of knowledge. Knowledge is not the result of an accumulation of facts and information but rather the result of an integration of information within some structure that gives it meaning. Facts are the raw data from which knowledge is developed, and as raw data, may be easily discarded once used. To create knowledge a person, whether adult or young child, must *do* something to these facts; he must become an active seeker and creator of knowledge. To be a passive receiver of what is told to him is not enough to make the child a true learner.

Unfortunately the instructional role of the teacher has been identified as focal by key educators as well as by lay persons. Much of the research on teaching focuses on teacher behavior in the classroom, often in the instructional roles. The analysis of teaching may only deal with the verbal interaction of teachers and children within an instructional framework. When this happens, much of the teaching role remains unstudied.

Viewing only the instructional role of teaching has also led to what many educators have called "competency-based" programs of teacher education. By identifying the instructional behaviors of teachers in the classroom, one can identify the "competencies" that teachers need for effectiveness in their instruction. These competencies, once identified, can be taught and practiced until fully assimilated.

The concept of the teacher as instructor is inadequate for an understanding of the role of the teacher, as is this concept of teacher training. Although the instructional aspect of teaching is valid and important, it is only part of the whole picture.

THE TEACHER AS A PERSON

While some educators view the instructional role of the teacher as crucial, others view the relational aspect of teaching as being of primary importance. The teacher is continually interacting with children during the school day, and the quality of these interactions may be more important than the specific instructional practices used by the teacher.

Combs defines the effective teacher as "a unique human being who has learned to use himself effectively and efficiently to carry out his own and society's purposes in the education of others."[2] The use of oneself in carrying out the purposes of education includes professional competency, but it goes beyond that. It requires that the teacher's total self, the personal side as well as the professional side, be involved in the

---

[2]Arthur W. Combs, *The Professional Education of Teachers* (Boston: Allyn and Bacon, 1965), p. 9.

education process. How the teacher relates to children, parents, and other persons becomes important. Developing ways of relating to and interacting with people is an important part of becoming a teacher.

In addition to providing instruction, the teacher serves as a guide and a helper to the children. She must create an atmosphere in the classroom in which children gain a sense of trust. The teacher helps the child feel secure as a learner and as a person; she serves as a guide, helping the child make his own decisions, and provides a rich environment for learning.

Above all, the teacher provides warmth and nurturance for the children. The relationship established in the classroom is not based on achievement alone. Children are accepted as they are—total human beings with strengths and weaknesses. Through her personal relationship with the child, the teacher helps him to grow.

Although teachers can be taught appropriate behaviors for classroom settings, the relational aspects of teaching are not based upon any set of teacher actions; what is important is that the teacher manifest her own personality in an authentic way. Teacher-training programs concerned with the teacher as a person must go beyond conventional courses in methods and foundations of education; they must help students explore the meaning that education and teaching has for them and help them understand the nature of their relationships with others.

**TEACHING AS
DECISION MAKING**
With the increase in the use of teacher aides and assistants, educators have been hard-pressed to differentiate the role of the professional from that of the paraprofessional. In many cases the aide acts almost as a junior teacher. The major difference lies not in the kinds of interactions that take place between the adult, professional or paraprofessional and the children, but rather in the responsibility taken for these actions. The paraprofessional acts, in many ways, as an extension of the teacher, who has ultimate responsibility for the class and who must make the major decisions about classroom activity. Some of these decisions are made prior to the time the children enter the class. Many decisions, however, must be made on the spot, in reaction to specific situations.

How does the teacher make decisions to immediate situations? She may, for example, decide that a group reading situation is appropriate at a particular time. A host of decisions follow. She may ask herself the following questions:

Should I read a story or tell a story?
Which book should I select?
Should the story precede the cleanup from the prior period of activity or should it be reserved for after the cleanup?

Should all the childen be expected to attend to the story, or should the story be read to a few, with alternative activities available?

Should the children sit on chairs, on the floor in a semicircle, or simply informally grouped around me?

Should I show the pictures in the book as I read?

If a child disrupts, should I interrupt the reading to focus on that one child, or should I ignore him until I have finished?

If the class seems restless, should I stop reading the story momentarily, lead the class in a few finger-plays, and then continue?

Should I stop the activity and move on to something else, or should I ignore their behavior?

Should I ask the children questions about the content of the story upon its completion to test what they have learned from listening, or should I simply let the story "sink in"?

Should I relate the story to other activities of the day, or should I allow the experience to remain isolated?

How should I move the children on to the next activity?

Within a rather simple five-minute segment of the school day the teacher may have had to make a dozen decisions. Multiply this by the 360 five-minute periods that might confront a teacher of young children during a school day, and one realizes the complexity of the decision-making process within any teaching situation.

A FRAMEWORK FOR ANALYZING DECISION MAKING

What are the legitimate bases for teacher decision making? Unfortunately, there has been little study done on the decision-making process in education. What few studies there are of the teaching process have focused on the *behavior* of teachers, the *reasons* for the behavior often being assumed. Teachers are not robots, however. Their behavior must be seen as a selection of possible alternative behaviors from a range of options.

The decisions that teachers make can be roughly organized into three categories: policy decisions, institutional decisions, and technical decisions. Policy decisions are related generally to the setting of goals for education. Institutional decisions are those related to the maintenance of the school. Technical decisions relate to the "nuts and bolts" activities of the teacher as she carries out educational policies.

Policy Decisions

Policy decisions, relating to the goals and purposes of education, may be stated in a high level of abstraction or may be more specific in nature. Goals of instruction are usually derived from statements of *values* as well as from *educational ideologies*. Values are statements about the worth of things and their desirability, often in societal terms. These may relate to concepts of the "good life" that a community holds.

An ideology refers to a belief. It is possible to hold specific beliefs about the nature of the childhood, the role of the teacher, and the purposes of schools that are independent of values but are basic to the policy decisions made about education. While a particular goal might be considered worthy in its own right, it may be viewed as inappropriate for the school or for a specific level of childhood. Teachers might consider it appropriate to support autonomous learning in children, but their ideology could lead them to believe that young children are necessarily dependent on adults and that opportunities for autonomous behavior should necessarily be postponed until later in the life of the child.

Historically, teachers in American schools have had little involvement in policy decisions. While for decades educational philosophers debated the purposes of school and the goals of education, the establishment of policy for a particular school or school system was always well-removed from the classroom teacher. Policy was to be made "downtown" and to be adhered to by teachers. Educational policy was viewed as being outside the "professional" sphere.

In school systems, policy is the domain of the board of education, a group of knowledgeable laymen who speak for the community. Even community nursery schools, outside the body of public education, often have their governing boards, independent of teacher or administrator, to set policy. The Head Start program, noted for its parent and community involvement, also requires the establishment of local Policy Advisory Boards.

The relationship of the professional to policy decision making is a tenuous one. The professional educator possesses knowledge of educational alternatives and is often in the position where he can weigh the possible outcomes of policy decisions. His role, however, is usually viewed as advisory—that of helping lay people see possible consequences of their decisions, although by controlling the lay person's access to information he can significantly influence policy decisions.

While policy decisions in school have been considered outside the domain of the teacher's responsibility, teachers have nevertheless become involved. In many school systems, they have been involved in the work of curriculum committees that set educational policy for the school, determining the goals of instruction in each program area and formulating the general strategies by which these goals are to be achieved. These committees are also charged with recommending the materials, printed and otherwise, to be used by the teacher in helping the children achieve these goals. Although the work of such committees still must have the approval of lay authorities, such approval is often more ceremonial than real.

On a less organized basis, teachers have also involved themselves in policy decisions. They have a major influence in seeing that policies are carried out; policy may be changed by the nature of its administration. A school may state a specific policy for promotion and retention, but this policy statement remains valid only as long as the teachers adhere to it. If, for example, specific criteria for promotion are stated but teachers refuse to recognize them, the actual school policy in this matter may be quite different from that stated by the school system.

Recently teachers have become involved in a more organized manner than ever before in the determination of policy decisions for schools. The whole area of professional negotiations for teachers is a relatively new one in American education. Unions and professional associations, through contract negotiations, have demanded a voice in the setting of salary and working conditions for teachers.

In many cases, the negotiations of teachers have moved beyond bargaining about "bread-and-butter" issues and are beginning to focus on school policy as well. Statements relating to school discipline, class size, and the selection of curriculum materials are becoming as much the basis for professional negotiations as is the salary index. Teachers are currently beginning to demand the same voice in educational policy that other professionals have in the determination of their professional behavior.

Institutional Decisions

Institutional decisions have no direct bearing on the achievement of educational goals, but rather are concerned with the maintenance of the school itself. Many of the decisions about staffing and grouping are institutional ones, for they cannot be understood in terms of the achievement of educational goals.

Similarly, classroom teachers make decisions about children which have nothing to do with the achievement of educational goals but which are directed toward the maintenance of the school as an institution. The teacher may demand that children remain quiet in classrooms, stay in their own seats, and speak only when spoken to. Such demands can only be related to policy if the policy of the school is the establishment of conformity in children. This is seldom the case. These decisions, however, can be understood in terms of the maintenance of order, which is deemed necessary for the operation of even the school in which conformity is not valued. Many classroom decisions that teachers make are institutional in nature. Gracey has suggested that many of the activities of the kindergarten are designed primarily to teach children appropriate student responses rather than to prepare them for academic or intellectual pursuits.[3]

[3]Harry L. Gracey, "Learning the Student Role: Kindergarten as Academic Boot Camp," in Dennis W. Wrong and Harry L. Gracey, eds., *Readings in Introductory Sociology* (New York: Macmillan, 1967), pp. 288–99.

The need to make institutional decisions is not good or bad in and of itself. Educational institutions need to be maintained as vehicles for the achievement of educational goals. Too often, however, institutions develop a life of their own and care must be taken that the institutional decisions that are made are not in conflict with the policy decisions of the school.

Technical Decisions

Technical decisions relate to the translation of policy into classroom activity and to the development of educational experiences that will help achieve goals determined in educational policy. Long- and short-range classroom planning belongs at this level of decision making, as does the selection and deployment of educational resources.

Ultimately technical decisions have to do with the matching of educational resources to the educational needs of children. This suggests the diagnostic model of teaching. The diagnostic teacher uses her knowledge and skill to elicit information from children through testing or observation, and she also uses her intuitive ability to sense nontestable sources of data. Like the good doctor, the teacher is able to prescribe as well as diagnose. There is no single effective program or method of instruction that is most suitable for all children at all times. A teacher must be able to match methods and materials to children in order to achieve goals. This requires that she have a range of techniques and materials available so that she may effect the match. She may find that she can be more effective with some methods than others, and may depend heavily on a few that reflect her style. Flexibility and sensitivity are still needed.

The teacher must know each child as a person and be aware of his learning abilities and style of behavior. She is then in a position to make differentiated educational decisions concerning individuals, decisions such as the educational activities in which they should be involved, the social interactions that should be supported, or the amount of freedom or structure in which activities should be framed.

A knowledge of alternative ways of achieving policy goals is important if the teacher is to operate in a diagnostic fashion. While all children may ultimately be expected to achieve the same goals, they may be starting from different positions based upon levels of maturity or differentiated background experiences. An approach to learning might be more appropriate for one child than for another because of these reasons, or even because of different personal styles. A range of alternative methods and materials available to the teacher allows her to make decisions based upon her judgment of individual appropriateness.

Finally, the teacher must develop means of assessing the consequences of school activities for individuals. Judgments made about earlier experiences should be used as the basis for providing later experiences. Such decisions require not only a knowledge of the child and the curriculum but also a knowledge of the teaching field. The teacher must be skilled personally and must be aware of the results of research, development, and practice activities in the field.

The discussion in this chapter has referred to teaching in general. Is teaching in the early years of school no different than teaching at any other level? Although the general processes of teaching can be found at all levels, how they are manifest, and which aspects of teaching are focal varies from one educational level to another.

Teaching as decision making is crucial at all levels. It is the basis for planned experiences. The basis for decision making, however, is different in the early years. What children can learn in the early years is more a function of developmental level than in any other period of schooling. In addition, the greater dependency of young children on the teacher requires different kinds of behaviors and organization. Similarly, the relational aspects of teaching, with its concern for providing support and nurturance, are of prime importance, while the instructional aspects of teaching are of lesser importance in these early years.

A BASIS FOR DECISION MAKING

What are the bases for the teacher's decision making? They are probably as varied as the decisions themselves. Some of the sources that teachers use are found in the history and traditions of the field, and others in the statements of accepted goals of early childhood education. Additional sources include the bodies of knowledge from which academic subjects have been derived and the bodies of knowledge related to the teaching of children: curriculum and method. Special consideration needs to be given to play as an educational method in early childhood education and the uses to which play can be put.

Other sources of decision making need to be identified as well. Institutional decisions are often related to the organization of the classroom and the deployment of resources and persons in school. Ultimately, one must judge the consequences of the decisions that teachers make, determining what has transpired as a result of earlier decisions as the basis for the making of future decisions.

This, then, is the organization of the rest of this volume. The next two chapters deal with the models of schools and the curriculum of early childhood education. These relate to teachers' policy decisions. The chapters that follow address themselves to content and method in the instructional area of reading, language arts, mathematics, science, social studies, music, and art. A chapter is also provided on play as a tool of learning.

These chapters relate to the technical decisions of teaching. Chapters on classroom organization and ways of working with children are related to institutional teaching decisions. Special consideration is given to programs for parents, since they, as well as the children, are the clients of early childhood education.

Because the education of disadvantaged children has become so important an issue in the field of early childhood education, a chapter is devoted to this area as well. The final chapter concerns the area of evaluation, which can help teachers judge their goals and their effectiveness in achieving these goals; adequate judgments of teachers' decisions can only result from adequate evaluation.

SUGGESTED READING

FRAZIER, ALEXANDER, ed., *Early Childhood Education Today*. Washington, D.C.: Association for Supervision and Curriculum Development, 1968.

FROST, JOE, ed., *Early Childhood Education Rediscovered*. New York: Holt, Rinehart & Winston, 1969.

HECHINGER, FRED M., *Preschool Education Today*. Garden City, New York: Doubleday, 1966.

HESS, ROBERT D., and ROBERTA M. BEAR, eds., *Early Education: Current Research, Theory and Action*. Chicago: Aldine Publishing Company, 1968.

HYMES, JAMES L., *Teaching the Child Under Six*. Columbus, Ohio: Charles E. Merrill, 1968.

WEBER, EVELYN, *Early Childhood Education: Perspectives on Change*. Worthington, Ohio: Charles A. Jones Publishing Co., 1970.

2

Schools For Young Children

Early childhood education in the United States is practiced in nursery schools, day-care centers, Head Start programs, kindergartens, and primary classes. While there are many common elements among these institutions, there are differences as well—differences in institutional setting, age of children served, traditions from which the programs developed, goals set for programs, and psychological theories subscribed to. A look at the traditions of early childhood education, contemporary models of early childhood schools, and some alternatives to these schools presently being advocated should help in understanding the field as it is presently organized.

Almost all children attend elementary schools, beginning at about age six in grade one. Currently, more than half of all five-year-olds attend kindergarten. The U.S. Office of Education figures that about 69 percent of all five-year-olds attended kindergarten in 1969, with nursery school attended by about 23 percent of all four-year-olds and over 8 percent of three-year-olds.[1]

Much of the material in this and the succeeding chapter has been adapted by the author from the following articles:

Bernard Spodek, "Early Learning for What?" *Phi Delta Kappan*, Vol. 50, No. 7 (March 1970), 394–96.

————, "What Are the Sources of Early Childhood Curriculum?" *Young Children*, Vol. 26, No. 1 (October 1970), 48–58.

————, "Alternatives to Traditional Education," *Peabody Journal of Education*, Vol. 48, No. 2 (January 1971), 140–48.

[1]Gordon Hurd, *Preprimary Enrollment* (Washington, D.C.: U.S. Office of Education, October 1969).

The fact that not all young children can be expected to attend school significantly influences any decisions related to a long-range sequence of learning. In addition, many children are in schools not influenced by public policy.

The sponsorship of an early childhood program may determine the emphases in the program. Nursery schools in social welfare agencies often stress welfare and nurturance concepts rather than academic concepts in their programs; church-supported schools may stress moral and religious training.

The administrative organization of a school or school system may well determine the kinds of decisions made, as well as the method of decision making. Some schools allow teachers to make important educational decisions. In other schools, decisions are handed down from a central authority. Often, decisions will be made in large systems that perpetuate the structure of the system, irrespective of their effect on children.

In many schools, the range of options available to a teacher is determined not by the administrator, but by the faculty. There may be a set of implicit guidelines that are shared by these teachers. Neither the influence of the administration or of a single teacher can effect change if the change falls outside these guidelines. Schools are communities, each with its inherent power structure. A recognition of the nature of the community and the values held by its members (teachers and administrators) can help a teacher understand how educational decisions are made.

THE ROOTS OF EARLY CHILDHOOD EDUCATION

Some of the differences in early childhood education stem from the distinct traditions and backgrounds that helped to develop the separate institutions of the nursery, kindergarten, and primary grades. Each institution was developed and influenced by educators and philosophers with different points of view and from different cultures. As the years have passed, the institutions have been modified, influenced by different schools of educational thought and different contemporary cultural contexts.

The Primary School

The primary grades have been conceived to provide instruction in the basic skills subjects. Reading, writing, and computational skills are the core of learning and teaching at this level. While other areas of study may be included in the program of the primary grades, these are never afforded the status of the skill areas, and may be removed, limited, or shifted around. A teacher would not have the same freedom to eliminate or even limit instruction in reading as she might in science or art.

The goal of contemporary primary education descends directly from the goal of colonial primary education. Especially in the New England colonies, the pressure of religious belief required that persons be able to read the scriptures in the vernacular. This led to the establishment of primary schools under the supervision of the community church. The content of the schools was the teaching of reading, with instruction in spelling, grammar, and arithmetic added later.

The preamble to the Puritan School Law of 1647 gives evidence to the religious roots of colonial primary education:

> It being one chief point of that old deluder, Satan, to keep men from the knowledge of the Scriptures, as in former times, by keeping them in an unknown tongue, so in these latter times, by persuading from the use of tongues, that so at last the true sense and meaning of the original might be clouded by false glosses of saint-seeming deceivers, that learning might not be buried in the grave of our fathers in church and commonwealth, the Lord assisting our endeavors,—It is therefore ordered that every township in this jurisdiction, after the Lord has increased them to the number of fifty householders, shall then forthwith appoint one within their town to teach all such children as shall resort to him to write and read.[2]

As the American colonies became a nation, the content of school learning lost some of its religious flavor as concern for developing patriotism in children grew. The content of primers used for reading instruction in the late eighteenth century shifted from excerpts from or about the Bible to tales of patriotism and morality. Now the school was viewed as a unifying force for the New America. In the nineteenth century, the education of children became a public concern, and schools began to receive financial support from the states. At this time, the concept of universal education began to take hold, and children of all backgrounds were admitted into the publicly supported schools.

While the primary school of the early nineteenth century was basically concerned with teaching the "Three R's," new elements of instruction were slowly added to the curriculum: arts and crafts, nature study (later to be supplanted by science), geography (later to be incorporated into the social studies), music, and physical education.

Teachers in the colonial primary schools were hired with little

---

[2]E. Nohle, in *Report of the United States Commissioner of Education* (1897–98), Vol. I., 24–25, as reported in C.S. Parker and Alice Temple, *Unified Kindergarten and First-Grade Teaching* (Chicago: Department of Education, University of Chicago, 1924), p. 6.

regard for professional qualifications or credentials. Often indentured servants or widowed women served as teachers. The method of instruction consisted mainly of recitation and rote memorization, with the limited number of textbooks available providing the core of the instructional program.

New educational methodologies were developing in Europe during the nineteenth century that were to have their impact on the American primary school. Interpretations of the Pestallozzian system of education, with its emphasis on education through objects, were leading to new developments in German primary education. Reports about these schools influenced American educators to modify their verbal methods of teaching and to enrich their curricula. The establishment of normal schools for the preparation of teachers helped to increase the concern of American educators about teaching methodology.

During the latter half of the nineteenth century, the educational philosophy of the German educator Herbart greatly influenced the American primary school. Educational lessons were organized into five steps of the Herbartian system: preparation, presentation, association, generalization, and application. All lessons were to start with preparation of the class and all learnings were to culminate in the child's demonstration of his ability to apply new learning. Remnants of the Herbartian method still remain in the organization of lesson plans, which may begin with "motivating the children" and end in a "culminating activity."

The American Progressive Education movement had a great impact upon the organization of instruction in the primary grades during the first half of the twentieth century. In many cases, the Herbartian lessons gave way to the more organic *project* method, which in turn led to the *unit* approach that one may find in some science and social studies programs.

The move toward urbanization and the development of large schools and school systems in the nineteenth century also led to a change in the organizational patterns of primary education. The nongraded structure of the one-room country school was supplanted by the multiroom school organized by grade, with instructional objectives determined and all children of like age being grouped together in a single class.

The Infant School, a form of primary education in Britain, was founded in 1816 in New Lanark, Scotland, by Robert Owen, the social reformer. The original principles of infant education were:

> that the children were to be out of doors as much as possible and to learn 'when their curiosity induced them to ask questions,' to dance and sing and not to be 'annoyed with books.' They were to be educated and trained without punishment or the fear of it, no unnecessary restraint was to be imposed on them and they were to be taught only 'what they could understand.' The

teachers were told to think about such matters as forming good habits and helping the children to treat each other kindly.[3]

Owen's school was designed for the children of workers in his mill and was conceived as a part of a broader program of social reform. Owen's conception of the Infant School foreshadowed the concerns of many contemporary educators. As the Infant School developed in England, however, it took on characteristics similar to those of the American primary school with its stress on book learning and the immobility of the children. Some of the English concepts of infant education of the last decade are closely related to the original ideas of Owen.

The Froebelian Kindergarten

The kindergarten was developed in Germany in the first half of the nineteenth century. Based upon a mystical religious philosophy relating to the unity of man and nature, man and God, and man and other men, Froebel designed a series of activities for children aged three to six to symbolize these relationships. The Froebelian kindergarten was composed, in essence, of the use of the *Gifts*, the *Occupations*, and the *Mother's Plays*, as well as the care of plants and animals.

The *Gifts* were a set of small manipulative materials to be used by children in prescribed ways. The first of these was a series of six yarn balls, each a different color. The single surface of the ball, a sphere, symbolized the unity and wholeness of the universe. The next set—a wooden sphere, a cylinder, and a cube—represented unity and diversity, as well as the mediation of opposites—the sphere and cube representing opposites, the cylinder representing a mediating shape. Other *Gifts*, including a cube broken up into smaller cubes, followed by square and triangular tablets, were presented to children in a prescribed sequence. At each presentation, children were supposed to build specific forms, each one representing some deeper meaning. Throughout the manipulations, little attention was paid to the physical properties of the objects, for sensation and perception of the real world were not considered important.

The *Occupation*, consisting of weaving, paper-folding, cutting, sewing, drawing, painting, and clay modeling, reflected the activities of primitive man. They also provided the children with opportunities for artistic expression. The *Mother's Plays*, specifically designed songs and games, were derived from the play of peasant women with their young children and from the activities of the social and natural world.

[3]D.E.M. Gardner, *Education Under Eight* (London: Longmans, Green and Co., n.d.), p. 6.

In time, the Froebelian kindergarten began to expand as an educational movement, and kindergartens were established in many German communities. With the extension of kindergarten education, there came a need for training "kindergarteners," as kindergarten teachers were then called. Soon kindergarten training institutions began to attract a number of young German women as their students. It is interesting to note that the original kindergarten teachers were men. Froebel approved of women kindergarteners later in life, after his marriage.

With the wave of German migration in the mid-nineteenth century, many German women with kindergarten training came to the United States. The desire to apply the principles of the Froebelian kindergarten to their own children led many of these women to establish kindergartens in their homes. Mrs. Karl Schurz, who was trained as a kindergartener in Germany, invited the children of relatives into her home to join her own children in what became the first American kindergarten in Watertown, Wisconsin, in 1855. Other kindergartens were established in the homes of German-American women and in German-American academies in various communities in the United States in the 1850s and 1860s.

Mrs. Elizabeth Peabody became interested in kindergarten education through her reading and through contact with Mrs. Schurz. She established the first English-speaking kindergarten in Boston in 1860. The philosophy of Froebel was compatible with that of New England Transcendentalism, a philosophic movement that provided intellectual support for the establishment of kindergarten programs in America. Although kindergartens were introduced into the public schools of St. Louis by 1873, the inclusion of kindergarten in public education did not become common for at least two more decades. Kindergartens were being established in many cities during this time, however, by various associations and mothers' clubs and by philanthropic agencies.

The kindergarten was seen as especially useful to the children of the poor in these early days. With the rapid rise of urban centers, the immigration of Europeans to America, and the growth of large city slums, philanthropic kindergartens were established in many areas. Arguments, not unlike those heard today in support of the Head Start program, were used to support kindergarten education for the poor:

> Centering among, and concerning itself with, the children of the poor, and having for its aim the elevation of the home, it was natural that the kindergarten as a philanthropic movement should win great and early favor. The mere fact that the children of the slums were kept off the streets, and that they were made clean and happy by kind and motherly young women; that the child thus being cared for enabled the mother to go about her work in or outside the home—all this appealed to the heart of America, and America gave freely to make these kindergartens possible. Churches established

kindergartens, individuals endowed kindergartens, and associations were organized for the spread and support of kindergartens in nearly every large city.[4]

By the beginning of the twentieth century, a significant rift developed in American kindergarten education. Traditional kindergarten educators felt that Froebel had discovered the significant elements of education for young children that were relevant to all children at all times. A more liberal group saw greater meaning in Froebel's educational philosophy than in the specific educational activities and methods derived from it. This liberal group felt that while the original kindergarten program was a step in the right direction, specific activities ought to be discarded when inappropriate. The emergence of the Child Study Movement, which was then establishing an empirical base of knowledge about childhood through the study and observation of children, and the progressive education movement, with its emphasis on freedom and activity in the classroom, lent support to the liberal kindergarteners.

The emerging philosophy of the reform kindergarten movement was probably best stated by Patty Smith Hill in the *Second Report of the Committee of Twelve of the International Kindergarten Union* presented in 1913. According to her, the content of the kindergarten program should be related to the present life of the child rather than to the life of children of another culture and another generation. The child should be helped to acquire the knowledge of the civilization, which is best done by using the child's personal experiences as a means of achieving insight into knowledge. Hill proposed concrete child-oriented experiences and classroom play that was based more upon the natural activities of childhood, in which the child was free to reconstruct his own reality. The reform movement tried to retain the philosophy of Froebel while doing away with the unnecessary formalism of kindergarten method.

Some of the elements of Froebelian philosophy supported by these educators included:

1. The concept of development in childhood. Froebel's basic concept that the young child is not a miniature adult suggested that education for young children ought to be different in form and content from that offered to older children. While Froebel's conception of child development is incompatible with present knowledge, the educational implications of the assumption that education ought to be developmentally oriented remains sound.

[4]Laura Fisher, Report of the Commissioner of Education as quoted in Vanderwalker, *The Kindergarten in American Education* (New York: The Macmillan Co., 1908), pp. 19–20.

2. *Education as self-activity.* Education takes place as the human organism unfolds. The child's involvement in educational activity supports this unfolding process. Here, too, we find that while child development has moved from an acceptance of an "unfolding" process, the concept of education as self-activity is still supported in education.

3. *The educational value of play.* Froebel saw play as an important activity in helping the child mature and learn. In play, Froebel observed the child's symbolic reproductions of adult activity. He attempted to abstract the significant elements of these and provide them in a meaningful order in his educational program. This idea of the use of play in the education of young children is still supported by educators.

The kindergarten reformers felt that many of the Froebelian occupations were too tedious and required hand movements too small to be appropriate for young children. They also felt that other arts and crafts activities could be profitably included in the kindergarten program. Since the play of the American child was different from that of the German child, different kinds of play activities should also be encouraged. In addition, the reformers felt that the child's current life should provide a source of learning. School play became freer and more reflective of the child's life. Large blocks replaced the *Gifts* for constructions, and dolls and miniature housekeeping materials were included in the program.

The reform of kindergarten education continued through the 1920s and 1930s, leading to the creation of the modern American kindergarten we find in many schools today. A number of factors have influenced the development of kindergarten education since the 1920s. The changing economy of the 1930s and 1940s saw a lessening in the number of public school kindergartens as shortages in funds and building space led to the exclusion of this level of education from the public schools. The influence of the mental health movement led to an increase in concern for social-emotional learnings and a deemphasizing of the "habit-training" of the 1920s. In the late 1950s and 1960s, kindergarten education began to receive more positive attention. A concern for intellectual development in children led to a reexamination of kindergarten curricula. In addition, psychological theory pointing up the importance of early education gave support to increased public aid for kindergartens and the extension of kindergarten education to large numbers of children in many states.

The Nursery School

The nursery school movement developed from a different culture context than did the kindergarten. Out of their experience in English health clinics for children of the poor, Rachel and Margaret Macmillan conceived of the nursery school as a preventive for children's illnesses, both mental and physical, that were so prevalent in the slums. The basic philosophy of nursery education was one of *nurturance.*

Nurturance was conceived of as dealing with the whole child, including the social, physical, emotional, and intellectual aspects of the human being. The responsibilities of the original nursery school included bathing the children, clothing them in clean outfits, resting them, and seeing that they got plenty of fresh air, all at the same time they were being educated. The original nursery schools established in the slums of London were single-story buildings with large doorways or French windows that opened into gardens and large play spaces. Children's play flowed freely between the indoors and outdoors.

The educational program developed by the Macmillans was social rather than religious in origin, concerning itself with helping the child learn the observable rather than the symbolic. The Macmillans were influenced more by Seguin than by Froebel in their educational approach. This French educator had developed many activities to improve the sensory education of retarded children. His influence can be seen in current programs for "special" children as well as in the Montessori method.

For the three- and four-year-olds, the program of the nursery school included learning the skills involved in caring for oneself (washing, tying shoelaces, and so forth) and taking care of special responsibilities having to do with plants, keeping animals, or cleaning the school. In addition, specific activities were included to develop the "senses," such as music and rhythmic activities, language activities, and activities that taught form and color. Activities leading to reading and writing as well as number work and science work were recommended by Margaret Macmillan, while Grace Owen, another nursery school pioneer, objected to the introduction of the "Three R's" and object lessons in the curriculum. Free play activities were included in the program, with opportunities for art construction and work with water, sand, and other nonstructured materials.

The work of the Macmillans with children was so successful that nursery schools were given an official stamp of approval by the Fisher Act of 1918, which allowed for the establishment of nursery schools in local school systems throughout England. Unfortunately, the funds needed to establish these programs were not forthcoming and the expansion of opportunities for nursery education was and is today a slow process.

In about 1920, a number of teachers who had worked with Margaret Macmillan and Grace Owen came to the United States to demonstrate the English nursery school. Nursery schools were started at Teachers College, Columbia University, the Merrill Palmer School of Motherhood and Home Training, and several other agencies in the United States. Many of these schools enrolled children younger than the presently accepted beginning age of three.

During the next decade the idea of the nursery school spread slowly throughout the United States. A survey of nursery schools in 1931 listed 203 in existence. About half these schools were related to colleges and universities, a third were privately controlled schools, and a fifth were related to child welfare agencies. This diversity of sponsorship, a continuing characteristic of nursery schools, paralleled their diversity of function. All nursery schools were concerned with educating children. Additional purposes varied with the sponsorship of the school:

> A large number of colleges and universities use the nursery school as a laboratory for the preparation of teachers and for research. The schools sponsored by departments of home economics in colleges and universities act as laboratories and demonstration centers for preparental education and instruction on home management. Relief of parents from daytime care of their children is chiefly supported by nursery schools connected with day nurseries and conducted by family welfare or philanthropic organizations.[5]

In the 1930s, the Great Depression overshadowed all other elements of American culture. The depression had its impact on the development of nursery education. With incomes low and the collection of taxes down, many school systems found that they had to curtail educational services and release teachers whose salaries they could no longer pay. These unemployed teachers became an additional burden to the economy. In 1933, the federal government, first under the Federal Emergency Relief Act (FERA) and then under the Works Projects Administration (WPA), provided money to establish nursery schools which would hire unemployed teachers. These nursery schools operated through normal public school channels. Emergency teacher training programs were instituted to provide teachers with the necessary skills for working with young children.

Many communities took advantage of the opportunity provided by the WPA nursery schools, which not only provided relief to unemployed teachers but provided a valuable educational experience to children as well. Federally sponsored schools were operated in most states in the United States. The number of schools established ran into the thousands, far outstripping the number of nursery schools that had been in existence in this country up to that time.

[5]Mary Dabney Davis, *Nursery Schools: Their Development and Current Practices in the United States,* Bulletin 1932, No. 9, U.S. Office of Education (Washington, D.C.: Government Printing Office, 1933), p. 31.

The end of the depression and the beginning of World War II brought an end to the WPA nursery school as teachers ceased to be an unemployed group. The burgeoning economy, along with the manpower needs of the armed services and the defense industry, required additions to the labor force. The answer to the labor problem was seen in hiring women for war work. Agencies were needed to care for the children of those women workers who were mothers as well. Under the Lanham Act, the federal government again became involved in servicing the needs of young children. Child-care centers were established in most centers of war industry, and care and education were provided to the children of working mothers. These child-care centers often provided services beyond what would presently be considered appropriate, with some of them open on a twenty-four-hour basis, paralleling the three work shifts of the war industries.

Shortly after the end of the war, federal support for these programs was withdrawn. In many cases, however, since the need for the day-care centers remained, they continued to operate under the sponsorship of local governments or philanthropic agencies. Even when operated by the local government, seldom did these centers become a part of the public school system.

The decade of the 1950s saw the expansion of the parent-cooperative nursery school movement. While cooperatives had been established as far back as the 1920s, their greatest growth was in the 1950s. The desire for high quality nursery education at a reasonable cost, as well as the desire for increased parent education, supported this development. In a parent-cooperative nursery school, the parents own the school and may serve as participants in the children's program as well. Often adult classes or parent meetings relating to child development, child rearing practices, or other topics are included as part of the program.

Nursery school education continued to develop slowly under its varied sponsorship until the mid-1960s, when the federal government again became involved in providing preschool education for disadvantaged children under the Economic Opportunity Act and the Elementary and Secondary Education Act.

While nursery school education went through a series of organizational metamorphoses, its development did not elicit the deep theoretical conflict that characterized the development of the kindergarten. This is not to say that nursery programs did not change, but rather that the original eclectic approach to nursery education was broad enough to encompass modification and diversity without serious conflict.

Among the important changes that took place in nursery school thought are the following:

1. The change from nursery education as a program for the poor to nursery education as a program for the affluent. The originators of nursery school conceived of their programs as an antidote for many of the problems of poverty.

In the United States, the nursery school became a source of knowledge about children, a place for young women to practice for motherhood and home management, a place to "keep" children, or a place to educate middle-class children. One of the first nursery schools in the United States was operated by faculty wives of the University of Chicago, a very different socio-economic group than the wives of the workers in the London slums, despite the fact that university salaries were lower in those days than they are today.

This change came about as a consequence of the sponsorship of nursery schools in the United States. Without government support, most nursery schools outside of philanthropic agencies were supported by individual tuition payments, thereby limiting opportunities for nursery education primarily to the children of the affluent.

2. A deemphasis of the health aspects of nursery education. Because the children served by American nursery schools had less need for the total care provided by the English nursery schools, programs were shortened to half-days or school hours and the responsibility for nutrition, health, and hygiene was omitted. Only in day-care centers and the Head Start programs of today, both concerned with providing nursery education to the poor, do we see a manifestation of the original concept of nurturance.

3. A shift from the emphasis on "training the senses" to a more broadly based education. The same conditions that led to the reform movement in the kindergarten led to the shift in emphasis in nursery education. There was less concern for cognitive learning and more for emotional and social learning in the kindergarten. With the current return to a concern for intellectual learning in young children, nursery educators have generally supported broad cognitive skills and strategies rather than the too-specific learning tasks of the original nursery school.

The Montessori School

Paralleling the development of the nursery school in England, there developed a similar institution in Italy, the *casa die bambini*. Dr. Maria Montessori, the originator of this new educational institution, attempted to break from traditional Italian education just as Macmillan had broken from the rigid formalism of the British primary schools. While Montessori education has had a separate development from nursery and kindergarten education, there are interesting parallels between the systems as well as an evident intertwining of ideas, especially in their early years of development.

Dr. Montessori began her work as a physician dealing primarily with retarded children. Impressed by her knowledge of the work of educators of retarded children, such as Seguin, she began to use and modify some of their methods and materials. Soon she moved from working with retarded children to creating an educational program for normal children in the slums of Rome. The target population and the root methods of the nursery school and Montessori school were basically the same. They both worked with children of the poor, they were both influenced by the work of Seguin, and they both saw sensory education as an important development in the education of children. The British nursery school was more broadly conceived, however, and took responsibility for aspects of development and work with parents that was absent to a great degree in the Montessori system. The freedom of nursery educators from a specific dogma also allowed them to develop programs more fully and more flexibly, utilizing new knowledge that became available and responding to new social situations. The Montessori method, however, strongly influenced the content and method of nursery schools.

An investigation of Montessori philosophy also shows some interesting parallels with Froebelian educational thought. Montessori saw the development of the young child as a process of unfolding, a concept found in Froebelian writing. Montessori saw education as self-activity, again an idea found in Froebel's work, as was the idea of self-discipline, independence, and self-direction. Significant differences in philosophy included the Montessori emphasis on sensory education, which was less important to Froebel than symbolic education and the identification of sensitive periods of instruction in the development of the child.

Montessori education caught the imagination of many persons concerned with the welfare of children. The movement expanded, first in Italy and then throughout the world, with Montessori schools being established in several communities in the United States in the 1920s. While Montessori schools remained well-established in Europe, most of them disappeared in the United States during the 1930s and 1940s, when they either closed down or when the schools watered down the Montessori elements in their program and became nursery schools not unlike others around them.

At the beginning of the 1960s, a resurgence of Montessori education could be seen in the United States. An American Montessori movement was reestablished and Montessori schools for children as well as training programs for teachers were founded in many communities. Visits to some of these schools show a wide range of activity in the name of Montessori education. Some schools adhere exactly to the regimen of activity set down by Dr. Montessori in her original writings; others modify these activities or include additional activities found in non-Montessori nursery schools, such as block-building and dramatic play activities.

The revival of the Montessori method has had its impact on the continued thinking about educational activities for young children. Currently, Montessori programs have again been suggested for children of the poor.

The genius of American early childhood education has been in its eclectic nature. Rather than reject new or foreign methods and theories, American educators and the public to which they are ultimately responsible have been willing to accept them at least in some limited form. Seldom, however, did any "pure" form of early childhood education remain uncontaminated. As a result of the interaction of often opposing ideologies as well as the pragmatic approach of many American educators, an American form of early childhood education, consistent yet flexibly developed, taking the best from Froebel, Montessori, Macmillan, and other European theorists and incorporating American theories and techniques. For just as the above-mentioned European educators influenced the emergence of early childhood education, so did Americans such as Dewey, Hill, Pratt, and a host of others.

Today many educators view the kindergarten and the nursery school as a downward extension of the primary school. The goals for the nursery school and kindergarten are exactly those goals set for all schooling. The differences in activities found at these earlier levels stem from developmental differences in the clientele rather than philosophic differences or differences of purpose. Presently the form and content of early childhood schools must be related to how we define the goals of the school and how we conceive of schooling.

Models for Schooling

While many models for schooling exist, the following seem to be the most prevalently supported today. Often the goals of the models are not made explicit by those who advocate them, but they are identifiable. In some cases an existing school will not reflect any single model, but may combine elements of several.

THE SCHOOL AS AN ACCULTURATOR. This model was reflected in the Mission Kindergarten Movement at the turn of the century, in the

1922 compulsory public education law of Oregon, and in many current programs of compensatory education. Within this model the school's role is to teach a single acceptable pattern of behavior and values, often identified as the "American Way," to all children. In the Mission Kindergarten Movement, children of recent immigrants were taught the English language as well as American values and patterns of life. The school became the means of including these children and their families in the "melting pot" of American society.

The Oregon law of 1922 in effect outlawed all private schools. The public schools were viewed as a means of teaching "Americanism" as a single set of beliefs and values to all children regardless of background. For many supporters of the law this was a way of lessening the influence of minority religious, cultural, and political groups.[6] In many programs of compensatory education the admonition to teach children "standard" English and to eradicate the children's native dialect, as well as the emphasis on teaching middle-class values and behavior systems, represent a more contemporary example of this same model.

At the early childhood level, such a model requires that all children, but especially children from deviant and minority groups, be brought into the school early to be influenced by what could be characterized as a "Wasp" (White Anglo-Saxon Protestant) curriculum. Early childhood education becomes singularly important because of the possibilities of significant language learning at this level of development and the fact that teachers have a greater impact on children's values and behavior patterns in the early grades. Early schooling means that children can be acculturated early in the behavior patterns and value systems that will continue to be the central focus of the school. Teachers in schools reflecting these models are careful not to allow any child's prior background or experience to enter into the classroom, since it might cause disruptions in the achievement of proper school learning.

THE SCHOOL AS AN AGENCY FOR VOCATIONAL PREPARATION. This model values the school for its utilitarianism rather than for its acculturating effects. The school is an avenue for teaching those skills needed by persons entering the world of work and for selecting children for the appropriate levels of vocational aspirations. Many current programs of compensatory education fit into this model of the school. These programs also concern themselves with teaching the disadvantaged student the language skills and technical subjects necessary to enable him to compete in the contemporary job market. Subjects that do not produce marketable

[6]David B. Tyack, "The Perils of Pluralism: The Background of the Pierce Case," *American Historical Review*, October 1968, pp. 74–98.

skills are of secondary importance in these programs; thus such subjects as art or history may be downgraded or even eliminated in a program in which many subjects compete for available school time and resources.

At the early childhood level, vocationally oriented programs emphasize those activities that provide a readiness to learn marketable, job-oriented skills.

THE SCHOOL AS A PREPARATION FOR COLLEGE ENTRANCE. Schools fitting this model concern themselves with preparing students for more schooling. The prime goal of the elementary and secondary school is to ready the individual for entrance to college. (Since many colleges are vocationally oriented, this model may in some instances be an extension of the vocational model at the higher levels of vocational aspiration. The difference lies in the fact that schools prepare students for "careers" rather than "jobs.") The rationale for the inclusion of school subjects in secondary schools within this model is that these subjects are required for college admission. By downward extension, elementary school subjects and early childhood education are affected, being prerequisite for learning at the succeeding level.

Sometimes the content of the class or the school is less important than the prestige of the school, especially when the concern is to get into the "right" college. The competition of parents in large cities to get their children into selective nursery schools as a first step toward a proper college education is evidence of parental support for this model.

THE SCHOOL AS A MINIATURE UNIVERSITY. Within this model the school is conceived of as a transmitter of accumulated human knowledge. Significant human knowledge has been organized into disciplines that closely approximate the academic departments of a university. Only aspects of the human experience that are organized within the "scholarly disciplines" are worthy of attention in the school. While other content areas may be found in these schools, they are merely tolerated and do not represent the focal concern of the school. Emphasis on language and literature, science, social science, and mathematics characterizes this school, with less attention paid to the teaching of social skills, expressive skills, values, or aesthetics.

At the early childhood level, schools within this model might be organized around the Brunerian admonition that any subject can be taught to any child at any level of development, leading to a developmentally correct academic curriculum.[7]

[7]Helen F. Robison and Bernard Spodek's *New Directions in the Kindergarten* (New York: Teachers College Press, 1965) emphasizes this model.

THE SCHOOL AS A "SYSTEM." School bureaucracies, like other bureaucracies, develop a life and a rationale of their own, completely independent of any set of external goals. Some of the new critics of American education suggest that within American education one can identify many schools that fit this model of the school as a "system." The content of schooling is primarily designed to help children fit into the system with a minimum of conflict and to allow for perpetuation of the system.

A recent article by Noyes and McAndrews reports several high-schoolers describing school:

"It's a system, you have to understand that. I guess it's because they have so many kids and they all have to be in school so many days a year, for so many hours."[8]

"Schools are like roulette or something. You can't just ask, well, what's the point of it? . . . But you have to figure the system or you can't win."[9]

Jackson's *Life in Classrooms* describes elementary school activities that are inherent in this model, including learning appropriate classroom behavior.[10]

Gracey's study of the kindergarten, cited in Chapter I, suggests that even at the preprimary level there are classrooms where the main concern is also to teach children to fit into the system.

ALTERNATIVES TO CONVENTIONAL MODELS   A number of signs on the social scene have raised serious criticism of American schools. Charles Silberman, for example, has characterized American schools as dull, lifeless institutions that oppress children.[11]

Evidence from other sources also suggest the inadequacies of the public schools. The recently mounted "Right to Read" program gives evidence that schools have failed to help all persons attain basic literacy skills. The push for "compensatory" education programs, special programs

---

[8]Kathryn Johnston Noyes and Gordon L. McAndrews, "Is This What Schools Are For?" *Saturday Review*, December 21, 1968, p. 58.

[9]*Ibid.*, p. 59.

[10]Philip Jackson, *Life in Classrooms* (New York: Holt, Rinehart & Winston, 1968).

[11]Charles Silberman, *Crisis in the Classroom* (New York: Random House, 1970).

for disadvantaged children, give similar evidence that schools have not educated large segments of our society.

Given the seriousness of the crises in American schools, a number of alternative approaches to schooling are being suggested. Some of these relate to the sponsorship of schools; others relate to the content of schooling.

Alternative School Sponsorship

Some critics suggest that the problems of the schools stem primarily from their sponsorship, and that schools created by members of the majority group in society can never be sensitive enough or responsive enough to the needs of members of minority groups. Some who take this position, often blacks, American Indians, or Spanish-speaking citizens, often advocate the establishment of community schools—schools run by and for small elements of the larger society. Since schools reflect the societies that maintain them, discrimination continues in public schools supported by communities that practice discrimination. The solution to the problem of the downtrodden, it is felt, is to give them the power to control their own schooling.

The advocates of the community school represent one position in the creation of responsive schools. Others suggest that the proper way to increase responsiveness of schools is to look outside the educational estab- lishment for groups to sponsor schools. Private corporations are becoming involved in providing educational service, often under a "performance contract." The contractor must demonstrate that the service he performs is of good quality, usually through an analysis of children's scores on standardized achievement tests. Contractors who can demonstrate that children partaking of their educational service are achieving above grade level may receive a bonus over the agreed-upon cost of service, while if the children score below grade level, they may forfeit a portion of their fee.

A third alternative to conventional school sponsorship has been the establishment of "Free Schools." These are schools organized by parents and others, outside the public school systems. While the content, organ- ization, and methods of teaching vary in these schools, which are highly individualistic, they all tend to be child-oriented and dedicated to pro- viding a less prescriptive curriculum than that found in public schools.

In many ways the free schools resemble cooperative nursery schools, but are designed for older children. The local lay sponsorship and the maintenance of control by the parents and teachers allows for the determination of basic policy by each school and for flexibility in dealing with issues and problems.

A fourth suggested alternative to conventional schooling is the elimination of schools as they presently exist. Illich, for example, has called for the disestablishment of schools in our society, or the "deschooling" of culture. The suggestion made is that schools today hold a virtual monopoly on education. Illich suggests that there are many more desirable ways to educate children and youth outside conventional schools.[12] The proposal to "deschool" society leads to the development of a number of educational alternatives, most of which are appropriate to older children. A viable alternative to some form of schooling for the education of young children has not yet been developed.

Alternative School Content

The concern for the failure of schools has also led to the creation of alternatives for the conventional content of education. A number of educators are suggesting that the way to solve the problems of the schools is to define more narrowly the goals of education and to teach these goals more directly and in a more controlled fashion.

An example of this is the advocacy of classroom use of programmed instruction. The Individually Prescribed Instruction (IPI) system developed at the University of Pittsburgh and presently being tested in a number of areas in the United States is a good example of this approach. While most of the work in IPI is currently being done in reading and mathematics, the advocates of the system suggest that IPI can be just as effective in teaching science and social science.

With IPI, the skills of reading and mathematics are identified and the goals of instruction are stated in behavioral terms. These goals are ordered in a hierarchical fashion so that the simple skills that are needed to learn more complex skills are taught earlier. Children are given diagnostic tests, and as a result of the analysis of these tests, individual "prescriptions" are provided for each child. These prescriptions take the form of work sheets which the children must fill in. The work sheets are checked by a clerk.

On the basis of an analysis of the children's responses, they may be moved on to the next level of learning or given additional practice or remedial work. The role of the teacher is to manage the system and provide individual assistance to children. When the IPI system is not in

[12]Ivan Illich, "The Alternative to Schooling," *Saturday Review*, June 19, 1971, pp. 44–48 ff.

effect, teachers may work on art and music activities, group discussion, and other more socially oriented educational activities.

The IPI model fits very nicely with the level of technology that currently characterizes educational evaluation. Children's progress along an educational continuum can easily be identified. Because of this ease of evaluation, forms of programmed instruction are often used by the performance contractors.

A number of educators, also concerned with the failure of the schools, reject this approach to educational reform. They see it as being inadequate because it merely offers more of the same in a more systematic way. They suggest that the structure of educational experience needs to be changed if schools are to succeed.

While no one particular approach to education may be fitting for all children, possibly a range of educational models ought to be provided. There is no reason a school system could not support a number of alternatives within its confines. One of these alternatives that seems to make sense to a number of us has been characterized as informal education, or *open education*, suggested by recent developments in some English Infant Schools.

In visiting an English school one first becomes aware of its organization. Many of the classes are *family grouped*; children of two or three different ages are in the same classes. The time schedule is also different from that of American schools and, apart for special periods like lunch and time for the use of the "hall" or multipurpose room, there may be no periods. Instead, there is a "free" or *integrated day*. Many different subjects and activities take place at the same time, with the children working individually or in small groups; the teacher seldom lectures, but often weaves in and out of groups, helping children learn in their own fashion.

While the class may not seem to be structured in time, it is structured in space. Many of the classrooms are divided into *interest centers*. In each area materials, supplies, and equipment are organized for the children's independent use. There is a reading center with perhaps few primers in view, but many different and delightful children's books. A "maths" center includes Cuisenaire rods, Unifix materials, or other manipulative materials, as well as instruments for weighing and measuring things. There are play materials and a "Wendy house," as their housekeeping corner is called. There are other play materials such as blocks and trucks. Each room is different and each represents the interests and styles of the teachers and children who live in these rooms.

The mode of learning is an active one. Academics are taught but children inquire rather than being told. Play is seen as a legitimate mode of learning and the purposes of the children are taken into account in planning for learning.

Each child is considered an individual. If a five-year-old is ready to read, the teacher starts him on reading instruction. If he is not—well, he has another year or two to learn in the class and the teacher will meanwhile present him with activities that give him the necessary requisites. Learning takes place as a result of expression, and children are always encouraged to write, paint, draw, act, or dance—modes of expression that are used to move the child's level of understanding forward.

Nor is the teacher to be considered the only instructor in the class. With as many as forty children under her tutelage, the teacher learns to use other resources. Assignment cards and the like extend the teacher's instructional role. But in addition, the other children in the class also find themselves in the role of teacher, for children easily learn from other children and teaching an idea to others is an aid to understanding.

A number of educators in the United States have been attracted by this form of education. It is not that different from the ideas promulgated by progressive and early childhood educators in the United States in the past; the writing of Caroline Pratt and Patty Smith Hill, pioneers of American kindergartens, are consistent with the writing of British Infant Educators.

To attempt to superimpose an English institution on an American community would be foolish, though. Rather, American models of *open classrooms* need to be developed. This would require breaking down many artificial barriers that get in the way of children's learning—barriers related to time, activities or subjects, expectations, and institutional structures.

Defining Open Education

Open education is difficult to define, since it is not an educational system or model in the traditional sense. It does not adhere strictly to any single dogma. There is no single organizational model that it characterizes, and it does not narrowly determine the behavior of either teachers or children. Perhaps it can best be understood in terms of the assumptions underlying it and the mode of decision making used within it.

One of these assumptions states that learning takes place as a result of an individual's encounters with his environment, and that understanding is abstracted from these encounters. Concepts develop in the mind of the child as a result of continued encounters with like and unlike phenomena. This assumption suggests that conceptually oriented education requires an active mode, especially for young children. The child is seen as constantly bumping into people, things, and relationships as he attempts to understand. He develops understanding by observing these things and thinking about them. Verbalizations need to take place after the child encounters reality, and verbal learning, especially in the early years, is never a substitute for experience.

An open classroom contains much more than textbooks and work sheets. Children need to be provided with opportunities to "mess about" with materials, to explore, to try out new ideas, to hypothesize, and to make mistakes—to play. The classroom must be full of a variety of materials, to which the children must have free access. The world outside the classroom is also seen as a resource for children's learning. School experience goes beyond the four walls, bringing the world into the classroom and taking the class out into the real world.

Another assumption is that learning is not necessarily linear. Programmed instruction is, in its way, a caricature of school organization. The content of school learning is generally divided into a number of bits, each bit being assigned to a grade level for children to master sequentially. We assume that if a child has not mastered an early bit of learning he will fail in later learning. Prerequisites are clearly defined.

In an open educational environment there is no single way to master a concept or learn a skill. A single educational goal can be achieved using many avenues, and a child may move toward the mastery of a single concept from a number of different paths at the same time. Individual learning style is as important in determining instructional methodology as is the definition of goals.

The single-textbook approach to learning is alien to the open classroom. Not only might different children be learning different things at the same time, but the same learning might be approached in a variety of ways. In reading, for example, some children might be learning phonetic analysis as an early word attack skill while others might be using whole words. At the same time all the children might be involved in a language-experience approach to reading. The utilization of multiple approaches to learning does not lead to confusion on the part of the children, for each child to some extent controls his own learning encounters.

A third assumption underlying open education is that expression is a source of learning. In most traditional classrooms children are viewed primarily as receivers of learning. The teacher is the prime sender, using many ways of telling children what they must learn.

In an open classroom there is more than inquiry-learning taking place. Children use arts and craft activity, movement or dancing, creative dramatics, the writing of stories, or the retelling of experiences as sources of learning. Out of expression grows understanding and these activities are given prime importance in the classroom, not relegated to Friday afternoons.

A corollary of this assumption is that feelings have a legitimate place in the classroom. It is impossible to express ideas without expressing feelings. Children who are involved in learning show intense interest. They also occasionally show joy, anger, resentment, and fear. These expressions of feelings are accepted as natural in the classroom, and the teacher doesn't attempt to sweep feelings under the table, explain away all expressions of emotions, or serve as a child therapist.

Teachers' feelings also have a legitimate place in the classroom. If a teacher feels angry, particularly enjoys an activity, or comes in one morning feeling out of sorts, she need not hide this from the children.

A final set of assumptions relates to children being viewed as competent, desirous of learning, and trustworthy. Many older views of children suggest they can learn only when they are prodded from without, as if the natural state of children were to be inactive. In natural settings, however, it becomes evident that children are always learning, without being prodded either by external rewards or by external punishments. It is only when the purposes of the adult are antagonistic to the purposes of the child that controls in the form of rewards or punishment must be given. When children's purposes are given legitimacy, activities have their own rewards.

If children are considered incompetent, then their activities need to be carefully controlled; others who are more competent must make decisions for them. Error must be avoided and there is no way to correct them except by recourse to an external referee—either a human one or a set of criteria determined by others.

When children are not trusted, it is thought that their behavior must be controlled—once uncontrolled, children will naturally do bad things. In contrast, in a situation in which children are viewed as competent and trustworthy, they will continue to work on activities whether or not the teacher is in the classroom. Nor does the teacher always need to hover over each child. Children can be set to independent activities and then be allowed to move on their own. If they make mistakes, they can benefit from these as well.

As a result of the assumptions upon which open education is based, a new form of classroom decision making is created. One finds that the old dichotomy between "child-centered" and "adult-centered" classrooms does not hold for open classrooms. These are not classrooms in which children are allowed to "do their own thing" while the teacher acts as referee—rather, teacher and children both have major contributions to make in the decision-making process.

The availability of new models of schooling for children requires a reexamination of the assumptions and goals of early childhood education as well as of the methods used in achieving these goals. An analysis of the sources of early childhood curricula and goals of early childhood education is provided in the next chapter.

SUGGESTED READING

BROWN, MARY E., AND NORMAN PRECIOUS, *The Integrated Day in the Primary School*. New York: Agathon Press, 1968.

DENNISON, GEORGE, *The Lives of Children; the Story of the First Street School*. New York: Random House, 1969.

ENGSTROM, GEORGIANNA, ed., *Open Education*. Washington, D.C.: National Association for the Education of Young Children, 1970.

FOREST, ILSE, *Preschool Education: A Historical and Critical Study*. New York: The Macmillan Company, 1927.

GARDNER, D. E. M., *Education Under Eight*. London: Longmans, Green and Company, n.d.

GOOD, H. G., *A History of American Education*, 2nd ed. New York: The Macmillan Company, 1962.

HARRISON, JOHN F., *Utopianism and Education; Robert Owen and the Owenites*. New York: Teachers College Press, 1968.

HILL, PATTY SMITH et al., *A Conduct Curriculum for the Kindergarten and First Grade*. New York: Charles Scribner's Sons, 1923.

LILLEY, IRENE M., *Freidrich Froebel: A Selection from His Writings*. Cambridge: Cambridge University Press, 1967.

MACMILLAN, MARGARET, *The Nursery School*. London: J. M. Dent and Sons, Ltd., 1919.

Montessori in Perspective. National Association for the Education of Young Children, Washington, D.C., 1966.

MONTESSORI, MARIA, *The Montessori Method*. New York: Schocken Books, 1964.

PARKER, S. C., AND ALICE TEMPLE, *Unified Kindergarten and First-Grade Teaching*. Chicago: Department of Education, University of Chicago, 1924.

ROGERS, VINCENT, ed., *Teaching in the British Primary School*. New York: Macmillan, 1970.

SILBERMAN, CHARLES, *Crisis in the Classroom; the Remaking of American Education*. New York: Random House, 1970.

WEBER, EVELYN, *The Kindergarten: Its Encounter with Educational Thought in America*. New York: Teachers College Press, 1969.

WILLCOTT, PAUL, "The Initial Reception of the Montessori Method," *The School Review*, Vol. 76, No. 2 (June 1968), 147–65.

3

Early Childhood Curriculum

Schools for young children serve a purpose. They are expressly designed to achieve certain goals for children. Although different models of schooling may have different goals, once a model is chosen, it becomes the responsibility of school authorities to fill the school day with activities designed to achieve these goals—to develop a school curriculum. How does one derive a curriculum? The curriculum may be defined as the organized experiences designed to provide opportunities for learning to children in a school setting. In this chapter the sources of an early childhood curriculum and the appropriate goals of the curriculum are discussed.

THE SOURCES OF EARLY CHILDHOOD CURRICULA During the past half-dozen years, many innovative programs have been proposed for the education of young children. Each purports to provide the *right* kind of educational experience. Each contends that the experiences provided within it are best for young children. While many of the programs were originally designed for special subpopulations of children, such as the disadvantaged, the proponents of at least some of these programs have generalized the appropriateness of their curricula to all young children. Although some programs described as "new" are primarily modifications of existing practice, the difference between a number of innovative programs and traditional nursery school and kindergarten practice is great. Even greater than the difference in practice is the difference in the sources of these curricula.

Children As a Source of Curricula

According to some theorists, early childhood curricula should originate from children themselves. If you read the works of Friedrich Froebel or Maria Montessori, you will quickly note that both these pioneers of early childhood education used their observations of children as the main source of their curricula.

The kindergarten of Friedrich Froebel consisted of the ordered use of manipulative activities, or *Occupations*, and the use of songs and finger plays, his *Mother's Plays and Songs*. Froebel conceived of these activities as they were revealed to him by the children themselves.[1] Similarly, Dr. Montessori developed her educational approach by observing the uses children made of didactic materials provided them, abstracting the essential elements for learning and ordering them into her famous *Montessori Method*. The observation of children was for Dr. Montessori the essence of scientific pedagogy.[2] Froebel's analysis of child behavior was more mystical than scientific.

The use of "natural" childhood activities as the source of curricula is a romantic ideal. Such educational arguments can be traced as far back as Rousseau. The ideal of the unsocialized savage whose best instincts are destroyed by the surrounding culture is echoed as much in Goodman's *Compulsory Mis-education* as in *Emile*. Educators who use such arguments take comfort in the feeling that they are not violating the child in any way but are rather "doing what comes naturally."

Unfortunately these arguments do not hold up well. There is nothing natural about any school, even a preschool. Nursery classes and kindergartens cannot be directly derived from the natural activity of children. Even the play activities provided children in these settings is modified by teachers who allow certain activities to take place, disallow other activities, and regularly intervene in the play of children in direct and indirect ways in order to make these activities educational. The very nature of the educational process requires, if it is effective, that the child be different as a result of his experiences within it. The child should exit from the program in a less natural state than the one in which he entered it. All schools, as a matter of fact, are cultural contrivances to *do* things *to* children; to change them.

Looking more closely at the curricula derived from the natural observations of children, one becomes aware of the selectivity of the observations and the uses to which these observations have been put. When one observes an object, one must define certain attributes of the object as critical. This definition provides a focus for the observation and the descriptions that follow. Other attributes besides those observed may

---

[1]Friedrich Froebel, "The Young Child," in Irene M. Lilley, ed., *Friedrich Froebel: A Selection from His Writings* (Cambridge: Cambridge University Press, 1967), pp. 68–119.

[2]Maria Montessori, *The Montessori Method* (Cambridge, Mass.: Robert Bently, Inc., 1964), pp. 47–88.

exist, but they are overlooked because they are considered uncritical. The purpose for which one is observing determines what one is looking at and what one will see. For example, a young lady preparing for a date may consider the color and cut of a dress in her observations of that dress. The mother of the same young lady may observe the fabric and stitching with which the dress has been assembled. Ralph Nader might be more concerned with the flammability of the garment, as well as its price, while a sociologist might be more concerned with the effects of the garment on the wearer and on outside observers. Who has seen the real garment?

In analyzing the arguments about the natural activity of childhood as a source of the curriculum, one becomes similarly aware that the purposes of the observer or educational theorist often determines what is seen and the products of such observations are far from natural.

The same child may be seen by a variety of educators in many different ways. One educator may see a set of potentials while another sees only deficits; one may see only the intellectual behavior of children, another only the emotional or social behavior. One educator may view a particular child as a problem solver, while another may see the same child as a respondent to external rewards. The natural child ceases to be natural and becomes a product of the theoretical scheme that helps to determine which observations should be attended to and which discarded in a complex organism.

Few contemporary educators can fail to see the contrived nature of both the Froebelian kindergarten and the Montessori school. If one is to understand the curricula determined by Montessori, Froebel, or any other educational developer, one must go beyond simple natural observation and identify the basis for selecting the observations and the conceptual framework used to give meaning to these observations in developing educational experiences for children.

Developmental Theory As a Source of Curricula

A second source of curricula used by early childhood educators has been the child development theory. One such theory is derived from Arnold Gesell's research, and considers child development as primarily maturational. Children are studied to determine the process of the unfolding of childhood. The developmental norms produced by Gesell and his colleagues are based on many observations of children of various chronological ages. As a result of this theory, children have been grouped by age in nursery and kindergarten classes and have been provided with experiences that are considered specifically appropriate for their age level.

Arguments derived from Gesellian theory have been used to exclude activities thought to be inappropriate and to insure inclusion of appropriate experiences in the school life of children. The argument that we must "protect the right of the child to be five" has often been heard in answer to the suggestion that reading instruction be included in the kindergarten program. However, the nature of "fiveness" is difficult to determine, for age norms do not adequately describe the range of heights, weights, skills, abilities, or other attributes of children at any age. Nor would these attributes remain constant at all times for all persons in all cultures if they could be identified. Average heights and weights of children have risen in the last fifty years and vary from one geographic area to another, not necessarily as the result of natural differences but rather as the result of environmental differences. Other attributes of childhood also vary as a result of the environment—cultural as well as physical. What a child is at any level of development is to some extent a result of what a culture says he ought to be.

Psychoanalytic theory, concerned primarily with the personality, has also been used to formulate curricula for young children. Interpretations of the work of Freud, Jung, and Erikson have led to emphasis on expressive activities, dramatic play, and group interactions. Sometimes as a result of psychoanalytic theory teachers were admonished not to interfere with the activities of children. In excesses such as this, educational practices based upon this theory resembled child therapy sessions as much as educational activities. With the increased emphasis on ego development, however, psychoanalytic thinkers became less concerned with catharsis and more concerned with building an integrated self requiring personal competencies, and many of the excesses eventually disappeared.

More recently, the work of Piaget has been used as a source of curricula. Gesell is no longer as fashionable, and Freud is considered suspect by some educators. While Piaget is primarily a developmental epistomologist, his theories have been used by many American psychologists and educators.

A number of recent projects have used strategies to enhance intellectual development as the basis for creating specific curricula for disadvantaged children. Lavatelli reports on a project she directed that developed a number of intellectual schema in children. These included one-to-one correspondence, classification, and seriation. Additional activities involved children in conservation of quantities.[3] Feigenbaum has also described activities that nursery-school teachers can use to teach conservation.[4]

[3]Celia Stendler Lavatelli, "A Piaget-Derived Model for Compensatory Pre-School Education," in Joe L. Frost, ed., *Early Childhood Education Rediscovered* (New York: Holt, Rinehart & Winston, 1968), pp. 530–44.

[4]Kenneth Feigenbaum, "Activities to Teach the Concept of Conservation," *Young Children*, Vol. 24, No. 3 (January 1969), 151–53.

A Piaget-based curriculum developed in Ypsilanti, Michigan, has also been described by Sonquist and Kamii. Using a Piagetian scheme of analysis, activities are designed to move children through levels of representation from the index level to the symbol level to the sign level.[5]

Is child development theory, Piagetian or otherwise, a legitimate source of educational curricula for young children? The "child development point of view" has been a popular one in early childhood education for many years. However one may seriously question its appropriateness as the prime source of curricula.

Child development is a descriptive science. At its best it can tell us what *is*. Education by its very nature deals not with what is, but with what *ought* to be. Choices and preferences are involved in creating educational experiences that cannot be rationalized by recourse to child development theory. If anything, it can provide us both with useful information, often of a negative kind, about what we cannot do to children at a particular point in their development if we want them to learn, or with information about readiness stages for learning.

Too often the uses made of developmental theory by educators of young children have been to determine the goals of education through an analysis of the theory. In excess, this has led to teaching children the tasks used by the researcher to test his theory. Children in a Piaget-oriented nursery school, for example, might spend hours "learning" conservation tasks. This is as much a distortion of child development theory as is preparing children for specific items on the Stanford-Binet test of intelligence as a way of demonstrating that an educational program can boost IQ.

Child development knowledge might be used most productively in education as an analytic tool. Educators could identify consistencies and inconsistencies in what they do, as well as develop ways of judging the consequences of their programs and the "match" of program activities to the developmental level of the children.

This role is not to be understated. In the last few years, increased recognition of the theories of Piaget have had a significant impact on early childhood education. This recognition has been partly due to the framework of intellectual development provided by Piaget which provided educators with a broad concept of readiness for intellectual learning in the early years. Piaget identifies four broad stages of intellectual development, each containing many identifiable substages. These broad stages are as follows: a sensorimotor, preverbal stage; a stage of preoperational representation; a stage of concrete operations; and a stage of formal operations.

[5]Hanna D. Sonquist and Constance K. Kamii, "Applying Some Piagetian Concepts in the Classroom for the Disadvantaged," *Young Children*, Vol. 22, No. 4 (March 1967), 231–40.

Piaget suggests that there are four main factors that explain the development of new intellectual structures in the child: maturation, experience, social transmission, and equilibrium or self-regulation.

The third factor, social transmission, is the one about which educators are concerned. Piaget highlights the teacher's need to be aware of children's readiness for educational experiences:

> The third factor is social transmission—linguistic transmission or educational transmission. This factor, once again, is fundamental. I do not deny the role of any one of these factors; they all play a part. But this factor is insufficient because the child can receive valuable information via language or via education directed by an adult only if he is in a state where he can understand this information. That is, to receive the information he must have a structure which enables him to assimilate this information. This is why you cannot teach higher mathematics to a five-year old. He does not yet have structures which enable him to understand.[6]

While social transmission, a part of which consists of formal education, is identified as having an important role in intellectual development, Piagetian theory provides no guidelines for improving its effectiveness.

Learning Theory As a Source of Curricula

Child development theory is only one form of psychological theory that has been identified by program developers as a source of curricula; learning theories and theories of intelligence have also been used. Developmental theory deals with change in the human being over long periods of time. Learning theory attempts to account for short-term change. The recourse to learning theory as a source of curricula has been manifest in several different ways.

The "conduct curriculum," developed in the early childhood program at Teachers College under the leadership of Patty Smith Hill, gives evidence of the influence of Thorndike's school of behaviorism.[7] Kindergarten was seen as a place for habit training to take place. Lists of appropriate "habits" and recommended stimulus situations for five-year-olds were developed for kindergarten teachers at this time.

Today the theories of behaviorist B. F. Skinner are having similar influence. Skinner's learning theory contains six major concepts:

1. Operant Conditioning. Skinner's conditioning consists of reinforc-

---

[6]Jean Piaget, "Development and Learning," in Richard E. Ripple and Verne N. Rockcastle, eds., *Piaget Rediscovered* (Ithaca, N.Y.: Cornell University Press, March 1964), p. 13.

[7]Patty Smith Hill, et al., *A Conduct Curriculum for Kindergarten and First Grade* (New York: Charles Scribner's Sons, 1923).

ing operations or responses that occur normally. Learning increases at the rate at which they occur.

2. *Reinforcement.* A new stimulus that increases the rate at which an operation occurs is called a reinforcer. A wide variety of reinforcers can be used in education: food, toys, money, tokens, or praise. Knowledge of results (feedback) might also be considered a reinforcer.

3. *Immediate Reinforcement.* There should be a minimum delay in time between the operant behavior and its reinforcement, otherwise some other response might be emitted and reinforced.

4. *Discriminated Stimuli.* Behaviors that should be emitted under specific circumstances are reinforced only under those circumstances.

5. *Extinction.* Any response that has been increased by reinforcement can be decreased by its failure to be reinforced.

6. *Shaping.* Complex behaviors can be analyzed into simple components. A sequence of reinforcement procedures can be designed to build up to the complex behavior.[8]

The technology of programmed instruction is rooted in this theory. Through a procedure that breaks down complex learning into a series of simple sequential steps, children can be taught a range of things. Programmed instruction might use a teaching machine, a book, a series of tasks with manipulative materials, or a set of human interactions as the context for learning procedures.

A number of psychologists have rejected behaviorism as the prime way of looking at psychological phenomena, including learning. Often referred to as "third force" psychologists or phenomenological psychologists, this group views behaviorism as too mechanistic and simplistic to provide an adequate framework for understanding complex human processes. They suggest an alternate approach in dealing with human learning.

Snygg and Combs, for example, view the process of education, and implicitly of learning, as a process of change in the phenomenological field. How a person behaves, they suggest, is a function of his understanding of a situation. Understanding, rather than responding, becomes the important goal of a learning setting. The meanings of behavior and of situations become the focal point of learning. Learning, therefore, requires not simply recall of words or actions, but developing organizing frameworks that give meaning to situations. Meanings are personal and therefore vary from individual to indivdual. (Meanings, by the way, cannot always be fully verbalized.) The goals of learning are also indi-

---

[8]B. R. Bugelski, *The Psychology of Learning Applied to Teaching* (Indianapolis: Bobbs-Merrill Co., 1964), pp. 208–12.

vidual. What a person learns depends upon his own goals and needs, which are not always externally manipulable.

Within phenomenological psychology, the *self* plays an important role. How a person views himself affects his behavior and what he learns. A child who views himself as competent will be more ready to learn and will learn more than one who thinks of himself as incompetent. The school, it is suggested, needs to concern itself with developing adequate selves in its pupils.[9]

Phenomenological psychology, when used in classrooms, leads to a different set of instructional strategies than does behavioral psychology. Complex learning situations are used intact, with children being helped to develop their own meanings of them; their behavior is not "shaped," nor are specific behavioral goals predetermined. Instead, the teacher is concerned with moving children in the direction of appropriate behavior, a wide range of behavior being acceptable. Such an approach allows a greater degree of freedom for children, enabling them to select alternatives and develop personal responsibility for their learning and their growth.

Another form of learning theory that has been addressed to early childhood education is social learning theory. Bronfenbrenner has summarized the basic concepts of social learning theory and some of its applications to education.[10] He suggests that social psychologists have demonstrated that behavior is contagious—that children learn by watching others. This process is called modeling. In this process children acquire specific behaviors or patterns of response through observation; this is more than simple imitation because the behaviors learned are "symbolic equivalents" of the models' behavior rather than absolute mimicry.

The modeling process can take place without external reinforcement, since the imitative behavior is its own reward. Modeling, along with social reinforcement gives approval or affection when the child manifests a desired behavior, is an even more potent learning tool.

The school is an acculturating institution. Many of the behaviors we wish children to learn can be taught through modeling and social reinforcing. The issue of which behaviors we wish children to learn is outside the realm of this theory.

The use of behaviorist learning theory carries with it the admonition to develop behavioral objectives. Actually there is nothing psychological about the use of behavioral objectives, nor are objectives more profound because they are stated in behavioral terms. The translation of curricula

[9]Donald Snygg and Arthur Combs, *Individual Behavior* (New York: Harper and Brothers, 1949), pp. 204–25.

[10]Urie Bronfenbrenner, *Two Worlds of Childhood: US and USSR* (New York: Russell Sage Foundation, 1970), pp. 120–51.

goals into behavioral objectives, however, allows for an easy, though often misleading evaluation of achievement.

Psychological processes are not directly observable; they must be inferred. Behaviors are observable. Psychologists sometimes forget that the *meanings* of behaviors must still be inferred. A psychologist may identify as a legitimate goal of nursery school or kindergarten education the ability to attend to auditory signals. This might be translated into the following criteria behavior: "The ability to sit still for ten minutes and listen to a story as part of a group." Whether or not a child is actually gaining meaning from the auditory environment is not directly observable. The relationship between sitting still and listening (certainly not a one-to-one relationship) has led psychologists to list as the goal a behavior that might better represent *conformity* than *attention.*

Psychological theory focusing on behavior and behavior modification has determined the structure of a number of curricula in early childhood education. While short-term change is easily observed and evaluated, there are seldom any attempts to study long-term effects of these curricula. In the final analysis, such programs may be based as much on ultimate faith as are any of the more traditional programs. The description of a program in psychological terminology and the great emphasis on the evaluation of effectiveness without analyzing ultimate goals may, in the long run, obscure the ultimate consequences of these programs.

Nor can phenomenological psychology or social learning theory help us to determine what should be taught to children, a problem often ignored by psychologists involved in educational programs. At best, learning theory can help us in developing new instructional methodologies and in analyzing and assessing established methodologies. This, in itself, is no small role.

Test Items As a Source of Curricula

One other facet of psychology that is often used for formulating curricula is psychological testing and evaluation. This is used more in practice than in theory. Many of the programs in early childhood education, for example, are justified as ways of increasing intelligence, and one way of judging the intelligence of children is through the administration and scoring of intelligence tests. Such tests consist of items which purport to sample a broad range of intellectual behaviors in children. Each item achieves its validity from the fact that it represents many other kinds of behaviors that might have been elicited from the total number of intelligent behaviors.

Since the effectiveness of educational programs can be demonstrated by students' achievement of higher scores on intelligence tests, it is easy to use tasks taken from or related to intelligence tests as the actual content of the program. Justification for this approach to curriculum development often takes the form of an argument that suggests that since these items are selected as samples of intelligent behavior, having children practice these behaviors is the same as having children practice behaving in an intelligent manner. Such logic is devastating—rote learning of responses to particular stimuli cannot be called intelligent behavior.

Such distortions of psychological testing and curriculum development are not limited to the area of intelligence testing. They may take place in the realm of language development or in any other area where samples of behavior are mistaken for the total population of behaviors they represent. The small number of items that determine the difference in age or grade placement for a child make this form of justification all too attractive for persons who have developed short-term intervention techniques for young children.

Organized Knowledge As a Source of Curricula

About a decade ago, Bruner suggested that the organized fields of knowledge should become the basis of educational curriculum for children at all levels. The "structure of the disciplines," it was argued, could provide a vehicle to insure that school learning would be intellectually significant.[11] Key ideas in each area of knowledge would be revisited in more sophisticated ways as children moved through their academic careers. These key ideas could be taught in an intellectually honest way at every level of development. *New Directions in the Kindergarten*[12] provides examples of how this proposal could be translated into an early childhood program in the fields of science, social science, and mathematics.

The proposal to develop school curricula based on the structure of knowledge was an attractive one. During the 1960s quite a large number of curriculum development projects were organized along these lines. A number of new elementary textbook series also based their work upon this proposal, as did the curriculum guides of many school systems. As the work in these projects continued, a number of problems became evident. For one thing, it became difficult to identify the actual structure of the disciplines.

Scholars identified many different structures, but some disciplines, such as social science, did not seem unified. Another problem was that

---

[11]Jerome S. Bruner, *The Process of Education* (Cambridge, Mass.: Harvard University Press, 1960).

[12]Helen F. Robison and Bernard Spodek, *New Directions in the Kindergarten* (New York: Teachers College Press, 1965).

the mere identification of intellectual structures did not help to determine what in school experiences would help children attain significant understandings in a field.

In addition to this, the structure of many areas of knowledge seemed to elude the curriculum developers. The strategies for understanding the sciences did not seem to help in understanding the arts and the humanities. Fewer projects dealing with these areas and with the expressive elements of school learning were mounted, leading to a distorting thrust in curriculum development.

The relationship between the conceptual structures of mature disciplines and the less mature understandings of which children are capable is more complicated than was originally thought. Issues dealing with relevance to children, individual learning rates and style, personal interests, and so forth, complicated what had once seemed a simple task.

While the content of the disciplines—the areas of knowledge—could help to determine the significance of school content, by itself it was inadequate for determining school curricula at any level, but especially at the early childhood level.

School Content As a Source of Curricula

Although psychological theory represents one area used in justifying curricula proposals, it is by no means the only source; another used popularly is the content of later schooling. "Reading readiness," for example, is considered important because it prepares children for reading instruction. Though readiness skills have no importance by themselves, they and certain other kinds of learnings are considered good because they prepare children for later school expectations. Thus the pressures of later life and later schooling are heaped upon the child in anticipation of what is to come.

A caricature of such a justification is to be found in the Bereiter-Engelmann Program. The content of the program (reading, language, and mathematics) is considered important because it is required of children in primary grades. The organization also prepares the child for behaving appropriately for his school life ahead. The legitimacy of such a justification is questionable; whether or not such preparation will benefit students later on is debatable.

One of the few long-range studies of the effects of education, the *Eight-Year Study* of Progressive high schools, demonstrated that children in open school situations did better than those from more restrictive school environments when they went to college.[13] While extrapolation

[13]William M. Aiken, *The Story of the Eight Year Study* (New York: McGraw-Hill, 1942).

to a lower age level may not be appropriate, the study certainly raises some questions about the desirability of providing children with rigid early schooling as preparation for rigid later schooling.

Unfortunately, such preparation for later learning also obscures the concern for the sources of curricula. For later school learning is not a goal in and of itself, but is again a means to a goal. Using such a justification only pushes decisions about curriculum content back further. As it is, too little concern is given to the proper source of curricula.

THE PROPER SOURCE OF CURRICULA   The sources of curricula-formulation theories that have been used through the years have been reviewed and analyzed. A number of them must be rejected. Neither test items nor school content can be viewed as proper sources of any curriculum. Using either of these presents a circularity of thought which supports existing practice merely because it exists. School content is devised to achieve societal aims, no matter how ill-defined they might be. To support school content as an end in itself is to deny the purposes of schooling and to legitimize activity solely on the basis of tradition.

Test items themselves are part of evaluation procedures. The role of such procedures is to help in judging the educational experience, but to use them to determine curriculum content is to distort both the educational process and the process of evaluation. Rather the reverse should occur—test items should be determined by educational practices.

A third source of curricula formulation might also be questioned—that which uses children themselves to determine educational programs. Since what we see in children is determined by prior conceptions, it might be more fruitful to legitimize these conceptions and make them explicit. This is done when we define the developmental theories and learning theories to which we adhere when we observe children's behavior. Learning theory, developmental theory, and conceptions of organized knowledge and ways of knowing are all sources of curricula that must be used in concert. But even together they are inadequate to determine a curriculum. Only within the context of human values can these sources function properly.

Schools at all levels serve two functions. On the one hand, schools help children learn those behaviors that will help them adjust to an effective role in society. This we might call socialization. On the other hand, they help children develop sensitivities and competencies that will help them lead personally satisfying lives. This we might call self-fulfillment. To the extent that schools help to define the "good life" and the "good society," they are moral enterprises. It is the set of values growing out of this enterprise that determines how we should use our knowledge of human development or human learning, or for that matter our knowledge of *knowledge* in determining educational experiences for young children.

Our view of the role of the school and the relationship between the individual and his society identifies goals for education. Dearden, for example, has suggested that the goal of education is "personal autonomy based upon reason." He describes this autonomy as follows:

> There are two aspects to such an autonomy, the first of which is negative. This is independence of authorities, both of those who would dictate or prescribe what I am to believe and of those who would arbitrarily direct me in what I am to do. The complementary positive aspect is, first, that of testing the truth of things for myself, whether by experience or by a critical estimate of the testimony of others, and secondly, that of deliberating, forming intentions and choosing what I shall do according to a scale of values which I can myself appreciate. Both understanding and choice, or thought and action, are therefore to be independent of authority and based instead on reason. This is the ideal.[14]

The concept of autonomy is not alien in the education of young children. Erikson's framework for human development includes the stage of autonomy early in the scale, just after the development of *trust*.[15] The child's autonomy in these early years may not, however, be based upon reason. As the child's intelligence continues to develop, the basis for personal autonomy becomes more rational.

Dearden's goals derive from a conception of the individual as a contributor to a democratic society that is not unlike that found in the progressive education movement in the United States some years earlier.

If we accept the goal of "personal autonomy based upon reason" as legitimate for early childhood education, then of what use is psychological theory to the educator? For one thing, it helps us determine ways of testing the effectiveness of a program in achieving the ideal. Second, knowledge of developmental processes can help us order the activities we provide for children in terms of what can be of use to a child at a particular level of development, and suggest what activities might precede or follow others. Developmental theory becomes a tool for the analysis of curricula rather than its source, and the content of school programs must be recognized as a product of the imagination of educators to be tested by psychological means rather than as natural consequences of children's behavior, adults' thinking, or institutional organization.

[14]R. F. Dearden, *The Philosophy of Primary Education* (London: Routledge and Kegan Paul, 1968), p. 46.

[15]Erik H. Erikson, *Childhood and Society* (New York: W. W. Norton & Co., 1950).

A "TRANSACTIONAL CURRICULUM"   Generally, curriculum development is conceived of as the very careful working-out in advance of goals and procedures for educating children. Often the more predetermined the activities, the more specific the goals, and the more detailed the educational evaluation, the better the program is considered. In such a program, individual differences in children may be dealt with through differentiated pacing—increasing or decreasing the rate at which new experiences are provided to children.

If we conceive of a model of a school in which the primary consideration is not fitting all children into a particular mold and not having all children achieve the same aims, such a model of curriculum development is not viable. School can be considered a partnership affair in which children, from the moment of their entry, are involved in determining purposes and goals as well as procedures. The early nursery schools, some of the kindergartens of the 1920s and 1930s, and the presently popular English Infant School reflect to some extent this concept of schooling. Such a school would require a form of curriculum that might be labeled a "transactional curriculum"—that is, one determined for each child through transactions between the child, as client, and the teacher, as professional. At the early childhood level the teacher's role as professional would be to set the stage for learning, to provide legitimate alternatives for children's activities in school, and to serve a guidance function in the classroom. The teacher would provide alternative goals, help children clarify their needs and desires, help them anticipate the consequences of their acts, help them evaluate their activities, and help to see that the school provides productive learning situations for all children.

As viewed within this model, the child is not a passive participant in the curriculum process. He will not simply be acted upon as the client in the situation. Nor will he dominate the decision-making process. The child, however, will have a role in instigating learning, in determining its direction, and in terminating any learning situation. In this transactional process, not only can the child achieve the traditional academic goals, but he can also learn to be self-determining. There can be outlets for creative thinking in the ongoing activities of the school. Divergent sets of values and patterns of behavior need not be squelched, nor will anarchy reign in the classroom. For in the transactional process, the goals and desires of the child can be modified and restructured.

The involvement of the young child in the decision making suggested in this transactional curriculum need not cease when the child leaves the nursery school and kindergarten class, but should continue as he moves through the many levels of schooling. The current student demand for a voice in educational policy making at the college level closely parallels a similar need at the early childhood level.

In order for a teacher to implement this transactional curriculum, she needs to have an understanding of the basic goals of education and the many ways in which they can be achieved. She needs to be aware of the various areas of knowledge and what they can offer children at each level. She needs to be aware of children's abilities and interests, and must be able to develop a guidance function in the classroom, helping to marshal resources, both material and human, and to keep a classroom going so that children can achieve satisfaction and can grow within it.

GOALS OF EARLY CHILDHOOD EDUCATION

In devising a curriculum for young children, the goals of education may be identified in the following areas:

Socialization
Values
Intellectual competency
Language systems
Self expression
Aesthetic appreciation
Physical skills
Personal autonomy

The first two of these goals are learned not through any formal, prescribed curriculum, but as a result of the sum total of the school experience, formal and informal. The achievement of the last of the goals is to a great extent a result of achievement in all the other areas. The rest of the goals are often delegated to specific portions of the school program. Children's learning is not that compartmentalized, however, and learnings tend to spill over to all times of the day and all portions of the program.

Socialization

The prime socializing agency in our society is the family. In everything from toilet-training to teaching the skills of eating, dressing, and relating to others, the parents are primarily responsible for the socialization of the child. In as diverse and as complex a society as ours, with children needing to be in contact with so many different social groups, the family needs to be helped to complete this extensive job. The school, along with other institutions, must enter into a partnership with the family in extending the socialization of the child. Teachers can help the child develop skills in working with different groups and living within various social settings. They can help the child learn the rules and regulations for behaving in various settings. In addition, teachers can help the child to learn how to relate to a variety of authority figures.

The school situation is a good place for children to learn ways of behaving that are different from the ones learned in the home. The school presents a different setting. There are new authority figures, whose role and range of authority is different from the parents'. The teacher's role is school-bound and related to the classroom setting. There are many children in a class who have to be treated fairly by the teacher and with whom the child must vie for attention and rewards. There is also a different set of expectations the child must meet. He finds that there are new expectations and satisfactions to be found outside the home, and is ultimately socialized by being helped to establish himself as a person in this new environment. Thus, readiness for school learning is closely related to the socialization process.

Of course the child does not become a fully socialized person in these early years. There will be more new situations to face, more roles and relationships to master through the years. The nursery school, kindergarten, and primary grades can become a buffer zone for the child, helping him make the transition to the larger world outside the family. They can also help the child learn strategies of social interaction that can be transferred to new situations as they arise.

Values

The young child is a self-centered individual at the time he enters the formal educational process. His motivational system consists of meeting his own immediate needs and wishes and responding to the demands of his parents. This system needs to be broadened so that he becomes sensitive to what others think and feel. He must also assimilate the value system of the adult culture.

The school has its own value and reward system. The young child must learn to value those things that the school and his teachers value. While most of what a child learns in elementary school is important in later life, it may not seem important to the five- or six-year-old. The valuing of achievement in school activities is a learned characteristic. While the child might have learned to value this achievement before entering school, teachers cannot assume that this has happened. Sometimes motivational systems are learned by the child in modeling the behavior of those around him. At other times, teachers may wish to develop systematic programs to help the child approximate accepted motivational systems.

Intellectual Competency

One of the main goals of education at all levels is to help people deal intelligently with their surroundings. This requires that an individual have access to certain information about the world. It also requires that the individual has skills in processing this information, organizing it appropriately so that he can generalize from it and fit new information into a developing knowledge system. This means going beyond perceptual training or sensory education to helping the child derive meaning from sensations.

The young child perceives the world. He must know what aspects of his perception are important and worthy of focus, and what aspects are unimportant and should become background. Only by selective focusing can the child abstract information from an otherwise booming, buzzing mass. He learns that certain objects have common attributes and that these objects can be grouped together for certain purposes. These groupings or concepts allow the child to deal more efficiently with ideas and more readily with new phenomena which can be placed into existing categories. The child's conceptual system needs to be related to society's way of organizing knowledge, and the child needs to learn the skills involved in comparing his ideas with those of others. The skills necessary to build the child's basic knowledge system provide a foundation for later learning. The young child needs to learn how to learn in school as well as how to learn to abstract meaning from the perceptions he receives from the outside world. Much of what he needs to know about appropriate learning behavior in school is gained through the socialization process. The child must order perceptions and somehow symbolize them in order to develop his own knowledge system.

Language Systems

While many children arrive in school already having mastered the basic structure of the English language and having acquired a broad speaking and listening vocabulary, others do not. From the beginning, the school needs to identify the needs of children in language acquisition and help them learn the system as well as extend the language skills of the more capable. This may require teaching standard American dialect to some children, or helping children learn to use language for self-expression. While most early language experiences are with the spoken word, written language has an increasingly important place in the school program. But even writing is no longer the sole means of recording language, and therefore children need to have experiences with mechanical devices for recording language early in their school careers.

Self-Expression

Young children are extremely expressive under ordinary circumstances. While language is one of the prime means of expression, it is not the only means available to children. Arts and crafts, music, and movement provide additional avenues of expression. Children need to learn basic skills in using these media to serve their purposes. They also need to develop a degree of self-awareness and understanding. In the area of self-expression, both the content expressed and the effectiveness of communication is important.

Aesthetic Appreciations

It is one thing to be involved in creating expressions through the arts and music, but quite another to learn to be receptive to the creations of others. Both require the development of a feeling of beauty. Aesthetic appreciations are culture-bound and are learned by children in diverse ways. Aesthetics ought to be a part of any program for young children, developed in such a way that they can achieve their own standards of beauty and their own ways of judging it.

Physical Skills

The teaching of a range of physical skills needs to be a part of the nursery-kindergarten program. These skills involve large muscle movements, as found in the activities of running, climbing, or riding wheel toys. Skills in small-muscle activities are also important. The use of crayons and scissors builds many of the skills necessary for writing and reading. Basic skills in movement and balance are important for academic achievement as well as for physical development.

Personal Autonomy

To a great extent, this goal subsumes all the other goals previously stated. To become autonomous, the young child must develop competency, a sense of independence of action, and a set of values upon which to base his actions. Competency might be conceived of in the early years as the ability to care for oneself. Even such skills as dressing and undressing, while primitive, are important to the child. Later, competency will require literacy and the ability to make rational judgments.

As the child becomes competent, his actions become less dependent upon the wishes and demands of the adults around him and more a function of personal decisions. A set of values are important to help the child develop positive behaviors. It is the child's internalized value system that allows him to take more independent action while still remaining a productive member of a collective group, be it class or culture.

USING GOALS AS   A statement of educational goals can serve
GUIDES FOR ACTION   a variety of purposes. It can be a public
                            relations device, a justification for current
practices, a rallying point for practitioners, or a guide for action and decision making. If educational experiences are to help children achieve these goals, then every aspect of the experience may be judged by the degree to which it supports the child's achievement. Often one conceives of the curriculum as the determining factor in the child's achievement of educational goals. Actually, every aspect of the educational experience has a contribution to make towards this achievement.

SUGGESTED READING

BLOOM, BENJAMIN, *Stability and Change in Human Characteristics*. New York: Wiley and Sons, 1964.

DEARDEN, R. F., *The Philosophy of Primary Education*. New York: Humanities Press, 1968.

ELKIND, DAVID, "Preschool Education: Enrichment or Instruction," *Childhood Education*, February 1969, pp. 321–28.

FRAZIER, ALEXANDER, ed., *Early Childhood Education Today*. Washington, D.C.: Association for Supervision and Curriculum Development, 1968.

HEADLEY, NEITH, *The Kindergarten: Its Place in the Program of Education*. New York: Center for Applied Research in Education, 1965.

RIPPLE, RICHARD E., AND VERNE N. ROCKCASTLE, eds., *Piaget Rediscovered*. Ithaca, New York: Cornell University, 1964.

ROBISON, HELEN, AND BERNARD SPODEK, *New Directions in the Kindergarten*. New York: Teachers College Press, 1965.

ROGERS, VINCENT R., *Teaching in the British Primary School*. New York: Macmillan, 1970.

Language Learning
In Early Childhood Education

Perhaps the most important area of learning in the education of young children is that of language. While reading is obviously crucial to all school learning, other aspects of language learning, such as listening and speaking, are equally important. As a matter of fact, learning to read is predicated upon a great deal of prior language learning.

From the moment the child enters the classroom he is bombarded with verbal messages from many sources, some giving him specific directions for actions, others providing him with information about the world, still others offering him opportunities for enjoyment and aesthetic appreciation. The child is also sending messages to others. He responds to the teacher and attempts to influence the behavior of his peers. He makes his needs and wishes known to those around him. He expresses the ideas and feelings that have developed inside him. The continual verbal give-and-take of the active school day has endless opportunities for speaking, listening, reading, and writing.

THE CHILD COMES TO SCHOOL
School does not provide the child's first language learning situation. The most important part of the child's language learning has taken place before the child even arrives at school. The role of the school is to extend and enrich the language learning of the child and to provide remediation if necessary.

By the time the child reaches the first grade he has probably mastered a listening and speaking vocabulary of several thousand words. While estimates of the average vocabulary of young children vary, there is general agreement that they are capable of understanding and using an extensive repertoire of words and have learned the syntax of the language. Although it would not be possible for a young child to parse a sentence or recite the rules of grammar, he has by this time developed an intuitive sense of the structure of the language. For most young children have learned to use the basic sentence forms of their culture and to use words correctly. Through interaction with others they have somehow learned, for example, that adding "-ed" to a verb places that verb in the past tense. The mistakes that teachers so often report in the conversations of young children grow out of the children's applying rules logically to words that happen to be exceptions to those rules. Rules are seldom misapplied by young children, however. You may hear a child say, "He dided it," but you will seldom hear a young child add the "ed" at the end of a noun.[1]

Individual children vary greatly in their language development. There are early talkers and late talkers, loquacious children and quiet children. Some differences are a function of the way children react to a specific environment, others are developmental. Psychologists report that sex, class, position in family, and ethnic group membership are all related to the child's rate of language development. Differences reported by psychologists are usually differences in *group trends*. Individuals may differ markedly from the norm of their group.

It is unfortunate when teachers become so blinded by expectancies based upon reported research evidence that they become insensitive to the individual child as a data source.

How Does Language Develop?

While there is a long tradition of research in language development, we still do not know exactly how children develop language or what elements in the environment are most crucial for optimal language development. We do know that there is a maturational base for language development and we can identify some of the things that children do in the process of acquiring language. Bellugi and Brown, for example, describe the process by which children develop syntax in language as a process of interaction between mother and child.[2]

[1]Extensive reviews of research in language development are available in many resources. Among them:

Susan Ervin Tripp, "Language Development," in Lois W. Hoffman and Martin L. Hoffman, eds., *Review of Child Development Research*, Vol. 2 (New York: Russell Sage Foundation, 1966), 55–106.

Susan Ervin and Wick R. Miller, "Language Development," in *Child Psychology*, 62nd Yearbook of the National Society for the Study of Education (Chicago: University of Chicago Press, 1963), pp. 108–43.

Dorothea McCarthy, "Language Development in Children," in Leonard Carmichael, ed., *Manual of Child Psychology* (New York: John Wiley and Sons, 1954), pp. 492–630.

[2]Ursula Bellugi and Roger Brown, *The Acquisition of Language*, monograph of the Society for Research in Child Development, 29, No. 2, 1964.

The parents studied did not develop a series of prescribed lessons that they presented to these children. Rather they seemed to use a process called *expansion*. When the child uttered a communicative though incomplete sentence, the parent responded by repeating the statement in syntactically expanded form. The child's utterance, "Mommy, lunch," might be expanded by the parent to "Mommy is having her lunch." Vocabulary might be more directly taught than syntax by parents.

Just how educators can best use the research in language development is not completely clear. Early researchers were concerned with normative studies, attempting to find the regularities in the development of language in children or attempting to discover the language acquisitions of children at different age levels. Later researchers focused more on the theoretical aspects of language development, studying the process of language acquisition or the factors that affect the development of language in children.

Eric Lenneberg has developed a theory of the biological foundations of language; he analyzes knowledge of language development in human beings alongside biological knowledge about animals, human and nonhuman, synthesizing them into a theory. He suggests that latent language structures are biologically determined and that they need to be actualized within a sound setting through exposure to adult language behavior. The period of language readiness for such actualization, it is suggested, is from two years to the early teens. In this period, the child recreates the language mechanisms of the culture.[3]

While Lenneberg's theories are fascinating to read and provide great opportunities for speculation, they give little guidance in how best to "actualize" language structures—the key role of language education. Education and child development specialists have developed research related to the engineering of the social setting to enhance language development.

Whether or not specific studies related to language education are directly related to any single theory of language development is questionable. Developmental theories can, however, provide the basis for theorizing about what will work in social engineering that can be transformed into educational hypotheses to be tested in classrooms.

Dialect

No matter how simple or complex it is, the child will learn the language he hears most often spoken by the significant adults around him. Most American children learn English, and children in Japan learn Japanese just as easily. But the various forms of the English language heard in different subcultures in America may differ markedly from one

[3]Eric H. Lenneberg, *Biological Foundations of Language* (New York: John Wiley and Sons, 1967).

another. These differences are called dialects. Naturally the young child learns the dialect spoken most prevalently around him.

The speech patterns of children may differ in many ways. There can be differences in the pronunciation of words or in speech inflections. There may be differences in the labels ascribed to familiar things, so that what is called a "sack" in one area may be called a "bag" elsewhere. There may also be syntactical differences among dialects. Syntactical differences make understanding difficult across dialects, for the structure of statements carries much of their meaning.

The dialect prevalent in the schools and generally heard over radio and television has been called *Standard American English*. Children may come to school more or less familiar with this dialect. Many of the children entering our schools have been raised in an environment in which different dialects prevail. Often they come from different ethnic backgrounds or from cultural groups isolated from the mainstream of American culture. It has also been postulated that dialect differences exist between social classes.

Bernstein has suggested dialect differences based upon social class, with the lower classes speaking what had been called a *restricted linguistic code* and the middle classes speaking an *elaborated linguistic code*.[4] These dialects differ not only in vocabulary and syntax, but in the way meaning is conveyed. The elaborated code makes more extensive use of language elements than does the restricted code.

Erickson has suggested that many of the apparent differences in the way in which meaning is communicated is actually a function of the context in which statements are communicated.[5]

The fact that many children enter school with a language background not shared by their teacher and significantly different from the language upon which most school learning is based has many implications for programs and for teaching.

Dealing with Language Differences
in the Classroom

Some educators suggest that differences in the language background of children are irrelevant in determining instructional goals; therefore, since the school uses Standard English, one might as well get on with it and teach Standard English even if it means suppressing the already acquired language of the child. Others suggest that the child's personal language is important and should be reflected in the school; one ought

---

[4]Basil Bernstein, "Language and Social Class," *British Journal of Sociology*, Vol. 11, No. 1 (March 1960), 271–76.

[5]Frederick Erickson, "Figet, you Honkey. A New Look at Black Dialect and the School," *Elementary English*, Vol. 46 (April 1969), 495–99.

not teach a single system of language, but instead teach the use of language appropriate to the situation in which the language is used. Using the Spanish language in school would be justifiable if there were a number of Spanish-speaking children in the class. The black dialect of the urban ghetto would also be recognized as a valid and useful form of verbal communication appropriate to the classroom.

Language serves many purposes in the lives of human beings. These purposes become the basis for establishing the goals of a language arts program in school. One of the purposes of language that may unfortunately be of less concern to teachers is its role in establishing personal and group identity. Speaking a particular dialect or using a particular style of language establishes an individual as a member of a specific group, and to attempt to change an individual's language system might have significant implications beyond learning the use of proper syntax. Arguments against teaching Standard English may stem as much from pride in minority-group membership as from any other reason.

While both approaches focus on teaching a standard dialect in the classroom, in one case this would be to the exclusion of all other language systems in school. Within either approach, Standard English might be taught in a number of ways.

USE OF NATURALISTIC METHODS.   One way to approach the teaching of Standard English is to model a program on the natural processes of language acquisition. This could be done by surrounding the child with people, both adults and children, who speak the majority dialect. The natural interactions of the child would help him acquire this majority dialect. The language of the school might be different than the language of the home and children would still have the problem of learning to be fluent in two language systems as well as continually having to determine which system would be most appropriate in each situation. In addition, the language the child learns in school would not be reinforced either in the home or the neighborhood, thus compounding the problem of learning the new language system.

Cazden reports using a process known as *expatiation* in improving language of disadvantaged children.[6] This process requires the adult to react to the child's utterances by expanding them ideationally rather than linguistically. The child's remark, "Dog bark," may be responded to by, "Yes, he's mad at the kitty." Blank and Solomon also report a naturalistic strategy that is successful in elaborating children's language.[7] Their pro-

[6]Courtney Cazden, "Some Implications of Research on Language Development," in Robert Hess and Roberta Bower, eds., *Early Education* (Chicago: Aldine Publishing Co., 1968), pp. 131–42.

[7]Marion Blank and Francis Solomon, "How Shall Disadvantaged Children Be Taught?" *Child Development*, Vol. 40, No. 1 (March 1969), 47–63.

posal suggests a one-to-one relationship with the children, basing instruction on the child's utterance but reflecting open-ended questions that have the children move beyond their original statements. This strategy allows the tutor working with the individual child to make judgments about his level of language development by listening to specific utterances. This information is used in framing the next question, which is designed to move the child along a developmental continuum. This program was not designed to teach child language per se but to develop within the child the linguistic base for thinking.

Naturalistic methods can be used with disadvantaged children in the primary grades as well. The model developed by Dr. Marie Hughes for Mexican-American culture tends to reflect this point of view. Children are given continuous opportunities to speak, and the language they bring to school is valued. The teacher develops a self-conscious style of responding to the child in Standard English that acts as a model for the child. Through the interactions of adult and child, the language of the child is expected to be transformed in a naturalistic school setting.[8] While this is one way of helping children increase their verbal facility, other models are also possible.

USE OF SYNTHETIC TECHNIQUES. The Bereiter-Engelmann approach to teaching young disadvantaged children rejects naturalistic strategies.[9] The teacher uses a series of basic statement forms in Standard English. The instructional model is closer to that used in teaching foreign languages to children. It makes no use of the language the children bring to school.

Nedler[10] and Reeback[11] use synthetic approaches to teach English to non-English-speaking children. In their patterned drill approaches, the teachers state a sentence or ask a question and the children must return the response desired by the teacher.

Approaches to teaching Standard English are generally geared to the disadvantaged child, but the normal child also needs help in expanding his language. The language problems of middle-class children are generally not as severe as those of disadvantaged children and the solutions suggested are seldom as drastic. Nevertheless, the focus on the dis-

---

[8]Arlene Hobson, "Systematic Language Modeling," *Contemporary Education*, Vol. 40, No. 4 (February 1969), 225–27.

[9]Carl Bereiter and Siegfried Engelmann, *Teaching Disadvantaged Children in the Preschool* (Englewood Cliffs, N.J.: Prentice-Hall, Inc., 1966).

[10]Shari Nedler, *Early Education for Spanish-Speaking Mexican-American Children*. Paper presented at AERA, March 2–7, 1970.

[11]Robert T. Reeback, *A Teacher's Manual to Accompany the Oral Language Program*, 3rd ed. (Albuquerque, New Mexico: Southwestern Cooperative Educational Laboratories, 1970).

advantaged ought not to detract from the concern for the needs of all children in language learning.

GOALS OF LANGUAGE LEARNING

Language arts programs in the early years have multiple goals. In general, the goals are as follows:

1. The development of verbal communication skills. The young child is constantly transmitting and receiving messages. His ability to function in the world is determined to a great extent by his ability to communicate his wants, needs, ideas, and feelings, and to receive and interpret similar communications from other persons. These two skills make up a large part of the goals of language arts programs. As the child matures, the communications sent and received are put into written as well as spoken forms. Reading and writing become important skills.

2. Development of rich language repertoire. Language is an extension of the person. In order for the young child to function effectively in the community, he must have a sense of the shared meanings of words and of the structure of the language that allows him to be linguistically effective.

A language repertoire is important not just for communication but as an aid to thinking as well. Since mature thought processes are so closely related to language both in structure and in content, the child's growth in language will also support his growth in thought.

3. Development of an ability to use language to influence and be influenced. Until the time a child reaches nursery school age, he is manipulated and manipulates others physically. As he enters school, he is manipulated and manipulates others more by the use of words. The teacher, for example, gives instructions in words. Language, in this sense, is a tool. The child satisfies social needs more by talking to other children. The give-and-take of human relationships becomes a function of language. Even in the dramatic play of children, verbal statements soon take the place of actual physical movements. All this suggests that the appropriate use of language is one of the most important social skills the young child can learn.

4. Developing personal satisfactions and aesthetic appreciations of language. Although much of the language arts program in the early school years is primarily utilitarian in nature, aesthetics should not be excluded. The use of literature, poetry, creative dramatics, and other forms of expression can provide great personal satisfactions for children. Reading is important for utilitarian purposes, but it is also a source of rich aesthetic and emotional satisfaction, as are listening to stories and viewing dramatic presentations.

EXPRESSIVE AND ORAL LANGUAGE LEARNING   There are many opportunities for oral language learning in the early years of school. Specific times are set aside for group discussion, story reading, and sharing, or "show and tell." While such large group activities may be suitable for teaching some receptive language skills, they are not efficient for teaching expressive skills, since too much time is spent by each child in a large group in waiting his turn. Alternate approaches need to be developed. Some of these approaches require a teacher's sensitivity to the time when language learning can occur naturally in a small group setting or in individual interaction. These small settings are usually more appropriate for language learning than are total class instructional settings.

The Activity Period

Most nursery-kindergarten programs set aside a good portion of the day for an activity or "work period." When primary grades are organized as suggested in Chapter X, these opportunities are also available. Some of the activities of the work period provide greater opportunities than others to support language learning. The teacher should use the opportunities to plan for the support of language learning.

Dramatic Play

One important area for language learning is the dramatic play area. Dramatic play involves the children in role playing in which there is no predetermined script or plot. It might include family play in a housekeeping area or the playing out of other societal roles reflecting a range of social institutions such as supermarket play, garage play, or other types of social situational play.

Although dramatic play is supported most often in nursery-kindergarten activities, similar play interactions can be developed by primary children. These may be more narrowly focused and closely guided and related to specific learning situations. Often social studies activities include dramatic play incidents to explore social roles. Dramatic play is symbolic play. It requires the interaction of children together in interlocking roles. The children taking these roles must communicate with one another to carry on the play. Language often substitutes for the actions of the playing. Smilansky found that there are specific techniques a teacher may use that work to enrich the dramatic play of disadvantaged children.[12]

[12]Sarah Smilansky, *The Effects of Sociodramatic Play on Disadvantaged Preschool Children* (New York: John Wiley and Sons, 1968).

The teacher needs to provide increased information about the themes of play. These could be provided through field trips to significant sites in the community. Such sites might include a supermarket, car wash, service station, television repair shop, dentist's office, or railroad station. Additional information may be provided through information books or films. Resource persons who visit the classroom also bring information to the group.

Prior to the involvement of the children in the play, the teacher must assemble the props to be used. Parents and children can be recruited to help in this task. If the theme of the play is the supermarket, a cash register, shelves, food boxes and cans, and perhaps a supermarket cart might be assembled. If planning play concerning a service station, a collection of props related to auto maintenance could be assembled, such as a bicycle tire pump, spark plugs, empty oil cans, distributor caps, wrenches, and screwdrivers—these will serve to stimulate play. Each theme will suggest its own props. Some props for dramatic play are available commercially through educational equipment companies. Others may be improvised by the teacher. The setting of the stage by the teacher often acts as a motivation for the children to play.

Educational play requires active guidance by the teacher, although she should allow the children to structure their own play activities within the theme and the setting that has been established. Through observation, the teacher becomes aware of possibilities in the play that are not evident to the children. She may move into the play, momentarily assuming a role, and move the children's play along in positive direction through a series of verbal interactions. She may simply come over to the children and ask key questions of the play participants that will suggest new alternatives. She may provide additional props if she feels that their inclusion will move the play forward.

The key to supporting language learning in dramatic play is not in simply setting up the children's play activities and leaving them alone in their corner. Robison and Spodek used the term *directive teaching* in describing how a teacher might guide the play of children.[13] The teacher functions not only as an observer but also as a guide and a source of information and play materials. In functioning in this manner the teacher must be careful not to impose too much of herself on the play of children.

Other Areas

While few areas are as productive for language learning as dramatic play, there are other opportunities in the activity period for language

[13]Helen Robison and Bernard Spodek, *New Directions in the Kindergarten* (New York: Teachers College Press, 1965).

learning. More mature block-building often involves verbal and social interaction.

As the children mature and move beyond the manipulative stage of block-building there will be a strong dramatic element to the play. When play takes on this dramatic quality and involves more than one child, it may be used in much the same way as dramatic play to support language learning. Arts and crafts and work in manipulative materials offer fewer opportunities to practice language skills. Teachers can add to available opportunities, however, by holding intimate conversations with the children.

Children who are shy and reticent in a large group situation will often speak more freely when alone with the teacher. Conversations can be started related to the activities in which the children are involved or to the materials they are using. Such conversations have the advantage of allowing the child to focus on something outside himself. It also allows him to refer to things immediately in front of him as a source of speech content. Teachers can use open-ended questions like, "Tell me what you have there," or "Are there other ways you could make something like it?" to elicit language expressions. These questions can be followed up in a probing fashion to continue the conversation. Techniques similar to the ones suggested by Blank, referred to above, can be effectively used in these situations.

Having the teacher immediately available as a respondent, with the child not having to wait his turn, make these small verbal interactions very useful. If there is a teacher aide or volunteer in the classroom, the amount of teacher-child interaction that can take place in an activity period is formidable, since two persons can be deployed to support verbal behavior.

Discussion Sessions

Most classes set aside periods of time during the day for discussion sessions. Often these sessions involve the entire class, as in sharing and "show and tell" periods. While such discussion sessions have many advantages, there are also disadvantages inherent in their organization.

The sharing period generally requires that each child, in turn, speak to the entire class. He may bring an object from home or he may discuss something that has happened to him. Such periods, if properly used, can effect a bridge between home and school as the child relates incidents or brings a valued object to school for display.

If the child is reticent, the teacher can ask questions about the object. During the sharing period, the children should be encouraged to ask questions, comment, and make observations on their own.

Teachers using this sharing period must avoid its inherent pitfalls. In some communities, the gap between home and school is so great it is difficult to bridge in such a situation. The rejection by the teacher of objects or incidents from home that might be considered inappropriate at school may actually widen the gap. It may also teach the child that it is safer not to expose oneself in school and thereby limit language learning possibilities.

There is also the danger that having the children take turns, limiting the length of each contribution, or having children wait for their turn longer than they can bear, may have negative influences on language learning. The children should be learning to be listeners and speakers and this is not easily learned in a situation that supports the negative responses of "turning off" and "tuning out."

There are several alternatives to the traditional sharing period that can increase the benefits of this type of activity for language learning. One method is to limit the number of children who will speak at each session. Going through the class alphabetically and assigning five children per session, for example, can keep the sharing period to a reasonable limit. Asking that children bring items to class associated with a specific theme might also limit the range of items discussed and relate the discussion time to other learning situations in the classroom. Children can be asked to bring in something of wood, or something that is attracted by a magnet, or something very old. Pictures of objects clipped from newspapers and magazines can be allowed as well as objects themselves. The need to focus on some special area or class of object turns the home search for an object into a problem-solving activity for the child as well as the family.

Another way of limiting the discussion is to change it from a whole class activity to a small group activity. This would allow a degree of voluntarism to the child's involvement in the activity as well as a greater degree of participation among all the children and for more interaction between children in the discussion situation. The children themselves might take turns asking about objects and events.

Finally, the discussion session might be changed from a situation in which children talk about things outside the school to a situation in which children talk about what happened in school. If a sharing time were held at the end of the activity period, for example, the children could then talk about what they made or did during that time. Holding the discussion immediately after the activities are over and before cleanup would allow the children to refer directly to things they had made, such as a block building or a picture.

The children can be called together in a suitable place that is regularly designated for assemblies. Each child can then be asked to talk about what he did or what he made that day. If a product is involved, then the child can show the product. The teachers or any of the other children may ask questions about it. If there is no product, then the child can be asked to describe the activity or activities in which he participated. Such discussions have the advantage of avoiding stereotyping, unless the entire program is a stereotyped one.

As the activities vary, the content of the discussions must also vary. The child and teacher share the same reference so that if there is distortion, misrepresentation, or confusion, the teacher is able to deal with it, since she was witness to the events. *Sharing* in this situation takes on new meaning, for not only does the child have an opportunity to relate things that are important to him, but the interaction and reporting of activity in the school setting can help establish a feeling of community in the classroom, without separating the "haves" from the "have nots."

Many other opportunities for discussions also can be found in the classroom. Informal discussions between the teacher and a single child or a group of children can take place on any occasion and should be regularly encouraged by the teacher. The greater the amount of verbal expression on the part of the child and the greater the number of adult-child interactions that take place, the greater the opportunities for language learning in the classroom. Teachers should encourage the initiation of such discussions by children.

Special occurrences such as the visit of a resource person or the return from a field trip are excellent opportunities to initiate such a discussion. The children can review the events that have passed and help bring focus to the situation. The careful framing of questions and listening for responses can help the teacher determine what areas of misconception exist. If discussions allow for a free interchange of ideas, they will provide children with opportunities to test their perceptions of the outside world against those of their peers. Questions asked of children should be answerable by them. If the teacher is the only one who has access to the information necessary for response, then the discussion deteriorates into a guessing game. Discussions held prior to an event can often be used for planning. Young children's planning will be rudimentary, since their lack of experience limits their ability to anticipate things ahead of time.

Creative Dramatics

The school should provide many opportunities for children to interpret the stories, poems, and songs they hear, in a variety of ways. Creative drama allows for such interpretations. Unlike dramatic play, which builds upon the general knowledge of children and can move in any direction, this focuses on a particular plot, such as that of a familiar story with a relatively simple, straight-forward plot line. The children can be assigned characters and then can go through the story, making up their own dialogue, and keeping the story line intact. The creative aspect of the dramatic presentation lies in the interpretations of the children, the dialogue they develop, and the actions they assign to particular characters. Children can also base dramatic presentation on their own original stories, which provide them with a greater latitude of plot and character.

Creative dramatic presentations need no audience. They can be organized as a part of the activity period, either started spontaneously by the children or encouraged by the teacher. The teacher and children can assemble the few props needed, and the furniture and equipment of the classroom can be made to represent anything: a pair of chairs can be an automobile, a table becomes a bridge, a piece of carpeting turns into an ocean. Odd pieces of drapery material, skirts, and floppy hats can be made to represent all kinds of costumes.

As the teacher directs such a dramatic presentation, she should be careful not to have the children memorize pieces of dialogue or action. Instead, she should allow the content of the play to be the child's product. Her job includes providing a story that can become familiar to the children through repeated telling, suggesting actions and sequences, and referring to the original story as a source of dialogue and action. Often a suggestion such as, "What happens next?" or "What did he say in response?" is the only guidance a teacher needs to give.

Simple dramatic presentations can be repeated again and again. Children can be encouraged to try new roles and, once assigned a role, to play it in their own way. While such productions ought not to be organized primarily as shows for others, if a particular dramatic presentation seems good, there is no reason not to invite another class, the principal of the school, or the children's parents to view it. This can provide the children with a great sense of accomplishment.

As children mature, dramatic presentations can become more elaborate, using more extensive stories, more extensive characterizations, and more elaborate props and settings. The same story can often be dramatized in a variety of ways in a class. After interpreting a story in creative dramatics, the children can try it with puppets or flannelgraph illustrations. They could also try acting out the story in pantomime—attempting to communicate with actions alone.

Puppetry

Young children enjoy playing with puppets. The use of puppets is a good way to get a shy child to vocalize, for the puppet becomes the center of attention rather than the child. While a variety of excellent commercial hand-puppets are available in supply houses, simple puppets can be constructed by the teacher or the children.

Stick puppets can be made by pasting faces the children have drawn on paper to a flat stick. These can be held in the children's hands and manipulated by them in a play situation. Puppets can also be made out of paper bags on which a face has been drawn. If the mouth is drawn on both sides of the point at which the square bottom of the bag is folded, it can be held between fingers and thumb so that the mouth opens and closes. Such sophisticated puppet manipulations are not really necessary for young children, however.

Teachers and parents can also make interesting puppets out of socks. Buttons can be sewn on to represent eyes and a piece of felt to represent the mouth. Puppets can be improvised in many other ways. All that is needed is an object to be manipulated by the children that is suggestive of a character. For very young children there is even no need for a puppet stage, for even if the puppeteer is visible, as in Japanese puppet shows, the audience will focus on the puppets themselves.

The making of puppets ought not to be a whole class craft activity. Puppets should be constructed because a need for them is felt by some children. Nor should puppet shows themselves involve the whole class. Children can be easily bored if they must sit for periods of time watching the unrehearsed and often uncommunicative manipulations of puppets by each member of the class simply because they all have made them and must therefore use them. Puppet shows are best developed in small classes; nor is an audience always necessary.

With older children, puppet making can become a more extensive craft activity with children using papier-mâché or wood for shaping the puppets' heads. Marionettes—puppets that move by the manipulation of strings—can also be used by children in the upper primary grades. As with creative dramatics, there is no age ceiling on the use of puppets, for they can be used by adults as well as by young children if their use is varied with maturity.

Children's Storytelling

While one generally considers the teacher to be the storyteller in a class, young children should also be encouraged to tell stories. These can be the children's original stories or the retelling of stories they have heard. Closely associated with children's storytelling is the children's reporting of occurrences of importance to them. These stories can be told to the other children or dictated to the teacher, who may write them down to be read back later.

Children can also be encouraged to tell stories by being asked leading questions. The teacher might also read part of a story and ask the children to complete it or to fill in portions of it.

Children can be encouraged to report on important events. A child may return from a vacation or a trip and be bursting to share his experiences with others. Time should be provided for him to do so, for the sharing of experience is one of the important reasons for developing good language facility. These reports may be given to a small group rather than to the entire class. On occasion these reports, too, should be written down by the teacher to be read back at a later time.

Teachers should be encouraged to take dictation from children. The children's observations of the process of dictating, recording, and reading back stories gives them an understanding of what reading and writing is. The phrase "writing is talk written down" comes vividly to life in this process. The children gain insight both into the reading and writing processes and the reasons for our concern for learning these skills. Meaningful associations between their own verbal utterances and the books around them are created in this process.

RECEPTIVE ORAL LANGUAGE LEARNING   The skills of a receptive language become increasingly important. Most children spend less time speaking and acting and more time listening and watching as they move through school. Opportunities must be provided for children to listen.

Children listen at different times for different purposes and with varying degrees of depth. Listening has been classified as marginal, appreciative, attentive, and analytic.[14] Listening to sounds in the background can be characterized as marginal; listening to music or to a story is appreciative listening; attentive listening is listening for directions; analytic listening requires a more active role of the individual, who dissects and evaluates what is heard. Unfortunately the activities in too many classrooms support marginal listening alone.

When children are constantly bombarded with messages and instructions, not all of which may seem relevant to them, they tend to "tune out." In many crowded, noisy homes children learn this skill of "tuning out" as a survival mechanism that may be brought to school and applied indiscriminately. While we seldom involve young children in analytic listening, the processes of appreciative and attentive listening may be developed in schools, and storytelling will help.

---

[14]National Council of Teachers of English, *Language Arts for Today's Children* (New York: Appleton-Century-Crofts, Inc., 1954).

Telling Stories to Children

Storytelling, both with and without books, has a firm, well-deserved place in the programs of the schools. A large body of children's literature providing a wealth of resources for storytelling has developed in the last few decades in our country. Unfortunately, the availability of books for children often creates a situation in which the teacher only reads stories to the children rather than telling them. While this is probably easier from the point of view of not having to worry about content or plot, the reading of books should never completely substitute for the telling of stories. Teachers can familiarize themselves with stories from children's books which they can retell in their own words.

The story told might be a fanciful, contemporary tale or the retelling of a traditional story culled from the folk literature. Stories may also be the outgrowth of the children's experiences. The retelling of the happenings on a trip or another experience the children have had, or even an occurrence from the childhood experience of the teacher herself, all provide excellent resources for stories.

Teachers often find that props or pictures help them dramatize a story and can use commercially available simple figures backed with sandpaper and used on a flannel board or simple objects or pictures.

Reading to Children

Any nursery or kindergarten class should have a good stock of well-written and well-illustrated books for children. Collections of stories, or anthologies, even when not illustrated, are also useful. Teachers can get help in selecting books from other teachers and supervisors, librarians, and local colleges and universities. In addition, several printed resources are available for teachers to help them select books. These include

Best Books for Children. New York: R. R. Bowker.

Bibliography of Books for Children. Washington, D.C.: Association for Childhood Education International.

Books for Children. Chicago: American Library Association, n.d.

Eaken, Mary K. *Good Books for Children*, 3rd ed. Chicago: University of Chicago Press, 1966.

Guilfoile, Elizabeth. *Books for Beginning Readers.* Champaign, Illinois: National Council of Teachers of English, 1962.

Larrick, Nancy. *A Parent's Guide to Children's Reading* (rev.). Garden City, New York: Doubleday, 1964.

Reading Ladders for Human Relations. Washington, D.C.: American Council on Education, 1963.

Rollins, Charlemae H. *We Build Together*, 3rd ed. Champaign, Illinois: National Council of Teachers of English, 1967.

Books should be selected carefully; it is important that they be of interest to the children. When information books are read, they should be accurate and authoritative—accuracy of information may take precedence over literary style in selecting them. Stories may also be read to prepare children for a future study; or a book might be selected because the theme concerns the teacher herself. Books are also read simply for good fun.

Good children's literature has within it themes that are the central focus of young children's concerns. Books provide a way of learning about things outside the immediate in time and space, thus expanding the child's horizons. Persons different in manner and dress can be introduced to children through books. And certainly the world of whimsy and fantasy should be a part of the child's literary experience.

Books can often help young children deal with the resolution of their own problems and conflicts. Reading these stories often has a mentally healthful effect by showing the child that the problems he encounters are not his alone. In addition, books that depict children from minority groups in realistic ways are becoming increasingly available. While such books are no substitute for an integrated classroom, they help the majority culture member realize that people who may seem different are really not that different. Providing such books in school also indicates that members of his group are worthy of being depicted in the national literature.

It is important that the teacher be familiar with the book she is reading to the children. New teachers often find it helpful to take books home and practice reading them aloud. The stage should then be set for a pleasurable reading experience with the children. An informal arrangement helps; having the group sit informally on a rug so that each child has an undisturbed line of vision to the teacher is helpful. Chairs can also be informally arranged for reading—especially if a picture story book is being read.

It is also helpful not to have to constantly interrupt a story to admonish a child who is misbehaving or inattentive. Teachers sometimes use the tactic of placing obstreperous children very near them to forestall the need to interrupt. Making story listening a voluntary activity, with choices of other non-noise-producing activities available for children to select, is also useful. It is interesting to note how often a child will begin to pay attention simply because he is not required to do so.

While teachers generally read stories to children themselves, it is helpful to have an aide or a volunteer parent come to school and read. If there is more than one person available, a story-reading time need not involve the entire class. Actually, making the story-reading period a more intimate one is helpful in developing language learning. Children in the upper classes may be invited to read to the class, as may the better primary readers.

The reading of a story will often engender a discussion. Teachers sometimes also like to ask questions of the children to see if they have understood the story. While this is a good technique for ferreting out the misconceptions of children, it can be overdone. Care must be taken to see that the story-reading activity remains a pleasant one and does not become burdensome to children.

Browsing Through Books

Children need opportunities to look at books themselves, to get the feel of books even before they are required to learn to read them. A good library area will have books attractively displayed and available for children. Books may be laid out on a shelf or placed in a rack so that the child can easily see covers in order to select books that seem interesting. There ought to be a place where the child can comfortably look through the books, examining the pictures, reading, and discussing them with other children. A rocking chair, a table and chairs, a group of pillows on the floor, or even a small rug all make inviting settings for browsing through books. Of course, lighting must be adequate and there should be a degree of isolation to the area. The books available in the classroom can be organized for children to care for them. When books are changed at frequent intervals there is always some new and exciting reading material available to the children.

It is useful to allow children to take books home if at all possible. Particularly when there is a suspicion that the child has few books at home, the teacher should try to arrange to loan books or see that in some way reading material is given the child to take home. There are inexpensive reprints of good children's books presently available that make the cost of this activity less prohibitive. If books are to be taken home, it is a good idea to encourage the parents to read to nonreading children. Sometimes a simple instruction sheet sent home to the parent is enough; at other times, teachers might wish to devote a parent meeting to working on the specific skills needed by the parents in reading to their children.

Poetry for Young Children

Children enjoy listening to poetry, for it combines the rhythmic flow of words with a concern for their sounds. A range of poems for young children, from Mother Goose rhymes and A. A. Milne to the works of many contemporary poets, can be introduced. The repetitive quality of much of children's poetry will sometimes help the children learn the poems themselves.

Often, the reading of poetry in a class will lead children to an interest in the sounds of words. Rhyming and alliteration may fascinate some children who simply enjoy the sounds of the words and the way the words feel on their tongues. Play with words should be encouraged, but teachers should be forewarned that young children can be terrible punsters. Poems should be read aloud so that the rhyme and rhythm become more apparent.

Teachers of young children often use poems along with finger plays. While these activities often lack literary value, they are useful as time-fillers and, as such, may be used with children while waiting for the bus or on similar occasions. Finger play has a venerable tradition in early childhood education, originating in Froebel's kindergarten.

Using Audio-visual Aids

In most classrooms the teacher, being alone, is limited in her ability to provide a great variety of listening activities for the children. If she reads a story to the children, her entire attention is consumed and she can do nothing else; thus, story times too often become total class activity times because the teacher finds that having all the children attend allows her to keep the class under her control. This is not necessary in a well-organized classroom. Many teachers have found that using audio-visual aids can extend their ability to provide receptive language activities under a variety of conditions and with smaller groups of children.

Commercial recordings of many children's stories are available. In addition, teachers have found it helpful to make their own sound recordings of stories, reading them into a tape recorder, enabling the children to listen independently. Most children at the nursery level can learn to handle a cassette tape recorder on their own. Providing them with a tape recording of a book along with the book itself allows the children to listen to the story and look at the pictures at the same time. Recording an auditory signal for turning the page is helpful.

Many classes are now becoming equipped with *listening centers*. Such a center consists of headphone attachments to a phonograph or tape recorder. Multiple jacks are available so that more than one child can listen at a time. While some listening centers are designed with carrels to separate the children, such separations are unnnecessary, and possibly even a hindrance unless there is a severe attention problem. Listening to a story can and ought to be an experience a child can share with others. The headsets are used primarily so that the sounds of the record do not interfere with other activities that may be occurring in the classroom.

Motion pictures and sound filmstrips can also be used to extend children's receptive language experiences. A number of excellent children's stories are now available in these media and rooms can be arranged and equipped to allow viewing by a single child as well as by a large group.

Television and Children

While most children spend a large proportion of their waking hours viewing television, we are still not sure what they learn from it; certainly they seem to learn a lot. Any parent can report stories of young children identifying packages of advertised products, or of having the children badger them for toys they have seen advertised on that medium. While educators may not be sure of the impact of television on children's learning, advertisers seem to have a lot of faith in it.

We know that children's vocabulary is affected by television, because many of the words young children use daily are accessible only through this medium. It is doubtful that television similarly influences syntax, however. Although Standard American speech is heard continually on television, children of minority groups who are constantly exposed to it still do not master the syntax. This exposure apparently does not effect their speech patterns. Perhaps this is due to the lack of interaction in televiewing, which is a relatively passive act, as well as to the fact that much of the listening is on a marginal level.

Educational programs have, on occasion, been developed for young children, but often these are local shows operated on meager budgets. Few national programs of educational value exist for children. *Sesame Street* and *Misterrogers' Neighborhood* are distributed nationally on educational television, and *Captain Kangaroo* is distributed commercially; these have all demonstrated that television programs can be entertaining, educational, and mentally healthy while reaching large groups of children. It is still too soon to determine the educational impact of such programs, however.

Existing programs for children are designed primarily for home viewing. Whether it would be profitable to provide television instruction in school is open to question. The amount of time available to most early childhood classes is little enough as it is. It would be unfortunate to limit interactional possibilities by substituting passive listening and viewing that can be done in the child's home. Television scheduling also limits the teacher's flexibility in class, although this may change as video tape recorders become more readily available.

Using the Normal Occurrences of the Day

Teachers can find many opportunities in all situations to support language learning throughout the school day. Continual language instruction requires, however, a sensitivity to the potentials of learning hidden in each situation.

A cooking activity might start with a planning discussion. "What needs to be done?" "How will we go about it?" "Who will do each task?" "What materials and equipment are necessary?" These questions can be used to elicit responses in a planning discussion from all the children. Recipes need to be read several times, both during the planning and the cooking. The entire cooking sequence can be reviewed at its termination and perhaps a chart can be written by the teacher describing the experience.

In dramatic play situations, signs can often be made by the teacher and used by the children. In music, the teacher might have the children listen carefully to the words of a song, then talk about the sounds of the words as well as their meaning. She might even use the singing of a repetitive verse of a song to teach new words, or she might ask the children to create their own verses. The need for finding rhymes will help the children learn to listen to the word endings and to compare the sounds of words. Each activity needs to be plumbed to determine the depth of language learning that can be found therein.

OTHER LANGUAGE-RELATED ACTIVITIES   In addition to the areas already discussed, there are many other opportunities for language learning in the classroom. In most classrooms, there are a number of manipulative materials that are provided in support of language learning. The use of these materials can extend an understanding of specific language attributes.

Lotto games are a good example of one of these. In playing lotto, children have to identify a picture, label it, and match it with another picture on a card—thus lotto games can be used to teach the names of categories of objects, the names of objects, or the names of actions, in addition to teaching visual matching skills. *See-Quees* puzzles, in which the scenes from familiar stories must be placed in proper order, help children learn the sequence of events in a story. Then they may be asked to relate the story after the pictures are ordered. There are also many reading readiness materials that can be used. Three-dimensional letters allow children to make up words and learn the names of the letters without needing to cope with the problem of forming the letters themselves. They also provide a tactile experience in perceiving the shape and form of letters. A number of reading readiness games and materials can also be included here.

Many of the games in the manipulative material area can be used by children individually or in small groups. Once children have mastered the skills needed in using the materials as well as the classroom rules for their use, they can often be used independently, with the teacher periodically checking on the accuracy of the activity. This independence of operation allows the manipulative materials to be used during many different times of the day.

The child's continued involvement in oral language activities, discussions, creative dramatic productions, listening to stories and poems, and all the other language activities described, has a direct connection with his involvement in written language activities. There is less separation of the language arts in life than there is in school programs, which are too often segmented and compartmentalized. Reading and writing must go hand in hand with listening and speaking in the classroom.

WRITTEN LANGUAGE LEARNING

Primary teachers in particular are concerned with the mechanics as well as the expressive content of reading and writing. Much activity in the area of written language learning can be approached in an informal manner. However, the teaching of the skills of reading and writing requires some systematic approach to learning.

Writing

Most schools today teach young children to write in manuscript, a simple form of calligraphy using unconnected letters. The switch to cursive writing, in which all the letters in a word are connected, usually comes at the end of the primary grades or the beginning of the intermediate grades—most typically in about the middle of second grade. Children often begin writing in kindergarten by learning to write their names. Sometimes they have learned this skill at home. It is helpful if kindergarten children can learn to use manuscript rather than block printing in writing their name in order to avoid an additional transition.

The beginnings of letter writing actually start even earlier. Children in nursery school and kindergarten have already had experiences using crayons and paint brushes. If the teacher has helped the children learn to hold and use these implements properly, the transition from drawing to writing is simplified. Children can be provided with pencils in the kindergarten for both drawing and beginning writing. They can be helped in informal situations to make the strokes necessary for manuscript writing—these strokes include the circle and the horizontal, vertical, and slant strokes. They can often be identified in the child's existing paintings and drawings. The child's ability to control his painting, drawing, or writing implement will aid him later in forming letters.

A variety of techniques can be used to teach the formation of letters, including the use of template, wooden, or sandpaper letters allowing a feel for the shape and form of letters. Children can then copy letters the teacher writes or those printed in work sheets or exercise books, or go over letters formed by the teacher. Letters can be formed in the sand or on a blackboard before using paper and pencil. Teachers may also give children models printed on paper placed under acetate sheets so that the child's first writing is directly on the model. When such activities are provided in the classroom, it is important that they be provided only to those children who are interested and who can benefit from them. It is unwise to make such printing activities a whole class assignment.

In many cases, children will be able to *use* writing long before they have perfected the ability to write each letter clearly, legibly, and without error. They should be encouraged to do so, since unnecessary attention to the mechanics of writing without any concern for its use may lead them to lose interest. It is useful to have the children write words, sentences, and stories as early as possible.

Many kindergarten and primary classrooms have primer typewriters available. The large type and simplified form of the letters made by these typewriters makes them an extremely useful addition to the classroom. Children can begin early to type their own stories on these machines, and the stories can be read by other children with ease. The typewriter frees the young child from his concern with coordinating the muscles of his hand to form the letters. Words come out with ease. In its introduction, the typewriter often stimulates children to play with the forms of letters and punctuation marks. This can be allowed. Soon children will move from this exploratory stage to a more goal-oriented stage, using the typewriter as a writing implement. More than one child might wish to be at the machine at the same time, for dialogue as well as discourse can be typed by children.

If the teacher has been taking down the dictation of children, it is an easy matter to move slowly to the children's writing. She might begin by having the children dictate a short story, using only a few words which the children can copy. The children might also be given the opportunity to illustrate the story on large sheets of paper. The copying of short stories can be extended as stories are elaborated and lengthened. Groups of children can write stories together. They should be encouraged to begin to write their own stories as soon as possible.

The stories children write should be used. They should be read, either to the teacher or to other children. They may also be sent home. It is helpful to collect the writings of children to show progress in school and to read for pleasure. These writings can be stapled together into a book with covers made by the children. Illustrations can be drawn and the total volume be displayed or put into the reading area so that others can read these stories as well. If the work of children is read by others, the need for clarity and precision in writing becomes quite evident, for the other children's convenience.

Providing the children with thin writing tablets at the beginning of the year gives them a sense of writing their own book. Care should be taken that there are not too many pages in these tablets, for otherwise, completing them will seem an overwhelming task.

The school day is filled with opportunities for writing and children should be encouraged to write as much as possible. They can write about experiences out of school as well. Starting with the reporting of incidents may help the children become writers. As time goes on, they can become more creative in the writing and add the composition of fanciful tales and poetry to their accumulated skills.

In the beginning, spelling is not too important and should not be stressed. Children need to feel comfortable in writing and this is not easily accomplished at first. Premature criticism can stifle the child's early attempts. The work can be corrected later by the teacher or by other children. Eventually children will develop the habit of proofreading their written work before submitting it to the teacher. It is helpful to provide them with primary dictionaries so that they can begin to look up the spelling of words on their own. They can also develop their own dictionaries or word lists. Providing each child with a file box and a set of cards or a notebook with each page devoted to a single letter of the alphabet can initiate this. Children can put into their dictionary new words that they have learned to spell and define. They will soon begin to use one another as well as the teacher as resources for proper spelling. In the primary grades more formal work in spelling can be included in the program.

There is not complete agreement in the field as to when a systematic program of spelling construction ought to begin for children, nor is there agreement as to the nature of such a program. In the past, many spelling programs consisted of providing children with lists or books of words used in their particular age-groups. Since it was felt that English spelling was highly irregular, most programs consisted of having the children memorize the spelling of lists of words in some fashion. Sometimes pretests were given weekly and children wrote the words they could not spell periodically until they were retested at the end of the week. Often the length of the word was the criteria for determining its suitability for children, with young children asked to learn shorter words. They were often helped to focus on the visual aspects of the word to enhance retention.

Recent studies by Hanna and others have shown a high degree of regularity in the spelling of English words.[15] This would suggest that spelling patterns can be abstracted and words taught to children in a more rational manner than has been the convention. It also suggests that the errors of children who spell words as they sound could also be used to greater advantage by teachers, for even when mistakes are made, there may be some errors that are more logical than others.

Grammar

Recent changes in linguistic theory have had a profound effect on the teaching of grammar at the secondary school and college level. It is only possible to speculate about the extent to which these changes call for modification of early childhood programs. Current theory conceives of grammar as a process by which an infinite variety of sentences can be derived by transformation from a limited number of basic sentence forms.[16] The theory of transformational grammar as postulated by Chomsky and others would suggest that grammar ought not to be taught as a series of rules that lead to "proper" language usage, but as a series of rules from which new structure can be generated.

In the early years we are concerned about having children become good users of language rather than scholars of the structure of the language. From this point of view, the teacher's concern needs to be about how the newer grammar could provide insights that would help to extend children's language.

One possible approach that might be taken is to provide children with opportunities to "play" with the structures of language just as they often play with the sounds of words. Children can be given simple sentences and asked to transform them in a variety of ways. Given a declarative sentence, children could be asked to state it as a question or as a command. They could be asked to add modifiers to noun or verb phrases as ways of becoming more specific in their language use. They could also be asked to place words in different sequences to see if they could change the meaning of sentences or to become sensitive to grammatical and ungrammatical structures.

Teachers need to be aware of the beauties of the language that can be found in the personal ways that children express themselves. Often the idiosyncratic phrases of children in the nursery years are subdued because they do not fit into the formal structure of the language program.

[15]Paul R. and Jean S. Hanna, Richard E. Hodges, and E. Hugh Rudorf, "A Summary: Linguistic Cues for Spelling Improvement," *Elementary English*, Vol. 44 (December 1967), 862–65.

[16]Noam Chomsky, *Syntactic Structure* (The Hague: Mouton and Co., 1957).

Subcultural groups have expressions that have enriched our language, yet we often exclude these from our schools. Teachers should support and cherish these rather than try to eliminate them. The beauty of the language is enhanced when communication is a personal statement rather than a stereotyped series of phrases.

Reading

Reading and writing are two sides of the same coin. As we wish to develop writers through our primary programs, we also wish to develop readers. In order to do this, reading has to become a meaningful and personally satisfying experience. This can only happen when the child reads because he wants to rather than because he has to. If a child is to become "hooked on books," the book has to be introduced early in the child's reading experience.

As mentioned earlier, children need to be provided with opportunities for free browsing and reading. They should be able to determine what they will read, when they will read, and for how long. Even nursery-school children need opportunities to look at books themselves to get the feel of books before they are required to learn to read them. Once children develop reading skills they should have many opportunities available for independent study.

The books available in a class should range broadly in topics and reading levels. If a book is interesting, a child will be able to read beyond his reading level as well as beneath it. There needs to be a place where a child can sit or stretch out and read undisturbed. Nor should conversation be limited in a reading area, for if a child is truly interested in a book, he will want to share its contents with others. If the school has a library, it is important to schedule times for children to read or select books in it. A school library is a supplement, not a substitute, for a classroom library. Children need continual access to books. If children are reading independently it is helpful for them to have a record-keeping system to enable the teacher and child to keep track of books read.

Children learn as much by observing the behavior of teachers as by listening to their admonitions. If a teacher wishes to teach children to enjoy reading, she must be a reader herself and must be able to communicate her enjoyment of reading to the children. The reading of stories to the class is one way of showing this enjoyment. There are other ways as well. A teacher can bring special books into class on occasion and tell the children about them, or feature them in a display. She can have conferences with the children, asking them to describe the books, telling whether or not they enjoyed them and why. She can allow the children to write about the books they read. The teacher needs to show that she values the books in the room by keeping the reading center attractive, featuring interesting books, and insuring that children have time for free reading of books of their own choice during the school day.

More than anything, the climate of the classroom and the values the teacher's behavior reflects will determine the nature of the language program. The same room with the same materials can be a dull setting or it can be an exciting place with children eagerly learning, listening, reading, talking, and writing. It is what the teacher does with the materials at hand that makes the difference.

SUGGESTED READING

ANDERSON, PAUL S., *Language Skills in Elementary Education*. New York: Macmillan, 1964.

APPLEGATE, MAUREE, *Helping Children Write*. Evanston, Illinois: Harper and Row, 1963.

ARBUTHNOT, MARY HILL, *Time for Poetry*. Chicago: Scott Foresman, 1951.

BEREITER, CARL, AND SEIGFRIED ENGELMANN, *Teaching Disadvantaged Children in the Preschool*. Englewood Cliffs, New Jersey: Prentice-Hall, Inc., 1966.

BURNS, PAUL C., AND ALBERTA L. LOWE, *The Language Arts in Childhood Education*. Chicago: Rand McNally, 1966.

CAZDEN, COURNEY, "Some Implications of Research on Language Development," In R. Hess and R. Bear, eds., *Early Education*. Chicago: Aldine Publishing Company, 1968.

CHUKOVSKY, KORNEI, *From Two to Five*. Berkeley: University of California Press, 1963.

COHEN, DOROTHY H., "Language and Experience: The Setting," *Childhood Education*, Vol. 42, No. 3 (November 1965), 139–42.

DAWSON, MILDRED A., AND GEORGIANA G. NEWMAN, *Language Teaching in Kindergarten and Early Primary Grades*. New York: Harcourt, Brace and World, 1966.

HANNA, PAUL R. et al., "A Summary: Linguistic Cues for Spelling Improvement," *Elementary English*, Vol. 44, No. 7 (December 1967), 862–65.

HORRWOTH, GLORIA L., "Listening: A Facet of Oral Language," *Elementary English*, Vol. 43, No. 4 (April 1966), 359–64.

HUCK, CHARLOTTE S., AND DORIS A. YOUNG, *Children's Literature in the Elementary School*. New York: Holt, Rinehart & Winston, 1967.

PITTMAN, G., "Young Children Enjoy Poetry," *Elementary English*, Vol. 43, No. 3 (March 1966), 247–51.

RUSSELL, DAVID H., AND ELIZABETH F. RUSSELL, *Listening Aids Through the Grades*. New York: Teachers College Press, 1959.

SIKS, GERALDINE B., *Creative Dramatics, an Art for Children*. New York: Harper and Row, 1958.

STERN, CAROLYN, "Language Competencies of Young Children," *Young Children*, Vol. 22, No. 1 (October 1966), 44–50.

STRICKLAND, RUTH G., *The Language Arts in the Elementary School*, 3rd ed. Lexington, Massachusetts: D. C. Heath, 1969.

5

Teaching Beginning Reading:
Issues and Activities

Any discourse about reading in the early years can be full of pitfalls. The area has been marked by controversy throughout the history of early childhood education. It is interesting to note, for example, the disagreement about the place of reading instruction in the nursery school found in the writing of pioneer nursery educators. Margaret Macmillan states:

> Reading—The letters, which I originally had made for the trays, were kept in big wooden boxes, each with 26 letter places. These we still use and I think they form the best means of teaching reading and spelling, their use making appeal as it does to three distinct senses, the muscular, the tactual, and the visual. Falling back on these, particularly on the earlier senses, many of our pedagogical difficulties fall away.[1]

On the other hand, Grace Owen is definite in the opposing point of view:

> No mention has been made of instruction in the Nursery School because in any formal sense it has no place. No reading, no writing, no number lessons should on any account be allowed, for the time for these things has not yet come.[2]

One can find similar positions being stated today in the United States, fifty years later.

Controversy over the proper age for beginning reading instruction has been with us for a long time. Ought we wait until a child is six or

[1]Margaret Macmillan, *The Nursery School* (London: J. M. Dent and Sons, Ltd., 1919), p. 11.

[2]Grace Owen, *Nursery School Education* (London: Methuen and Co., Ltd., 1920), p. 25.

seven to begin reading instruction, or should we teach our babies to read, without even waiting until they reach the appropriate entrance age for nursery school? There is controversy over the method of reading instruction as well—should reading be taught using a phonics approach, a linguistic approach, a basal reading approach, or a language experience approach? Should the child be instructed as a member of a group or should instruction be individualized? Should beginning reading instruction put the child immediately in contact with the traditional system of writing the English language or should this first contact be with a more rational transitional orthography?

Each opposing point of view in the area of beginning reading has its following of educators who are sure they have *the* answer, often brandishing reports that demonstrate the effectiveness of *the* method, and almost always having materials available to be used to teach children to read in that particular way.

In recent years, the number of alternative approaches to beginning reading instruction seems to be increasing, and new textbooks and programs appearing with increasing regularity. To the legion of reading specialists producing instructional materials have been added linguists, psychologists, specialists in exceptional education, and many others. The recent national concern for the failure of schools in educating disadvantaged children has heightened developmental activities for the teaching of reading, especially in the area of early instruction and prereading education.

For all the interest and activity, the fact is that *there is relatively little dependable knowledge about how children learn to read and what instructional programs seem to be most effective.* Recently the U.S. Office of Education conducted an extensive study of reading in the first grade designed to collect data about the effectiveness of many programs. In general, the findings suggested that there was no single approach to reading instruction that was outstanding compared to others in all aspects of reading. While there were differences in results, children learned certain phases of reading better by one method, and other phases better by other methods. Furthermore, it was suggested that there was more variability among teachers than among programs in terms of successful reading achievement.[3] This would suggest that it is quite possible that variables other than the particular methodological approach used in reading instruction are crucial in getting children to read. This presents an interesting point for speculation and research. What are the crucial elements of an effective reading program? Are there classroom character-

---

[3]Guy Bond, "First Grade Reading Studies: An Overview," *Elementary English*, Vol. 43, No. 5 (May 1966), 464–70.

istics, teacher characteristics, pupil characteristics, or community characteristics that must be taken into account in developing an optimal program? More careful analysis needs to be made of classroom variables other than the instructional method before we can make use of these findings.

DEFINING READING   Some of the controversy about reading instruction arises from the way in which the reading process is defined. Some educators contend that it is basically a decoding process—a process of learning the relationship between written symbols and spoken sounds. Once these associations are learned, the child is a reader. Since the young child already has a body of knowledge available to him in relation to meanings and processes in oral language, beginning reading teachers need not worry about these. What the child does with the information gleaned from the written page is not considered the domain of reading. Further, the goal of reading instruction, according to this point of view, is to provide children with the key letter-sound associations that will unlock the written code.

While few will disagree with the need for the successful beginning reader to learn letter-sound associations, there are many who suggest that the reading process is more than "code cracking" alone. Different experts extend their interpretations of the reading process and include much more. Some claim that reading is "gaining meaning from the printed page." They take reading one step beyond the first approach, suggesting that the process of *interpreting* the sounds associated with the letters is also a part of the reading process and needs to be included in any program of instruction. Educators supporting this theory even suggest that the derivation of meaning for the printed word, rather than "code cracking," be emphasized in any reading instructional program.

Still others suggest that the reading process is really an extension of intellectual processes, for the interpretation of meaning is a significant part of reading also. Critical reading, problem solving, and other complex processes need also to be included in any reading program.

These points of view are not contradictory to one another, for they deal with the relationship of the skill of reading to the language and thinking process of the individual. It is quite possible that the reading process is different at different age or grade levels. For the teacher of young children, some of the discussion about the reading process may seem irrelevant, for much of it relates to the nature of this process in more mature individuals. The teacher of young children, though concerned mainly with the beginning processes of reading, needs an understanding of the relationship between early processes and more mature modes of reading to put beginning reading instruction in the proper perspective.

Relationship of Reading to Language

When language is discussed one needs to include the four modes of communication: speaking, listening, reading, and writing. The linguists study written language as a way of expressing oral language in visual symbols. The writer takes oral language and encodes it into a series of characters which can be decoded in order for their meaning to be ascertained.

There are ma.1y ways of encoding language. Early man used pictures to illustrate the things he wished to communicate. Some men eventually developed abstractions of these pictures, replacing them with a set of symbols, each symbol reflecting a single idea. The advantage of this ideographic approach was that the symbols could be combined to create representations of abstract ideas and actions. The Chinese written language is composed of ideographs of this order. While the written symbols relate to the spoken language ideationally, they have no relationship to the sounds of the language. The advantage of such a written system is that it allows one to communicate across languages and dialects without the need to share a common spoken language. The disadvantage lies in the large number of symbols that need to be learned to establish basic literacy, let alone the vast number needed for a person of scholarship.

In our own system, one can read any material, no matter how complex its nature, by mastering a set of twenty-six symbols and their multiple sound relationships. The symbols reflect sounds in the spoken language rather than ideas or objects. The need to crack the code of letter-sound association, therefore, becomes obvious, for the written symbols carry no meaning outside of their oral counterpart. Some reading specialists suggest that one of the major problems in reading stems from the fact that a sound can be represented by more than one letter, and letters or combinations of letters can represent a multitude of sounds. While there is some irregularity in this relationship, there is a high degree of regularity between the sound symbols and the visual symbols of our language.

Reading is a part of the language process that deals with the decoding of written symbols. In its simplest form it is a translation of written symbols into their equivalent sound symbols. Since this is a linguistic process, however, it is incomplete until meaning has been derived from those symbols. In the early years of schooling, the meanings gained from the written word are usually meanings the young child has already learned in relation to his knowledge of the spoken word. Only as he approaches maturity does his reading vocabulary outstrip his listening vocabulary. Few books developed for reading instruction under any system contain a vocabulary that is beyond the listening vocabulary of the children for whom the book is designed. In some cases, advocates of the code cracking approach to reading have described very young children reading Shakespearian plays or other similarly sophisticated written matter. This type of reading is a distortion of the reading process, for few reading experts at any level would support a child's learning to read to the exclusion of his understanding.

Defining the process of reading does not solve the issues inherent in reading instruction, though it is a necessary first step. The crucial issues relate to *how* the child can best learn the reading process. Is meaningful or meaningless material best for teaching the code cracking system? This is one question that even the proponents of "phonics only" or linguistic approaches to reading raise. Another relates to the appropriateness of using cues other than letter-sound associations in gaining meaning from the printed page. Yet other issues relate to the form, organization, and materials of instruction in reading. Some of these issues might be clarified if we fully describe the process of reading.

The Reading Process

Even in its simplest form, the reading process seems to involve a broad range of perceptual, associative, and cognitive elements. While these may be analyzed and described separately, the processes themselves are intertwined so that the individual does not practice each one separately as he reads. Nor is the process simply a matter of making a series of letter-sound associations. The scene of the preschool child roaming the aisles of a supermarket and identifying and reciting labels of packages made familiar through television commercials is not an unfamiliar one. While such a process might not be labeled as *reading*, much early reading seems to mirror this process, for in attempting to gain meaning from the written page, the young child uses a variety of approaches and clues.

Young children can learn a reasonable number of words without using any analytic techniques. The associative learning technique used in the "look-say" method has proved successful and is probably responsible for the very young child being able to read product labels. The continually repeated association between the picture of the product and its name on television helps the child learn the words and recall them when he sees the symbol. Other techniques as well can be used for associating visual cues with the sounds of words.

The shapes of beginning and ending letters provide clues to the word. Using these visual cues requires that the child be helped to make the association between the written symbol and the spoken word. Children also learn to use the context in which a word is placed as a clue to reading the word. The structure of the language and the meaning of phrases have a degree of regularity that creates a fairly high chance of success in the use of context clues.

As the child begins reading instruction he learns other techniques of word recognition. Structural analysis—the breaking of large words into their parts—is an important one. Phonetic analysis, one way the child can identify letter-sound associations, is another important technique. Phonetic analysis is not the *only* method, however, that the young child can use in learning to read, nor is it necessarily the first one he may learn. It would be unfortunate if we did not provide the children with as many different ways of unlocking the mystery of the written word as he can use, for it is the synthesis of many skills that helps make a competent reader.

It is important to note that while the skill of word identification is an important part of beginning reading, it is just one part. It is the meanings that must become evident to the child. He must associate the written words with the spoken words and move quickly from reading *symbols* to reading *ideas*.

APPROACHES TO READING INSTRUCTION
While there are a multitude of different reading instructional programs available today from which teachers may choose, many of them are actually quite similar to one another in approach, if not in the skills developed. In analyzing reading programs, it is helpful to look at the dimensions upon which these programs might differ. Essentially the differences can be categorized into the following scheme:

1. Differences in the stress on letter-sound association
2. Differences in the conception of reading in relation to other language arts
3. Differences in the organizational pattern of instruction

The various approaches to reading instruction can be analyzed along these three dimensions.

Programs that Focus on Letter-Sound Associations

There are several kinds of programs that can be grouped in this category, including the various phonics programs, the newer linguistics programs, and the programs that use a transitional alphabet or orthography in an attempt to provide a greater degree of regularity in the relationship between letters and sounds.

PHONICS. Teaching reading through phonics may require the children to sound out the letters in a word and then blend the sound to create the word, or to analyze speech sounds in words and then relate them to letter representations. While some programs depend upon phonics entirely, it is usually taught in combination with other reading skills. One often finds a phonics workbook added to a basal reading program. Phonics lessons are also outlined in teachers' manuals and in most basal series reading textbooks.

LINGUISTICS.   In recent years a number of programs labeled "linguistic" or "modified linguistic" approaches to reading instruction have reached the market. These programs attempt to teach the child the rules of letter-sound associations in the language. They often start with those letters that have a very regular relationship to specific sounds in the English language, progressing slowly to letters with less regular relationships and from there to those letters with the most irregular relationship. Instruction in this approach may place little reliance on using meaning as a way of learning to read, so reading might be taught through the use of nonsense words as well as meaningful words.

ARTIFICIAL ORTHOGRAPHIES.   These approaches cannot truly be classified as programs that teach letter-sound associations, since an orthography can be used in many ways. Because these orthographies tend to produce a greater degree of regularity between written symbols and the sounds they represent, and because this aspect has been highlighted by most of the developers, they are discussed here. The most widely known of all the artificial orthographies is the Initial Teaching Alphabet (*ita*). First introduced into British schools, this approach to reading has had a good deal of exposure in American schools in recent years. It consists of a 44-symbol alphabet that, while not completely regular, is more regular in its letter-sound associations than our traditional 26-letter alphabet. The child is introduced to both reading and writing instruction with materials using this alphabet. After he has achieved a degree of competency in using it for reading and writing, he is helped to make the transition to the traditional form of reading and writing. At present, one can find both simple trade books and reading textbooks available in *ita*.

While *ita* is the most popular of the artificial orthographies being suggested as aids to beginning reading instruction, it is only one of several similar approaches. Although different in its operation, the *Words in Color* approach to reading also fits into this category. In this approach a sound is associated with a color in which it is presented no matter what its spelling, thus providing a regularity of relationship between spoken sounds and their presented counterparts.

Relating Reading to Other Language Arts

The one program of instruction that seems more than any other to relate reading closely to the other language arts is the Language Experience Approach. Basically, this approach conceives of reading as integral with writing, speaking, and listening as a unified whole of language experience in the life of the child. Of all the possible approaches to reading, this one places the least emphasis upon learning the skills of code-cracking in some systematic fashion. Some proponents of the Language Experience Approach would caution teachers that premature focus on the skills of reading will thwart rather than help the child's acquisition of reading skills. Since focusing on a single word or part of a word would slow down the child's rate of reading and is counter to the natural way in which mature readers function, teachers are cautioned not to start the child with improper reading habits. Word attack skills are often taught to individuals and small groups as the need arises.

The Language Experience Approach works most effectively in a classroom that is filled with stimulating learning opportunities. As the child involves himself in the activities of the classroom, he feels the need to communicate what he is doing. Early communication takes the form of speaking and listening, so a natural transition to reading and writing then takes place. The child first dictates stories about his experience to the teacher, who will write them on experience charts; the child learns to read from these charts.

The child is also encouraged to write early. Soon he is writing his own stories rather than having the teacher do the writing for him. These stories become the content of the child's reading. Since he has written the material himself, he seldom has difficulty with vocabulary, for even difficult words are remembered.

The next transition is from reading one's own writing to reading someone else's writing, and the child is encouraged to read other children's work as well as to read many books available in the classroom. Stories can also be written as a group endeavor, and experience charts as well can be the work of more than one child.

The language experience approach to reading does not deny the need to crack the code of letter-sound associations. Rather than being learned from lessons designed specifically to this end, however, they are learned through the organic activities provided. The process of learning to read more closely parallels the learning of a native language rather than a second language.

Differences in Organizational Patterns of Teaching Reading

The most popular of the two basic organizational patterns in the teaching of reading is the *group* method, most often exemplified in the use of the basal reading approach. The other, less popular, is the *individualized* reading program.

The basal approach consists of instruction in reading through a series of ordered reading textbooks. Along with the textbooks and often available from the same publisher are workbooks and other instructional aides, such as flash cards, pictures, films, filmstrips, and records. In most classrooms, the children are divided into groups for instructional purposes based upon reading ability; one group of high reading ability, another of low ability and a third, usually the largest group, in the middle. Group instruction is organized in order to limit the range of ability within each instructional unit, a range that would be great in most classrooms.

Most basal reading programs are carefully designed, eclectic ones. Teachers are provided with a manual of instructions that includes a great degree of detail about the content of the program and the method of instruction to be used. The use of textbooks and related activities may be carefully prescribed for the teacher. In addition, the books are carefully graded so that a teacher needs only to take her class through the books and related exercises provided her to successfully carry on her program. Generally, all groups are offered the same reading program, but the pace of instruction differs.

Some basal reading programs are changed from edition to edition over the years to mirror the changes that take place in current reading instruction theory. Recent changes include a greater focus on phonics and a concern with the linguistic analysis of initial vocabulary. Changes in the content of some basal readers also reflect the changing social scene. Many basal readers have begun to change their illustrations to reflect more honestly the multiracial nature of our society. Newer reading series (such as the *Bank Street Readers, Skyline Readers,* and the *Chandler Reading Series*) have been developed in which the story lines relate to an urban context not found in the more popular readers. Additional changes relate to the uses of newer format designs for basal reader series, especially the use of smaller books and integrated audio-visual aids.

Most basal reading series begin by providing pupils with a limited sight vocabulary of words and names of characters in the stories used in the reading program. The vocabulary is carefully limited and constantly repeated. As the child's sight vocabulary reaches a minimal level, he is introduced to a variety of word recognition skills, including phonics and structural analysis.

While basal reading programs have been discussed as a group here, there is considerable variation in methodological emphasis and textbook content among basal reader series.

Individualized reading programs have been conceived of as a way of dealing with the inherent problem of the inappropriate fit of instructional programs to the diverse needs of children in any group. Within a single group of children there are differences in learning skills, styles, and interests, as well as differences in reading abilities. While grouping might limit the range of differences in one dimension, differences in children continue to exist in other dimensions.

Individualizing reading instruction provides neither a single medium nor a single organizational framework for instruction. Instead, a great variety of books are provided for the children, both trade books and basal readers. Trade books vary in topics and level of difficulty, and are selected individually by the child, who also sets his own learning pace.

Central to the organization of the individualized reading program is the pupil-teacher conference. Several times each week the teacher meets with each child in conference. The conference is used to review the child's progress in reading and to plan new work for the future. The teacher often asks children to read aloud to her, and asks questions about what the child has read to check on his degree of comprehension of the material he has been reading.

An individualized program requires an extensive amount of record-keeping and planning. The teacher keeps records on the books the child has read as well as on the content of her conference. These records might include notes about the child's progress in reading as well as about the problems that are encountered and need to be dealt with. Planning consists of selecting and providing an adequate array of books as well as suggesting specific books for particular children. Planning for individualized reading requires that the teacher have some degree of familiarity with a wide range of books and is knowledgeable about the reading level as well as the content of each book.

If the need for instruction in a particular set of reading skills is manifested by more than one child, the teacher may organize a group for instructional purposes. The group is convened for a particular task and may include children of different levels of reading ability but with the same instructional need. When the instructional task is completed, the group may be disbanded. Practice in reading skills may also be provided through worksheets and other materials. While some teachers may begin a program of instruction with individual lessons, more often such a reading program is designed to extend from some form of group instruction. As the children show competence in reading skills, they are allowed greater degrees of freedom in reading.

While significantly different from the individualized reading program described above, another method that has been developed for individualizing instruction is called Individually Prescribed Instruction (IPI). This system is organized to provide for individually paced instruction in a classroom setting. The focus is on reading skills rather than on other aspects of the reading program. At the beginning of each instructional unit, the child is given a diagnostic test, and on the basis of the results of the test, he is provided with his own instructional prescription, a work-sheet which he completes and which is then checked by a classroom clerk supervised by the teacher. He may then be allowed to move to the next set of instructional tasks or be provided with remedial work.

In the IPI model, no child is asked to work on a lesson if he has already mastered the skills that are the goals of that lesson. In addition, he may move at his own pace through the set of instructional tasks without concern for the progress of others.

Computer-assisted instruction and *programmed instruction* have also been used to individualize reading programs. Each of these approaches allows the child to move through a set instructional program at his own speed. Computer-assisted instruction also has the potentiality of greater flexibility in the presentation of material based upon the analysis of learning weaknesses in the individual child.

These two types of instruction are vehicles for teaching, and represent no single instructional approach. Phonics, linguistics, contextual analysis, and other skills can be taught through this kind of teaching program. Programmed instruction may use a teaching machine or may be incorporated into a workbook. Computer-assisted instruction may make use of both visual and auditory channels and may require many different forms of children's responses.

While these approaches to individualization have shown themselves to be effective teaching tools, they are probably best used in conjunction with other program elements. The high cost of computer-assisted instruction and the continual need for adult intervention raises a question of its practicality. Program writing and the rental of computers and coaxial cables often makes computer-assisted instruction prohibitive for use in early educational programs. At present, the computer does have a role to play in researching early education. Its role in producing continual instruction to young children still needs to be demonstrated, though.

**EVALUATING
APPROACHES TO
READING INSTRUCTION**   Considering the number of approaches to beginning reading instruction that are possible and the number of programs available within each approach, it becomes exceedingly difficult for the classroom teacher to decide which program she should institute in her classroom. In many school systems there is little choice actually available to the teacher, for the decision has already been made by the administration or by a curriculum committee. Schools and school systems usually select one reading program to be instituted in all classrooms rather than allow each teacher free choice in her selection. This plan insures a degree of continuity in the program as the child moves

through the grades, and allows for some increased efficiency in the purchase of books and supplies.

One would hope, however, that a teacher will have a voice in the selection of a program and will also be allowed to make modification in the program she is required to implement in her particular classroom. In many school systems, teachers may have the freedom to test new instructional programs under certain conditions.

Assuming the relevancy of the question, however, how does a teacher make a professional judgment in selecting a reading program for her class? Each program and series of books professes its superiority over the others. In addition, proponents of a particular approach are usually able to quote some research as to the effectiveness of their program. While effectiveness is one criterion, other considerations also need to be taken into account, including the practicality of the program, its cost, and the ability of a teacher to use it effectively. It is helpful to study each of these attributes of a program separately.

Effectiveness

While it is difficult to get measures of effectiveness of reading instructional programs, a number of recent large-scale studies may shed some light on that area. Chall's recent book reviews studies of reading instruction that have been conducted in the last thirty years. Her findings suggest the superiority of systematic phonics programs.[4]

The First Grade Reading Studies sponsored by the U.S. Office of Education, mentioned briefly at the beginning of the chapter, is one of the first concerted large-scale research projects, combining the results of a number of studies which used comparable measures. The results of this study found no significant difference in basal and linguistic texts. The prereading knowledge of letter names was concluded to be the best single predictor of reading achievement in the primary grades. Even the best predictor of reading achievement, however, could not predict accurately how well any given child will succeed in a reading program, nor was there a difference in the predictive ability of any measure of reading readiness for the many types of reading programs used.

The study showed sex differences in reading readiness as well as in first- and second-grade reading and spelling achievement. Girls were generally superior to boys as far as methodology was concerned. Instruction in phonics seemed to be highly related to word recognition and

---

[4]Jeanne Chall, *Learning to Read: The Great Debate* (New York: McGraw-Hill, 1967).

spelling achievement in the primary grades, but the way in which phonics was taught did not appear to be very important. Direct instruction in comprehension was deemed essential in beginning materials and a writing program seemed an effective addition to a primary reading program.[5]

There were no clearcut conclusions on effectiveness to support any single program to the exclusion of others. Since reading, as defined earlier, is a complex process, different activities probably best nurture the various aspects of the process. The conclusions suggest that a combined program of basal reading, phonics, and language experience could be extremely effective as a beginning reading instructional program. They also suggest that the determinants of an effective classroom reading program are not the sole function of the method used. Teacher competence and classroom climate are also very important.

Practicality

While teachers may find one program superior to others under certain circumstances and for particular populations, there are issues of practicality that need to be taken into consideration. A Language Experience approach to reading seems to be more practical in a classroom that contains an activity-based program, since the children will have experienced interesting activities worth communicating to others. An individualized reading program requires an extensive classroom library and the teacher's knowledge of the contents and reading levels of many books. *Ita* or a similar program based upon the use of an artificial orthography may be difficult to implement in a nongraded classroom because of the need to provide duplicate reading material for those children in the program and those who have already made the transition to the traditional orthography.

The cost of implementing a program may also be a consideration of a school system if it has limited funds; the implementation of a new program would necessitate large expenditures for new materials and supplies. Teachers need to survey the program and their particular situation in any selection procedure.

Teacher Effectiveness

A teacher's effectiveness is usually related to her competency or her training. In an area of such great controversy as that of beginning reading instruction, it might be useful to postulate another antecedent of effectiveness: the teacher's belief system. A teacher who believes her pro-

[5]Robert Dykstra, "Classroom Implications of the First-Grade Reading Studies," *College Reading Association Proceeding*, Vol. 9 (Fall 1968), 53–59.

gram is a good one will generally experience a high degree of success. Teachers who are less sure of their program, who feel they are forced to teach a program that is not one in which they can believe, will probably experience less success in their teaching. While the teacher's expectancies might create a self-fulfilling prophecy, there is also probably a difference in what a teacher will do to support an instructional program in which she has faith. Teacher involvement in the process of selecting curriculum components can help to develop confidence in the program finally selected.

A READING PROGRAM FOR THE EARLY YEARS   The First Grade Reading Studies described above suggests that the best results could probably accrue from a program that used a combination of approaches for teaching beginning reading. This might lead a teacher to organize her class instruction around a basal reading series. In addition, a supplementary program of phonic materials could be used. To round out the program, elements of a Language Experience approach could be included, such as the writing of stories by the children and the use of experience charts for instructional purposes. Finally, ways of individualizing the program could also be devised. Such a program could be implemented by the majority of teachers who are best able to use published instructional materials.

A teacher with a greater knowledge of the reading processes and the methods of reading instruction, a greater desire to provide creative experiences in her classroom, and a greater willingness to develop her own methods and materials could probably do just as well by eliminating the basal readers and relying more on providing a wide range of language experience and using many trade books. If the class she is teaching is average or above-average in intelligence, such an alternative might significantly increase the children's reading abilities. It would also allow for increased creative expression and independence in reading. Because this alternative program is a difficult one to implement, especially for teachers who are unsure of their own ability to teach reading, it is not recommended for all.

Nor should a combined approach as suggested be merely a basal reading program with a few chart stories used at the beginning and a few trade books made available for children to read as time fillers. In the program proposed, the range of classroom activity available at any time would be great. The combination program would not be a basal program, but would use basal reading materials. Spache and Spache, in their book, *Reading in the Elementary School*, describe what could be considered a realistic combination program and provide an excellent description of its content.[6]

BEGINNING A READING PROGRAM
A reading program begins long before the child attempts to make sense out of the first preprimer. Reading is an extension of the language process. As such, reading instruction begins in the infant's babbling stage. The child's first reading teacher is usually his mother, who has a profound effect on his reading achievement in many ways, both through helping him develop language skills and through providing the motivation for learning to read. While few schools concern themselves with attempting to influence the child's reading patterns so early in life, the idea is not as far-fetched as it might seem. Several projects are currently developing ways to reach the child as an infant and provide him with home instruction through teaching the parent specific ways of handling him, playing and interacting with him in order to increase his intellectual and language skills.

Most schools, however, wait until the child is old enough to be enrolled in an institutional group program before beginning any kind of formal instruction. The age at which a formal reading program might be provided for the child is open to controversy, and it is doubtful if any single age limit would be appropriate for all children.

Beginning Reading Instruction

When should reading instruction begin for the child? This is a question for which it is impossible to provide legitimate answers, although there are those who provide glib answers for the public. As has been mentioned, articles in lay magazines in the past decade have suggested that even infants can learn to read. Research reports have been circulated describing reading instruction for two-year-olds. Montessori programs have been held in esteem by some because, as described, reading instruction begins when the child enters the program. (Actually, much of what is labeled "reading instruction" by some Montessorians is what other educators have called a "reading readiness program.") In many school systems where dissastisfaction has been felt with the current reading program beginning in first grade, a program of reading instruction has been instituted in the kindergarten with reported positive results. All

[6]George D. Spache and Evelyn B. Spache, *Reading in the Elementary School* (Boston: Allyn and Bacon, 1969), pp. 189–481.

this suggests that it might be possible to begin reading instruction at some point earlier than has been traditional.

On the other hand, a large number of educators suggest that reading instruction should begin no sooner than the first grade. In some kindergarten classrooms of the recent past, teachers were not even allowed to display any written material, for written language was the province of the first grade. Few basal reading programs are designed to begin formal reading instruction prior to first grade, although they might include readiness materials for use in the kindergarten.

In the United States, the traditional age for beginning reading instruction is at some time during the child's sixth year. Some countries postpone reading instruction until age seven, while still others begin at age five. Generally speaking, the age at which children begin to be taught reading is related to the age at which most children in the community enter the public school system.

In the area of beginning reading instruction, one also can see the operation of an "educational mythology." In many books on early childhood education and beginning reading instruction, it has been traditional to state that children cannot benefit from beginning reading instruction until they have achieved a mental age of six years and six months. An attempt to find the source of this statement leads to a single study done in a Chicago suburb many years ago in which it was found that children in the Winnetka schools with a mean age of six years and six months benefited from reading instruction.[7] A study conducted a short time later by Gates, however, suggests that the necessary mental age for beginning reading instruction is not rigid, but is related to the size of the group and the flexibility of the program.[8]

The answer to the question of when to begin reading instruction is complex. It depends, to begin with, on the child's maturity, his level of intelligence, and his language background and capability, which is also related to intelligence. The decision to begin instruction must also depend on the particular program of reading instruction and the way in which it is organized. Not all classroom situations nor all teachers can provide the individual attention or flexibility needed to support an early reading program.

A question might also be raised about the amount of effort that must be expended to teach young children to read and the ensuing benefits that would accrue from an early reading program. There is research to support the contention that children who are taught to read early do seem to

[7]M. V. Morpell and C. Washburne, "When Should Children Begin to Read?" *Elementary School Journal*, Vol. 31 (March 1931), 496–503.

[8]Arthur Gates, "The Necessary Mental Age for Beginning Reading," *Elementary School Journal*, Vol. 37 (March 1937), 497–508.

benefit from such instruction. These research studies seldom, however, compare formal reading instruction with other attempts at enriching the program. And whether or not the results of an early reading program fade in the years beyond the primary grades is still open to further research. Certainly, a program of early reading that provides an educational advantage that is not exploited by later programs is a worthless one. Too often the cry for early reading instruction is a substitute for the more difficult task of reforming the programs of primary and intermediate education in our schools.

Nevertheless, the question of when a child might begin formal reading instruction is best answered on an individual basis. If children can be taken individually or in small groups for beginning reading instruction at the time they seem most receptive to such instruction, this is probably the best method of matching a program to the children's capability.

Teachers can assess the readiness of the child to benefit from such instruction in a variety of ways. One way is to use reading readiness tests. But although they correlate well with successful results on reading achievement tests in first grade for *groups* of children, these are not accurate enough to predict the success of any single child. Teachers may also make their own personal assessment of a child's readiness to read. Spache and Spache present the following checklist as a guide to observation:

Readiness Checklist

Vision

Good binocular acuity, near
Good binocular acuity, far
Able to shift focus easily and accurately
Good binocular coordination
Good visual discrimination
Good hand-eye coordination, near

Speech

Free from substitutions and baby talk
Able to communicate in conversation and with group
Reasonable fluency and sentence structure

Listening

Able to attend to and recall story
Able to answer simple questions
Able to follow simple directions
Able to follow sequence of story
Able to discriminate sounds of varying pitch and loudness
Able to detect similarities and differences in words
Sufficient auditory vocabulary for common concepts

Social and Emotional Behavior

Able to work independently or in group

Able to share materials
Able to await turn for teacher's attention
Able to lead or to follow

Interest in Learning to Read

Show interest in signs and symbols
Interested in listening to stories
Can tell some stories and recite some poems or rhymes
Likes to look at pictures in books
Can attend to the continuity in a sequential picture book
Makes up stories about pictures
Asks to take books home; brings some to school
Tries to identify words in familiar books[9]

The results of the First Grade Reading Studies suggest that the attributes of children that correlate most with reading success include auditory discrimination, visual discrimination, familiarity with print, intelligence, knowledge of letter names, and the ability to discriminate between letter sounds. These attributes should be kept in mind and observed by the teacher when she is making judgments about beginning reading instruction for a particular child.

Reading Readiness

The term "reading readiness" might most simply be defined as the predisposition to benefit from reading instruction. The term has been used in so many ways that it is often unclear. To some, it has been seen as a maturational state in a child. If readiness is a function of maturation alone, the teacher who identifies a child as not yet ready to read has no recourse but to simply wait until the child gets older. There is little in the school curriculum that has any effect on the rate of maturation of the human organism.

Educators have, however, become aware of the inadequacy of the maturation approach to readiness. Success in reading achievement is correlated not just with intelligence, physical maturity, or wrist-bone indices of maturation, but with specific learned skills such as auditory and visual discrimination as well as familiarity with print and knowledge of letter names. These are not functions of maturation alone, but are a result of the child's specific learning before he is introduced to formal reading instruction. Our knowledge to date suggests that even intelligence as we measure it is not a function of maturation alone, but is also related to the learning opportunities available in the child's environment. A purely maturational approach to reading readiness is wholly inadequate today.

[9]Spache and Spache, *Reading in the Elementary School*, p. 63. Reprinted with permission of the publisher.

Actually, formal reading instruction should not be considered the beginning of a reading program but an extension of a program of learning, in the school or at home, that provides children with a large number of requisite skills and information that are put to use through reading instruction. Some children arrive at school already knowing what is necessary, having been taught by siblings, peers, or parents or having picked up this knowledge on their own. If they have not yet mastered the prerequisites for formal reading instruction, it is the responsibility of the school to create a program of instruction to foster this readiness.

Designing a Reading Readiness Program

Much of the composition of a readiness program for reading has already been described in the previous chapter on language learning. Reading needs to be seen as an extension of the language process. The child's ability to be involved in the production and reception of language is important in his ability to learn to read. He needs to develop fluency in speaking ability and listening abilities. The focus on oral language also helps the child develop an extensive speaking and listening vocabulary that can be a resource in developing a reading vocabulary. He will also have developed a familiarity with print and printed material. Stories will be read to him and he will have an opportunity to handle books and to see how one can get information from the printed page, if only from pictures at first. The child can develop simple skills such as how to hold a book, open it, turn its pages, and care for it.

Most important, the child will develop a concept of what reading is. He will have many opportunities to dictate his own stories to a teacher who will read them back at a later time. These many informal and formal language activities will help the child as he moves into actual reading.

In addition to these language activities, teachers can provide learning activities that help develop the specific skills upon which the reading process is built. Many of these will be in the area of visual and auditory discrimination.

VISUAL DISCRIMINATION. Many nursery and kindergarten classrooms include a wealth of materials that help to develop visual discrimination skills. In the use of parquetry puzzles, the shape of each piece must be related to the shape of the space in which it is to be inserted as well as to the rest of the picture. Pegsets, beads, strings, and similar materials can also be used in teaching visual discrimination. Teachers can develop design cards for children to model. A simple pattern of one red and one blue peg alternating along the length of a line of holes in the pegboard is one that children can model, with more complex patterns following. Similar patterns can be made with beads on a string. A series of cards beginning with simple patterns and including complex designs can be provided and used at the children's own pace, more complex tasks being offered as they succeed in the simpler tasks. Design cards can also be made to be used with parquetry blocks of different shapes and colors.

Children can also be asked to copy specific patterns from models using crayons or pencils. Etch-a-Sketch boards help children copy models provided by the teacher. Using an Etch-a-Sketch is a complicated task, since it requires coordination of both hands. Form discrimination tasks can be given children, starting with simple geometric forms and continuing to discrimination of letters. Form boards and letter templates may be useful in this connection. A number of visual discrimination and perceptual motor programs are available on the market that may be used for this purpose.

As children learn to discriminate letters, they should also learn the names of letters. Not only is this a good reading readiness task but it also improves communication between teacher and child in that it provides the class with a common verbal referent. While copying patterns and filling in outlines are suggested here, none of these activities are to be considered as a substitute for an art program concerned with creative expression.

AUDITORY DISCRIMINATION. Music affords many opportunities for this, since the child must distinguish and reproduce pitch in music as well as learn to listen to the words of songs. Instruments can be provided to allow the children to recreate patterns of sound that differ in pitch and rhythm according to models provided by the teacher. Again, this is not to be considered a substitute for a creative music program.

A number of other techniques for auditory discrimination can also be used. A number of books such as the *Muffin* series can be read to make children more aware of sounds. There are many records and sound film-strips that can similarly be used, *Sounds Around Us* (Guidance Associates) being a good example. Teachers can also create a number of games for teaching listening skills such as sound recognition and discrimination. They may create their own auditory discrimination materials using tape recorders or a *Language Master*.

Most importantly, teachers need to make children aware of the sounds they hear in the language around them. Word sounds can be the basis for much fun, because children enjoy alliteration and rhyming. While many opportunities for learning may be found in the classroom setting, teachers should be aware of the need to exploit situations as they arise as well as to create situations for particular purposes.

Not only do children differ in their ability to profit from formal reading activities but they also differ in their ability to profit from reading readiness activities. Requiring a child to participate in an activity for which he has no need is wasteful, as is the requirement for participation by a child who is not yet ready. Such formal requirements for total class participation is doubly wasteful, for, in addition to the loss of profit to the child, he is kept from being involved in a more useful activity for him.

FORMAL READING INSTRUCTION The move from a reading readiness program to a program of formal reading instruction should be a gradual, almost imperceptible one. If the children have been writing stories and charts, it is an easy move to have the teacher begin to use simple short charts for reading. This can be done with individual children or with small groups as they are identified by the teacher as being able to profit from reading instruction. Such a beginning will build upon the language knowledge that a child already possesses and will keep reading from seeming like an exotic skill. The charts can become longer and more elaborate as each child progresses. The teacher should have pupils write their own stories on smaller sheets of paper, rather than have all experiences transcribed in large charts. She can also begin to introduce children to reading books at this time.

Developing Word-recognition Skills

Chart reading should be more than sounding out words previously memorized by the children. With the presentation of charts, teachers must help the children develop a range of word-recognition skills. Many of these skills can be introduced in conjunction with reading experience charts. Because the content of the chart is so close to the child's experience, teaching the child to use context clues seems natural. The child's intuitive knowledge of sentence structure and the fact that he has shared in the experience recorded on the chart makes this an effective technique.

Informal phonics instruction can also be provided in the program. The child should be made aware of the sounds of the words. Initial consonants can be identified and related to sounds. Experience charts have the disadvantage or advantage, depending on one's point of view, of being relatively uncontrollable in terms of the systematic introduction of a limited word vocabulary. Children's experiences and interests are so broad that they cannot be limited to those that can be described with only a small number of words. A formalized linguistics or phonics program becomes difficult to introduce to children, although the products of linguistics studies help reading instruction. The writings and reading of children will also contain a sprinkling of fairly sophisticated, complicated words. This fact should be accepted by the teacher using these methods, who realizes that some words will not be fully learned by the children.

Using a Basal Reading Series

Most teachers in the primary grades will establish a reading program in their classrooms based upon the use of basal readers. While these books are not bad in themselves, they are often used in such a stereotyped fashion that the reading programs that result are boring to children. Basal readers must be seen as a resource to be used in the teacher's program rather than as a program by themselves. Slavish adherence to teachers' manuals and to the traditional grouping practices should be avoided.

Teachers need to take into consideration the abilities of their pupils in planning their reading program. The First Grade Reading Study suggested that bright children did better in more individualized programs, while slow readers seemed to profit from a basal reading approach. This might suggest that a teacher's use of basal readers needs to be differentiated. Brighter children will develop the basic techniques of reading rapidly and should be allowed the freedom to select books to read under the guidance of the teacher. Those children who need the help provided by the basal readers, with their controlled vocabularies, should be given the opportunities to use them. But even in the use of basal readers by the slower readers, there can be a great degree of flexibility.

When teachers use the basal readers, they do not need to operate in the traditional "three-reading-groups-everybody-reads-aloud-today" fashion. Opportunities can be provided for silent reading, and conferences can often supplant the group experience. Teachers can make use of the pupil-teacher conference even when their reading program is not fully individualized and task grouping can supplant ability grouping.

Nor does the teacher need to follow a workbook step-by-step. In the discussion of reading readiness, no mention was made of using readiness workbooks. Readiness skills can best be taught in an experience context where children learn to use their language skills through interacting with the human environment. Children as individuals differ in their educational needs and patterns of learning. While skill learning and practice ought to be a part of a beginning reading program, this does not necessarily mean that these skills are best taught by having all the children in a class systematically go through a set of prescribed exercises. Although some teachers prefer this so that children "won't miss anything," the practice is too often wasteful.

Spache suggests that instead of using a single workbook, the teacher should order a number of different workbooks and skillsheets.[10] These

---

[10]Spache and Spache, *Reading in the Elementary School*, p. 262.

can be organized into sets of related exercises for each skill area. The suggestion that these can be placed in heavy acetate folders on which the children can mark their answers is a sound and economical one.

Using a Classroom Library

The availability of a classroom library has been continually emphasized in this chapter as well as in the previous one. If children are to learn to read, they must not only learn the basic skills, but the uses of reading as well. Most reading is an intimate personal experience based upon a child's interest and need for knowledge. Classroom reading, from its moment of introduction, should reflect this. As soon as children have mastered a rudimentary vocabulary, they should be introduced to a range of books. Fortunately, there are books available that even the first-grade child can read independently. If he does not know how to read all the words in a book, such an experience will provide him with opportunities to practice his developing word recognition skills. Books should be carefully selected, with a relatively small number in the room at any one time, but with the selection of available books constantly changing during the year.

Use of Reading in Other Subject Areas

While the appreciation of literature is an important aspect of a reading program, there are other uses of reading as well. Reading in specific subject areas for particular purposes will help increase the children's comprehension and help them learn to use reading skills flexibly, reading differently for different purposes. Many information books are available in the various subject areas that are written at a primary grade level.

In addition, children can begin to use reference books. Encyclopedias, dictionaries, atlases, and other reference books are available in simplified children's forms. The use of reference books will require that children learn certain techniques for seeking information. Alphabetization becomes important, since topics are often listed in alphabetical order. Children also need to learn to use the table of contents and index of a book to seek out specific information. These skills, often a part of a reading program, take on greater significance when the child can see the need for learning the skill and when skill acquisition has a fairly immediate payoff.

As children use information books it is often helpful for teachers to phrase questions to guide their reading. At first these questions may be related to the specific content of the book, asking the child to repeat what has been learned in reading. As the children develop skills in informational reading, more critical elements need to be included in the questions so that the child learns to read carefully and to make judgments about what he has read. Often, asking the child to read and compare material from two different sources on the same topic is helpful.

Keeping Records

The further the teacher diverges from a standard basal reading program, the more she will feel the need for a comprehensive record-keeping system. It is all too easy to judge progress by the book the child is reading and even the page in the book that has been completed, although exposure cannot realistically be substituted for learning. Such a simplified way of making judgments is not available to a teacher who uses a variety of books, for children will read books at different levels and in different order. The page and book are *not* accurate indicators of progress and only provide the teacher with a comfortable delusion.

Records should be used by the teacher to keep track of what books the children have read. It also helps for the teacher to keep a record of the skills achieved and the reading difficulties encountered by each child. These records can be the source of planning for individual and small group skill-teaching sessions and practice activities. They also help the teacher guide the child's independent reading. Fortunately, children can share in the record-keeping tasks, for otherwise, accurate and adequate recording can become a burdensome chore. A chart will do as well as a card file in the children's own recording of the author and title of each book they have read. They should also make some sort of summary statement about the book and possibly even some evaluative statements. Such a list or file of books is a helpful indicator of the child's reading activity. Of course, the pupil-teacher conferences evaluating the child's reading progress is a check on the accuracy of the list.

Pupils can also keep a record of words with which they have had difficulty and of words they have mastered. An individual word list or dictionary organized in alphabetical order is a good instructional resource as well as a record.

Teachers can record the children's progress at each individual reading conference. The titles of the books the child has read at the time of the conference, independently selected from trade books or from a basal reading series, can be recorded, as well as the book's reading level. The teacher can then note comments about the child's reading ability, word attack skills, and comprehension of the material. Any suggestions for special work for the child can also be noted. This becomes a comprehensive record of the child's reading ability that can be used when necessary to report on the child's learning process.

Record keeping can be a chore. It is an important chore, however, in that it allows the teacher to be continually aware of the child's progress. It also provides the teacher with information upon which to base her future plans. The quality and depth of a reading program should be reflected in the records the teacher keeps.

SUGGESTED READING

BOND, GUY L., AND EVA BOND WAGNER, *Teaching the Child to Read*, 4th ed. New York: Macmillan, 1966.

CHALL, JEANNE S., *Learning to Read: The Great Debate*. New York: McGraw-Hill Book Company, 1967.

DURKIN, DOLORES, *Children Who Read Early*. New York: Teachers College Press, 1966.

FRIES, CHARLES C., *Linguistics and Reading*. New York: Holt, Rinehart & Winston, 1964.

GANS, ROMA, *Common Sense about Teaching Reading*. Indianapolis: Bobbs-Merrill, 1963.

LEE, DORRIS M., AND R. V. ALLEN, *Learning to Read Through Experience*, 2nd ed. New York: Appleton-Century-Crofts, 1963.

MONROE, MARION, AND BERNICE ROGERS, *Foundations for Reading*. Chicago: Scott, Foresman, 1964.

SMITH, NILA BANTON, *American Reading Instruction*. Newark, Delaware: International Reading Association, 1965.

SPACHE, GEORGE D., AND EVELYN B. SPACHE, *Reading in the Elementary School*. Boston: Allyn and Bacon, 1969.

STAUFFER, RUSSELL G., ed., *The First Grade Reading Studies: Findings of Individual Investigations*. Newark, Delaware: International Reading Association, 1967.

————, *Directing Reading Maturity as a Cognitive Process*. New York: Harper and Row, 1969.

6

Science in the Early Years

The young child, almost from the moment of birth, reaches out to his surroundings through his senses in an attempt to gain information about the world in which he lives. At first the child's understanding of the physical world is limited by his perceptual field. Things not perceived do not exist; things perceived often seem to have no explanation.

As the child begins to mature and his experiences with the world increase, he becomes aware of the existence of order in the world. There is a degree of regularity to events and objects with which he has contact. Some cause-and-effect relationships soon become evident. Items heretofore dealt with as discrete phenomenon are now classed with other similar items and are treated accordingly. The child will even try to create order where order does not exist. He develops concepts, both physical and social, about the world, which allow him to accumulate knowledge from experience and develop new powers of understanding.

It is easy to see how early observers in the field of child development conceived of the child's intellectual development as following the pattern of the development of cultural knowledge; the parallels are striking. Early man also viewed occurrences as discrete, attributing changes to magical powers beyond human understanding. From that point human society moved through a series of progressions whereby man could explain, understand, and, to some extent, deal with the world of people and things through the development of concepts. Their concepts allowed whole classes of objects to be treated as equivalent. Generalizations could then be developed about regularities of relationships among concepts. Systems of knowledge could be created by relating concepts and generalizations to one another.

As knowledge was created it could be accumulated and transmitted from generation to generation. In time, knowledge systems became quite complex, and divisions were created leading to an increase in specialization of inquiry and to a more efficient system of knowledge storage and retrieval. This specialization has led to the *scholarly disciplines* as we know them today, with separations based upon the subject studied as well as upon the basic sets of assumptions and agreed-upon ways of accumulating and verifying knowledge in each area.

One of the basic purposes of the school is the transmission of significant portions of this knowledge to the young. This allows each generation to grasp what we know at present about the world, so that they can deal effectively with it, building upon what is already known and, in time, accumulating greater knowledge about it. School subjects closely parallel the scholarly disciplines so that the sciences, social studies, mathematics, and other subjects have their parallel in the intellectual inquiries from which they are derived.

Recent activities in the area of curriculum development have illustrated the parallels between the ways children develop knowledge of the world and the ways in which the scholarly disciplines have developed. Science, mathematics, and the social sciences have been viewed as the results of intellectual processes by which the physical and social world can be explored. Hurd and Gallagher, for example, have identified the ability to comprehend science as:

> (1) the ability to grasp the central theme of a set of observations; (2) the ability to look at data from a variety of vantage points; (3) the ability to recognize the effect of changing one variable at a time; (4) the ability to discount irrelevancies and focus on the useful aspects of information; (5) the ability to formulate useful hypotheses and test them; (6) the ability to search for new evidence; and (7) the ability to reason logically from a model. A good imagination is also helpful.[1]

These intellectual skills represent a high order of intellectual development. As newer conceptions of intellectual development were promulgated, these higher mental processes have been seen as deriving from a long train of maturational stages and prior experiences. Thus, the ability to think scientifically does not suddenly appear in a youngster at maturation, but requires nurturing from the early years on. As a result of this realization, the new curriculum development movement began to turn its attention to programs in the primary grades. The theories of Piaget provided one framework within which science concepts could be gen-

---

[1]Paul DeHart Hurd and James Joseph Gallagher, *New Directions in Elementary Science Teaching* (Belmont, Calif.: Wadsworth Publishing Co., 1968), pp. 5–6.

erated in children; learning theory provided another. Models of curriculum development paralleled the beliefs about what and how children could learn. These models are evident in the newer science programs. Basic to this development in science education was the belief that schools should teach science as an intellectual activity.

THE NATURE OF SCIENCE   Science was one of the later subjects to be
EDUCATION IN THE PAST   included in the curriculum of early childhood education. In many of the pioneering approaches to early childhood education we do find nature study, the observation of natural phenomenon primarily for the sake of appreciation rather than comprehension. Teachers were admonished to keep a section of their outdoor play space reserved tor a garden to be cultivated by the children. Small animals were kept as classroom pets with the children caring for them. Interesting natural objects such as rocks and leaves were brought into the classroom and arranged on a table for the children to observe. Nature stories were read and pictures exhibited to further children's learning.

All this activity had as its prime purpose the development of children's reverence for the outdoors and appreciation of the wonders of nature to be found around them. In urban schools nature study was often considered as a form of compensatory education, needed because city children had less opportunity for encounters with nature than did rural children. Since young children were seen as being so natural themselves, nature study seemed a logical inclusion in the program. Although direct observation in a natural setting is one strategy of modern science, observations of the "wonders of nature" were seldom used in the past as the basis for thinking scientifically about the surrounding world.

After the first quarter of the twentieth century, the study of science began to replace nature study in the curricula of elementary schools and in early childhood education as well. Science education became less concerned with appreciation and more with understanding scientific concepts and the scientific method, even at a rudimentary level. Vestiges of nature study continue in early childhood classes today, with teachers still displaying materials for observation and appreciation on science tables, reading anthropomorphic nature stories to children, and using an incidental approach to science education.

While teaching an appreciation of nature, providing opportunities to observe natural phenomena, or using incidental occurrences to further children's learning are all worthwhile activities in a science program, they are not adequate as a total science program. Teachers, for example, need to develop activities that improve children's observational skills.

They also need to teach children that an appreciation of nature might require social action that must be based on an understanding of how to preserve nature and an understanding of the consequences of technological activities on nature. The ability to use a fortuitous occurrence as a basis for science learning requires the development of criteria to judge whether these occurrences can provide significant learning opportunities. A systematic approach to science learning, based upon a conception of science appropriate to young children, can help establish such criteria.

SOME MODERN CONCEPTIONS OF SCIENCE EDUCATION FOR THE EARLY YEARS

What and how one decides to teach in science programs depends to a great extent upon how science is conceived by the curriculum developer—what he sees as the purposes of science education and how he conceives of the nature of early learning. At the early childhood level teachers are not concerned with preparing children to be scientists. Rather science education is thought of as part of general education. All persons in our society ought to have some knowledge of science to use in their daily life's activities. Equally important is an understanding of the nature of scientific inquiry and the role of science in modern society. Scientific literacy is an educational goal for all children in schools today.

SCIENCE AS SYSTEM OF KNOWLEDGE

Science has been conceived of by some educators as a body of knowledge about the physical world. The curriculum, from that point of view, could contain selective scientific facts that would be most useful to children and adults. Determination of the scope and sequence of such a curriculum would be made by deciding which facts can be learned at what age and dividing up the information so that it is all covered by the time a child completes school.

The problem with developing a program based upon this point of view is that there are so many scientific facts that have been accumulated and that continue to be accumulated that it is difficult to select the most significant ones. The number of facts an individual would have to be taught and would later have to remember would make science education a formidable task. In addition, science is continually discovering new facts and discarding information that was thought to be true. Teaching a body of scientific fact to children becomes a cumbersome, never-ending task having questionable ultimate value.

Because of the difficulties within this approach to science teaching, it has generally been discarded in favor of a view of science as a set of organized concepts and generalizations. Most scientific information can be organized into a systematic set of concepts which help to order the facts of science. The concepts give meaning to the facts, putting them into a more generalized perspective that allows a person to relate pieces of information to a conception of knowledge about the world.

In addition, science is conceived as a method of generating and verifying knowledge. The method used by the scientist in observing phenomena and testing hypotheses in controlling variables and in careful reporting and replicating of experiments are all part of what may be considered the *structure* of science. It is the teaching of this structure that is the goal of the newer science programs.

The organizing of the content of science into a conceptual structure is not a completely new idea. Craig's research in science education in the 1920s was aimed at developing a unified science program for children based upon generalizations that cut across the boundaries of separate disciplines.[2] This work led to the development of a conceptual scheme for education that is still in use today.

1. The universe is very large—*Space*
2. The earth is very old—*Time*
3. The universe is constantly changing—*Change*
4. Life is adapted to its environment—*Adaptation*
5. There are great variations in the universe—*Variety*
6. The interdependence of living things—*Interrelationships*
7. The interaction of forces—*Equilibrium and Balance*[3]

This scheme became the source of a textbook series based on an elementary school science program authored by Craig and his associates that was adopted by many schools. Other textbook-based programs have also been built around conceptual schemes. For example, Brandwein and his associates recently developed a similar conceptual scheme for science teaching:

1. When energy changes from one form to another, the total amount of energy remains unchanged.
2. When matter changes from one form to another, the total amount of matter remains unchanged.
3. Living things are interdependent with one another and with their environment.

[2]Gerald S. Craig, *Certain Techniques Used in Developing a Course of Study in Science for the Horace Mann Elementary School* (New York: Teachers College Press, Columbia University, 1927.

[3]Craig, *Science for the Elementary School Teacher* (Boston: Ginn and Co., 1958), pp. 93–101.

4. A living thing is the product of its heredity and its environment.
5. Living things are in constant change.
6. The universe is in constant change.[4]

Within this framework, Brandwein and his colleagues have designed an integrated science program for the kindergarten through the sixth grade. While the conceptual organization may be similar to older ones, the science content and the approaches to teaching have been modernized.

Such conceptual schemes have great attractiveness for education. They are useful in integrating information into meaningful concepts and generalizations. In addition, almost all scientific knowledge and information fits into one category or another, programs at different levels can be articulated with one another, and the entire content of science education for the total school can be integrated by fitting each science experience into a concept and then determining the level at which it could best be taught. In this way what is taught in the kindergarten can be related to what is taught in the third grade, with little danger of too much overlap in the content of instruction from grade to grade.

This approach is, however, still based upon a conception of science primarily as a body of knowledge and information. Scientific concepts are not taught directly but through the teaching of elements of knowledge that reflect these concepts. The concepts, however, order this knowledge and allow for its greatest transferability.

Other programs of science education have focused on the phenomena of science, the concepts of science, or the strategies of scientific inquiry rather than on scientific knowledge. Karplus and Thier have characterized the differences in three science curriculum projects as follows:

> The interested reader is urged to examine in detail the course material produced by these three groups and by others. He will find a variety of approaches to the curriculum. For example, the units produced by the SCIS and the parts written by the AAAS form a complete and integrated curriculum, while the ESS is creating self-contained units that may be fashioned into a curriculum by local teaching groups. He will also find that there are significant differences in emphasis on the three elements—concepts, phenomena, processes—which make up the science course. Thus, the ESS stresses the child's involvement in the phenomena and is confident that he will thereby gain practice with processes and achieve understanding of valuable concepts even though these are not made explicit. The SCIS stresses the concepts and phenomena, with process learning an implicit by-product of the children's experimentation, discussion and analysis. The AAAS stresses the child's practice with the processes and uses the phenomena only as vehicles and the concepts as tools. An added difference is that the AAAS

[4]Paul F. Brandwein, Elizabeth K. Cooper, Paul E. Blackwood, and Elizabeth B. Hone, *Concepts in Science* (Grade I, Teacher's Edition) (New York: Harcourt, Brace and World, Inc., 1966), pp. 8–9.

program attempts to appraise the children's progress more systematically and in greater detail than do the others.[5]

Differences in programs, however, reflect not only differences in content emphasis but differences in ideas about learning and intellectual development, as well as differences in conceptions of schooling.

While it is easy to emphasize differences in programs, there are also a number of common attributes found among newer programs. Generally they are all based upon modern conceptions of science; they conceive of the child as an active learner and require his participation in science experiences; they provide materials for learning as well as instructions to teachers for developing activities with these materials.

A brief sketch of the three science programs discussed by Karplus and Thier should help to illustrate the likenesses and differences among newer programs. The American Association for the Advancement of Science (AAAS) has developed the program *Science—A Process Approach.* The *Science Curriculum Improvement Study* (SCIS) was developed at the University of California under the direction of Dr. Robert Karplus. The *Elementary Science Study* (ESS) is a product of the Educational Development Center.[6]

SCIENCE—
A PROCESS APPROACH

The American Association for the Advancement of Science, in the primary science curriculum it has developed, conceived of the processes of scientific inquiry as the essential element of science that one wishes to communicate to children:

The basic processes of science appropriate for children in the primary grades are identified by the following terms:

1. observing
2. using space-time relationships
3. using numbers
4. measuring
5. classifying
6. communicating
7. predicting
8. inferring

[5]Robert Karplus and Herbert D. Thier, *A New Look at Elementary School Science* (Chicago: Rand McNally, 1967), p. 8.

[6]More complete descriptions of the content of the various science programs and the materials developed are available from their educational publishers. For information, contact the Webster Division, McGraw-Hill Book Co., St. Louis, for *Elementary Science Study*; Raytheon Education Co., Lexington, Mass., for *Science Curriculum Improvement Study*; and Xerox Corp., New York, for *Science—A Process Approach.*

A principal aim of the program is to develop skill in the careful and systematic use of these processes in the primary grades as a necessary preliminary to undertaking more complex science learning in the later grades.[7]

The more complex science learning of the intermediate grades include the skills of formulating hypotheses, defining operationally, controlling variables, experimenting, formulating models, and interpreting data.

Activities in the AAAS primary program are carefully designed to teach children the above processes. Young children observe objects and identify color, shape, and texture within them. They observe weather phenomena and describe their observations. They also observe, among other things, the various parts of a plant. In the area of space/time relationships, children learn to identify two- and three-dimensional shapes and angles as well as to deal with concepts of speed. Number work includes identifying and comparing sets, finding the sum of two numbers, and dealing with number relationships. Measures of length, weight, area, and volume are explored by the children, who learn to make comparisons as well as use standard units of measurement.

Specific experiences are provided to help children classify objects by visible attributes, moving from single stage to multistage classifications. Communication requires identifying and naming objects, using graphs, and describing experiments to others. Children are required to draw inferences from information and demonstrate how inferences may be tested. They also learn to make and test predictions.

The program is a hierarchically structured one, with simpler activities followed by more complicated ones. Prerequisites for later activities are taught in earlier activities. In the area of observation, for example, early activities include identifying and naming textures of an object in terms of rough or smooth, large or small, or by primary and secondary colors. Later activities require the identification and naming of two or more characteristics of an object, such as rough and small. Similarly, early identification of two- and three-dimensional shapes leads to the identification of two-dimensional shapes that are the components of three-dimensional ones.

This approach conceives of science education as helping children learn the process of scientific inquiry that can be identified through a task analysis of the scientist's role. Although facts of science continually change, the basic processes of scientific inquiry remain relatively constant even though changes in technology affect the way the processes of inquiry are put to use.

[7]American Association for the Advancement of Science, *Description of the Program: Science—A Process Approach* (New York: Xerox Educational Division, 1967), p. 3.

The method by which scientific processes are taught in the program leans heavily on behaviorist learning theory rather than developmental theory. Maturation or levels of intellectual development are considered irrelevant. Upon successful attainment of one level of skill development, the child moves up to the next level. What a child can learn is a function of what he already knows. A child's inability to master a scientific process means that he needs to go back and master the prerequisite skills.

Behavioral Objectives

The AAAS program has been organized toward the achievement of specific observable behavioral goals. Each lesson or element of instruction has identified within it the goals the child is expected to achieve and these are specified in behavioral terms. Since these behaviors are directly observable by the teacher, immediate evaluation becomes possible and the teacher can then judge the effectiveness of the program.

"The process skills of the program are readily described in terms of component skills which correspond to observable performances or behaviors of the child."[8] The evaluation of learning for the whole class as well as for the individual child is related directly to these behavioral goals.

> Appraisal helps determine whether a majority of the children in the class have satisfactorily attained the behavioral objectives of an exercise. ... Tests designed to evaluate individual achievement are called competency measures. Each task included in a competency measure tests the attainment of one or more objectives of the exercise.[9]

An illustration of the goals and evaluation technique is provided from the lesson *Observing I—Perception of Color*. The objectives of the lesson are listed as follows:

> At the end of this exercise the child should be able to
> 1. IDENTIFY the following colors by sight: yellow, orange, red, purple, blue, and green.
> 2. NAME the three principal colors—yellow, red, and blue.
> 3. IDENTIFY other colors as being like one of the colors yellow, red, and blue.
>
> The appraisal of the group is based upon the following tasks:
>
> Ask each of about six children to bring a box of crayons and sit together in some place convenient for you. (The boxes of crayons must include red, green, yellow, blue, orange, and purple.)
>
> Ask each child to match one crayon with some article of clothing that someone else is wearing. For example: Find a crayon whose color is most

[8]AAAS, *Description of the Program*, p. 3.
[9]Ibid., p. 6.

like Jane's skirt. If Jane's skirt is pale blue, the child should point to the blue crayon.

Before each group of children leaves the activity, ask each child individually to name and point to the red, blue, and yellow crayons.

Competency measures for each child include:

TASKS 1–3 (OBJECTIVE 1): Show the child in turn each of three blocks: a yellow (1), a red (2), and a blue (3). Each time ask, "What is the color of this block?" Give one check in the acceptable column for each correct name.

TASKS 4–6 (OBJECTIVE 2): Name the colors of three blocks which are in front of the child: an orange (4), a green (5), and a purple (6) one. As you name each one, say, "Put your finger on the block as I name the color." Give one check in the acceptable column for each correct identification.

TASK 7 (OBJECTIVES 2, 3): Give the child three paper plates: one yellow, one red, and one blue. Show him a piece of pink paper and say, "Put this on one of the three plates—yellow, red, or blue. Which color is it most like?" Give one check in the acceptable column for placing the paper on the red plate.

TASK 8 (OBJECTIVES 2, 3): Repeat this procedure with a light blue piece of paper. Give one check in the acceptable column for placing the paper on the blue plate.[10]

Critics of this approach are concerned that it does not in fact teach the basic processes in science, which include thinking creatively about phenomena, inventing concepts, and developing divergent notions about aspects of the world. The lack of concern for children's stages of intellectual development has also been criticized. One may also criticize the teaching of science, which is an open-ended field, within a closed system of instruction.

SCIENCE CURRICULUM IMPROVEMENT STUDY   Another approach to teaching science relates to conceiving of science as a way of thinking about the world through developing and testing theories. The Science Curriculum Improvement Study of the University of California conceives of science education as a way to help children form "A conceptual framework that permits them to perceive phenomena in a more meaningful way. This framework will also help them to integrate their inferences into generalizations of greater values than they would form if left to their own devices."[11]

The Units of Study included in the SCIS program are reflected in the chart on page 123.

[10]AAAS. *Science, A Process Approach*, Part A, Observing 1. New York: Xerox Corporation, 1967.

[11]Karplus and Thier, *A New Look at Elementary School Science*, pp. 20–21.

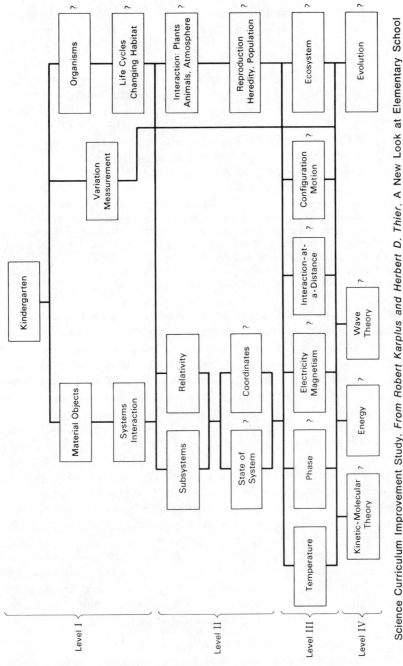

Science Curriculum Improvement Study. *From Robert Karplus and Herbert D. Thier, A New Look at Elementary School Science. p. 36 © 1969 by Rand McNally & Company, Chicago.*

123

The topics of the SCIS program have resulted from an indentification of basic concepts in science. The organization of units reflects an acceptance of a Piagetian framework of intellectual development. Level I in the diagram corresponds to the transition from preoperational to concrete operational thought in the child; level II reflects concrete operational thought; level III reflects the transition from concrete operations to formal operations; and level IV requires facility with formal operations.[12]

Materials, activities, and concepts are compatible with the child's reasoning ability at each level, and science learning is seen as providing a bridge between personal explorations and interpretations of the world and an understanding of scientific concepts.

> The child's elementary school years are a period of transition as he continues the exploration of the world he began during infancy and builds abstractions with which he interprets that world. With a careful introduction to scientific abstractions at this time, he will later be able to relate them to the real world in a meaningful way. As he matures, the continual interplay of interpretations and observations will frequently compel him to revise his ideas about his environment.[13]

Units in the SCIS program are designed to be taught in a specific sequence. Each unit includes a teacher's guide, student manuals, and a kit of equipment and materials to serve one teacher and thirty-two children. Each unit covers a number of topics and contains *invention* lessons and *discovery* lessons. Invention lessons allow the teacher to define new terms or concepts. Discovery lessons permit the children to apply these new ideas. Optional activities are also provided.

In each lesson children are given specific sets of materials and asked to experiment with them. All the children in the class are usually working on the same experiments, although they may be working individually or in small groups. The children may record the results of their experiments in their individual manuals. Some lessons in the program are left completely open-ended; others may terminate in classroom discussions. Teachers are often advised to guide discussions with questions and comments requiring reflection as well as response, such as, "Tell us what happened in your experiment," or "How did the objects change?" Since specific behavioral objectives are not stated, a range of outcomes could be expected from any of the experiences provided and often there is no specific immediate outcome that is expected from a single experience. Goals are to be achieved cumulatively over long periods of time.

[12]Ibid., p. 35.
[13]Science Curriculum Improvement Study, *Teachers Guide: Systems and Subsystems* (Preliminary Edition) (Lexington, Mass.: Raytheon Educational Co., 1968), p. 1.

In the *Interactions* unit, for example, each pair of children is given, to begin with, a box containing:

Cupped vial with water
Colored candy spheres
Scissors
Paper clips
Rubber band
3″ × 5″ card
Plastic clay
Small magnet
Battery
Flashlight bulb
Aluminum wire
Two "mystery pictures"
Sharpened pencil with steel eraser band

The children are allowed to experiment with the objects from the box, and the teacher guides individual experiments by asking questions and making suggestions. Later they are asked to record their experiments and a discussion is held in which children can demonstrate their experiments to the class. This work is preliminary to the lessons, in which the interaction concept is *invented* through reference to these experiments and there is a demonstration of interaction with magnets and roller skates and water, vinegar and bromothymol blue solution in tumblers.[14]

ELEMENTARY SCIENCE STUDY   The products of the Elementary Science Study are a series of units, each of which can be used at several grade levels, rather than a systematic program of science instruction. There is a particular model of science education that underlies the project. Hawkins, former director of ESS, defines three phases of science instruction in a program. The first phase is one in which children primarily "mess about," freely exploring the materials and making their own discoveries in an unstructured environment.

The second phase is one in which the work is externally guided but still highly individualized. This can be done, according to Hawkins, through the use of "multiply programmed" materials—materials that contain written or pictorial guidance for the student but which are designed for the greatest variety and ordering of topics, so that for almost any

[14]Science Curriculum Improvement Study, *Interaction and Teaching Guide* (Preliminary Edition) (Boston: D. C. Heath and Co., 1967), pp. 28–34.

given way a child may evolve on his own there is material available which will help him move along in his way.

The third phase of science instruction moves children from concrete perception to abstract conceptualization. This phase of theorizing must be built upon experience and experimentation, but abstraction does not develop without special attention given to it. While each of these phases is described discretely, actually they all represent central tendencies of the phases and each phase includes activities reflecting the other phases.[15]

The "messing about" phase can be illustrated in the directions for getting started provided in the *Teachers Guide for Geo Blocks*. In the *Geo Blocks* unit, children are provided with a set of blocks smaller than the traditional kindergarten unit blocks. These blocks are designed as units so that a number of small blocks equal the size of a larger one. Many small blocks and fewer larger ones are provided so that children are forced to develop equivalences. The blocks are used to build towers, ramps, three-dimensional maps, and other constructions. Specific problems are provided for the children to work through with the blocks. In the introductory instructions, however, the teacher is advised not to structure prematurely.

> Before beginning any formal work with Geo Blocks, the children should have ample opportunity to familiarize themselves with the composition of the Basic Set. We recommend, therefore, that you begin by making the blocks available to your class during periods of free time, without giving directions and without commenting on their use. Put the blocks in an easily accessible place with an open space (floor or table) nearby where your students will have room to spread out the blocks and explore their nature and possibilities. At times, these early investigations may be noisy, and they may last for months rather than weeks, but they are as much a part of the learning process as are the later activities in which you may participate more actively.[16]

Teachers are asked to observe but not intervene in these early explorations, although they may make informal suggestions for elaborating the use of the blocks. Later, more directed use of the blocks can be developed by the children as a result of the teachers' questioning of children. Questions may deal with building, counting, shapes, slopes, grouping, surface area, and volume. In addition to *Geo Blocks*, a number of other units have been prepared by ESS. Some of these are appropriate for young children, others are designed for the intermediate grades. Units include *Small Things, Growing Seeds, Batteries and Bulbs, Mirror Cards,* and *Light and Shadows,* among others.

[15]David Hawkins, "Messing About in Science," *Science and Children*, Vol. 2, No. 5 (February 1965), 5–9.
[16]Elementary Science Study, *Geo Blocks—Teachers Guide* (*Trial Edition*) (Newton, Mass.: Educational Development Center, 1967), p. 3.

While the AAAS and SCIS programs tend by their structure to support whole class activity, the ESS units can be used by a small group or a portion of a class. The ESS program also uses "discovery" techniques as an instructional strategy to a greater extent than do the other programs. Children are placed in direct contact with scientific phenomena with a minimum of prestructuring on the part of the teacher. Although the teacher does play an active role in helping children build scientific concepts, this role is reserved for later, rather than in the first phase of the learning situation. Her role relates more to the organization of the environment to facilitate "discovery" on the part of children.

SELECTING A SCIENCE PROGRAM   The three science programs discussed here represent only a sample of the programs in science available today. In addition to the programs resulting from the national curriculum development projects, textbook publishers are offering newer programs that reflect many of these new developments. The *Concepts in Science*, published by Harcourt Brace Jovanovich, is one example of these. The newer programs generally contain up-to-date science content. In addition, they make provisions for active participation of the child in the learning process so that science instruction goes well beyond rote memorization.

Selection of a science program could be based upon an analysis of available programs, as recommended in Chapter XV. Judgments could then be made upon the content emphasis of the science program (for example on content, concepts, or skills) as well as assumptions made about child learning and development.

Most important, the science program should be compatible with the rest of the classroom curriculum. The AAAS program as a whole, for example, would be more difficult than would the ESS program to fit into an open educational environment such as that suggested in Chapter III.

The Hawkins paradigm of science teaching closely parallels that of the *integrated day*. "Messing about" is followed by other elements of instruction as the child shows an interest and the ability to move ahead. The teacher can then provide him with formal or informal assignments that will move his inquiry into greater depth. The "multiply programmed" effect that Hawkins suggests is closely akin to that gained from the use of the *assignment cards* provided by many teachers in English primary schools. Each card raises a question for children to pursue or suggests some activity to further the child's learning. For the very young, these suggestions could just as easily be provided orally by the teacher.

Teachers can also sit down with children in group discussion sessions, asking questions about what they have been doing and leading them to develop generalizations and theories about their experiences. Such sessions can be brief, organized informally during activity period or integrated into a time when children are describing and evaluating their work. Such a discussion could take place with a single individual as well as with a group of children. The key in fruitful discussions rests in the teacher's serving a guidance function, leading the discussion and asking clarifying questions without offering conclusions to the child or structuring his thinking too much. Although not all teachers would select this program, the other programs available can also be modified to make them more *open*.

SELECTING A SCIENCE PROGRAM FOR YOUNG CHILDREN

At the kindergarten and primary levels, teachers have available to them a number of newly developed science programs from which to choose which have the potential of providing significant science learning for young children in the classroom. Often the decision of what to teach under such cicrumstances is not the individual teacher's, for a school system may adopt a single textbook series or program in order to insure continuity of learning through the grades with a minimum of unnecessary duplication of experiences. The newer science programs often provide better learning potential than some of the traditional school curriculum guides. In most instances, the newer programs were developed by teams of scientists, psychologists, and teachers, and have been tested and refined before final dissemination. Such professional services are often far beyond the resources of the curriculum committees of most school systems. These programs do, however, place limitations upon the teacher, who is expected to teach what may be a very prescribed content through a prescribed set of experiences.

A Program for the Nursery School

The nursery-school teacher has fewer guidelines to follow in selecting a science program. Some nursery-school teachers skim off a number of experiences from a science program intended for older children and offer these to their classes. This approach can lead to a lack of significant learning, since the activities are unrelated to each other and the intended meanings of the experience may actually be beyond the young child's capability for learning. Other teachers use a nature study approach, creating displays of leaves, rocks, or other "science material," including some small animals in the classroom, and also talk to the children about weather and seasonal changes.

Nature study can provide a good beginning if the teacher capitalizes on the possibilities of various activities. Displays can be designed in cooperation with the children who organize materials as a result of their observations. Rocks can be placed together to highlight likenesses and differences. Leaves can be highlighted so that the individual differences among a set of similar leaves can become apparent. The care of animals can provide a legitimate source of science study. Teachers can begin to ask questions that alert children to significant occurrences rather than *tell* children what they ought to know.

The new science curriculum projects can provide guidelines for structuring a science program at the nursery-school level, since they all seem to have common prerequisites.

Each program requires that the children be able to make observations of physical objects, be able to describe these observations, know how to categorize objects by certain attributes, and discriminate between groups of objects that fit into a category and others which do not. A significant program could be built around experiences which help children to observe, describe, and categorize physical phenomena. These activities could be balanced with other activities in which children could be allowed to freely explore scientific materials and the use of these materials in a range of classroom experiences.

Focusing on the Exploration and Description of Sense Perceptions

Each person receives his information about the external world through his five senses: sight, sound, touch, taste, and smell. This information can be identified and categorized. Visual properties of things can be differentiated in terms of size, shape, color, and other qualities. Sounds can be identified by pitch, intensity, quality, and regularity. Sounds can also be related to their producers. Touch sensations can also be described as hard or soft, rough or smooth, warm or cold, sharp or dull. The qualities of taste and smell, while not as precisely identifiable, can also be differentiated. These properties are listed as examples and are not to be considered exhaustive.

For each sense modality one can provide children with manipulative activities and related language experiences that would help them to identify, categorize, and differentiate experiences and begin to describe objects by their sensory properties. This is the beginning of scientific thought. Language activities can be related to manipulative activities so that children learn descriptive language that allows them to symbolize and to communicate their sense experiences.

At snack time, the teacher might want to vary the traditional serving of milk or juice and crackers and bring in a variety of foods for the children to taste. Children can eat these foods and talk about how they smell, taste, and feel. Fruits make excellent samples, as do many vegetables, including those which are often seldom seen by children in their natural form and not often tasted raw. Carrots, potatoes, celery, turnips, and spinach are some of the vegetables that can be used. A variety of breads and crackers, as well as many other foods, can be included.

The teacher might wish to cook some of these foods, especially the raw vegetables, to help children see the process of change that takes place as a result of the application of heat. Cooked spinach looks much different than raw spinach. Cooked carrots feel different than raw carrots. Even mixing foods together often makes significant differences in the way they look, taste, and feel. Sugar dissolved in water still tastes sweet, but it no longer has a granular feel. Flour also changes consistency when mixed with a liquid. The number of specific ways that foods can be used is endless.

Experiences with many other materials can also help children become aware of attributes of things. Providing similarly shaped objects of lead and aluminum helps children differentiate between heavy and light objects. A touch board made with sandpaper, velvet, absorbent cotton, a piece of aluminum foil, and other such everyday items can help children differentiate between textures. Setting up a "feeling box" containing an object that is hidden from view but can be touched by the children can help focus on tactile perception. Teachers can talk about the colors and shapes of a number of things, bringing in samples of primary colors and specific shapes as well as helping children identify color and shape in everyday objects around the school. Block structures can be identified as larger or smaller, wider or narrower than other block structures.

The opportunities for helping children focus on the different elements of their perception can take place in the free, less structured activities of play situations, or may be included in more structured activities specifically designed to help the children learn a particular category or name for an attribute. Once attributes are learned, children can be helped to make finer and finer discriminations and to begin to categorize things by their attributes. The same objects can be used to teach different kinds of categorization. A box of buttons, for example, might be given to a group of children to be separated by color. At another time the children might separate the buttons according to size, and at yet another time, on the basis of the material from which they are made.

Including Science Materials in Natural Activities

At the same time an "attribute" program is being conducted, the teacher should also be concerned with feeding science materials into the play activities of the children so that they can discover properties and relationships and use them. Setting up a pulley system in the block area for the children to use in building will help children learn about force and the way it can be increased or changed in direction. A doorbell and buzzer operated on batteries could be included in the housekeeping area, stimulating dramatic play as people come and go and also helping children see the effects of electricity and the need for a circuit in operating electrical devices. Battery-powered electric lights complete with switches could also be placed in a play house. A bulb, battery, and a couple of lengths of wire can be placed in a box for the children's free manipulations and discovery. Magnets, magnifying glasses, and other items can be made available to children for "messing about" or for inclusion in their play activities.

Children could also be given opportunities to grow things from seeds, tubers, and cuttings, in order to observe the process of growth. They should be able to describe things growing as well as what they and the teacher did to help them grow. Fish and small animals, in appropriate containers, can also be placed in a classroom for the children's observation.

It is important in all science inquiry that children be given opportunities to ask questions about what they see and to be able to find the answers to these questions. Sometimes the questions they ask of teachers are unanswerable. A question like "What is electricity?" might best be answered by the teacher who says, "I don't know, but we can see some of the things that electricity can do." It is better to answer questions honestly than to be caught in providing inaccurate answers or answers that border on the magical. Children need to become comfortable with the unknown.

SCIENCE ACTIVITIES
IN THE CLASSROOM
Whether or not a teacher selects a particular science program, she still must organize her classroom so that science learning can take place in an area that is identifiable by the children and that has a degree of isolation from the other activity centers of the room. Children can find materials and have space available to pursue scientific inquiry in such a center. The center should have within it or near it some closed storage space, such as a cabinet, in which the teacher can keep science materials not currently in use by the children. If these materials are

readily available, the teacher is able to use the children's cues to move into the study of a science topic that happens to interest children, thus exploiting the children's personal motivation for learning. If a range of materials is not available, the teacher may have to postpone an experience or even allow a critical moment for learning to pass right by.

In addition to storage, there ought to be some open shelf space where children have access to a range of science materials. A display area might be available in this center, including a bulletin board and a display table. There should be space available as well for children to work at problems of scientific inquiry. If the center is relatively isolated, a teacher can set up a problem for the children and allow them to come to the center to work on the problem individually or in small groups. Since scientific inquiry is the important goal of science instruction, most of the science work ought to be done by individuals or small groups.

Using Displays

Teachers of young children often place displays on a "science table" for their class to view. Simply *having* a display is inadequate for the purposes of science education in the early years, for the key to its effectiveness is how the display is used. Teachers should organize their displays for the children's use.

Bulletin-board displays can be organized to demonstrate a scientific concept. Leaves of the same kind of tree can be pinned up to show diversity of foliage. Pictures of a plant at different periods in its growth can be used to demonstrate the process of growth. Objects of varying size can be used to demonstrate the concept of "bigger than" or "smaller than."

Materials on a science table can be organized so that they can be actually used by the children. A group of rocks can be placed so that the children can feel the rocks and then do something with them, such as organizing them by texture, color, or form. Different types of lenses can be displayed so that children can use them to look at objects and discover the effect on the apparent size of the object. A magnet can be placed with both magnetic and non-magnetic material so that the children can manipulate it and discover from this the properties of magnets.

There are many other ways in which displays can be organized for children's use. The crucial element is in the use that the child can make of a display in learning to develop modes of scientific thinking. Simply placing materials out for children to look at without expecting anything else of it is a waste of materials and space in the classroom.

For displays to be effective, they should also be changed regularly. If the content of a display reflects the children's concern with particular areas of scientific inquiries, then the displays can be changed to keep up with the shifts that take place in the focus of science learning in the classroom.

Providing Demonstrations

Actual experiments, in the traditional sense, including the use of laboratory controls, are seldom carried out in the classroom. Often there is little to be gained from such experiments that cannot be gained from freer experiences with the same materials. Experiments using a certain degree of control over conditions in order to highlight comparison can be used as a way of answering a child's particular question about the consequence of certain variables in a situation, but teachers often use demonstrations instead.

Demonstrations can be a way of *telling* children about science, a variation on direct verbal instruction, or they can be a part of legitimate scientific inquiry, depending upon how they are set up. If the demonstration is performed and followed only by an explanation, this accomplishes no more than an illustration. Even when the demonstration is followed by a form of superficial inquiry during which the children are supposed to guess what the teacher wants them to know—a form of academic "Twenty Questions" often played in school—it remains a form of telling.

Demonstrations can lead to inquiry when followed by a legitimate questioning and discussion session. Teachers can stimulate such sessions by asking questions such as, "What happened?" "Why did it happen?" "How do you know?" "Did you see anything else happening?" "Can you think of other ways we can explain what happened?" "How can we tell that our explanation is a correct one?" These questions need to be a part of honest inquiry, because without them, there may be blocks that are unsurmountable, and improper answers might be accepted that are unsupported by some form of evidence. In order for honest inquiry to occur, the children must have access to the information that can be used to test their conclusion. If such information is not directly observable by the children, their responses may border on the magical rather than the scientific.

Recording the Results of Inquiry

One of the important elements of science is that the products of inquiry be recorded and communicated so that ideas can be retested and the results of earlier inquiries can be compared to those of later inquiries. Thus, children learn to record the results of their investigations in such a manner that these results can be communicated to others and may be referred to at a later time. With children in the upper primary classes this generally presents no problem, since they can write with a sufficient amount of competence to begin to develop science notebooks, which reflect the science activities in which they have participated. For the younger child, this requirement presents a bit of a problem, but teachers can devise many ways of helping children record their scientific activities.

Children can dictate materials to the teacher to record on experience charts or in individual books; they can also dictate the results of their activities into tape recorders to be played back at later times. Young children can use paintings and drawings to record their experiences in some symbolic fashion. It is important that the teacher set aside time for discussion, and for recording of the results of a scientific experience, because the language and symbolic aspects are important for the child's continued learning.

Providing Opportunities for Inquiries

This chapter has emphasized science instruction as a part of the curriculum that requires children to be actively involved in forms of inquiry. Science has been viewed not as a set of labels or concepts, but as a way of conceiving of the world—a way of thinking about things. This point of view makes it imperative that at every point in the curriculum children should be actively involved in thinking about the experiences that are provided for them and that their processes of thought about physical and natural phenomena parallel their acquisition of scientific information. The ramifications for classroom organization are that activities must be organized so that children can *act upon* materials and experiences and arrive at their own conclusions. This requires that most activities be organized for individuals and small groups of children. It also requires that the teacher not spend a great deal of time telling children about science, but instead continuously provide the children with opportunities in which they can find out on their own.

This approach requires that the teacher both be sensitive to the thought processes in which the child is involved and become an observer of what the child does in class. The important element of science learning is not necessarily the products of scientific inquiry—the conclusions that the child arrives at or the kinds of categories the child develops—but rather the process by which the child arrives at these conclusions and the reasons and methods of developing a set of categories. This approach should support a great deal of diversity in the classroom—diversity in achievement, in goals, and in activities. Such diversity can only take place when there is a degree of individualization in classroom work.

SUGGESTED READING

BLOUGH, GLENN O., AND JULIUS SCHWARTZ, *Elementary School Science and How to Teach It*. New York: Holt, Rinehart & Winston, 1964.

CRAIG, GERALD S., *Science for the Elementary School Teacher*, 5th ed. Waltham, Massachusetts: Blaisdell Publishing Company, 1966.

DUNFEE, MAXINE, *Elementary School Science: A Guide to Current Research*. Washington, D.C.: Association for Supervision and Curriculum Development, 1967.

FOWLER, WILLIAM, "Developmental Science Learning for Disadvantaged Children," *Elementary School Journal*, Vol. 68, No. 2 (November 1967), 76–87.

GEORGE, KENNETH D., "Science for the Preschool Child," *Science and Children*, Vol. 6, No. 1 (September 1968), 37–38.

HANEY, RICHARD E., *The Changing Curriculum: Science*. Washington, D.C.: Association for Supervision and Curriculum Development, 1966.

HAWKINS, DAVID, "Messing about with Science," *Science and Children*, Vol. 2, No. 5 (February 1965), 5–9.

HURD, PAUL D., AND JAMES J. GALLAGHER, *New Directions in Elementary Science Teaching*. Belmont, California: Wadsworth Publishing Company, 1968.

KARPLUS, ROBERT, AND HERBERT D. THIER, *A New Look at Elementary School Science*. Chicago: Rand McNally, 1967.

RUCHLIS, HY, "Scientific Thinking in the Lower Grades," *Science and Children*, Vol. 1, No. 3 (November 1963), 16–17.

7

Mathematics for Young Children

Many changes have taken place in the mathematics programs suggested for schools during the past two decades. The new curriculum development movement of the 1950s and 1960s had its greatest gains in the area of science and mathematics. These two subjects, possibly more than any others, were said to be out of phase with recent developments in their parent fields of scholarly inquiry. The mathematics developed in the last hundred years could not be found anywhere in the teachings of the elementary and secondary school. In addition, much of the mathematics that was taught in schools relied heavily on rote learning with the goal of developing computational skills. Little emphasis was placed on mathematics as a logical system, a symbol system, or a system of inquiry, and little was done to teach problem solving in mathematics.

The work of the new curriculum development movement started in the secondary school; as the new projects showed that many children could learn more than was expected of them in the standard curriculum, the work of reconstruction moved downward, affecting even the kindergarten and primary grades. Soon it was the fashion to teach ideas from "set theory" to the youngest children in school and have them learn to use new symbols for such operations as the "union" and "intersection" of sets.

Although the new vocabulary of the modern mathematics movement was quickly embraced by teachers, one often found the spirit of modern mathematics still lacking in classrooms adopting new programs. Instead of learning mathematical concepts as a result of inquiring into the nature of numbers and number relationships and abstracting generalizations and concepts from their own experiences, children were asked to memorize new sets of words and new operations. They often memorized the new vocabulary without having the opportunity to gain an understanding of it. The "new" mathematics differed from the traditional only in its use of less familiar language. In addition, topics for mathematics study were often added to the curriculum because they were exotic rather than because they were useful to children or could help build better mathematical understandings.

THE CONTENT OF
MATHEMATICS
PROGRAMS

What should be the nature of the mathematics program for young children? Fehr suggests that elementary mathematics should be a "study of number and of space, and the relating of these two ideas through the use of measurement . . . presented in a well-balanced program of mathematical concepts, computational procedures and problem solving."[1] These goals for elementary education could serve as well at the early childhood level. Such a program would include the study of "sets," or collections of objects, the learning of cardinal and ordinal numbers, one-to-one correspondence, the operations of addition, subtraction, multiplication, and division, as well as the concept of fractions, simple geometry, and developing concepts of measurement of two-dimensional space, volume, and weight.

Incidental Versus Planned Teaching

With the development of new mathematics programs, there was a revolt against the teaching of mathematics through "incidental activities" in the classroom. Earlier programs for young children had often admonished teachers not to be tied to a textbook but rather to use the environment of the child and his daily activities as a source for mathematics learning. Often the teacher was expected to wait for a significant natural occurrence that could be exploited for its inherent learning opportunities, too often a function of chance.

Newer programs did not rely upon chance classroom occurrences. Specific lessons or experiences were planned for the children with particular learning goals in mind. Courses of study were carefully detailed and the sequence of learning was specifically ordered. Specifically designed textbooks, workbooks, and manipulative materials were developed and incorporated into planned programs for children.

[1]Howard Fehr, "Sense and Nonsense in a Modern School Mathematics Program," *The Arithmetic Teacher*, Vol. 13, No. 2 (February 1966), 87.

Unfortunately, in their desire to remove themselves from the anarchy of incidental learning, many of these planned programs ignored the many rich opportunities that the child's daily life provides for mathematics learning. There are systematic ways of using the real world surrounding the child as a source of mathematics learning. These require a careful assessment by the teacher of the learning possibilities available in each situation, as well as a clear understanding of the goals of mathematics education for young children.

A planned program need not necessarily be a formal program. Teachers of young children can plan many fruitful mathematics experiences without recourse to textbook or to lecture and recitation sessions. Almost all areas of the early childhood program provide opportunities for children to group things and to count limited numbers of objects. The block-building area is rich with opportunities for making comparisons and showing one-to-one correspondence as children match two walls of a block construction. Similarly, the woodwork area can provide experiences in comparing lengths of wood or counting nails. Arts and crafts areas also allow for grouping and comparisons. The comparison of the volume of clay being used by different children, or providing them with different shapes of paper for collage and then having them discuss the various shapes and their attributes are two simple examples. Sand tables and water play areas can be planned to include a variety of containers so that children experience and compare different measures.

In addition, a great range of manipulative materials may be provided children in a game setting to give them opportunities to gain experiences with numbers, size, shapes, and the like. Various structured mathematics materials such as the Stern blocks, Cuisenaire rods, or Montessori beads may be used. Puzzles using geometric inserts, peg-sets, and sets of beads and strings can be used for counting, showing numbers, and patterning. The endless opportunities available in any classroom for counting, comparing, and measuring, provide children with a wealth of opportunity to do mathematics.

These experiences with real things in the children's environment, if used appropriately, can keep children from feeling that mathematics is something strange, totally theoretical and completely alien to their lives, a feeling that can be communicated when mathematics is taught in a rigid, totally abstract way. It is disheartening to see some young children labeled as incapable of understanding mathematics when these same children go to the store each day, order groceries for their family, pay the grocer, and count the change, being sure to check the transaction along the way so that they are not cheated. Often it is the way mathematics is taught rather than mathematics itself that creates learning difficulties.

TEACHING BASIC MATHEMATICS CONCEPTS IN THE EARLY YEARS

While it is simple to order the range of mathematics learning for the early years and to assign grade placements for each topic, such an exercise is not productive. One might approximate the age at which concepts might be taught, but there ought to be an acceptable degree of variability. The child beginning school earlier need not be held back from pursuing a topic because others do not have the necessary background. It is important to note also that concepts are not learned in an all-or-none fashion. Starting with intuitive responses to the environment, children go through a series of successive approximations of mature concepts. Continued experiences with an idea and with different manifestations and examples of that idea help children understand the concept in greater depth. Therefore, there are no age or grade placements suggested for topics discussed in this chapter. Teachers need to be sensitive to the level of understanding of the children in their classes and to the prerequisites for understanding a particular concept as they attempt to teach their pupils.

Assessing a child's level of understanding is more difficult than assessing his ability to produce specific responses. The teacher may find that a child can complete a page in a workbook but will not be able to perform similar operations in another situation. One way of assessing a child's level of understanding is to see if he can use what he has learned in other situations. Important clues to the child's level of understanding can be gained by listening carefully to children's responses to questions. These can be assessed as to the correctness of the response. If the response is incorrect, it is useful for the teacher to attempt to infer the child's level of understanding. Incorrect responses may be a result of inattention, but more often they reflect the child's inability to grasp concepts. Teachers can diagnose children's difficulties and either present activities that will clarify misconceptions or gear their teaching more closely to the child's ability to understand.

Grouping

In developing a concept of quantity with young children, it is helpful to begin by having them group things. Children could group all the pencils in a box, all the red beads in a bead set, the pieces of a puzzle, containers of milk, or the children in a class. Such a group may be called a "set." While sets can be made up of dissimilar things, it is less confusing for the children in the beginning to use objects with common elements in developing the concept of sets.

Young children can also begin to compare the number property of sets. This is probably done most easily by matching the members of a set. As the children set the table for snack time, for example, they can compare the set of napkins with the set of straws laid out. In matching, the children might discover that the two sets have the same number of elements, or they may find that one set has more elements while the other set has fewer. Learning the concepts of *more, fewer,* and *same* will precede knowing *how* many more or *how* many less there are. Such a use of sets and the comparison of sets has practical application for the children, making the uses of mathematics obvious to the children who may now have to modify their environment on the basis of increased mathematical knowledge (provide more napkins or more straws).

The matching of sets to teach one-to-one correspondence may be done with pictures and charts as well as with physical objects. It is helpful for children to have real objects to manipulate in the beginning. With manipulative objects, the children can line up two sets of objects, matching a member of one set with a member of the other, even before they can count.

Counting

Children often come into nursery school or kindergarten "knowing how to count." What too often passes for counting is the ability to recite the names of numbers in sequence without any understanding of the idea of the number that corresponds to a given name or numeral.

Children need to be provided with experiences that help them associate names or symbols with the numbers they represent. For the young child, there is little difference between a physical representation of number and the idea of number. They can be helped to make these associations through the experiences described above. Sets of two or three are helpful at first. Children can be given manipulative materials and asked to build sets of two and three. It is easiest for them to begin to match their constructed sets with those provided as models. The spoken symbol for the number can be learned immediately; the written symbol may be learned later. Although there has been much made about the differentiation of number and numeral, emphasizing such a differentiation may be confusing to the young child.

Children can be provided with many experiences in which they build sets of two, three, four, and so on. They can match these sets to other sets, either matching groups to other groups, or groups to pictures of groups. They can also match sets to symbols of these sets of objects. As children begin to write, they can write numerals as well as letters, and they can begin to match the numerals they write with the correct number of objects in a set.

From this point, children can begin to construct new sets by adding one more object to a set already constructed. They can also be given opportunities to order sets in relation to the number of objects in each group. Through a series of such experiences, children will learn that the numbers 'one' to 'ten' fit into a special order from smallest to largest quantity. This is the beginning of counting and the understanding of ordinality. While a range of materials may be used to move children along, a number line with numerals written from 0 to 10 may help the children in their final ordering.

The Number System

Once children begin to count beyond ten, and as soon as they begin to record these numbers, they must become aware of our numeration system. This system has its own peculiarities, but it is simple enough to allow notation of extremely large numbers with only ten digits. The children are already aware of the number named by each symbol or digit, 0, 1, 2, ... 9. They must now learn that the numeration system has a base of ten and that the place of each digit in a numeral represents its value. A whole range of activities in which children learn to substitute ten unit elements for an element valued at ten using rods, beads, chips, or markers can help children develop this concept of equivalence. They can then be given papers with columns, or pocket charts to work with, to help them understand the role of position in relation to value. The notation of two-place numerals can be presented at this time.

As children move on, they can be taught three-place numerals after having learned two-place numerals. They can also learn other ways of representing numbers. One-place numerals are easily represented by squares and sets of squares lined up to ten or by a variety of three-dimensional rods or sets of beads. Two-place numerals can also be represented in like fashion. A set of ten rods of ten values each equals one hundred.

Larger numbers become rather cumbersome in their concrete representation. The Montessori golden beads represents one thousand as a cube, ten beads long, ten beads wide, and ten beads deep. Children soon become aware of the need for more efficient representation of numbers, especially large numbers, and can become involved in the game of representing and reading large numbers in the arabic notation system.

Number Operations

It is a relatively simple matter to go from counting, comparing, and noting numbers to the basic operations on numbers. At the primary level, we are concerned mainly with the basic rudiments of addition, subtraction, multiplication, and division. By counting up or counting down the child can develop the basic rudiments of the addition and subtraction operations. For centuries man has used counting up and down as the basis for addition and subtraction, as evidenced in the use of the abacus. With this rather sophisticated yet simple device, the counting of beads allowed a person to go through complicated mathematical procedures.

Similarly, beginning addition and subtraction-type problems can utilize the process of counting of objects. Only later, when the child has developed an understanding of the process, does he move to the use of shortcuts, or *algorithms*. After understanding is developed, children can be offered practice activities to improve computational skills. The failures in early mathematics programs too often occur when teachers forget that the acquisition of mathematical knowledge must be based upon understanding, which will then lead to drill to achieve mastery. When drill alone is the basis for the program, simple facts are easily forgotten, since they were meaningless from the beginning.

Children should be provided with a large number of situations in which they can put together sets of objects so that they can establish the facts of addition. A large number of experiences with the manipulation of things can help children move to an intuitive understanding of the operation of addition. At this point, the process can be formalized and the appropriate language of mathematics can be introduced. Too early an emphasis on the formal aspect of arithmetic may thwart the children's intuitive acquisition of sophisticated concepts and operations. If children are too often told they are wrong, or that they are not saying it correctly, they may stop saying it altogether. Continued practice with the operations will lead to their mastery.

Similar approaches can be used in teaching subtraction, beginning with the opportunities to actually "take away" members of a large group and see how many are left. The children can then be moved to count down on an abacus or similar device, moving objects over, then comparing larger sets with smaller ones. The proof of the correctness of response is immediately available, as children can return and count the number of beads left and the number of beads taken away.

If children have already learned the concept of place and have understood the equivalence of one 'ten' to ten 'ones', for example, it becomes relatively simple to move from addition and subtraction of one-place numbers to work with two-place numbers, since the readiness for this learning has already been developed.

Multiplication and division are usually introduced in the primary grades. These processes, too, can be first approached by the use of concrete manipulative materials and by recourse to prior mathematics learning. Children have probably already learned to count by twos, fives, and tens before multiplication is introduced. They have also learned to add. If they are asked to put together five groups of two blocks each, for example, they can visualize the process of multiplication. Many experiences such as these are helpful to begin with. Later the multiplication facts can be organized into tables.

The asking of such questions as, "If I want to make groups of three out of this pile of twelve beans, how many groups will I have?" or "I want to give the same amount of pretzels to each of the five children here. I have ten pretzels. How many will each child receive?" is an appropriate beginning of division. Using real situations, involving the children in the manipulation of concrete objects, and having them act upon their environment provides the basis for later mathematics learning.

Geometry

In the geometry program young children can learn about basic shapes. They can begin early to identify and compare square, circular, and triangular shapes. Rectangles and other shapes, more difficult to identify, can be introduced at whatever point children are able to compare the measurements of sides and angles of objects. In identifying these shapes, the children learn to count sides and angles, or "corners." They can later compare sides, as well, so that they can differentiate between a square, with all its sides the same length, and a rectangle, with its two equal short sides and two equal long sides.

Later, as the children learn to measure, they can begin to compare perimeters and areas of different objects and shapes. Problems such as which shape of several has the greatest perimeter (giving the children two differently shaped objects) or how many things it takes to cover the top of a table (a problem in area) can be worked out by children who have been provided with the proper manipulative material and who have learned how to set out to solve problems of this nature. Children can also learn to classify objects by shape and to find geometric shapes in familiar objects around them. The concrete presentation of geometry can make it a natural part of the program since the children can handle things, ask questions, and test their ideas on elements of physical reality. While proper vocabulary is important in teaching geometry to children, the language should be an outgrowth of experience. Otherwise, the content becomes abstract and, unfortunately, meaningless.

DEVELOPING MEASUREMENT SKILLS   One way to integrate the mathematics learning of the early years and to concretize quantitative and spatial concepts is to use measurement. This allows the young child to use his developing mathematical knowledge as a vehicle for understanding his immediate world. Measurement can be approached simply and intuitively by young children. In teaching measurement one can move through teaching the comparison of things to one another, to comparisons of things to a common arbitrarily established standard, to comparison and quantification in relation to commonly established standards. Each area of measurement has its own unique set of problems.

Linear Measurement

When they are very young, children come up against problems of linear size. The problem of matching the height of two sides of a block structure or of finding a piece of wood that fits in a woodwork construction are examples of children's experiences with problems of linearity. It is a simple matter to give children sets of wooden rods and ask them to find the longer one or the shorter one, or even to have children stand alongside one another and judge who is taller. The words "tall", "taller", "short", "shorter", "long", and "longer" can be taught children in this connection.

A somewhat higher order of linear comparison is reached in asking children to compare things that cannot be placed next to one another; block structures on two sides of the block area, or the height of the sink and the height of the woodwork bench. In this case, the child has to somehow record the measurement and compare the recording of one object with another. A length of wood might be marked to record the height of one block building and later moved to the other block building in order that visual comparison can be made. After many such experiences, regular measuring devices can be introduced, such as primary rulers and yardsticks. As children learn to count they can be introduced to the numbers on the ruler and the unit "inch". They can then go around the room measuring objects in inches. Before fractions are introduced, length can be reported as "between _____ and _____ inches long".

After many of these experiences, concepts of the "foot" and the "yard" as units may be introduced. Unfortunately, our measurement system is not metric and the relationship between various units of measure are nonregular (for example, there are twelve inches in a foot, three feet in a yard and thirty-six inches in a yard). These relationships may take some time for children to master.

Once the child has learned to measure objects there is no end to the amount of measuring he can do and, with these measurements, no end to the amount of practice in addition and subtraction that can be the result of his activity. Floors, walls, furniture, materials, and people can all be measured. The measurements can be compared, and spoken and written statements about them can result.

Measurement of Weight

Weight is somewhat less directly perceivable than length. Placing an object in each hand and comparing weight is an exceedingly tricky matter, for the volume of the object distorts our perceptions. A pound of feathers, for example, does not *feel* as heavy as a pound of lead. External aids to judgment are most necessary in teaching children about weight comparisons.

A simple balance is a useful tool in helping young children begin to make weight comparisons. This can either be purchased from an educational equipment company or made by using a length of wood, some string, and a couple of pie tins. If the teacher makes such a device she should be certain that the two ends of the balance do indeed balance when empty.

Again, the measurement of weight can begin by comparing objects. Placing two objects in the pans of the balance allows the child to make a visual judgment about which is heavier and which is lighter simply by noting which of the two pans is lower. The child's next step can be to make comparisons with arbitrary standards with which the weights of objects can be measured. These standards can be anything—large metal washers, fishing line sinkers, or rocks are useful for this purpose. Later metal weights representing units of measure can be introduced—one-ounce weights, half-pound weights, and one-pound weights.

When children are introduced to measurement of weight they again find that the relationships between units are complicated. These relationships simply have to be learned arbitrarily. At this point, it is useful to bring in a scale with which the children can determine the weight of objects by reading the pointer on its face. This introduces children to indirect measurements, for in reading the scale, the children are observing weight translated into the distance or movement of the pointer from zero.

It is helpful if the children have the experience of direct measurement first before moving on to indirect measurement. There are a limitless number of objects that can be weighed in the environment of the school. These weights can be added up, subtracted from one another, or compared. Statements about these activities can be communicated orally and in writing. The language of measurement, including concepts such as "lighter than," "heavier than," and "the same weight" become important.

Measurement of Volume

In learning to measure volume, children can be provided with containers of all sizes and shapes and given an opportunity to fill them and to transfer the contents from one container to another. It is a good idea to include containers of the same volume, but of different shapes in the classroom. Using these can help the children learn that volume is not simply a function of the height or width of a container. In time, containers of standard volume should be introduced to the children. These would include one cup and half-cup, pint, quart, and gallon. The sand table and water play area are excellent places to introduce measurement of volume but many other areas of the classroom serve as well.

Measurement of Time

Much attention in the early years is given to the measurement of time. Time is measured indirectly, making it a difficult dimension for young children to measure. Teachers do a lot of calendar work and work with clocks. Unfortunately, the work is ineffectual in too many cases. All too often teachers are observed in calendar work in a kindergarten talking to a group that is inattentive or from whom only arbitrary responses are elicited.

There are two processes involved in learning to measure time which need to be addressed separately. One is the reading of clock faces and calendars. The other is measuring something that cannot be seen or felt. The passage of time is perceived in a subjective fashion. All of us have experienced periods of time that have dragged on interminably and others that have moved too quickly. Time is a difficult concept for a child to grasp. Until his entrance to school, the young child has seldom had much awareness of time, except for the passage of day and night and the regularity of daily occurrences, including the viewing of television programs. There have been few expectations for him to be "on time," or to do things at a particular time. He has also experienced exceedingly few cycles of seasonal change. With the beginning of school, the child's life suddenly becomes ordered in time, and time takes on increased psychological importance.

Many of the problems that children face in clock and calendar work stem from the fact that the children are being asked to read fairly sophisticated material on the face of the clock or on the calendar without their being taught the symbols and the systems by which these symbols are ordered. Other problems stem from the complicated relations of time segments to one another, as well as from the child's failure to have identified for him the benchmarks needed for the measurement of time. Often the only alternative left to the child is to memorize the material offered without ever really understanding it. It is amazing how few curriculum guides ever take the time to analyze and identify the elements needed to insure successful learning in this area of measurements. Gotkin's article demonstrates the systematic development of a curriculum to teach time to children.[2]

OTHER TOPICS
IN MATHEMATICS
A number of additional topics will be touched upon in our discussion of a mathematics program for the early years of school. Although they generally are not treated as extensively as the ones described above, they are still important elements of the program. Included in these are the study of fractions, the use of graphs and charts, and money.

Fractions

Once they have an understanding of whole numbers, young children can also be helped to understand simple fractions. Fractions are understood as equal parts of a unit. During these early years, it is possible to help children understand the meaning of one-half, one-fourth and one-third. Their first understanding is of the number of parts of a unit, without concern for their equality. The teacher will find many opportunities to use fractions in the classroom. The sharing of snacks, giving out materials for craft work, children's work in the block area or at the woodworking bench all provide opportunities for using fractions.

Understandings in this area, as in other areas, grow slowly in young children. A nursery school child's concept of "half" grows out of seeing objects divided into two parts. The fact that the parts must be equal to be considered halves is a part of the definition that comes later. Children's understandings, however, grow as a result of many encounters with their environment, beginning long before they are able to grasp complex sophisticated meanings.

Graphs and Charts

As children learn to communicate in writing they may become aware that some things are communicated more efficiently in ways other than through the use of words. Geography requires written communication of topographical information through maps. Quantitative information, similarly, might best be communicated using graphs and charts.

[2]Lassar G. Gotkin, "A Calendar Curriculum for Disadvantaged Kindergarten Children," *Teachers College Record.* Vol. 68, No. 5 (February 1967), 406–17.

Robison, in her study of economics in the kindergarten, used graphs to communicate quantitative information.[3] Heard also described her use of bar graphs and picture graphs in the kindergarten.[4] A variety of graphic representations can be used in the early years. They might start simply as ways of comparing children in the class in such areas as can be represented in just two columns, such as the number of boys versus the number of girls, those who go home for lunch versus those who stay at school, or those who live in houses versus those who live in apartments. Beginning graphs can be three-dimensional representations. A line of building blocks or wooden cubes representing each group, with each block or cube standing for one person, can be used at first, and later two-dimensional representations can be added.

The children can then move on to more complicated graphs: graphs of children's birthdays (by months), heights, weights, color of hair, interests. Line graphs can be made of the morning temperature of the room or the outdoors over a period of time, of the number of children absent each day, or of the number of cars passing the school in a five-minute interval. This will require the collection of information from which the graphs will develop and will often be a part of a more extensive study. Using graphs in this fashion demonstrates that the study of graphs is not an abstract, theoretical exercise, but a practical way of recording and communicating information.

Money

Another topic often included in the primary mathematics program is the study of money and money equivalence. Since our monetary system is based on the unit of ten, just as our system of numeration, once the relative value of coins and paper money is learned, little new knowledge or skills is required for children to develop skills of monetary computation. As a matter of fact, the use of money, real or fake, is a helpful resource in teaching the numeration system itself to the very young.

In the early years, the main concern is teaching children to recognize coins of different values and to exchange coins properly. Manipulations with real coins are necessary to some extent, although play money can be used. Opportunities for using coins in play, as in a mock supermarket, or in real situations, such as shopping trips, and experiences in purchasing, making, and selling objects is helpful.

[3]Helen F. Robison, *Learning Economic Concepts in the Kindergarten*, Unpublished Ed. D. Project, Teachers College, Columbia University, 1963.

[4]Ida Mae Heard, "Making and Using Graphs in the Kindergarten Mathematics Program," *The Arithmetic Teacher*, Vol. 15, No. 6 (October 1968), 504–506.

USING A MATHEMATICS VOCABULARY WITH YOUNG CHILDREN   Psychologists and educators have become very much aware of the importance of language development in children and the relationship of language to thinking. In the area of mathematics, there has been an increased concern with language because of the fact that the vocabulary used in many new mathematics programs is so different from that used in older programs. This strangeness has often created a "mathematics generation gap" as parents, brought up in an older arithmetic tradition, are unable to communicate with their younger children about school work.

It is important that children learn to use the language of mathematics with some degree of precision. It is also important that children find mathematics meaningful. New words will be used appropriately if children understand them and understand when to use them. When new vocabulary that is more appropriate for the graduate school than the kindergarten is given the children, the teacher has overstepped the bounds of reasonable innovation and may find the children rejecting the new words.

The understanding that mathematics is a language system is as important as computational skills. The children are provided with a whole new notation system. The symbols of mathematics allow persons to write rather complex statements in a simple form with a degree of clarity and specificity that would be difficult to match if they were limited to words alone. As children become appreciative of written communication, they can be helped to become appreciative of the language of mathematics and learn to use it appropriately.

USING REALISTIC EXPERIENCES   The nursery school and kindergarten are replete with opportunities for infusing mathematics learnings into the activities of the day. The entrance of children into school provides the chance to tally children in attendance. Marks can be made for each boy and girl and these can later be grouped and added. Other routine activities also hold similar promise. Setting up for snack time provides opportunities for seeing one-to-one relationships and for counting. Work in the block area requires a mathematical sense, as do woodworking and crafts activities. Music, dance, and games all provide opportunities for counting and matching. Dramatic play activities can offer a storehouse of mathematics activities; playing store requires using money, counting, and measuring, and playing at bus driving or housekeeping offers similar opportunities.

As the children move up into the primary grades, less fanciful activities are available to them in the classroom and the teacher needs to use realism for mathematics. Most classrooms are full of things that can be compared, counted, added, weighed, and measured. It is important to give children opportunities to involve themselves in these operations as well as direction in doing it. One of the instruments used in English Infant Schools for this purpose is the assignment card."

Assignment cards are cards upon which are written simple problems or activities in which children can engage. The provision of assignment cards in the classroom opens up the possibility of individualizing instruction and providing a great range of possibilities of learning activities without having the teacher continually telling children what to do. A small file box can contain a large number of assignment cards, which can be numbered in order of difficulty and then coded by topic. Such areas as weight, linear measure, clock work, counting, writing equations, measuring volume, and geometry can all be taught through assignment cards. Teachers can set up a simple chart for each area of assignment cards on which children can check off the cards they are using. This simplifies record keeping. The teacher also needs to devise a way to check the accuracy of the completed assignment.

While some assignment cards may list closed-ended tasks, others may be open-ended, allowing opportunities for creativity and discovery in mathematics. Examples of assignment cards are as follows:

WEIGHT

Place a cup of rice in one pan of a balance and a cup of beans in the other. Which is heavier? Write a story about these.

Choose two things which look the same size and weigh them. Do they weigh the same? Now choose two things which seem to feel the same weight, but are different in size. Weigh them. Are they the same in weight? Which is easier to guess, equal weights or equal sizes?

Take your shoe and place it in the scale. Weigh it to the nearest ounce. Record the weight. "My shoe weighs _____ ounces."

LINEAR MEASURE

Measure the length of your desk. Measure the length of the teacher's desk. Which desk is longer?

Measure the height of all the boys in the class. List the boys in order of height starting with the tallest.

VOLUME

Using a one-cup measure, fill up a quart container. How many cups does it take?

COUNTING

Count the number of windows in the room. How many can be opened? How many must remain closed? Do more windows open or close?

Count the number of books with blue bindings in the library.

GRAPHS

Make a graph using unit blocks for each person. Show the number of persons in the class that have a birthday during each month of the year. Write a story about it.

AREA

Cover the top of your table with index cards. How many are needed?

SHAPES

How many things can you find in the room that have circles in them? List them.

Draw a design using ten squares. How many different designs can you make?

Such assignments allow the children to grasp mathematical relationships in the world around them. It also provides them with opportunities to gain new mathematical insights and to practice the knowledge they have already acquired. Assignment cards, like other such devices, must be used wisely. When used in a stereotyped way, they are no better than workbooks. Used with imagination, they can point up the learning opportunities in the surrounding world. The uses of the environment as a resource of learning mathematics opens up new vistas for mathematical understandings for children.

Using Materials

While there are many opportunities for learning mathematics in the real environment, teachers cannot depend on natural occurrences as the only source of mathematics learning. Many additional sources should be infused into the program.

In the primary grades, one usually finds a great deal of dependence upon mathematics textbooks and workbooks. If used flexibly, these provide an excellent source of learning activities. Textbooks may offer the teacher as well as the children a guide to learning. The selection of a single textbook series may help to assure a certain degree of continuity of learning from grade to grade. Textbooks also provide a large number of instructional and practice activities.

Mathematics instruction should go beyond the textbook, however. A large number of manipulative materials to be used by children should be provided to help the children understand concepts and processes through practical application with concrete examples of the ideas taught. A large number of these materials are commercially made. Many teacher-made materials can also be developed and should be included. While the quantity and type of materials provided depends on the needs of the class at any time, it is helpful to have a *mathematics center* available in the classroom where mathematical material can be kept and used. The materials should be readily available to the children, easily accessible, and well-organized so that cleanup does not become cumbersome.

In spite of the material and supplies provided, it is still the teacher who remains the key to the success of the program. Although she needs to be knowledgeable of mathematics and of methods of teaching mathematics, more important is her sensitivity to children. For within the framework of her knowledge she is constantly in the decision-making role—planning activities, assessing progress, diagnosing difficulties, and providing additional sources of learning for some while looking for enrichment activities for others. It is the teacher who can make the subject of mathematics a vital and meaningful area of inquiry in the early years of schooling.

SUGGESTED READING

BIGGS, EDITH E., AND JAMES D. MACLEAN, *Freedom to Learn*. Don Mills, Ontario: Addison-Wesley, 1969.

COLLIER, CALHOUN C., AND HAROLD H. LERCH, *Teaching Mathematics in the Modern Elementary School*. New York: Macmillan, 1969.

DAVIS, ROBERT B., *The Changing Curriculum: Mathematics*. Washington, D.C.: Association for Supervision and Curriculum Development, 1967.

DEVAULT, M. VERE, AND THOMAS E. KREIWALL, *Perspectives in Elementary School Mathematics*. Columbus, Ohio: Charles E. Merrill, 1969.

DIENES, Z., *Building Up Mathematics*. London: Hutchinson Educational, 1963.

FEHR, HOWARD F., "Sense and Nonsense in a Modern School Mathematics Program," *The Arithmetic Teacher*, Vol. 13, No. 2 (February 1966), 83–91.

FEHR, HOWARD F., AND JO McKEEBY PHILLIPS, *Teaching Modern Mathematics in the Elementary School*. Reading, Massachusetts: Addison-Wesley, 1967.

GOTKIN, LASSAR G., "A Calendar Curriculum for Disadvantaged Kindergarten Children," *T. C. Record*, Vol. 68, No. 5 (February 1967), 406–17.

GROSSMAN, ROSE, "Problem Solving Activities Observed in British Primary Schools," *The Arithmetic Teacher*, Vol. 16, No. 1 (January 1969), 34–38.

GROSSNICKLE, FOSTER E., AND LEO J. BRUECKNER, *Discovering Meanings in Elementary School Mathematics*. New York: Holt, Rinehart & Winston, 1963.

HOLLISTER, G. E., AND A. G. GUNDERSON, *Teaching Arithmetic in the Primary Grades*. Boston: D. C. Heath, 1964.

PHILLIPS, JO., " 'Basic Laws' for Young Children," *The Arithmetic Teacher*, Vol. 12, No. 7 (November 1965), 525–32.

ROBERTS, DOROTHY M., AND IRVING BLOOM, "Mathematics in Kindergarten—Formal or Informal?" *Elementary School Journal*, Vol. 67, No. 6 (March 1967), 338–41.

VIGILANTE, NICHOLAS J., "Why Circumvent Geometry in the Primary Grades?" *The Arithmetic Teacher*, Vol. 12, No. 6 (October 1965), 450–54.

8

Social Studies for Young Children

Schools for young children attempt to help them understand the world around them and their relationship to that world. As the child makes sense of his surroundings, he develops knowledge and skills that are useful both for his everyday life and as a prerequisite for future learnings. The young child's approach to the physical world is direct. He can test what he knows about physical things by touching them, listening to them, or viewing them directly. Because of the transitory nature of human behavior, the social world is more elusive. Although he has direct contact with people and can observe their behavior directly, it is the *meaning* of behavior that is important rather than the observable behavior alone, and the meaning is not directly accessible. The products of social behavior and the context in which behavior takes place, however, are more accessible to him.

WHAT IS SOCIAL STUDIES? Some educators consider the social studies to be that portion of the school program that is derived from the social sciences. History, geography, economics, political science, anthropology, and sociology are the prime sources of the program, with additional contributions derived from the fields of social psychology, psychology, philosophy, and linguistics. The content of these fields, the facts, concepts, and methods of inquiry, all contribute to social studies.

Many educators suggest that this concept of social studies is too narrow. In addition to the content of the social sciences, it is suggested that schools need to be concerned with the application of this knowledge to social problems. Attention to problem-solving skills as well as to the nature of current social problems must be incorporated into school programs.

Other educators suggest that social learnings or the development of social skills must be taught along with any social science as a part of the social studies program. Learning to live in a group, to follow rules, resolve conflicts, and get along with other children should also be goals. An extension of this idea is the suggestion that social studies programs should concern themselves with the socialization process in children. Although concepts and skills might be important, the key to this program is helping the child become a full-fledged member of the larger society. Cultural values, traditions, and rituals need to be included to help children become better acclimated to the surrounding social scene.

A strong social studies program must actually contain all three elements: social science concepts and knowledge, applications of these concepts to social problems, and the socialization of children. The socialization and problem solving, however, are not the sole domain of the social studies area, but can be found in many portions of the school program.

Intellectual Processes

Much of the research related to the intellectual development of young children has been applied to the organization of their mathematics and science programs. A social studies program can, however, have an impact on children's thinking similar to that of science if an intellectually oriented approach is used. While the information gathered in a social studies program is different from that gathered in a science program, the *processes* used for organizing this information differ very little.

Children can go through the procedures of grouping things into concepts and relating concepts to one another as generalizations. The tests of knowledge and the need to verify knowledge exist in the social studies program as in the science program, as does the need to draw inferences and communicate results. Quantification, too, is a part of the social sciences. As a matter of fact, recent programs in the social studies have tended to increase their emphasis on intellectual content for young children.

Socialization

As stated in Chapter III, socialization is one of the prime goals of early childhood education. But though they can certainly contribute to the socialization process, it would be inappropriate to identify the social studies as the prime vehicle for the socialization of the child. There are too many other learning opportunities in the school day. The classroom teacher is concerned with two forms of socialization: helping the child find his role in the school community and helping him find his role in the larger community. While there is some transfer in learning socialization strategies from one area to the other, there are enough significant differences in these two forms of socialization to warrant their separate treatment.

Within the classroom, the teacher not only creates a range of conditions that helps the child learn his role of pupil in school but also teaches him the rules, expectations, mores, and values of the school. Awareness of the way the teacher organizes the class, the rules she makes, the way these rules are enforced, the amount of freedom provided, the kinds of activities rewarded, and the rituals of daily life all lead to the socialization of the child. But there is more to socialization. At some times group efforts are allowed in the classroom; at other times children are expected to work alone. They soon learn the need for sharing as well as the fact that physical conflict is frowned upon. Children also learn that there are appropriate ways of interacting with and addressing a teacher. The lessons of the socialization process are sprinkled throughout the entire program.

The social studies program can play an important part in helping the child find his role in the larger community. He needs to understand the way in which the society is organized. He also needs to learn the shared values, rituals, symbols, and myths. The school's attention to holidays, to stories of historic figures and heroes, to the reading of traditional stories and the singing of traditional songs all contribute to the process. Even social study inquiry activity can help the child better understand the organization of society and thus be better able to act out his role in appropriate ways.

Values

All education is concerned with values. The very fact that we provide an environment for children's learning and invest resources in materials and personnel is proof that we feel that what happens in school is important. In addition, a specific set of goals is identified for the children to achieve in school. These goals—the understandings, attitudes, and skills achieved by the children—are valued by our society. Requiring children to become involved in the activities of the school indicates to them that these activities are important.

The basic social values that we wish to communicate to children include concern for the worth of the individual, concepts of freedom and responsibility, the importance of democratic decision making, and concern for the safety of persons and property, and all these can be taught in the school. They cannot, however, be taught as a separate subject, for they are communicated as much by the way in which the teacher organizes her classroom and deals with individual children as through separate lessons. If children from minority groups are not respected and if they are not valued for the contribution they make in the classroom, then typical patriotic exercises take on little meaning. If rules of behavior are arbitrarily set by the teacher, children learn not to value rational decision making as a basis for developing behavior controls.

Children learn what to value from inferences drawn from the behavior of significant adults in their lives, by imitating their behavior and assimilating perceived values. Values are learned all day, not just in single segmented subject-oriented periods. The teacher, therefore, is transmitting her values to the children all day long. The social system within the classroom and the school operates as an educative force that may be more powerful than any curriculum in developing values.

Wolfson suggests that values can be learned by young children through role playing, creative dramatics, literature, and art experiences. She concludes that value development can be promoted by providing a wide variety of opportunities for individual selection of goals and activities and by allowing children to consider alternatives and possible consequences of acts as well as opportunities to consider their own feelings.[1] This may be seen as a beginning step in the analysis of value systems. The level of analysis that can be expected of young children, however, is a function of their level of intellectual as well as moral development.

In addition to teaching values in the traditional sense—that is, helping children become aware of acts considered proper or for which the culture has a high regard—schools have often been concerned with the moral education of children—helping children make distinctions between *right* and *wrong*. The issue of whether schools ought to deal with the moral education of children or to what degree they should deal with it is unresolved. While there is a common moral code, the sources of morality are varied in our country. The home and church are separate institutions concerned with the moral education of children. Nor are we at all sure as to how effective schools can be in teaching morality. Since moral issues cannot be resolved by recourse to a single source, some educators suggest that their teaching is not in the domain of the public schools.

In the education of young children one must also be concerned with their readiness to deal with learning. How much can young children gain from moral education in the traditional sense at this point? Kohlberg has identified six stages of moral development in children:

---

[1]Bernice J. Wolfson, "Values and the Primary School Teacher," *Social Education*, Vol. 31, No. 1 (January 1967), 37–38.

Stage 1: The punishment and obedience orientation
Stage 2: The instrumental relativist orientation
Stage 3: The interpersonal concordance or "good boy-nice girl" orientation
Stage 4: The "law and order" orientation
Stage 5: The social contract, legalistic orientation
Stage 6: The universal ethical principle orientation[2]

Children in nursery and preprimary classes are primarily in the first two stages of moral development. It is doubtful that they can learn moral reasoning at the highest stages of development, although they can learn to mouth appropriate phrases at this age level.

The role of the teacher might be less to teach moral behavior directly but more to set a moral atmosphere in the classroom that allows children to move beyond their present stages of moral development. This role, too, goes beyond the confines of the social studies or of any portion of the curriculum but must pervade the entire environment of the classroom.

TRADITIONAL APPROACHES TO SOCIAL STUDIES
Over the years many approaches to teaching social studies to young children have been used in schools. Early in the century, history and geography were taught separately to children and later fused into a single subject called social studies. Often these subjects were reserved for older children, since the primary school was thought of as a place for teaching literacy and computational skills. Ancient history was taught to the young, and modern history was reserved for older children. According to the psychology of G. Stanley Hall, the development of the young child was viewed as paralleling that of the entire race. Since the young child and his thinking most resembled man in his earliest stages, the study of prehistory and ancient history, when man was at his "simplest" stages, was considered most appropriate for the young child. As he matured and became more sophisticated, he could study more complex social phenomena such as those found in his contemporary life.

Because of this approach to curricula, the young child was asked to learn those aspects of human behavior that were the most remote and the most different from the world with which he was familiar. This approach was rejected in time because, in spite of its seeming logic in relation to subject matter and the child, it ran counter to the accumulating knowledge of child development.

In addition, history and geography were considered to have too

---

[2]Lawrence Kohlberg, "The Moral Atmosphere of the School," in Norman V. Overly, ed., *The Unstudied Curriculum: Its Impact on Children* (Washington, D.C.: A.S.C.D., 1970), pp. 124–25.

narrow a scope for social studies education. The integration and uses of knowledge became important for the schools. In addition, educators became aware of the concrete nature of young children's learning. The sequence of learning, consequently, was reversed and it was proposed that the young child deal with elements of his immediate world as a basis for social studies education, leaving the more remote in time and space to older children. The same areas of human activity could be studied within a more expanded concept of humanity as children matured. Out of this approach to the social studies grew the "Here and Now" school of early childhood education, this being the most immediate arena of human activity. Within this approach, young children were to use their immediate environment as a source of learning. Social studies understandings could grow out of analysis of observations of actions and relationships in the immediate setting and experiences of the child's daily life. The home, school, and neighborhood became the social science laboratories in which the children learned. Young children could emulate some of the behaviors of social scientists, developing simple hypotheses about their environment and testing these hypotheses through direct observation, recording, analyzing, and organizing the information received from the world outside the classroom.

Unfortunately, the "Here and Now" approach was distorted in time so that although the *topics* for study (home, school, and neighborhood) remained in the tradition of early childhood education, the *method* of study (acting as laboratory scientist) disappeared. Gathering data from the outside world, recording it, organizing it, and analyzing it were complex operations. They were time-consuming and, with other subjects competing for limited classroom time, they were often not seen as important enough to warrant attention. In addition, teachers who lacked basic knowledge of social science methodology saw many of these activities, including field trips, as wasteful and frivolous. Much of the information children collected on their own could be told to them orally or learned through books.

Textbooks provided to young children often so watered down the content of social studies that there was little relationship between the social studies programs in young children's classrooms and the actual social sciences. The "Here and Now" approach was divorced from the reality of the child's life and was treated in the most remote way possible in these books.

NEWER APPROACHES TO SOCIAL STUDIES

The activities of the new curriculum development movement described earlier in the areas of science and mathematics have had their parallel in the area of the social studies. A number of curriculum development projects in the social studies have been mounted in the past decade, and some of these projects include the development of social studies programs at the kindergarten-primary level. The results of many of these programs are presently being disseminated.

Many of the curriculum development projects attempted to look at the social studies as a total field, integrating ideas from the various social sciences within them. The University of Minnesota *Project Social Studies* and the Taba *Elementary Social Studies* program are examples of these. Other projects like the *Anthropology Curriculum Project* of the University of Georgia and the *Developmental Economic Education Program* of the Joint Council for Economic Education concerned themselves with only a single discipline. Some projects concerned themselves primarily with developing resource units, outlines that could be disseminated to teachers and schools, while others, such as *Materials and Activities for Teachers and Children (MATCH)* developed boxes of multi-medial materials, including books, films, and manipulative materials to be used in carrying out teaching units.

Some programs were primarily cognitive in orientation, such as Senesh's *Economic Education Program*, while others, like the *Intergroup Relations Program* of the Lincoln Filene Center for Citizenship and Public Affairs, concerned themselves with the affective domain.[3]

Each of these projects has its own rationale from which a unified, often sequential program has been developed, covering either a few grade levels or the entire spectrum of public education. In all the projects there is greater recourse to social science materials than has been the case in earlier social studies programs. Many of the materials are directly available from the projects themselves. A number of commercial publishers, however, are making available materials developed in many of the projects;[4] some program evaluations are also available.[5] In addition to the many specific projects, the movement has also brought about changes in textbook publishing.

[3]See Bob L. Taylor and Thomas L. Groom, *Social Studies Education Projects: An ASCD Index.* Washington, D.C.: Association for Supervision and Curriculum Development, 1971.

[4]See for example The Educational Research Council of Greater Cleveland, *Concepts and Inquiry* (Boston: Allyn and Bacon, 1970); Hilda Taba, *Elementary Social Studies* (Palo Alto: Addison-Wesley, 1967); Lawrence Senesh, *Our Working World* (Chicago: Science Research Associates, 1964); Vincent and Carol Presno, *Man In Action Series* (Englewood Cliffs, N.J.: Prentice-Hall, Inc., 1967); and Frederick H. Kresse and Ruth Green, *MATCH* (Boston: American Science and Engineering).

[5]Morris Serdus and Marlin L. Tank, "A Critical Appraisal of Twenty-Six National Social Studies Projects," *Social Education*, Vol. 34, No. 4 (April 1970), 383–449. Descriptions and evaluations of many social studies programs are also available from Social Science Research Consortium, 1424 15th Street, Boulder, Colorado 80302 (see Chapter XVI).

**DECIDING WHAT
TO TEACH**
In developing a social studies program for young children, decisions must be made about what to teach and how to teach it. Often these decisions are made in relation to research reporting children's present level of knowledge.[6] Such research assesses what children know without benefit of an educational program; it cannot offer guidelines as to what children can or should be taught. Goals for the social studies must be related to overall goals of early childhood education. Instructional programs in the social studies need to be based upon concepts of readiness. Children should be given material that is appropriate, in a way that is appropriate to their specific level of development. Knowledge of a child's readiness tells us to what degree we can expect him to master concepts and skills rather than what concepts and skills ought to be considered in the goals of a program.

Children at the nursery school level, for example, can begin to deal with sociological concepts such as *self* or *group* as they move into school and explore themselves in relations to others in school and at home. Their level of understanding of these concepts will be quite different from that which can be expected from a primary-grade child. Similarly, young children can deal with historical events, putting them into a framework of "now" and "long ago" before they can deal with chronological time and the periodicity of history. If teachers conceive of the goals of social studies instruction as achieving a series of successive approximations to more sophisticated cognitive structures, then a concept of readiness becomes a helpful tool of instruction rather than a limiting one.

Identifying Goals of Instruction

The process of defining what and how to teach studies in an early childhood class is a rather complex one. It involves setting goals for instruction, identifying topics to be used as vehicles for achieving these goals, and developing instructional units or programs based upon these goals and related to the topics. Materials and resources need to be gathered and activities need to be planned and implemented. Some way of judging the effects of the program on the degree of the achievement of the goals should also be a part of the process.

In many of the new social science curricula, the relationship of social studies to the social sciences has been emphasized. The goals of instruction identified may be less concerned with gaining factual knowl-

[6]See, for example, Louise N. Ames, "The Development of the Sense of Time in the Young Child," *Journal of Genetic Psychology*, Vol. 68, No. 1 (1946), 97–125, or Joy M. Lacey, *Social Studies Concepts of Children in the First Three Grades* (New York: Teachers College, Columbia University, 1932).

edge about the topic under study and more concerned with understanding basic concepts, generalizations, or conceptual schemes.

A conceptual scheme might be identified for the social studies as an integrated field. Brandwein has identified the following "cognitive scheme" in the social sciences:

1. Man is a product of heredity and environment.
2. Human behavior is shaped by the social environment.
3. The geographic features of the earth affect man's behavior.
4. Economic behavior depends upon the utilization of resources.
5. Political organizations (governments) resolve conflict and make interaction easier among people.[7]

Other conceptual schemes have been developed which underlie a number of curriculum guides or programs in the social studies.

The goals of the social studies cannot be conceived in terms of concept attainment alone. Taba, in her elementary social studies program, identifies four categories of objectives: (1) basic knowledge; (2) thinking; (3) attitudes, feelings, and sensitivities; (4) skills. Basic knowledge includes basic concepts, main ideas, and specific facts. Thinking includes concept formation, the inductive development of generalizations, and application of principles and knowledge. Attitudes, feelings, and sensitivities include the ability to identify with people in different cultures, self-security, open-mindedness, acceptance of change, tolerance of uncertainty and ambiguity, and responsiveness to democratic and human values. Skills include both academic skills, such as map-reading, and research and social skills, such as the ability to work, plan, discuss, and develop ideas in groups.[8]

Identifying Topics for Study

In the early childhood years there have traditionally been a limited number of topics for social studies programs. No topical themes are identified in the literature for the nursery school social studies, so teachers at this level have probably been freest to choose topics for study independently. At the kindergarten-primary level, topics have usually revolved about the immediate environment of the child in school. Generally accepted topics consist of home and family, the school (including the classroom), the neighborhood (including stores, supermarkets, filling sta-

---

[7]Paul F. Brandwein et al., *Principles and Practices in the Teaching of the Social Sciences: Concepts and Values* (New York: Harcourt Brace & World, 1970), p. T–16–17.

[8]Hilda Taba, *Teachers' Handbook for Elementary Social Studies* (Palo Alto: Addison-Wesley, 1967), pp. 7–10.

tions), and the community (including community services and agencies and community workers), as well as transportation and communication. Sometimes comparative studies of communities are suggested, such as the study of the urban community versus the rural or suburban community.

In recent years curriculum guides, textbooks, and curriculum development projects have suggested the widening of topics for study by young children. Topics suggested include family life in far-off countries such as Israel or Japan, broader comparative community study, and the study of specific concepts or conceptual schemes from the social sciences, such as the concepts of "consumers" and "producers" and how they are related, derived from economics, or an understanding of actions and interactions among people, derived from sociology. Many social science concepts can be adequately studied through observation of social phenomena within the immediate environment of the children.

While the expansion of topics for early childhood social studies to include themes not associated with the "Here and Now" approach is laudatory, there is a danger that concepts related to these themes will be learned shallowly by rote because of a lack of direct data sources available for the children's personal inquiry. When topics dealing with the remote in time and space are offered to young children, care must be taken that they have the requisite learning necessary to establish their own meanings from the experiences and that they also have access to appropriate data sources.

A unit on families in a foreign country can provide meaningful study if the children have some understanding of family structures, roles, and relationships. Such prerequisite learnings might best be achieved through a study of families in their own immediate environment. Teachers can alternate topics dealing with the immediate environment with related topics dealing with the remote in time and space, giving the children an opportunity to relate concepts and generalizations to new situations and to broaden their concepts as new and different data are fitted into already developed conceptual schemes. When dealing with topics unrelated to the immediate environment of the child, it is helpful to have a broad range of resources available for the children's study, including books, audio-visual materials, and collections of life materials.

**USING RESOURCES IN
PRIMARY SOCIAL
STUDIES**

Once decisions about goals and topics for study are made, teachers must organize for instruction. Planning at this point includes deciding about classroom activities and identifying and organizing resources to be used by both teacher and children in the instructional program.

It is important for the teacher to realize that she is probably the single most important resource in the classroom. The teacher serves as a model for teaching values and behaviors to the children through direct observation and imitation. The types of questions asked by the teacher can either further inquiry or lead to stereotyped responses. In addition, the teacher sets up the classroom organization. She decides on the activities to be included and the range of behavior permitted there. She uses her knowledge of the children, the resources available, and the topic under study to further the learning of the children.

Inquiry is important in early learning, but exposition still plays an important role. The teacher's role as teller, as source of information, is never to be underestimated.

Books also can provide a wealth of information not directly accessible to children. More children's information books are becoming available that are both well written at a level children can understand and that accurately reflect reality. Fiction books are useful in that they, too, reflect the social world, often with greater insight than is found in many information books. Children need to learn to use these important sources of information.

The oral tradition is also important in social studies. Verbal descriptions offered by children and adults are a useful source of information. Group discussions help children clarify ideas, and can provide the teacher with information about the concept as well as about the misconceptions that the children might have from their activities.

Although language is the most often-used symbol system in the social studies area, nonverbal symbol systems are also used, providing a useful resource for the children as both a source of data and a way of recording and communicating data. The most used nonverbal symbol systems are the map and the globe. Primary globes which show the world represented in simple form should make an early appearance in school. The globe is a more accurate representation of the world than a map because it is not flattened out. Charts and graphs are other nonverbal symbol systems children must learn to use.

Using Concrete Materials

The concrete materials of the social studies are representations of social science phenomena. The concrete materials we make available to children are either artifacts out of which we must infer behavior or symbolic representations of social science phenomena.

For the study of geography, a teacher may bring a map into the classroom, or, if she wants the children to obtain a more realistic view of the terrain to be studied, a three-dimensional model. She may bring in slides or a movie showing a particular area. These materials represent methods of making the children familiar with geographical areas which, more often than not, they cannot visit and explore.

In studying the family life of an Asian country or the culture of an African people, the teacher is again limited in what she can present to the children for study. She can describe different family patterns, roles, and relationships for the children. She can present pictures of the families in action, but seldom can she bring them into the classroom for interaction with the children, or even have the children visit families in the field. Even if they could visit, the children would not necessarily have access to the behavior being studied or to the meaning of the behavior.

The earliest development of concrete materials for use by young children in social studies education was found in the Montessori Method. In addition to tactile globes, Montessori devised map puzzles representing the world's political units. By playing with the map pieces, children became familiar with the names of countries and their boundaries. Each puzzle piece had a small knob attached to it to facilitate the children's handling. Similar geographic puzzles are available today (without the knob) from educational equipment suppliers.

With the development of the reform kindergarten movement in the United States during the first third of the twentieth century came the development of new educational materials. One of the most useful and flexible of these are *building blocks*. Two basic variations of these were developed. In the "Conduct Curriculum Classes" of Patty Smith Hill, a set of large floor blocks was devised. Long blocks could be fastened to corner posts with pegs to create structures for the dramatic play of children. The structures so created were large enough to allow children's play within them, and sturdy enough to take the occasional knock that might occur when a group of robust five-year-olds became involved in play activities. The stability of any structures built with these blocks allowed the children to use buildings over a period of time so that their dramatic play could be extended and elaborated. Several variations of this type of block are available today, including the hollow blocks, the variplay sets and Sta-Put blocks.

Unit blocks were developed by Caroline Pratt at about the same time. The unit block, looking much like a length of 2″ × 4″ lumber, is based upon a unit of measure. Each block is either the size of the unit, a multiple of the unit, or a fraction of that unit. Thus there are half-units and quarter-unit blocks as well as double units and quadruple unit blocks. Various shapes are added, such as columns, wedges, curves, and semicircles, to make a set. A good set of unit blocks is constructed of hardwood so as not to splinter or wear excessively, and is finished carefully so that each block is in exact proportion to the unit. This allows the children to construct complicated buildings that will stand securely for a time.

Because unit blocks are much smaller than the larger floor blocks, they cannot be used for dramatic play, since the children do not fit into the constructions. Instead of involving his whole self in the dramatic play with unit blocks, the child miniaturizes the world and plays with, not *in*, this miniature world. In the early stages of block play, found in the nursery school, the young child is content to build abstract structural designs. This type of block-building gives way to the building of individual structures, then large elaborate interrelated structures. These may represent either the child's fantasy world or the reality world, depending upon the kind of guidance that has been offered, as well as his present mood or needs.

Block constructions can be used in social studies learning to help children represent a home or a school. More elaborate structures can be used to represent a complex such as a shopping center, a neighborhood, a harbor area, or an airport. There is virtually no limit to the extent of elaborateness available in block representations, providing there are enough blocks and freedom of ideas available to the children, and provided that the construction activity can be allowed to continue over a long period of time. Block-building of this kind has a legitimate place in the primary grades as well as in the nursery school and kindergarten.

Children can incorporate other materials in order to elaborate on block construction; a variety of supportive materials can be purchased or improvised by the teacher. Miniature wooden or rubber people representing different family or community roles can be utilized, as can toy cars, trucks, boats, and airplanes. Traffic signs and street lights add to the reality orientation of a construction. Signs written by teacher or children can be used to identify places. Strips of paper or plastic can represent streets or rivers. A ball of twine can help the children build a suspension bridge. Imaginative uses of many everyday materials can enhance the building and provide an outlet for the children's creativity.

Blocks are simple things. They become arbitrary symbols to be used as the children and teacher see fit in representing portions of the world. Blocks have meaning only when we ascribe meaning to them. A block construction as a concrete representation provides a good transition to the children's use of maps as well as to other forms of symbol learning in the classroom.

Blocks are only one kind of concrete material used in early school to support social studies learning. Teachers can help children make models of places using cardboard cartons, papier-mâché constructions, or other kinds of materials. Commercially available sets such as *Kinder City* or *Playschool Village* can also be used by the children, as can tabletop construction sets such as *Lincoln Logs* and *Lego*.

Other concrete materials used in support of children's dramatic play also provide a useful resource for social studies education. The traditional housekeeping area of the nursery school and kindergarten can help in the exploration of family roles and relationships. Dress-up clothes and dramatic play props that suggest many situations are useful in supporting the dramatic play; hats representing different occupations, in particular, are helpful. A ladder and a length of hose can help children working as firemen. A table, cash register, some paper sacks and empty food containers suggest a supermarket. Sometimes the article in play does not even have to look like what it is representing. A bicycle pump, for example, can be used as a gasoline pump in a service station, or a fireman's hose. If the teacher is imaginative in her uses of concrete materials, the children will soon match this imaginativeness in play, if not surpass it.

Audio and Visual Representations

A range of simple to complex audio-visual representations can also provide resources for social studies teaching. Still photographs can be used in classrooms for stimulating discussions as well as for providing information. A number of sets of pictures for use in developing discussions are available from commercial sources.[9] Pictures should be large enough to be viewed by a group of children and contain enough detail without clutter so the children can easily focus on what is important. The availability of commercial picture sets simplifies the teacher's job of hunting through old magazines for useful pictures. Pictures can be shown to children in a group discussion setting or placed on bulletin boards. If bulletin boards are used, care should be taken that the arrangement helps the children see what is important. Pictures may also be combined with other display materials on the bulletin board.

Magnetic and flannel boards are also useful, because they allow the children or teacher to manipulate the materials and change the organization, thus allowing a more active use than simple picture displays provide. Commercial flannel board and magnetic board materials are presently available.

While commercially produced pictures provide easily accessible resources, they may not contain the specific elements needed to study a particular environment. These materials can be supplemented by locally developed and often teacher-developed materials. Fortunately, audio-

[9]For example, see Allonia Gadsden, *Concept Picture Charts: Exploration in Beginning Social Studies* (New York: Harcourt Brace & World); Fanny and George Shaftel, *Words and Actions: Role-Playing Photo-Problems for Young Children* (New York: Holt, Rinehart & Winston); Betty Atwell Wright, *Urban Education Studies* (New York: John Day Co.).

visual technology has arrived at the point where much good material can be produced by persons having little technical skill.

Polaroid cameras allow teachers to take still pictures which are immediately available, allowing the class to use the pictures without the delay that normal photographic processing takes. Relatively simple cameras such as the Kodak Instamatic also allow teachers to take color slides to be projected on a screen and viewed by an entire class, or placed in a viewer to be looked at by an individual at a time. Eight-millimeter movies can be made just as easily. The relative cost of motion pictures over slides unfortunately often limits their classroom use.

Sound recordings also provide a good resource for learning. Commercial recordings of songs and stories can provide an authentic mirror of a culture. These records can be supplemented by tape recordings the children can make themselves of their own songs and stories. A trip can be recaptured in a classroom through the sounds and pictures recorded on that trip. Upon return from an airport visit, for example, children could listen to the announcements of flight arrivals and departures and the roar of the jet engines as a plane taxis to the runway and takes off. Tape recordings can also be made of interviews with resource persons or of class discussions. Audio and visual resources can be combined very effectively.

Planned arrangements of materials are often useful in communicating information. Exhibits should vary with the topic under study. Studying a service station, for example, might suggest an exhibit of things used and sold in service stations, or an exhibit about petroleum and petroleum products. The first exhibit might include containers for products sold for automobiles and collections of small spare automobile parts, road maps, and simple hand tools used by mechanics. The petroleum exhibit could include a chart of petroleum products and refining processes. Containers of crude oil, lubricating oil, diesel fuel, home heating oil, kerosene and gasoline, or pictures of the vehicles which use these products could also be included in the display.

A study of families in Israel might include materials reflecting the culture of that country, with pictures of the area as it looked long ago, as well as other materials to help the children understand the past. Displays should be used by the children rather than simply becoming a decorative part of the classroom.

Teachers generally collect materials and arrange displays by themselves, but children and their parents can profitably be involved in this enterprise. Sometimes commercial sources are willing to provide display materials for school use. A survey of resources available in a community is helpful to the teacher. Care must be taken that commercially available materials are not distorted by advertising messages, however.

In some areas, local museums loan displays of social studies materials to schools. Dioramas or artifacts may be provided in kits, some of which are commercially available.

Using Community Resources

Teachers need to look beyond the classroom for learning resources. Resource persons are often quite willing to come to school to meet with a group of children. Such people could be representative of community workers (such as a garbage collector or a fireman), have a particular skill or area of knowledge (such as a weaver or an anthropologist), or possess something of interest to the children. A hobbyist, a visitor from a foreign country, a member of a particular ethnic group under study, or an older person who has first-hand historical knowledge might be of great interest.

In using resource persons, it is important that both the children and the visitor have some knowledge of the purpose of the visit and that basic ground rules for participation are laid down. Children enjoy acting as hosts in their own classrooms.

Field trips into the community need to be properly planned. In addition to the technical planning needed for any field trip, the children should be aware of the purpose and particular focus of the trip. Although chance occurrences can enhance a trip, it is not wise to leave the organization of a trip to chance. Field trips need not be elaborate excursions. Often the simplest trip is the most meaningful one to young children. A walk to the corner to watch the traffic control operation or a visit to a local supermarket can provide a fruitful experience. Even though children may have had the same experience outside of school, the focus provided by the teacher and the preparation taken for the trip can open new learning opportunities as new aspects of a familiar situation are unfolded before them. Significant learnings often occur through the asking of new questions in familiar situations.

Using Textbooks and Curriculum Guides

An increasing number of social studies textbooks are becoming available at the kindergarten-primary level. Often a textbook series at this level takes the form of workbooks with pictures for the earliest units, and becomes a social studies reader at later levels. While many texts follow a story line, newer textbooks present social science materials directly to young children.

A textbook can provide only a limited amount of information and should not be the only resource for learning, however. Textbooks can be used as resources for a program, as a way of providing common knowledge for all children or for pulling together knowledge from a variety of sources. A good teachers' manual may also provide helpful suggestions for resources and instructional procedures. Rather than simply reading about concepts from a book, however, it is more useful to have the children actively involved in inquiring about and developing concepts on their own. While teachers may not want to order a single set of textbooks for an entire class, it is often useful to have available several copies of many textbooks for the children's use.

Curriculum guides are seldom considered as instructional resources because they are not used directly by the children. A teacher's adequate use of a good curriculum guide can help develop significant instructional activities, however. Curriculum guides vary in scope and organization. Some provide a generalized scheme of the subject matter area and are more suggestive in nature; others can be highly prescriptive, describing in detail the work that is supposed to take place in a classroom. Still another kind of guide takes the form of resource units. Such units contain outlines for classroom study as well as information a teacher can use in planning classroom activities. Often resource units contain much more information than a teacher can use at any one time, thereby allowing the teacher greater freedom and flexibility without imposing too great a need to seek out materials and instructional ideas.

In most states and large local school systems, curriculum guides and resources are generally developed and made available to teachers. In school systems where such materials are not available, teachers must use their own resources. Teaching units are available commercially and can also be found in such magazines as the *Grade Teacher* and the *Instructor*. Teachers need to assess the worth of available units in terms of the significance of the goals, the practicability of the suggested activities, the availability of resources, and the applicability of the program for the particular class of children. At the preschool level, few resource units are available and teachers must generally rely on their own ingenuity for developing classroom activities.

Insuring Significance in the Use of Resources

A lot of activity can take place in schools without much learning or with children learning the wrong things. Merely amassing resources and materials and providing children with activities does not insure learning. While children's involvement is important, the achievement of instructional goals is the prime criterion by which we judge the success of schooling. Teachers need to select carefully from the range of resources available to them, using only those that help children achieve significant and worthwhile goals.

Teachers frequently make use of free and inexpensive materials because they are readily available, but the worth of materials needs to be judged as much by the benefits that accrue from using them as from their initial cost. Criteria for selecting resources include the usefulness of the materials for achieving instructional objectives, the possible effectiveness of some materials compared to other resources, and the appropriateness of the materials to the maturity level and background of the particular children. In addition, teachers need to look at the ease of use or operation of the resources and the cost of the materials in relationship to gains, both in terms of initial expense and in time and effort expended by children and teachers.

INTEGRATING SOCIAL STUDIES WITH OTHER ASPECTS OF THE CURRICULUM

Although the social studies program has been described independently, it often loses its distinctiveness as it becomes merged with other portions of the program.

In the nursery-school and kindergarten, portions of the social studies program should be integrated into a general activity period. Children can build with blocks, act out social roles, and look at pictures as a part of the social studies program at the same time other children are busy in other curriculum areas. Even in the primary grades, social studies can integrate a wide range of learning so that the school day is not made up of a string of distinct disparate activities. Other parts of the early childhood programs have much to offer the social studies.

Social studies activities often include the construction of models or dioramas by children. Many arts and crafts activities can be related to social studies, providing the children with opportunities to develop expressive skills at the same time the products become useful tools for social studies education. Drawing a picture of a supermarket, devising a decorative chart, or involving the children in Indian handicrafts are examples of how this can be done. The children can also use paintings, drawings, and constructions as a way of telling what they have learned.

Music and literature of a culture can provide a key to the understanding of the symbol system and values of that culture. Ethnic music, songs, stories, and poetry have an important place in the social studies program. Good literature for children (and adults) can provide insight into people, institutions, and social relationships that are hard to describe in an expository way. Children can empathize with persons by sharing their feelings long before they can intellectually understand them.

Language arts in general provide an excellent resource for the social studies. Children can create dramatic presentation or puppet shows in relation to a social studies unit. They can use dramatic play to act out roles and relationships, as well as tell or write stories that express the insights gained in a program. They also need to develop command of language skills to be effective in gathering information and in communicating the fruits of their learning to others.

Example of a Social Studies
Unit for Young Children

The following is offered as a generalized approach to a social studies unit that could be taught at various age levels. It is offered as an example of what it is possible for teachers to do, and is not meant to suggest that this is the only way or even the best way to organize a social studies unit.

TOPIC: The Community
CONCEPTS: From Geography—Perpetual Transformation
GOALS OF THE PROGRAM:
A. Concepts and generalizations
  1. Change takes place in the geography of an area through man's social processes.
  2. These changes can be understood in a framework of time, and they become evident through observations spaced in time.
B. Competencies
  1. Developing a sense of the passage of time.
  2. Learning to use observation as a source of information.
  3. Learning to compare observations made at different times.
  4. Learning to use pictures, films, and models as sources of information.

Activities
1. The teacher may begin this study by reading to the children from Virginia Lee Burton's *The Little House*. After the reading, a discussion can be held with the entire class about the changes that occurred to the house and the area around the house. The discussion should attempt to elicit from the children the concept that things change over time. Children's own recollections of moving in their neighborhood or of changes they have seen can personalize the experience and make the concept of change more meaningful. The children can then draw a list of changes that have taken place in their community. These changes can be drawn or described in stories the children write. These descriptions can be grouped under *man-made changes* and natural changes, or changes in houses, changes in the street, and changes in people who live in these houses. The groupings provide a basis for a display.
2. Plan a field trip to some place in the community that is undergoing change. This could be an area of urban renewal, a new subdivision, a place where a superhighway is being constructed, or some similar kind of construction that can dramatize change for the children. Have the children observe the site and the work that is in progress. If possible, try to get a worker from the project to talk to the children about what is happening and why it is happening. Take pictures of the site as it looks at the time of the visit. Plan

to visit the site at some time in the future. If a visit with the children is impractical, the teacher can go alone taking more pictures of the work as it presently looks and report to the children, showing the pictures and comparing them with the ones taken earlier. If it is possible to procure a picture of the site before the work began, this is also helpful. Have the children look at the different sets of pictures and discuss what is the same and what is different in each set. See if they can visualize what the completed project will look like. Pictures the children draw may be discussed. Since none of the children will really know how the project will come out, there will be no one right picture. A display of different pictures might be interesting.

3. Set up a similar work project in the classroom using toy machines and blocks or a sand table. If possible, help the children fashion machines of their own. Simple trucks, cranes, and bulldozers might be improvised at the woodwork bench. Allow the children to play freely with the materials. You might wish to talk with them as they play, asking questions about the uses of the machines and the purposes of their play. You could also suggest uses of the machines similar to those seen on the field trips. Books and filmstrips about machines can be brought into the classroom for display at this time (e.g., Zaffo, *The Big Book of Real Building and Wrecking Machines*.) Children may then draw or describe in words different kinds of machines, different in both purpose and operation.

4. Identify a resource person from the community who has lived in the area a long time. Invite him into the class to talk with the children about the neighborhood as it looked a long time ago, comparing it to the neighborhood as it looks today. If he has photographs or old newspapers, ask him to bring them along to class. Develop a display of pictures and relics from the neighborhood as it once looked. In many areas one does not have to go too far back to get at observable change.

5. Ask the children to talk with their parents about what they remember about the neighborhood as it was long ago. If the community is a stable one, it will be easy to get information and memorabilia from families. Ask the children to dictate or write stories about the things they were told. Have them illustrate their stories with their own pictures or pictures they get from other sources, so that each child has a personal history book. The stories and pictures could be placed along a time-line so that children begin to visualize the chronology of change.

6. A local museum or historical society may have displays of things from long ago available that are related to the locality. A visit to such a display or the inclusion of such a display in the classroom could be coupled with the showing of the personal history books.

This unit deals with the neighborhood in a geographic framework. Many other topics could have been used and other social sciences could have provided equally adequate frameworks for study. Many of the topics traditionally studied in early childhood classes can provide opportunities for significant social studies learning. Additional topics can also be used, such as a unit on Black Americans, taught within a framework of anthropology and presenting significant learnings from a social science point of view and an important area of human relations at the same time. In making education efficient for young children, more and more teaching will have to be done with multiple goals in mind.

SUGGESTED READING

ARNOFF, MELVIN, "Introducing Social Studies Concepts in the Primary Grades," *Social Education*, Vol. 30, No. 7 (November 1966), 537–39ff.

CLEMENTS, H. MILLARD, WILLIAM R. FIELDER, AND B. ROBERT TABACHNICK, *Social Study: Inquiry in Elementary Classrooms.* Indianapolis: Bobbs-Merrill, 1966.

CRABTREE, CHARLOTTE, "Inquiry Approaches to Learning Concepts and Generalizations in Social Studies," *Social Education*, Vol. 30, No. 6 (October 1966), 407–11ff.

EMMONS, FRANCES, AND JACQUELINE COBIA, "Introducing Anthropological Concepts in the Primary Grades," *Social Education*, Vol. 32, No. 3 (March 1968), 248–50.

ESTVAN, FRANK J., *Social Studies in a Changing World.* New York: Harcourt, Brace and World, 1968.

HANNA, LAVONE, GLADYS POTTER, AND NEVA HAGAMAN, *Unit Teaching in the Elementary School.* New York: Holt, Rinehart & Winston, 1963.

JAROLIMAK, JOHN, "Skills Teaching in the Primary Grades," *Social Education*, Vol. 31, No. 3 (March 1967), 222–23ff.

———, *Social Studies in Elementary Education*, 3rd ed. New York: Macmillan, 1967.

KENWORTHY, LEONARD S., *Social Studies for the Seventies.* Waltham, Massachusetts: Blaisdell Publishing Company, 1969.

MEIL, ALICE, AND EDWIN KEISTER, JR., *The Short-Changed Children of Suburbia.* New York: Institute of Human Relations Press, 1967.

MICHEALIS, JOHN U., *Social Studies for Children in a Democracy*, 3rd ed. Englewood Cliffs, N.J.: Prentice-Hall, Inc., 1963.

———, *Teaching Units in the Social Sciences: Early Grades.* Chicago: Rand McNally, 1966.

MITCHELL, LUCY SPRAGUE, *Young Geographers.* 1934. Reprint. New York: Bank Street College of Education, 1971. Distributed by Agathon Press, New York.

MORRISETT, IRVING, ed., *Concepts and Structure in the New Social Science Curricula.* West Lafayette, Indiana: Social Science Education Consortium, 1966.

MUGGE, DOROTHY J., "Are Young Children Ready to Study the Social Sciences?" *Elementary School Journal*, Vol. 68, No. 5 (February 1968), 232–40.

SERDUS, MORRIS, AND MARLIN L. TANK, "A Critical Appraisal of Twenty-Six National Social Studies Projects," *Social Education*, Vol. 34, No. 4 (April 1970), 383–449.

WOLFSON, BERNICE J., "Values and the Primary School Teacher," *Social Education*, Vol. 31, No. 1 (January 1967), 37–38ff.

Music and Art in the Early Years

9

Music and art have traditionally held honored positions in early childhood education. The early Froebelian kindergartens included music and art activities in the form of the *Occupations* and the *Mother's Songs and Games*. Both of these were carefully patterned according to explicit directions and actually provided no outlets for creative expression.

Such is the case in the arts and music found in many contemporary programs for young children. The kindergarten that gives every child exactly the same paper construction, or that asks students to fill in the spaces outlined on a sheet of paper by the teacher leaves no room for the child's interpretation of reality or the outpouring of ideas and feelings. Nor is creativity nurtured by stereotyped rhythm band activity, in which each child is supposed to carefully follow the basic beat established by a teacher playing the piano and adding stress at preassigned points in the composition. Music and art serve as vehicles for creative expression, but used improperly, they can only support conformity and the suppression of individual style. Properly used, they can enhance individuality and creativity, as can other subjects and activities in the early years.

CREATIVITY   Marksberry identifies three types of creative products: unique communications, plans or proposed sets of operations, and sets of abstract relations.[1] Music and art activities generally produce creative products in the first category.

[1]Mary Lee Marksberry, *Foundation of Creativity* (New York: Harper and Row, 1963), pp. 10–13.

A painting, a piece of sculpture, a musical selection, or a series of movements are of this nature. Other areas of the curriculum, such as language arts, including the child's own stories, poems, or special descriptive phrases, are unique communications also. Personal interpretations of other people's works might also be considered as unique communications.

To speak of creativity in the classroom is really to refer to the total program. But the teaching of music and art cannot be understood only in terms of creativity, for in dealing with them, one must deal with concepts of aesthetics as well. The young child needs to be surrounded with beautiful things in order to begin to appreciate and understand beauty. He also needs to learn to constructively criticize his own work and the work of others to develop criteria of aesthetic appreciation. Such criticism need not be negative in nature, nor does it require that the children have sophisticated tastes and mature sensitive appreciations, for these too develop as a result of experience and guidance. Richardson describes how children develop sensitivity to aesthetic components as a result of the criticism of their art work. Such criticism heightened their appreciation of the individuality of others and helped them develop more artistic approaches to materials.[2]

The Creative Process

Andrews suggests that the creative process involves three phases: "(1) The child and his creative power, feelings and imagination, (2) the action or interaction of this experience, (3) and his outward form of expression."[3] Too often teachers focus almost exclusively on the third phase of the creative process to the exclusion of the others. The experience of putting one's expressions into concrete form through the use of words, paints, musical rhythms, or movement through space is the culmination of a chain of events and cannot be considered in isolation. The teacher who wishes to foster creative expression must do much more than provide paint and paper. It is in the attitude pervading the class and in the uses she makes of the child's perceptions and experiences that creativity begins.

Each of these three aspects of the creative process needs to be supported in the classroom in its own way. The child's feelings and imagination are, in many ways, outside the teacher's reach. It is in indirect ways that she can support their development. The child must be given opportunities in which he can freely use his imagination, with the products of this imaginative thought accepted and cherished. The child, in order to use his power, must feel a degree of acceptance in a climate in which he is viewed as a competent individual, important and worthy. This

[2]Elwyn S. Richardson, *In the Early World* (Wellington, New Zealand: Council of Educational Research, 1964), pp. 15–48.

[3]Gladys Andrews, *Creative Rhythmic Movement for Children* (Englewood Cliffs, N.J.: Prentice-Hall, Inc., 1954), p. 21.

acceptance of the uniqueness of the individual and the importance of each person's contribution to the classroom can boost creative power.

The teacher should provide the children with the stimulation of a broad range of experiences. The child who is given opportunities to see, hear, taste, smell, and touch a great variety of things has access to the raw material of creative expression. These sensory perceptions are meaningless, however, when provided in isolation. Giving the child a set of color chips, a range of tone blocks, or a board covered with various textured materials may help him become aware of differences in sensory experiences or learn to name and categorize the experiences, but the creative process may be thwarted if these isolated sensory explorations become the sum and substance of his education. Creativeness grows out of experiencing the rich fabric of sensory images woven into the complexities of real life. The child who is taken to the docks of a seaport and can perceive not only the visual images of ships, cargo, and machines but also have his experience heightened by the smell of salt water, the feel of damp air on his skin, and the sounds of seagulls and shouting men has a rich experience from which he may select those portions most meaningful for him to represent through the use of the art media.

Similarly, the child who is allowed to sit for long periods of time watching the movement of a lonely insect in a field, seeing how it travels from place to place, how it eats and collects its food, has a perception of the natural world far richer than that provided through a book. The opportunity to experience the world in its realistic state is an important part of the creative process.

The opportunity to interact with his environment is just as important for the child. This interaction may be physical in nature as he moves out and talks to people or touches things. It can also be intellectual, an internal process that allows him to reflect on his experience and abstract significant aspects for further study. He can compare a recent experience with one he remembers from an earlier time, or compare his perceptions and interactions with those of other people. The abstraction of personal meaning from the world surrounding him provides the raw material from which creative expressions are derived.

As the child develops an outward form of expression, he learns to master media so that the expression is deliberate rather than accidental. This means that he learns to use himself—his body for movement, his hands for painting and modeling. He learns to control the media with which he works. Paints and brushes become an extension of him, as do musical instruments, words, and all the raw material out of which he creates artistic products. This is not to say that he becomes insensitive to the attributes of the materials he is using or that he rejects ideas stimulated from experiences with the medium alone. The child who is given modeling clay needs to explore the dimensions of the material and test ways of using it in order to achieve mastery.

The young child is to some extent stimulus-bound. His use of a medium of expression becomes a significant experience that in effect transforms itself. The experience of colors dripping into each other on a painting may elicit new forms and new colors which will stimulate him to explore opportunities that were not even present when he first stood at the easel. These explorations should be supported, for it is through the individual exploration of the medium that the child develops control.

DEVELOPMENTAL STAGES IN ART AND MUSIC   Improving artistic expression is not merely a matter of teaching children control. The stages of human development influence the creations of the child as much as anything else. A concept of stages in development suggests that there is a substantive difference between the child and the adult that cannot be explained on the basis of experiences alone. He goes through a series of metamorphoses in development so that each level is different in kind from the one preceding it and the ones following it.

Levels of artistic development have been identified as being similar to those of intellectual development. Lowenfeld, over two decades ago, devised a scheme of stages in the artistic development of children. The levels of development that are roughly approximate to the early childhood period would include the *scribbling* stage (age two to four), the *preschematic* stage (age four to seven), and the *schematic* stage (age seven to nine).[4]

Between the ages of two and four, the child, usually in the scribbling stage, experiences a kinesthetic experience through drawing. He moves through longitudinal, then circular motions, becoming more coordinated as he matures. While there is no representation in the child's pictures, he usually gives names to the drawings.

Between the ages of four and seven the child, in the *preschematic stage*, discovers the relationships of drawing, thinking, and reality. There is a continuous change in the symbols he creates in his drawing. He begins to develop representational forms, although they may not be related in the picture as they are in reality. He also is developing form concepts.

When the child moves to the schematic stage, between ages seven to nine, he begins to create realistic representations of people and things. He learns to use color and space realistically, and movement is depicted in his pictures. He then moves on to more mature stages of development in art. Lowenfeld's conception of stages in art closely parallels Piaget's stages of intellectual development. It is quite possible that art as an ex-

[4]Victor Lowenfeld, *Creative and Mental Growth* (New York: Macmillan, 1947).

pression of the child built upon his perceptions and conceptions as well as on his level of muscular control and coordination is to some extent a function of general intellectual development.

The implications of the stage theory of development apply to other areas of creative expression as well. Children may go through various stages in the use of movement and music. Aronoff uses Bruner's conception of three modes of learning—*enactive, iconic,* and *symbolic*—in her framework of music education: "(1) the enactive through action and manipulation; (2) the iconic through perceptual organization and inquiry—aural, kinesthetic and visual; and (3) the symbolic through words and symbols."[5] She suggests that the enactive and iconic modes are the ways in which young children know music. This use of Brunerian framework, which is built upon a Piagetian conception of development, also suggests the development of concepts in music as a function of general intellectual development.

What a child does or how he develops does not predetermine how he should be taught or what the content of instruction ought to be. It does, however, establish a framework within which goals can be determined and expectations set. It also *suggests* directions for education, for the teacher should be concerned with helping the child move through present stages to more mature stages. A child in nursery school, for example, should not be expected to create representational paintings and drawings. Nor should a kindergarten child be expected to be able to draw his room with all of the objects shown in proper size and place relationship to one another.

The concept of stages does not suggest that the teacher ought to simply sit back and wait for the child to mature. The teacher must guide the child and help him arrive at more mature ways of dealing with media and creating expressions. The guidance function of the teacher is as important with young children as with mature adults. A knowledge of stages of development provides a series of benchmarks that the teacher can use in directing the child's learning.

ARTS AND CRAFTS   Arts and crafts activities are often considered less important in the primary grades than in the nursery school and kindergarten. Too often the arts and crafts work is designed solely to insure that a finished product will be presentable and each child will have something to take home. This makes for good public relations, for parents can see that the children are doing *something* in class.

There is no denying the importance of sound public relations in a

[5]Frances Webber Aronoff, *Music and Young Children* (New York: Holt, Rinehart & Winston, 1969), p. 7.

school district. There are also times when it is appropriate to have the children produce a product for the home such as the Christmas or Mother's Day gift. It is unfortunate, however, when concern for the image of the school takes precedence over the learning of the child, for it is not the product itself that is the important goal of the school, but the child's growing mastery over materials. Using them to express feelings, perceptions, and ideas is important, though intangible. The completed work of the child has significance only in that it provides the teacher with insights into what he has learned and what difficulties he still must master.

The media of art that are the most productive for children in the early years are those that can be used at any age level. Paints, clay, and collage, for example, can be used by the three-year-old as well as by the mature artist. One does not limit a medium to a particular age level. Nor does the child's prior experience with the material need to concern the teacher, because in his developing competency, the young child will continue to see fresh possibilities in these media that represent an outgrowth of his increased mastery over them and the more mature stage of artistic development he is entering. The materials, however, do need to be introduced in fresh ways through the years.

Two-dimensional Art Work

Much of the art work we provide for children in the early years relates to the use of materials on a flat surface. Paints, crayon, and collage material are concerned with only a single plane, although collage work can have depth to it as a result of overlaying various materials and textures. The child's concern is primarily with form and color.

Painting is one of the mainstays of the early childhood program. In many classrooms, one can find an easel accessible to the children for a good part of the day. While an easel is handy for painting, the top of a table or a bit of floor space is just as good. The flat surface, as a matter of fact, will limit the amount of dripping that occurs during the painting. Teachers should organize the area used so that cleanup is as simple as possible, having papers spread under the child's painting and sponges and paper towels readily available. Keeping paints in containers that can be covered enables art work to continue with a relative degree of administrative simplicity.

Tempera paints may be either powdered or liquid in form. If powdered, they should be mixed thickly enough so that the colors will be rich and the paint opaque. With young children, a few colors provided at a time is adequate; more and different paints can be added later. Colors other than the primary ones can be purchased or mixed in class. The mixing can lead the children to make new discoveries about color.

The children at this stage prefer to experiment with form and color, allowing the movement of their own arms to stimulate the shapes that form on the paper. As they mature, pictures contain more representative forms.

While the young child should be encouraged to explore and experiment, simple techniques can be demonstrated for him. Wiping the brush so that it is not overloaded with paint, cleaning brushes before using them for other colors, mixing colors in specific proportions to achieve desired results, and placing the right brush into the right container of paint are simple skills that young children can learn. Teachers need to be willing and able to make use of the accidents of painting, however. A color mixture that results from an improperly placed brush or an accidental drip can lead to exciting learnings.

Brushes should be large and rather stiff so that they respond easily to the movements of the child. It is helpful to have more than one size brush available. Most of the painting in classrooms is done on unprinted newsprint. The standard size used is 18″ × 24″. Teachers ought not limit themselves to this kind of paper, for a different size, shape, or even texture of paper will stimulate new ways of painting. The classified section of a newspaper or a piece of wrapping paper with a small design might even be used for painting.

Tempera painting is usually considered a quiet, individual activity. Each child has his own paper and paints and there is little interaction with others. Even when two children are painting together at the easel, they are seldom interacting, for their work is separated. Children often enjoy painting side by side or in groups. A double easel or the floor supports painting as a group activity. Involving the children in mural painting is another way of making painting a group experience.

Mural paintings can be done on large sheets of brown wrapping paper, which many schools keep available. At first, the murals of young children will actually be a collection of individual paintings, with any consistency growing out of the teacher's organization rather than their work. There is usually little group planning, and teachers often find it useful to simply allocate space on different parts of the paper to different children. As the children mature and gain experience in this work, they can begin to plan toward a unified product.

The teacher's role in painting is not to have the children copy models she provides but to encourage them to explore the media; to observe their progress and to guide it, providing new techniques consistent with the child's development and needs.

Many teachers of young children shy away from the use of transparent water colors in the classroom. Although this media is more difficult to control, young children can use it and benefit from it. The flow of color over color can also add interesting dimension to the child's art work. Oil paints are much more difficult to use and are best avoided.

Wax crayons are almost universally found in most early childhood classrooms. Their use requires little teacher preparation; they seldom create much of a mess, and they are easily available. Large hexagonal or half-round crayons are available that allow the very young child to make bold controllable strokes and won't roll off the table. Children may be given their own sets of crayons, or crayons may be kept in a class pool. Large sheets of manila paper are useful to provide for coloring with crayons, but other kinds of paper can be used as well.

As the children learn to use these crayons, they can also be encouraged to mix crayoning with other media. The waxy crayon drawing provides a surface to which tempera paint will not adhere, so covering the surface with a single coat of paint allows the crayon drawing to stand out in interesting relief.

Using colored or white chalk at the blackboard allows the child freedom to cover a large surface without concern for creating a product, for he knows his work will soon be erased. Chalk can also be used on paper; wetting the paper with water or buttermilk allows the colors to show up more brilliantly, and spraying a fixative on the chalk drawings will keep them from rubbing off the paper.

Cutting, tearing, and pasting paper to create interesting designs has long been a school activity. Papers of adequate stiffness can be folded to create three-dimensional shapes; the Japanese art of Origami creates three-dimensional forms out of a single piece of paper without any cutting. While this form of art work is usually too complex for the young child, it does give one an idea of what can be done. Interesting designs at the two-dimensional level can also be created. For very young children, the teacher can prepare various-shaped pieces of colored paper to be pasted on a background, and as children develop competency in using scissors, they can create their own shapes. White school paste is all that is needed for children's collage work.

Other kinds of materials can be added to the pool of colored paper to increase the variety of textures, colors, and shapes in collage. A teacher might pick up many scavengered materials in her daily travels rather than order them from a supply house. A variety of these, organized so that teachers and children can select them without too much difficulty, can enhance an art program.

Various kinds of special paper and cardboard, pieces of fabric of various sizes, shapes, colors, and textures, bits of rope and yarn, feathers, buttons, colored sawdust, metal foil, and almost any other kind of material can be shaped, cut, pasted and otherwise included in a creation. Children can be offered a limited variety of these materials at any one time, but can also be encouraged to think of new materials they can use. As new materials are used, the teacher must provide other ways of attaching them, since school paste may be inadequate. Rubber cement, white glue, staples, and cellophane tape may need to be added to the resources of the class.

While finger paints are often difficult for children to control, they offer the child a release that cannot be matched by other media. The child has direct contact with the medium since he has no brush, scissor, or other implement between him and the paper. Often a child's finger painting is important because of the process of exploration it provides rather than his ability to gain control over the media.

For finger painting, a glossy nonabsorbent paper is available from school supply houses; glazed shelf paper may also be used. Sometimes the painting can be done on the plastic surface of a table; this allows the finger painting to go through many design changes. When the child is through painting, he may wash the surface of the table to complete the cleanup, or if the teacher wishes to preserve the finger painting, it is an easy matter to print the product by carefully placing a paper over the painting, pressing it down firmly all over, and carefully lifting it off.

There are many ways of printing designs; many can be printed simply by finding an interesting textured or shaped object, dipping it into a shallow dish of tempera paint, and pressing it firmly on a sheet of paper. Sponges, grainy ends of wooden boards, and vegetables such as carrots or potatoes are among the many materials that can be used. A design can be carved into these materials to enhance the printing. The process is similar to that of a linoleum block printing or a woodcut, but not as complicated. With the youngest children, the teacher can create the designs and let the children print. Varying designs through the use of different colors and the patterning of prints on the paper makes this an interesting medium.

Three-dimensional Constructions

Although one can often add the quality of depth to the two-dimensional media discussed above, for example by adding whipped soap suds to tempera paint so that it dries with a degree of depth, the three-dimensional constructions created by children are quite different. In the early years, the three-dimensional media include woodworking, cardboard box constructions, clay modeling, and the creation of mobiles and stabiles.

Children get a great deal of pleasure out of working with wood— the simple activity of hammering and sawing is often enough to satisfy the very young child. It is not uncommon, for example, to find children in a nursery class sawing piece after piece of wood from a board until there is nothing left of the original; they may even bring home wood constructions that seem to contain more iron in the form of nails than wood.

It is unfortunate that in so many classes teachers hesitate to include this medium. Too often the absence of woodworking is caused by fear on the part of the teacher; this is usually because of lack of experience with carpentry and tools. Hammers, saws, and other tools, if improperly used, can cause injury to children, as can other school equipment. The greater the ignorance of the teacher, the greater the fear of possible bodily harm to children. But young children can develop a respect for tools and skills and learn to use them safely.

An important advantage to the inclusion of woodworking in the program is its obvious appeal to boys. So much of early childhood education reflects feminine tastes and needs; in addition, the teachers are usually women. Woodworking is a predominantly masculine activity, but girls should participate and learn, just as boys can learn from cooking activities. Providing woodworking activities is supportive of the developing sex role identities of the young boys in the classroom.

A woodworking area needs to be organized to promote positive activities and avoid danger; it requires a certain amount of isolation from other activities. Tools and supplies need to be stored so that they are readily accessible, and should be in good order and in proper repair, with saws sharp and hammer handles firmly in the heads. A good supply of soft wood such as common pine should be provided. Wood can often be collected from the scraps of local lumber yards. A number of accessories can be included as the children mature in their ability to use wood and tools.

Lightweight but good quality hammers should be provided, as well as short crosscut saws. Sandpaper and block planes help children smooth out their woodwork, as do rasps or wood files. A brace and drill bits and hand drill are useful to include. Screwdrivers can be added as children learn to use screws as well as nails for fastening boards together. A woodworking vise and workbench or saw horses and "C" clamps are useful, as well.

Children usually start out by building simple constructions. These can often be put together with nails. Other means of fastening can be added, including screws with large heads and white glue. As the woodworking constructions are elaborated, teachers can add dowels, empty paper rolls, spools, and just about anything she and the children find useful. Woodworking projects can be painted with tempera and then covered with shellac or lacquer so that the color will not run. More responsible children might be given enamels for painting. These, however, are harder to work with and to clean up.

Clay modeling has been a mainstay in early education for many years. Potter's clay is soft and malleable and responds easily to the child's handling. In addition, it can be used over and over. If dried out, water can be added; if wet, it can be left to dry.

Very young children enjoy the sheer fun of manipulating clay. They knead it, pound it, roll it into balls or snakes, flatten it out, break it up, and push it all together again. Just working with the clay often takes precedence over actually creating something with it. As children develop, they learn to make pinch pots, pulling the clay into shapes and tearing off pieces. They create figures, adding pieces of clay to a rolled body to create men and animals with heads, arms, and legs. After a while, they can even learn to build pots, using the coil or slab method.

After the children are through working with clay, they are often content to put it back into the crock. When they wish to save what they have made, however, the clay can be dried slowly and then painted. If a kiln is available in the school, it is exciting to watch the clay become transformed by the heat. Care should be taken, however, that work to be fired in a kiln is sturdy and the chances of its exploding or coming apart in the heat are slight. If the children have worked over the clay for a while, it may not need to be wedged. The pieces should not be too thick and the appendages should be securely attached. The teacher might even wish to glaze some of the children's work.

In some classrooms, other modeling material such as Plasticine, an oil-based clay, is sometimes substituted for clay. Although Plasticine is not as responsive to modeling, and the children's work cannot be preserved, it can be used again and again and will not dry out. Some teachers also use modeling dough in the classroom. It can be purchased commercially or made out of simple household ingredients—salt, flour, and water.

Simple constructions can be made out of cardboard boxes and cartons that are cut up, pasted together, elaborated with paper, and painted and colored. Houses, cash registers, rocket ships, or model automobiles can be made. The skills the children have developed in two-dimensional work can be elaborated and used, so there is no end to the constructions that can be created by the children. Thick corrugated cardboard is now available that can be worked like wood to create sturdy constructions. This "cardboard carpentry" is a welcome addition to the resources of schools.

Mobiles and stabiles are three-dimensional designs. Mobiles are designed to move; stabiles remain stationary. They can be created by combining a variety of material in interesting fashions, using dowels, tongue depressors, wire coat hangers, pipe cleaners, metal foil, yarn, bells, sponges, rubber bands, and anything else the teacher wishes to provide. Bases for stabiles can be easily fashioned out of clay or styrofoam, but mobiles are designed to hang, thereby eliminating the need for a base.

Young children can weave on simple looms early in their school career. "Loopers," using cotton loops and simple metal looms, can provide a beginning. Teachers can also make simple looms out of squares of corrugated cardboard. Cutting slots about one-half inch deep in two opposite ends allows the child to thread the loom; the yarn can then be woven back and forth until a square is completed. Simple looms can also be made by driving nails into the edges of wooden boxes or frames.

If children are provided with tapestry needles, they can begin to sew designs onto pieces of burlap. In time, these can be combined with sewing pieces of felt or a similar fabric to create interesting pictures.

The Classroom as a Studio

In using arts and crafts activities in the classroom, the teacher is concerned with teaching techniques, but techniques need not be taught in isolation. A child needs opportunities to explore each medium and set of materials. Skill in use of materials and respect for their potentialities and limitations grows out of personal exploration. Technique can be provided as the child feels the need to push his use of the material beyond what he has already accomplished. This is true for the mature artist as well.

The teacher should not be concerned that every piece of work the child works on leads to a finished product worthy of display. If a child experiments, he should be allowed to experience failure, and if he is busy practicing one technique in a complex project, he may not even be concerned with product completion.

The classroom should be a place where a child can explore his own abilities and the uses he can make of material. Accomplishment can be acknowledged and criticism can be provided, but only in the spirit of guidance and to move children to further accomplishments. The work of the child is his way of expressing himself. As an extension of himself, his art work becomes personally important.

Displaying Art

Children in the early years must do more than simply produce their own creations. They can be made aware of the artistic products of others: the work of other children in their own class and the work of mature artists as well. Thus it is helpful if the teacher sets aside a portion of the room as a display area for artistic expressions. Works can be displayed there and changed regularly. A bulletin board and an adjoining table make useful display space, allowing the display of both pictures and three-dimensional constructions. Children's work can be mounted simply on mats and pinned to the bulletin board. The teacher might wish to create an attractive surrounding for the picture by draping colored burlap over the bulletin board or cover it with colored construction paper that will enhance the colors in the painting.

Not only should the works of the children be displayed, but, if possible, the works of professional artists should be brought to the class as well. Museums sometimes make original works of art or reproductions available for loan to schools. Inexpensive prints may also be purchased. A class visit to a museum is an appropriate trip for young children, and if the teachers knows of a practicing artist in the area, it might be possible to arrange a visit to his studio or to invite him to class. Watching an artist at work can be very exciting for young children.

The children can talk about what they see in artistic representations and can try to explain what strikes them as attractive. Although such discussions might not be possible in nursery or kindergarten classes, primary grade children can begin to verbalize their intuitive sense of beauty.

The teacher can stimulate critical discussions through the use of questions that require responses beyond "I like it" or "I don't like it." Such questions as "How does it make you feel?" or "What does it make you think about?" might help generate personal reactions to the representation. Questions can also help children focus on the use of form or color, the degree of simplicity or complexity, the sense of representativeness or uniqueness, and other qualities of design. These questions should be used to goad children beyond their present state of perception and appreciation.

Children need to be aware that they are not competing with the mature artist. While elements of similarity exist, their main concern is in discovering and extending their own ability rather than in attempting to match that of an outsider.

MUSIC AND MOVEMENT   Aronoff, building upon the work of Reimer, identified the discipline of music to include "concepts of music, skills and knowledge for applying them, and concepts about music dealing with the uses of music in the past and ongoing culture. Their interrelationship is in fact the structure of music."[6] Music study, then, involves the development of factual knowledge and concepts, analysis, and skills and repertoire. Skills include listening, singing, playing, moving, and reading and writing music. A music program in early childhood education, therefore, should provide children with opportunities to listen to music, learn to understand its elements, and reproduce these through singing and playing instruments, as well as to provide opportunities for children to relate bodily movement to musical expression. Creation of musical compositions or movements should also be included. The music program should also be related to other parts of the curriculum. especially the language arts and social studies, in order to help children learn about the uses of music in any culture. Such a program provides opportunities for them to deal critically with music, to learn to reproduce it, and to learn to express themselves through it.

Creative music and movement are difficult to teach because they are noisy activities—a teacher cannot allow a child to experiment with the sounds of a drum while a reading lesson is in progress. Specific times

[6]Aronoff, *Music and Young Children*, p. 19.

should be set aside, and musical noise and movement controlled so that real learning can occur.

Too often music and movement are organized as large group activities. While such organization may be valid, there also need to be times for children to work alone or in small groups. In an activity-based program at the primary as well as the preprimary level, these opportunities can be provided during the activity period. A portion of the room can be set aside for movement. Musical instruments can be provided for use by a few children, and some can be allowed to listen to a phonograph, possibly using earphones if they are available. The music that children create in their ongoing activities can also be collected by the teacher by means of tape recording or written transcription. A multipurpose room, the play yard, or an auditorium or gymnasium can often be commandeered for a portion of the day for such activities.

Music in school during the early years generally consists of singing, playing simple instruments, listening, and creative movement. Often creative movement can be used as a way to involve children in mime and creative dramatics. Although musical activities may be primarily the responsibility of a music teacher, the classroom teacher always has some obligation to the music program. There are too many opportunities in a school day that support music education and too many ways to integrate music into the learning of children to allow teachers to avoid this area of instruction.

Singing

Almost all children enjoy singing. They sing loudly, often with more exuberance than skill. Young children pick up songs they hear and repeat them to the best of their ability, sometimes repeating a phrase over and over, and mispronouncing or not completely learning the words. At times the pitch is off, but this seldom deters a young child in his continued production of singing. A teacher should capitalize on this enthusiasm and exuberance. Greater adherence to melody and verse comes with experience and repetition. Teaching songs to children can be fun as well as educational.

Robert Smith has designed a singing program to develop and improve children's vocal accuracy, range, and quality. Songs chosen to help this development, according to Smith, should continue to appeal to children after many repetitions; there should be melodic phrase repetition, repeated word phrases, and the appropriate range for the child's particular stage of vocal development.[7]

The piano and other instruments such as the autoharp, guitar, or ukelele, can be used to accompany the children's singing. However, some

[7]Robert B. Smith, *Music in the Child's Education* (New York: Ronald Press, 1970), pp. 10–24.

music educators feel that instrumental accompaniment is unnnecessary for singing, even with young children. The Kodaly Method suggests that human voices be used to accompany other human voices, leading to a program of unaccompanied singing and simple two-part singing for primary children.[8]

A number of elementary music textbooks as well as books of children's songs are available on the market and can provide an excellent resource for the teacher. Some of these are listed at the end of this chapter. Teachers who cannot read music may be able to learn children's songs from records. Some music textbooks have accompanying records available.

Sources of children's songs are varied. Many, of course, are written especially for children. Popular songs should also be welcome in class. The folk tradition is rich in children's songs, which include the nursery rhymes as well as the vast array of folk songs from all over the world. Many of these songs are quite simple and contain much repetition of musical phrase and words, making it easy for children to learn them.

Too often, unfortunately, the music of the school is far removed from the music the child hears at home. Children should have opportunities to explore music of many kinds. Much contemporary music is rich in line, harmony, and meanings. Jazz, folk, and rock should not be avoided by the teacher, but should be included in both singing and listening activities.

Many of the ethnic traditions of which American culture is composed ought to be used as a resource for songs as well; for example, the music of black Americans, Spanish-speaking people, American Indians, and people of various European heritages should be included in the repertoire of the class. It is helpful if the teacher selects songs that she herself likes, and these should meet Smith's criteria, stated earlier. Songs can also be selected to fit a particular area of study in the program, such as African songs as related to a Black Studies program, or holiday songs at appropriate periods of the year.

Although most portions of the singing program are concerned with the recreation of musical experiences, singing can have creative aspects as well. Children can be given opportunities to compose their own verses to familiar songs. Teachers can note these songs in musical notation, reading them back to the children, or use tape recorders to capture the children's creations.

Playing Musical Instruments

Early childhood classes should provide opportunities for children to play many musical instruments. Group playing may be desirable at

[8]Geoffrey Russell-Smith, "Introducing Kodaly Principles into Elementary Teaching," Music Educators Journal, Vol. 54, No. 3 (November 1967), 43.

some times, but the children should not be restricted to this, for they need to explore the use of musical instruments independently. It is a good idea to make a few instruments available at different times for the children to use. On these occasions, they should not be required to beat out a particular rhythm, but should be given the freedom to experiment. Drums, tambourines, rhythm sticks, maracas, and tone blocks are all instruments simple enough for young children to use.

Some commercially made instruments should be provided, because many homemade instruments do not achieve a high quality of tone. Children can be given opportunities to create their own instruments as well, though. These can be as simple as shakers made out of milk containers or plastic boxes into which have been placed a number of beans or grains of sand; different objects in the box give different tones to the shaker. Sandpaper attached to wooden blocks and rubbed together makes a suitable instrument. Many objects found around the house or salvaged from the trash heap can also be fashioned into instruments—pot covers and automobile brake drums can be used as percussion instruments, for example. An imaginative teacher can come up with a long list of such items.

In many classes for young children there is a heavy emphasis placed upon the use of rhythm instruments. Simple tonal instruments should also be included. Although teachers should avoid any instruments that must be placed in the mouth to be played, since this could spread infection in a class, many tonal instruments can be used. Tone blocks in small sets, xylophones, marimbas, and tuned bells can be provided for the children. The use of these instruments encourages the exploration of tonal as well as rhythmic relationships, and the children often begin to play simple tunes by themselves.

If the classroom has a piano, the children can be taught to use it with care and then be allowed occasional access to it. Often in a classroom in which a piano is accessible, there is much experimentation with the keyboard, sometimes with only black or only white keys played, scales up and down the keyboard, or even attempts to pick out simple melodies.

Musical instruments can be used to accompany the children's own singing or movement, to reproduce rhythmic or melodic patterns, or to create original compositions. They also provide an avenue for free musical exploration. Sometimes merely leaving an instrument on a table is enough to stimulate a child to begin to "mess about" with sound. A teacher can provide direction to this type of activity by helping the child extend from simple explorations. Sometimes patterns can be abstracted by the child from the world around him; the sound of running, the noise of the mimeograph machine, and activities in the streets can be identified by sound patterns. The pattern of the names of children, objects, or words in a story can also be reproduced on a percussion instrument.

Children can also listen to songs, abstracting the meter or the accented beat and reproducing it. Changes in tempo should be felt and produced by the child. Individual explorations lead to group playing, with children joining and playing in union, or even playing against one another as in a dialogue.

As children play instruments, they should become aware of the range of sounds that can be made with each instrument. A drum struck with the hand sounds differently than when it is struck with a stick. When it is struck in the center it elicits a different tone than when struck at the edge. Children can learn to create different effects using the same instrument.

As children move into the primary grades, the teacher who is capable can begin to teach children aspects of musical notation. The children can clap out different note values, or run, walk, and skip to different rhythms. They can even learn to follow the melody line of a song as the music rises and lowers in tone. The teacher can use her hand, moving it up and down to illustrate changes in tone, or mark a blackboard accordingly. The extension of the child's musical ability at this level is as much a function of the teacher's capability and creativity as of the children's.

Children should not be forced into a rigid pattern of music production. Activities with instruments should be a function of the children's interest and willingness to try out new ideas in sound. In the early years, the teacher should help the children explore and discover the rich area of music through the use of instruments.

Listening to Music

Listening is a basic skill in the music program. Children can listen to the world around them to abstract the sounds heard as a way of knowing about the world. They can also learn to listen for elements of music such as pitch, intensity, and rhythm, as well as for patterns and themes. Attentive listening can help characterize music and determine its mood. In addition, listening is a skill needed for other musical activities such as singing or developing creative movement.

As children listen to music, live or on records, they soon become aware of various qualities. Some music is loud—some is soft; some music is fast in tempo—some is slow; musical pitch rises and falls. Teachers can help children become aware of these differences and learn to characterize elements of music as well as its design and texture.

Children can also learn to distinguish the various musical instruments and identify their sounds. Differences between families of instruments—brass, woodwinds, strings, and percussion—can be made first, with differences among the instruments in each family identified later. Records of musical pieces highlighting the various instruments are useful, as are pictures and charts of the instruments. The teacher might also be able to bring live musicians to class to play for the children.

Teachers can develop discussions that enhance attentive listening and lead to critical listening. Children can begin to talk about the feelings generated by pieces of music as well as the kinds of activities that might be evoked. They can also begin to talk about the *uses* of music. Music is used for relaxation, to accompany dancing, to facilitate work; music sets a mood, accompanies a story, and sometimes exists solely for sheer pleasure.

Children can also begin to talk about music they like and do not like. The teacher should help the children explore their preferences and help them understand what elements of music appeal to them most.

Almost every aspect of the music program is built on the development of listening skills. If children are to learn to sing properly, they must accurately reproduce pitch and rhythmic pattern of a song, and this requires that they have attended to it and are able to recall it. Creative movement requires attending to the music as a prerequisite for response.

While recorded music for children is plentiful, it is helpful for children to have opportunities to hear live musicians as well. Sometimes a teacher is talented enough to play for her class. At other times, parents or older children might be found who are willing and able to perform. In some communities, local symphony orchestras or ensembles are contracted to perform in schools. Sometimes young children are considered too immature to be included in the audience, but this is an unfortunate attitude, for the young child can profit from this experience as well. The one problem that may be encountered grows out of the fact that young children sometimes do not manifest "proper" audience behavior. They may make noise during a performance or move rather than sit still. Some skills in audience behavior can be taught; although children naturally move in response to music, they can learn that there are times when it is appropriate to sit quietly.

Movement

As children learn to respond to music and to their own feelings about it, they can become quite creative in using their bodies as vehicles for expression. This requires that they become aware of themselves in different ways and learn to control their movements. As in other areas of creative expression, movement develops out of children's intuitive responses and explorations. These should be nurtured as children are provided with opportunities to expand their physical capabilities.

Teachers can help children explore the various dimensions of movement, which Russell has analyzed under four main headings: the body—the instrument of expression; effort—how the body moves; space and shape—where the body moves, and relationship—relationship of body parts to each other, of dancers to each other, and of groups to each other. Russell has built upon the work of Laban to develop a program of creative dance aimed at helping children develop competency in movement through a series of basic themes.[9]

Movement can be taught as a means of creative expression, but it can also be used to help children explore the structure of music. The Eurythmics of Émile Jaques Dalcroze has provided the basis for the music program developed by Aronoff, whose work has been mentioned earlier. Although most teachers lack the specialized training of a Dalcroze teacher or a dance instructor, there are many ways to encourage children to explore movement. Simply playing music on a phonograph or piano often stimulates them to move, and varying the pitch, intensity, and rhythm leads them to move in different ways. Sometimes just a drum beat stimulates them to move freely. It is even possible to encourage movement without any accompaniment at all by using descriptive phrases, or asking them to show a soft movement, a hard movement, high steps, or a close-to-the-ground movement—all allowing them freedom of expression within a framework established by the teacher.

Such experiences are often enhanced with simple props. Giving children hoops or fine silk scarves to use as they move affects their motion, often enabling them to make more flowing movements. Asking children to move in ways that represent specific things can also extend their movement. A child can be a jet or a slithery snake, a boat, or a flower growing. Each object calls forth certain associations for the child, which he should be able to interpret in his own way. Having the children all move in the same stereotyped way stifles rather than supports creative expression. Individual interpretation is essential in these rhythmic activities. The teacher's role in the early years is to elicit movement and to encourage new ways of using one's body rather than to teach specific forms and techniques.

Creative movement should be encouraged in young children, but there should be opportunities for other kinds of dance activities as well. Rhythmic games coupled with songs or chants are enjoyable and can be learned by young children. Such games as "Looby-Loo" or "Bluebird, Fly Through My Window" are simple to direct and so full of repetition that young children can master them with ease. Many of these activities grow out of folk tradition, and teachers sometimes find that children know somewhat different versions than the one she is teaching. This may also occur when she introduces a folk song. These differences are interesting to study, for they represent a portion of the folk tradition in American society. It may be easier, however, for the teacher to learn the local version than to teach a foreign version.

[9]Joan Russell, *Creative Dance in the Primary School* (London: Macdonald and Evans, 1965), pp. 19–30.

Play party activities can soon give way to folk dancing, of both American and European derivation. Children can learn the simple basic steps of folk or square dances and then do the patterns as called by the teacher. Records and books are available that provide music and directions for the simple dances. More formal dances should probably wait until later in the child's school career.

Exploration in one's use of oneself and the extension of one's ability to express feelings and ideas through the controlled use of the body and through instruments and media are the goals of this portion of the program in the early years. Children are not being prepared to become musicians or artists any more than they are being prepared to become scientists and mathematicians. Learning to express oneself and to appreciate the expressions of others, and learning to find beauty in oneself and in one's surroundings is a contribution that can last throughout the child's life.

SOURCES OF MUSIC MATERIALS

Children's Music Center, 5373 West Pico Blvd., Los Angeles.
Educational Record Sales, 53 Chambers St., New York.

BASIC MUSIC TEXTS

Birchard Music Series. Evanston, Ill.: Summy-Birchard Co., 1962.
Discovering Music Together. Chicago: Follett, 1968.
Exploring Music. New York: Holt, Rinehart & Winston, 1969.
Growing with Music. Englewood Cliffs, N.J.: Prentice-Hall, Inc., 1966.
The Magic of Music. Boston: Ginn & Co., 1965.
Making Music Your Own. Morristown, N.J.: Silver-Burdett, 1966.
Music for Young Americans. New York: American Book Co., 1966.
This Is Music. Boston: Allyn & Bacon, 1965.

SONG BOOKS FOR YOUNG CHILDREN

Dietz, B. W., and T. C. Parks, *Folk Songs of China, Japan, and Korea.* New York: John Day, 1964.
Jenkins, Ella, *The Ella Jenkins Song Book for Children.* New York: Oak Publications, 1969.
Landeck, Beatrice, *Songs to Grow On.* New York: William Morrow Co., 1950.
————, *More Songs to Grow On.* New York: William Morrow Co., 1954.
MacCarthey, L. Pendleton, *Songs for the Nursery School.* Cincinnati: Willis Music Co.
Seeger, Ruth Crawford, *American Folk Songs for Children.* Garden City, N.Y.: Doubleday, 1948.

SUGGESTED READING

ANDREWS, GLADYS, *Creative Rhythmic Movement for Children.* Englewood Cliffs, N.J.: Prentice-Hall, Inc., 1954.

ARONOFF, FRANCES W., *Music and Young Children*. New York: Holt, Rinehart & Winston, 1969.

BLAND, JANE C., *Art of the Young Child*. New York: Museum of Modern Art, 1957.

D'AMICO, VICTOR, *Creative Teaching in Art*, rev. ed. Scranton, Pennsylvania: International Textbook Company, 1963.

GAITSKELL, CHARLES D., *Children and Their Art*. New York: Harcourt, Brace and World, 1958.

GROSSMAN, MARVIN, "Art Education for the Young Child," *Review of Educational Research*, Vol. 40, No. 3 (June 1970), 421–27.

HOOVER, LOUIS, *Art Activities for the Very Young*. Worcester, Massachusetts: Davis Publishing, Inc., 1963.

JEFFERSON, BLANCHE, *Teaching Art to Children*. Boston: Allyn and Bacon, 1959.

LANDECK, BEATRICE, *Children and Music*. New York: William Sloane Associates, 1952.

LOWENFELD, VICTOR, AND W. LAMBERT BRITTAIN, *Creative and Mental Growth*, 4th ed. New York: Macmillan, 1964.

MARKSBERRY, MARY LEE, *Foundations of Creativity*. New York: Harper and Row, 1963.

MATTIL, E. L., "Children and the Arts," *Childhood Education*, Vol. 40, No. 6 (February 1964), 286–91.

McILVAIN, DOROTHY S., *Art for the Primary Grades*. New York: Putnam, 1961.

MELZI, KAY, *Art in the Primary School*. Oxford: Basil Blackwell, 1967.

NELSON, LOIS, "Maximizing Creativity in the Classroom," *Young Children*, Vol. 21, No. 3 (January 1966), 131–35.

NELSON, MARY J., AND GLADYS TIPTON, *Music for Early Childhood*. New York: Silver-Burdett, 1952.

RICHARDSON, ELWYN, *In the Early World*. Wellington, New Zealand: Council of Educational Research, 1964.

RICHARDSON, MARION, *Art and the World*. Peoria, Illinois: Charles A. Bennett Company, 1952.

RUSSELL, JOAN, *Creative Dance in the Primary School*. London: Macdonald and Evans, 1965.

SHEEHY, EMMA D., *Children Discover Music and Dance*. New York: Teachers College Press, 1968.

SMITH, ROBERT B., *Music in the Child's Education*. New York: Ronald Press, 1970.

SWANSON, BESSIE R., *Music in the Education of Children*, 2nd ed. Belmont, California: Wadsworth Publishing Company, 1964.

10

Child's Play As Education

Traditionally, the field of early childhood education has been characterized by its support of play as an educational tool. Teachers at the nursery and kindergarten level organize their classrooms for play activities in the belief that through these activities young children can best learn what they are expected to learn. Even in the primary grades, where direct verbal instruction is a more acceptable mode of instruction, play is still considered to be an important educative device and many of the instructional activities are developed in the form of learning games.

PLAY IN EARLY CHILDHOOD EDUCATION Play activities or their derivatives have been a part of early childhood educational programs since these programs were first implemented in any systematic way. The original Froebelian kindergarten included the manipulation of *Gifts*, the use of craft activities or *Occupations*, and the involvement of children in the *Mothers' Plays and Songs*, all described in an earlier chapter. Although the children did not engage in the freely expressive forms of play we find in many kindergartens today, the activities were manipulative and were derived from the free play of children. The source of kindergarten activity was the natural play activity of German peasant children. The essential elements of the play were abstracted and systematized to insure that the important elements of the play activity, as identified by Froebel, would be given to all children.

Dr. Maria Montessori, in the development of her educational method, similarly abstracted the essential elements out of the natural play activities of children, reconstructed them, and systematized them as an instructional method. Activities in these two instances were meant to achieve different instructional goals. Froebel wanted children to gain the spiritual meanings symbolized by the materials and the activities. Montessori, however, wanted them to gain a greater understanding of the properties of the objects themselves as well as the achievement of specific skills gained through manipulating them. In both instances, although the activity of play remained, actual *playfulness* was eliminated from the educational method.

By *playfulness* is meant the *fun* aspects of play activities—a quality which pervades all types of real play. Lieberman has identified five characteristics of playfulness: physical, social, and cognitive spontaneity, manifest joy, and a sense of humor.[1] All of these should characterize the play activities of children to some extent.

It was only with the advent of the reform kindergarten movement and the modern nursery-school movement in the first quarter of the twentieth century that the organic play of children became accepted as a vehicle for learning. No attempt was made in these educational systems to abstract distinct separate elements from the play of children for transmission in the school. Instead, the children's natural play activities were supported and nurtured in the classroom as being educationally significant in their own right. In neither of these newer educational institutions was play considered the only way for children to learn.

The use of children's play for educational purposes created some changes in child's play. Neumann suggests that the educational use of play places constraint on the child's play activities. These constraints are a result of creating a specific setting for play and providing adult supervision, as well as selecting specific objectives and specific objects for play.[2] The reform kindergarten movement accepted these constraints of children's play while taking care, at least theoretically, that the child's play was not completely distorted in the school.

With the advent of these new forms of early childhood education, equipment and materials were designed for fostering play in classrooms, intended to be used by teachers to stimulate and elaborate rather than deflate the play activities. Even a cursory glance into a nursery school or kindergarten classroom reveals many of these play properties. Almost all classrooms at the preprimary level have some sort of doll corner or housekeeping area. In these areas miniature representations of kitchen

---

[1] J. Nina Lieberman, "Playfulness and Divergent Thinking: An Investigation of Their Relationship at the Kindergarten Level," *Journal of Genetic Psychology*, Vol. 107, No. 2 (December 1965), 219–24.

[2] Eva A. Neumann, "The Problem of Play," unpublished doctoral dissertation, University of Illinois, 1971.

equipment and household furniture as well as play pots and pans, dishes, dolls, cleaning equipment, plastic food, and other similar items are made available to the children to help them act out their representations of home life. The block area is another place in which equipment designed to foster children's play is available. In addition to the equipment in these areas, one might also find dress-up clothes, steering wheels, toy cars and trucks, and innumerable other devices that have the primary purpose of supporting play activities.

In recent years, new programs in early childhood education have been developed that question the place of play in the school curriculum. This is especially true of those programs concerned with the achievement of intellectual goals, the remediation of learning deficits, and compensation for early deprivation. While play may be all right for normal children when we are not concerned with their intellectual development, the argument states, play has no place in an intellectually oriented program, for it does not foster intellectual development or, if it does, not with any great degree of potency. Alternative approaches to play may be supported on the basis of the self-evident nature of learnings possible through more direct methods or, at most, on the basis of relatively short-range evaluations. A review of the theories of play and an analysis of the ways the teacher can use play in support of intellectual as well as other forms of learning will be useful.

THEORIES OF PLAY

Play is not only hard to understand but it is extremely difficult to identify and define in any systematic way. Play appears in the behavior of adults as well as of children, and even in the behavior of animals. Attempts to define play have ended in the diffusion of definitions. Play can generally be identified easily when observed, however. Mitchell and Mason have gathered many of the definitions of play which have been used traditionally. These include:

SCHILLER: The aimless expenditure of exuberant energy.

FROEBEL: The natural unfolding of the germinal leaves of childhood.

SPENSER: Superfluous actions taking place instinctively in the absence of real actions ... Activity performed for the immediate gratification derived without regard for ulterior benefits.

LAZARUS: Activity in itself free, aimless, amusing, or diverting.

HALL: The motor habits and spirit of the past persisting in the present.

GROOS: Instinctive practice, without serious intent, of activities that will later be essential to life.

SEASHORE: Free self-expression for the pleasure of expression.

DEWEY: Activities not consciously performed for the sake of any result beyond themselves.

SHAND: A type of play directed at the maintenance of joy.

DULLES: An instinctive form of self-expression and emotional escape valve.[3]

Neumann has attempted to develop a definition of play that synthesizes elements from other definitions and that is useful in defining play in a variety of settings. This definition includes the *criteria* of play—characteristics which differentiate play from nonplay; the *processes* of play—their form and method; and the *objectives* of play—the elements toward which play is directed.

The *criteria* for play include internal control, internal reality, and intrinsic motivation. To the extent that these characteristics are dominant in an activity as opposed to external control, external reality, and extrinsic motivation, that activity may be considered play. The *processes* of play include the operations, which are repitition, replication, and transformation and the *modes*, which may be sensorimotor, affective, oral, or cognitive.

The *objectives* of play include subjects, functions, and locations. The *subject* may be the player himself, other children, or adults. The *objects* of play may be real objects, toys, instructional materials, or multipurpose materials. The *functions* of play may be information seeking, social learning, sensorimotor activity, emotional expression, or sensorimotor expression. The *location* of play may be internal (within the organism) or external (within the environment).[4]

Mitchell and Mason have identified six classes of theories of play. These include the surplus energy theory, relaxation theory, pre-exercise theory, recapitulation theory, cathartic theory, and self-expression theory.[5] Gilmore, building upon this taxonomy, has divided the theories into two groups: the classical theories and the dynamic theories. While the classical theories attempt to explain why children play, the dynamic theories concern themselves with the content of the play.[6]

The Classical Theories

SURPLUS ENERGY THEORIES.   This theory postulates that there is a quantity of energy available to the organism and a tendency of the organism to expend that energy either through goal-directed activity (work) or through goalless activity (play). Play occurs at any time the organism has more energy available than it needs to expend for work.

---

[3]Elmer Mitchell and Bernard S. Mason, *The Theory of Play*, rev. ed. (New York: A. S. Barnes, 1948), pp. 103–104.

[4]Neumann, "The Problem of Play."

[5]Mitchell and Mason. *The Theory of Play*, pp. 48–85.

[6]J. Barnard Gilmore, "Play: A Special Behavior," in R. N. Haber, ed., *Current Research in Motivation* (New York: Holt, Rinehart & Winston, 1965).

Within this theory, the content of the play activity is not important and one form of play could easily be substituted for another.

RELAXATION THEORY.   This theory postulates that play is used to replenish expended energy. After a period of fatiguing activity (work), the organism needs an opportunity to be involved in a relaxing activity (play). According to this theory, play occurs when the organism has little energy left rather than when it has too much energy. Again, one kind of play activity could be substituted for another as a replenishing device.

PRE-EXERCISE THEORY.   Play, according to the pre-exercise theory, is instinctive behavior. The child instinctively involves himself in play activities which are, in essence, a form of some more mature behavior he will later have to assume. The content of play is therefore determined by the content of mature future adult activity. Play may be conceived of in this theory as preparation for future work.

RECAPITULATION THEORY.   From this theoretical position, play cannot be understood in terms of the future activities of the individual organism, but must be understood in relation to past activities of the race. Play becomes an instinctive way of ridding the organism of the primitive and unnecessary instinctual skills that have been carried over through heredity. The stages of play, according to this theory, correspond to the stages of development of the human race, going from the most primitive to the relatively sophisticated. Play, by allowing the person to rid himself of primitive activities, prepares him for modern work activities.

It is interesting to note in these examples how the same activity, play, can be understood through a series of opposing theories. Play either represents surplus energy or an energy deficit. Play can either be a form of pre-exercise for sophisticated action or the purging of primitive action forms found within the organism. Either alternative offers a legitimate and testable possibility.

The Dynamic Theories

The dynamic theories of play do not attempt to understand why children play. They accept the fact of children's playing. The focus is on attempting to explain the *content* of the play of children. The two most elaborated dynamic theories of children's play are found in the works of Freud and Piaget.

PIAGETIAN THEORY.   Piaget viewed the development of the human intellect as involving two related processes of *assimilation* and *accommodation*. In the process of assimilation, the individual continually abstracts information from the outside world and fits that information into the organized schemes representing what he already knows. The individual also modifies these organizational schemes when they do not fit adequately with his developing knowledge. This latter process is called accommodation. Play, according to Piaget, is a way of taking the outside world and manipulating it so that it fits a person's present organizational schemes. As such, play serves a vital function in the child's developing intellect and remains, to some extent, always present in human behavior.

Piaget has defined three distinct stages in the development of play. The first is the sensorimotor stage of infancy based upon existing patterns of physical behavior. The second is a level of symbolic play. This represents the stage of dramatic play that we find in young children. The third stage is the stage of playing games that have rules, representing the play behavior of older children.

FREUDIAN THEORY. Freud considered play a cathartic activity allowing children to master difficult situations. The child can use the fantasy play situation to act out adult roles, providing him with a feeling of mastery in fantasy situations that allows him to cope with reality situations. The child can use play to act out personally painful occurrences and to master the pain by coming to grips with it in the fantasy of the play situation. This same mastery in fantasy can allow children to cope with the affective elements of more positive life situations as well. Lois Murphy, in her book, *The Widening World of Childhood*, presents some vivid descriptions of young children using play activities to cope with problems of living.[7] (Mead)

These dynamic theories of play, if properly understood and used, can provide us with an understanding of the power of play in human development that can be useful in designing educational programs that support development in children. Our concern as teachers needs to be with the content of play and how to move it in desired directions. From Freud we learn that the content of play has a strong affective tone. From Piaget we learn that play has a strong cognitive tone. Learning can be supported in both these domains. Play can also have an important socializing role, a third significant domain.

According to Mead, children use play as a way of developing their concept of *self*—what they are. They learn this by actually trying on the roles of those about them in the dramatic play of early childhood. The concept of the "generalized other," upon which mature socialization is built, develops in the next stage as children play games. The games are based upon rules, and require, for the child to perform properly, that he internalize the role behavior of others as well as his own in the game.[8]

A final note on the school and play may be derived from Lieberman's research. In her study of kindergarten children, she found a rela-

---

[7]Murphy, *Widening World of Childhood* (New York: Basic Books, 1962).
[8]George Herbert Mead, *Mind, Self and Society* (Chicago: University of Chicago Press, 1934), pp. 152–73.

tionship between playfulness in children's behavior and their divergent thinking ability, or creativity. This research suggests that it might be possible to use play activities to improve creativeness in children.[9]

EDUCATIONAL USES OF PLAY

The theories of play discussed here are descriptive theories; that is, they attempt to explain play as it exists, but provide no guide for action. Teachers are not interested as much in how children play in natural settings as in how to modify the child's play to achieve certain goals. An understanding of these theories can allow us to extrapolate guides for action which would be appropriate to use in teaching situations.

Play occurs in the lives of young children whenever they are able to be active and have some degree of freedom, whether alone or in a group. Evelyn Omwake has made the distinction between *spontaneous* and *structured* play activities for children.

> Spontaneous play by younger children is universal wherever children happen to be. It can develop in an empty basement, city dump, elaborately furnished living room, expensively landscaped lawn, or a nursery school especially arranged and equipped to invite and promote play. A unique feature of such spontaneous play is the subtle, frequently nonverbal communication among the players as to theme, the assignment of roles and the rules. While an adult may be needed as a stage hand, prompter, audience, or to make certain the cues are understood, the inspiration and ideas come from the children's own interests and experiences. Another characteristic of such play is the children's ability to endow whatever is at hand with the features and functions of the things they want it to represent . . .
>
> Although the organized setting in the nursery school provides opportunities for spontaneous play, its curriculum also features structured play suited to the educational needs of young children. These structured play activities are especially planned and presented with regard to the developmental capacities, interests and experiences of the group of children. At the same time such planning depends upon attention to the differing developmental rates of the individual children.
>
> The two forms of play can be differentiated by the degree and nature of adult participation. In this structured form, teachers decide the time and place and provide the materials to be used, establishing appropriate limits for their use.[10]

Omwake's distinction between structured and spontaneous play is a very attractive one. In analyzing the kinds of activity that would be

[9]Lieberman, "Playfulness and Divergent Thinking," pp. 219–24.

[10]Omwake, "The Child's Estate," in Albert J. Solnit and Sally A. Provence, eds., *Modern Perspectives in Child Development* (New York: International Universities Press, 1963), pp. 581–82.

labeled as *structured* or *spontaneous* play, however, we find that her distinction seems to be between dramatic play activities (activities in which a child assumes a role in a situation and plays it through) and all other activities that might be included in a nursery school or kindergarten curriculum. Dramatic play has been labeled spontaneous; all other activities are labeled structured play. Many activities that Omwake has labeled structured play may not be play at all, such as science projects or stories, while other play activities, such as block-building, might contain a high degree of spontaneity. In addition, dramatic play loses some of its spontaneity when it occurs in a school situation, for the teacher decides the time and place of such activity, provides the appropriate materials, and sets the limits. The guidance that a teacher provides limits the spontaneity of the play situation even further.

It may very well be that for the teacher, spontaneous and structured play are not too useful a pair of concepts.

A more productive distinction might be made between *educational* play and *noneducational* play. The difference between these two types of play is not in the activities or the degree of enjoyment that a child may receive, but rather in the purposes ascribed to the play by those persons responsible for the activities of the child. Educational play has as its prime purpose the child's learning. Such play will still be fun for the child, for without the prime personal satisfaction received, the activity stops being play. Educational play activities are supported, however, primarily because they serve an educational purpose rather than because of their personally satisfying qualities. Thus a child in the housekeeping area of a classroom is receiving personal satisfactions from playing out the particular role he has ascribed to himself, interacting with persons in other roles, and using various play properties in innovative ways. The value of this play is that it helps the child explore and understand role dimension and interaction patterns, thereby supporting his further understanding of the social world and helping him to build a realistic sense of *self*.

Educational play may take many forms. The key role of the teacher here is in taking the natural spontaneous play of children and modifying it so that it has educational value, as well as setting up less spontaneous educational play activities. Evaluation of such play must include not only the child's degree of involvement but the worth of these activities in achieving educational aims.

In most nursery school and kindergarten classrooms one can usually find four kinds of educational play: manipulative play, physical play, dramatic play, and games. Manipulative play involves the child's handling of relatively small pieces of equipment such as puzzles, Cuisenaire rods, or peg sets. The manipulations are relatively self-contained; that is, there is no necessary interaction between the manipulative activity and other kinds of activities, nor is there a dramatic element to the play. The goals of manipulative play activities are achievable directly through the child's handling of the material. The use of Montessori apparatus provides a good example of educational manipulative play. A child may be given a series of wooden cylinders and a case into which they fit. By comparing cylinders and attempting to fit them in the case, the child begins to learn to make size comparisons and to seriate. Manipulative play activities generally have fairly narrowly defined educational goals.

Physical play involves large actions of children, such as running, jumping, or riding a tricycle. The goals of these activities are to help children increase their physical skills or learn to use them in new situations. Physical play can have a dramatic component to it and teachers can elaborate the child's play activities either by making the physical activities more challenging or by providing social content to the play.

Dramatic play requires that the child assume and act out a role in relationship to other children playing their roles in informal dramatic situations which often represent true life experiences. The housekeeping area (or doll corner) is the most readily observable setting for play. In this area children act out the roles of family members in actions representing home situations. Other dramatic play situations may be set up by the teacher to enable the children to play through an infinite number of roles.

At times, rather than the child becoming the performer in the dramatic play situation, he manipulates things that represent the characters in the dramatic situation. Informal puppet play often allows him to act out a role through a puppet. Building with unit blocks can also allow children to be involved in miniature dramatizations if the teacher provides adequate properties, enough time for them to go beyond the manipulative building, and ideas as sources for dramatic themes.

Games are a form of play activity but of a different kind from those discussed above. They are highly structured play activities which include specific rules that must be followed. Often games have been excluded from early childhood activities because they were considered inappropriate for this age level. Actually children at the four- and five-year-old level are beginning to move into a stage where game playing is possible. Simple games or musical activity containing elements of games are quite appropriate for children. When games are played with young children, certain elements must be included if they are to be played successfully and if they are to be educational. They need to be taught the strategies of game playing (gamesmanship) and the teacher needs to be continually involved in guiding the game, for she is the only one mature enough to maintain the rules of the game and to help the children understand rule-appropriate behavior.

Although many educators accept play as a part of nursery school or kindergarten classroom activities, they are hesitant to recommend it as a part of the primary school program, with the exception of that play which is incorporated as part of the physical education program. Play, however, has equally valid uses with primary children as with children at lower educational levels. The "messing about" of the science program is a form of play, as are many of the newer materials-oriented programs in mathematics. Dramatic play is often a useful avenue of social studies education and a support for language learning. Appropriate play activities can be integrated in almost all areas of learning in the primary school.

Manipulative Play

It is helpful to set up a manipulative play center in the nursery or kindergarten class. In the primary grades, manipulative materials are generally organized along subject-matter lines. A manipulative play center may have materials placed on open shelves, so that they are readily accessible. A set of tables and chairs can also be included, but many of the materials can be just as easily used on the floor. A rug makes working these materials on the floor more comfortable. On the shelves can be placed the following materials:

PUZZLES. A wide range of jigsaw puzzles are presently available for children's use, including puzzles that have just three or four pieces, each representing a single item, and rather complex puzzles made of two or three dozen pieces. The "See-quee" puzzle, which contains a set of pictures that children put in sequence to represent a story, is another useful type of puzzle. Sturdy puzzles can be purchased which are made out of wood or masonite and can stand much use. It is a good idea to have a number of puzzles ranging in difficulty available for the children's use. If a puzzle rack is used for storage, the children can easily learn to take out and replace puzzles and to see that puzzles are complete when replaced. Such care can limit the number of puzzle pieces that get lost in a classroom. Marking the backs of all the pieces of each puzzle with a common symbol also helps to locate missing pieces. When losses do occur, teachers can often shape substitutes out of wood putty, painting it to match the rest of the puzzle.

It is helpful for the teacher to have the puzzles organized according to their order of difficulty and to check the children periodically to see how they have progressed in their ability to complete puzzles. Although most children have had some experience in working with puzzles prior to their entrance to school, some children have not learned the appropriate skills. Teachers should not take skills for granted, and a session or two at the beginning of the year explicitly teaching children the procedures of puzzle completion may be useful.

PARQUETRY BLOCKS AND PEGBOARDS.   Parquetry blocks with wooden pieces of varying shapes and colors and pegboard sets with pegs of different colors are useful materials for teaching form and color discrimination and retention. Many of the skills gained in the use of these materials can later be used for formal reading and mathematics instruction. Although children need opportunities to manipulate these materials freely, teachers can make model cards for the children to replicate with their manipulative materials. These cards can also be ordered from the simplest to the most complex and presented to children in their order of difficulty to support mastery. Pegboard sets can also be equipped with elastic bands with which the children can create various shapes.

CONSTRUCTIVE MATERIALS.   Small sets of constructive materials such as "Lego" or "Lincoln Logs" are useful additions to the manipulative play area. Children can either make fanciful creations or construct small buildings with these materials. A large variety of construction materials is available from manufacturers for this purpose.

SCIENCE MATERIALS.   Plastic boxes containing sets of science materials can be profitably included in the manipulative materials center. A battery, bulb, and a couple of lengths of wire could constitute one set. A magnet with some small bits of material, some of which is attracted to a magnet and some of which is not, could constitute another set. A plastic jar covered with a rubber membrane, half-filled with water, and containing a medicine dropper is another type of science material that could be included. A small basin of water and some materials that float and some that sink; a box full of materials that have different feels to them—all are examples of the wide range of manipulative materials that can be included for science exploration.

MATHEMATICS MATERIAL.   Cuisenaire rods, Stern Structured Mathematics Materials, simple measuring devices such as a balance, primary ruler, a set of measuring cups and spoons, and materials to be measured or counted can all be fruitfully incorporated into the manipulative materials center.

MONTESSORI MATERIALS.   Many of the Montessori didactic materials are ideally suited for the manipulative play center. They can generally be used independently by the children and are self-correcting in nature. Montessori materials that are included need not necessarily be used according to orthodox Montessori prescription.

OTHER MANIPULATIVE MATERIALS.   In addition to those materials listed above, many other manipulative materials should also be included in the center. A quick glance through an educational equipment supplier's catalogue can provide some ideas for this center. Teachers can think of other ideas as they rummage through their own homes or through hardware stores and see materials that can be purposefully included in the classroom. Often some of the most stimulating and exciting materials for educational purposes result from the teacher's ingenuity.

MANIPULATIVE PLAY WITH NATURAL MATERIALS. While generally not included in a manipulative materials center, play with natural materials such as sand and water is an important part of an early childhood program. Although specially designed sand and water tables are available commercially, a galvanized tub or a plastic wash basin can also be used. Children need to be given freedom in using these materials, but must also learn how to care for them and know the necessary limitations on their use. A number of accessory materials including containers, spoons, and shovels should be available with the water and sand. Sand that is wet can be molded in many shapes; dry sand can be sieved and run through funnels. Equipment for cleanup such as sponges, a floor brush, and dustpan should be readily available, and children should learn to use them.

Physical Play

Physical play generally requires the allotment of much more space than manipulative play. Much of the outdoor play of children in early childhood classes falls in the category of physical play.

OUTDOOR PLAY. The content of outdoor play depends as much upon the climate and weather conditions as upon space and other considerations. In some schools in the United States, the content of outdoor play consists mainly of sledding and building with snow during the bulk of the school year. In other areas of the country there are possibilities for free exploration and a wide use of materials, because the weather remains temperate during the school year. Teachers should vary the content of outdoor play with the possibilities created by local conditions.

Outdoor space should be available that is easily accessible to the classroom. There should be both soft- and hard-surfaced areas available for play. Storage space for equipment allows teachers to include a greater range of play in the outdoor space, but they can also bring classroom materials outdoors.

Outdoor play activities should include opportunities for climbing, running, jumping, riding on large pieces of equipment, and digging. Equipment provided for the children should support these activities. Many school yards contain either no equipment at all or just the stereotyped slides, swings, and jungle gyms. These severely limit the range of children's play activities and should be supplemented or replaced by many other kinds of materials. Recent concern with playgrounds for young children has brought about the design of many more exciting pieces of equipment to support creative physical activities and social interaction in outdoor play. Some of these may be permanently installed and require little maintenance. (*Playscapes* are an example of a more stimulating approach to the equipping of outdoor play areas.) In addition to permanent structures, other equipment should also be available. These include:

> Sand pit for children's digging
> Play houses and platforms
> Wheel toys, including tricycles, wagons, wheel barrows, and boxes on casters
> Movable equipment for climbing, such as saw horses, walking boards, barrels, packing crates, and ladders
> Balls and jump ropes to be used for games

INDOOR PLAY. Many of the same physical play activities that are offered to children outdoors can be provided indoors as well. Sometimes the activities need to be scaled down, for the extent of physical play indoors is determined by the amount of space available. In some schools a multipurpose room is available for the children to use for more vigorous play, especially on days when inclement weather keeps children inside. In other situations, classes are limited to their own rooms. In any event, some physical play can take place indoors.

Teachers are often able to include some climbing apparatus in their classrooms. Combining boards, sawhorses, and ladders into rather elaborate exciting edifaces which require relatively little storage space can be fun for the children. Wheel toys can also be provided indoors for younger children, but these should be smaller than the ones used outdoors and could include sturdy wooden trucks or variplay boxes rather than tricycles and wagons. In many cases schools have built playhouses with elevated platforms, ladders, staircases, slides, and other artifacts into small spaces in a classroom.

BLOCK PLAY. Falling somewhere between the categories of physical play and dramatic play is block play. Basically two kinds of blocks are used in early childhood education; the smaller *unit blocks*, which allow the child to miniaturize his world, and the larger hollow blocks, or comparable variations on the Patty Hill blocks, which allow the children to build large structures suitable as stages for dramatic play.

Pratt and Stanton describe children going out into the neighborhood of the school and returning to symbolize their perceptions of the neighborhood in block structures.[11] Mitchell,[12] and Robison and Spodek[13] provide examples of blocks being used to further the geographic understanding of young children.

If blocks are to be used effectively, teachers must provide a large number of them as well as adequate space for block-building. In addition, it is helpful if children can work on a block structure for longer than a single period or a single day, for as block buildings are used by the children they are often further elaborated.

Mont. disagree.

Dramatic Play

Dramatic play is most often seen in the housekeeping areas of nursery schools and kindergartens. The children assume various adult roles in their play, which unfolds with a great deal of spontaneity. In these situations the children are generally acting out roles as they are perceived and understood by them, although often elements of fantasy can move the play far from reality.

The classroom teacher, in setting up an attractive housekeeping area, stimulates the role playing of the children. The materials used reflect the home life of a family and little else, the ensuing play generally remains in the realm of family play. The total world of the adult's life is the legitimate scope of school play situations. This includes the world of work as well as the world of family living.

For a play situation to be educationally useful the teacher needs to guide it. This guidance does not require the teacher's interference in the play actions of the children. It does, however, require an awareness of and sensitivity to the children's play activities, a sense of what the teacher hopes the children will derive from the play, and an ability to move into the children's play on occasion, make suggestions, even become a player if that can be done without distorting the children's play.

Most important, the teacher's responsibility is to provide the information that will move the play ahead; the reading of books or the showing of films and filmstrips often provides this information. The use of discussions, the availability of resource persons, and the taking of trips are all legitimate ways of feeding new information to the play activities of children, allowing their school activities to shuttle between fantasy and reality in a wholesome way.

[11]Caroline Pratt and Jessie Stanton, *Before Books* (New York: Adelphi Co., 1926).

[12]Mitchell, *Young Geographers.*

[13]Helen F. Robison and Bernard Spodek, *New Directions in the Kindergarten* (New York: Teachers College Press, 1965).

Games

A wide range of games can be used in early childhood classes. Some games are oriented only toward physical movement; others require little movement but a great deal of attention to problem solving. Different games can be used for different purposes.

In the nursery school and kindergarten years, games should be rather simple, with uncomplicated rules. Games at this level can include activities accompanied by singing as well as simple physical games in which children must follow a few directions. Lotto and other table games also have a place at this level. As the children move into the primary grades, more complicated physical activities requiring strict adherence to rules can be incorporated into the school day as well as many of the traditional games of childhood. In the classroom, teachers can use games to provide practice opportunities in the academic areas. Games such as these are often suggested in the teacher's manuals of textbook series as well as in teacher-oriented magazines such as *Instructor* or *Grade Teacher*. Board games can also be incorporated into portions of the school day. Those games requiring evolving strategies and planning before making moves, such as checkers, can help children develop thinking skills.

Although some games require specific equipment or sets of materials, a large number of games require little besides direct instructions from the teacher and her supervision of the game. Often a small piece of chalk or a ball is all that is needed to keep children involved in playing a game for a long period of time.

GUIDING EDUCATIONAL PLAY

Most discussions of play necessarily focus primarily on the activities of the children themselves. Earlier in this chapter, however, the concept of educational play was presented. If play is to be educational, the teacher has a prime role in setting the stage for play, in guiding its direction, and in modifying it. She must be aware of this important role and of the way she can facilitate the extension of educational play. Preparation for educational play and careful planning are necessary, as is providing guidance during the children's active play.

Planning for Educational Play

Although extremely satisfying play can erupt spontaneously in almost any class, the chances of fruitful play activities occurring is greatly increased with adequate preparation. The teacher must be aware of topics for play—topics that are of interest to the children and have within them the possibility for rich educational experience. Play activities revolving around various social roles can help children explore the functions of these roles and their limitations. Store play can help children understand economic principles. Block play can help them become aware of geographic relationships in their community. Play at being a builder can provide them with practice in measurement skills.

In planning for play the teacher should first assess the learning potential of the play activity. A search for resources to help children gain information about the play activity may then follow. The teacher may look for informational books on the topic. Films, filmstrips, and recordings may also be found. Picture files can provide children with graphic information on a topic. A search of the community might help to identify field trip possibilities or resource persons who can be brought into the classroom. A phone call to a museum or educational resource center may bring the promise of dioramas or other resource materials that can be loaned to the classroom.

Not all the resources a teacher identifies will be used in the classroom, and the teacher will certainly not introduce everything that has been collected at one time to the children. But a careful search will allow her to deliberately choose those materials that can provide enough information to stimulate the play and to carry it forward over time. In planning, the teacher should also identify the play materials that will be used by the children. Articles of clothing to be used in dramatic play, manipulative materials, and raw materials to allow the children to create their own props should all be collected before the play activities start. Many of these things can be used from year to year by different classes, so teachers often develop extensive collections of play materials over time.

The teacher should also think through the strategies that can be used for stimulating play, and the goals of the play activities that ought to be achieved. An understanding of these goals can provide her with guidelines for the constant evaluation and guidance of the play activities.

Initiating Play Activities

Simply setting out new materials in the classroom is often enough to start the children's play. If new materials are introduced into a situation in which children are offered choices, the teacher might initiate new play activities in two areas at the same time. This will keep the whole class from focusing on just one exciting area and will allow small group play to develop without undue coercion.

The introduction of new materials and equipment frequently requires a certain amount of direction. Teachers may want to talk with their students about how the materials are used and what limitations are to be placed upon their use. A short meeting prior to the introduction of the materials can prevent problems from occurring later.

In generating play activities, the teacher can look for ways to stimulate the imagination of children. Dramatic play activities are often initiated through a field trip, the showing of a film, or the reading of a book related to the topic of play. This initial infusion of information gives the children ideas for the use of materials that are being provided and will also suggest themes for play.

Role of the Adult

Guiding the Play of Children

Insuring the educational significance of any play activity requires that the teacher be actively concerned with the play. While this does not require her to hover over the children's activities at all times, it does suggest that she should not conceive of the children's play periods as the time for the completion of records or a personal withdrawal from the classroom. Teachers should be aware of the processes of play that unfold and should use the cues they get from their observations as the basis for supporting or modifying the play.

The teacher may guide the play of children by modifying the play situation. In dramatic play this might mean either adding new materials or withdrawing some materials when their use no longer seems productive. In manipulative play this might mean terminating one form of play and suggesting another. The teacher may also modify the situation by doing some social engineering; children left out of the play situation might be eased in by the suggestion of important roles for them, or simply by modifying the play situation to include them. Children who are disruptive might also be eased out of the play situation. At times teachers might want to determine the membership in play groups of the children in order to support specific social learnings. They might also use a play situation for what Omwake has called "play tutoring."

The infusion of more knowledge helps guide children's play activities. Observing the play of the children sometimes shows the teacher that they lack some necessary information or are operating under certain misconceptions. The provision of information by telling, by reading information books, or by looking things up in resource books can effectively clear up the children's confusions. Sometimes a field trip or the visit of a resource person also provides significant information that will modify the play.

There are occasions when the teacher becomes a player, actively involved in the play activities of children for varying periods of time. She may have to remain an active participant in the games introduced in early childhood classes. This can allow her to modify the direction of the play by introducing new elements to the play situation. It can also limit disruptive behavior that may be occurring. The teacher can also provide a role model for the play of the children. She can ask clarifying questions in this way that will allow for a greater understanding of the content of the play and the meanings of certain behaviors. In becoming an active player in dramatic play situations, care must be taken not to distort the play of the children and to leave them ultimately in command of the play situations, otherwise the teacher's involvement becomes a disruption and the play activities may terminate.

Evaluating Educational Play

Although teacher guidance is an important element in the play activities of the school, teachers need to be careful about the degree to which they impose on the play. It is easy to distort the play of children, taking it out of their hands entirely and subjugating it to the extent that it looses its spontaneity and is no longer personally satisfying. Play must continue to be *play* in school even as we use it to achieve educational objectives. It must remain the property of the children who have a role in instigating it, in determining its direction, and in terminating it at any time. And, most important, the element of playfulness should never be relinquished.

SUGGESTED READING

AARON, D., AND BONNIE P. WINAWER, *Child's Play: A Creative Approach to Play Spaces for Today's Children.* New York: Harper and Row, 1965.

ALMY, M., "Spontaneous Play: An Avenue for Intellectual Development," *Young Children,* Vol. 22 (May 1967), 264–77.

BALDWIN, A. L., "A is Happy—B is Not," *Child Development,* Vol. 36 (September 1965), 583–600.

BIBER, BARBARA, *Play as a Growth Process.* New York: Bank Street College of Education, 1959.

ERICKSON, E. H., *Childhood and Society.* New York: Norton, 1950.

FRANK, L., "Play in Personality Development," *Journal of Orthopsychiatry,* Vol. 25 (1955), 576–90.

GILMORE, J. BARNARD, "Play: A Special Behavior," in R. H. Haber, ed., *Current Research in Motivation.* New York: Holt, Rinehart & Winston, 1965, pp. 343–55.

HARTLEY, RUTH E., AND R. M. GOLDENSON, *The Complete Book of Children's Play.* New York: Crowell, 1957.

LIEBERMAN, J. NINA, "Playfulness and Divergent Thinking," *Journal of Genetic Psychology,* Vol. 107, No. 2 (December 1965), 219–24.

MATTERSON, E. M., *Play and Playthings for the Preschool Child*. Baltimore: Penguin Books, 1965.

MEAD, GEORGE H., *Mind, Self and Society*. Chicago: University of Chicago Press, 1934.

MILLER, SUSANNA, *The Psychology of Play*. Baltimore: Penguin Books, 1968.

MITCHELL, E. D., AND B. S. MASON, *The Theory of Play*, rev. ed. New York: A. S. Barnes, 1934.

MURPHY, LOIS, *The Widening World of Childhood*. New York: Basic Books, 1962.

OMWAKE, EVELYN B., "The Child's Estate," in Albert J. Solnit and Sally A. Provence, eds., *Modern Perspectives in Child Development*. New York: International Universities Press, 1963.

PIAGET, J., *Play, Dreams, and Imitation in Childhood*. 1945 reprint. London: William Heinemann Ltd., 1951.

SUTTON-SMITH, B., "Role of Play in Cognitive Development," *Young Children*. Vol. 22 (September 1967), 360–70.

WHITE, R. W., "Motivation Reconsidered: The Concept of Competence," *Psychological Review*, Vol. 66, No. 5 (September 1959), 297–333.

11

Organizing for Instruction

Teachers generally conceive of the content of schooling as the formal curriculum. But all the goals of early childhood education cannot be achieved through a specific set of activities that can be offered in a single time period each week. The goals are also reflected in the way the teacher organizes the class to provide opportunities for developing autonomy, trust, and competence in dealing with the surrounding world. This becomes the unwritten curriculum of the school.

In the early years, the child's autonomy is a goal rather than an established fact. We wish the children to become independent, knowing full well that they will continue to be dependent upon the adults in their surroundings well beyond the primary grades. The development of autonomy is important and is nurtured by teaching children to assume responsibility while still providing them with the security and needed guidance of a knowledgeable adult.

Teachers should give much thought to the activities they provide their children. Both long-range and short-range planning are important. Long-range planning helps the teacher organize classroom activities so that they accumulate in such a way as to help the children achieve their educational goals. Short-range planning is required for anticipating the many details of day-to-day teaching. Objectives of this type of planning are less extensive and some of them may be defined in terms of observable behavior. As a result of her planning, the teacher needs to organize her day into some form of activity schedule, deploy the children into manageable groups, and organize her room so that children can make the best use of space, materials, and equipment.

The teacher should begin her planning to help the child function adequately, even before he enters school, thus creating a smooth transition from home to school. The organization of activities and lessons should be planned in a way that will provide children with opportunities to grow in responsibility and autonomy; and each child must be known in terms of what specific learning opportunities he is ready for. The child must be helped in learning to use resources for learning both in the school and outside its domain. Finally, the teacher must provide opportunities for every child to learn to become a member of the classroom group, learning to use the group and respond to it without having his wishes submerged by it. The child also needs to learn to develop greater self-control and ways of dealing appropriately with his own needs and feelings.

PLANNING   Although there are wide differences of opinion as to the most effective type of planning, most educators agree that a certain amount of preliminary activity should take place before the teacher engages the children in a program.

There is no way to evaluate the effectiveness of a program unless there are goals, the achievement of which can be assessed. There are also certain predictable elements in programs that can be anticipated through the year. Though it is possible to purchase fully completed lesson plans which include all the activities, songs, games, and finger-plays for each day of the entire school year, this is not the most effective type of long-range planning for early childhood education, for it cannot take into consideration the learning needs and styles of individual children.

Long-range Planning

Effective long-range planning is vital in a program that is aimed at achieving any sort of large-scale goals. Without planning a teacher is apt to simply pile experience upon experience without any thought as to how the experiences relate to one another. The teacher's motivating factor becomes "how to interest the children and keep them busy for a morning." Long-range plans attempt to identify threads that will tie the various elements of the program together throughout the year. These can be conceptual schemes that the teacher wishes to introduce to the children or specific skills and traits she wishes to foster. She must then decide the degree to which she expects each child to achieve these goals.

Long-range plans are also necessary to achieve flexibility. As the children move through the program, the teacher, out of a greater awareness of the children, must make modifications in her plans to insure that the program is continually appropriate. Without prior thought and preparation day-to-day learning activities are necessarily limited.

Only the teacher knows the particular background of the group of children assigned to her. No textbook author or curriculum development specialist has that personal knowledge of the clients for whom the program is developed. Only the teacher, knowing the children—their strengths and weaknesses, their backgrounds, and the school environment—can modify the program, tailoring it to fit her group of children. She may be aware of weaknesses in the language backgrounds of the children and may wish to develop some special language experiences for them or order additional material. She may be aware of places in the neighborhood that would provide fruitful field trips for the children in relation to a planned unit.

Program planning needs to be flexible enough to be modified on the basis of children's spontaneous requests. The teacher may also wish to use her own developing interests and skills as her ideas change through reading books, listening to lectures, or rethinking her own educational approach.

The identification of plans for the year, however, allows the teacher to think through her program in advance and to gather the necessary resources to carry it through. Films and filmstrips may have to be ordered in advance. Trips need advance planning. The ordering of new books or supplies often takes time. It is always easier to cancel a trip or postpone a visit, or even to decide not to use a film, than to want to carry out an activity and find schedules filled or materials not available.

Short-range Planning

Teachers must organize for classroom work on a daily, weekly, or periodic basis as well as on a yearly basis. This planning includes the determination of what resources will be necessary for particular learning situations. The procurement and allocation of resources must follow. It is necessary to think ahead so that the tape recorder is available when needed, so that there are enough copies of a worksheet available, or so that a particular parent can visit the class to speak about his hobby at the proper critical moment.

Too often teachers' language goals seem to have little relationship to short-term plans. The day-to-day activities designed by teachers should be conceived of as the mediating element between the present, often pressing needs of the day and long-range plans. Although the pressures of running a class must be considered by the teacher in her planning, activities should not be designed simply as a way of coping with administrative necessity.

The daily balance of the program and the relationships that can be established among diverse subject areas should be considered in short-term planning. It is helpful for the teacher to look at the ways in which different areas of the curriculum can be related to one another. Children can write sentence stories that correspond to number facts or that tell about measuring experiences, thus integrating mathematics with language activities. Stories read in a book can be acted out in pantomime or with puppets. Science experiences often require quantification. The possible ways of relating learning areas to one another are endless. Each allows the teacher to extend the child's experience beyond the obvious.

Many school systems expect teachers to file weekly lesson plans. These weekly plans are supposed to aid the teacher in organizing her teaching in advance and in relating the instructional program from day to day. Weekly plans usually allow the teacher to develop a progression of learnings so that what a child is taught on one day is related to and may grow out of the experiences of the previous day. While there are differences of opinion about the specificity with which plans should be made and goals established, goals are necessary. Some educators suggest that each detail in an instructional program should be worked out in advance with ample opportunities provided for gathering information about its impact on the children.

Though it may be fashionable to talk about teaching in terms of specific learning objectives, the concern of early childhood educators has been more one of trying to get children involved in a broad general range of activities. If the activities presented are varied enough and if children can differentiate their own roles in each activity, then they will somehow find areas of the program that are related to individual needs and that will help them grow. The element of self-selection within carefully prepared alternatives is an exceedingly important part of education. Adequate planning can insure the availability of legitimate learning alternatives. This also suggests that the goals of the program need to be different for each child and cannot always be identified far in advance.

Developing Activities

The unit of instruction in the nursery school and kindergarten is the *activity*. Unlike the *lesson*, which is the unit of instruction in the elementary school, the activity need not have a formal beginning, middle, and end. In fact, activities are often open-ended, coming to no neatly packaged conclusion, but possibly beginning again at some later time. The activity is not teacher-dominated. The teacher may plan the activity and make materials available, provide time and even influence its direction, but it is the children who carry the activity forward and in the final analysis determine its content. Each activity may be conceived as a solitary unit having no relationship to any other activity, or it may more often be conceived more broadly with a series of activities being interrelated. One can have block construction, music, and story activities that are related to a single theme on the same day, or one can have a series of activities that continue from day to day in which each is an elaboration of the last one. Activities may be organized into units or planned so that basic concepts and ideas recur in some cyclical fashion.

The teacher should plan her program to support a broad range of activities. In order to do this, she must organize each session so that children are involved in different areas of the curriculum. She must also organize her room so that each activity has the necessary space, materials, and equipment available when needed, and so that several activities can take place simultaneously without interfering with one another.

The Feedback Loop

The discussion of planning has referred often to the need for flexibility and modificaton. This need cannot be overstressed, for an effective program is one that is sensitive to the children and can change when necessary. The teacher must be aware of the effectiveness of the program and the consequences of the activities she is developing with the children. This requires a periodic check on what the children are learning—the equivalent of quizzes or examinations given in more advanced classes.

The development of electronic devices has led to the establishment of a different model for monitoring outcomes. In electronics we often hear the term "feedback." A device that emits a signal may have a portion of that signal sent back into it so that it can constantly correct itself and maintain its own effectiveness. Translating this into the classroom suggests that, rather than provide for periodic checks, the teacher should seek ways of continually analyzing the activities of the classroom and modifying the program toward the goals she has set. This requires that she deliberately set aside time on a regular basis for classroom observation. By observing ongoing behavior, she should be able to make appropriate judgements about what is happening in her class and to continue following through on her plans or to modify them. The continued nature of this information seeking is vital for effective teaching. Some of the methods that can be used for gathering information are discussed later.

**DEPLOYING CHILDREN
TO ACHIEVE
EDUCATIONAL GOALS**
The placing of fifteen, twenty, or more children of like age into a single room for many hours each day creates many problems. There is a constant conflict between the needs of the individual and the group. That we consider teaching children in groups rather than individually suggests that we are more

concerned with conformity than with individuality, for to a great extent the tyranny of the group when coupled with the goal-directedness of the teacher tends to support conforming behavior.

We expect young children to give up their natural rhythm of daily activity when they enter school. We demand that they all come to school at the same time, sit in place for the same period of time, take care of bodily functions at prescribed periods, eat and play together at specific periods of the day, and learn at the same pace. We expect all children to conform to an appropriate model of school behavior irrespective of their earlier patterns of behavior or the particular expectations of that outside world to which they belong. Some degree of conformity is necessary for a child to get on in the world and is to some extent a form of acculturation, but how *much* conformity is really necessary is an open question.

Many educators have been aware of the inherent conflict between the individual and the group in school and have looked for ways to lessen it. Some children learn faster than others and are more competent in certain areas of learning. Children have different styles, different interests, and need different kinds of learning supports. To ignore these differences and to gear all teaching and classroom practices to the middle of the range of differences, expecting the other children to somehow accommodate, limits children and punishes them for being different. Many techniques have been used to cope with this conflict that grows out of individual differences.

One way of dealing with this problem is to provide a broad range in the choice of activities offered to children. A good portion of the day may be assigned to an indoor or outdoor "activity" period during which children may select from structured or unstructured tasks and may change tasks at will. Only during a relatively short period of the day are they required to be with the group—for "routine" activities, such as snacks or rest, or for large group instructional activities like music, story telling, or discussion times.

Too few early childhood classes provide an adequate range of choice. Conformity to group activity and a lessening of the range of learning opportunities available too often characterize these classes. In many classrooms, the range of activities available may even be totally nonexistent. The child's continued assignment to prescribed activities may heighten the conflict between group and individual.

Homogeneous Grouping

One way that some educators have proposed to lessen the conflict is to assign children to classes so that the range of differences within each class is narrowed. Traditionally, the criterion used for assigning children has been academic achievement; often it has been reading performance alone. Although such classes might be more comfortable for teachers who wish to work only with the total class, they present certain problems for the children involved. For one thing, narrowing the range of differences in one area of behavior may have no effect on the range of differences in other areas of behavior or performance. The conflict between the group and the individual still exists. In addition, the placement of a child in a homogeneously grouped classroom creates an expectation of performance for that child that may become a self-fulfilling prophecy. Putting a child into a slow group (and the children know which groups are considered slow no matter how teachers attempt to camouflage the fact) often leads the child to perform according to what is expected of that group. This is probably the least satisfactory way of grouping children. Other alternatives accept difference within groups of children and try to organize resources to deal with these differences.

Team Teaching

One way of dealing with differences is to use an instructional team rather than a single individual teacher in a classroom. Nursery classes that use a head and an assistant teacher in each classroom represent one example of a team. A team may be created in a kindergarten or primary classroom by adding a teaching aide—this allows two individuals to work together and facilitates splitting the classroom in various ways, so that adult attention can be provided to several individuals or groups of children at all times.

A more extensive team can be created by merging classes of children into larger instructional units, allowing the resources of the school to be deployed more flexibly. Some activities require little teacher supervision and a teacher might have responsibility for more children than would normally be found in a self-contained classroom during these activities. Other learning situations might be better organized as small group activities, independent activities, or as conferences. Members of a teaching team have greater freedom to work with individuals and small groups.

A larger instructional unit can also make good use of diversified team members, because all teachers do not have to be equivalent in competency or responsibility. A master teacher may be better used in a self-contained classroom, and fledgling teachers thus have opportunities to learn from others without having the total responsibility for teaching a class placed on their shoulders. Part-time teachers can also be incorporated into the team and additional skills, technical or clerical, might be included. Teaming eliminates the problem of teacher isolation, for each teacher constantly interacts with other teachers rather than always working alone. A team organization may require a different type of physical facility than the "egg carton" school one generally finds if it is to be optimally effective.

In creating a large instructional unit, care must be taken that the unit does not become so large as to overwhelm the child. Especially with young children there is the danger of creating a mass in which strong relational bonds between adult and child as well as between child and child are submerged. Large groups also tend to be handled in a more bureaucratic fashion than small groups. Although there is no reliable knowledge upon which it is possible to make judgment about the optimal size of a group, there are guidelines that some school systems and licensing agencies have established. These judgments should be made in relation to educational goals, facilities available, teacher competency, and basic conceptions of education, in addition to the absolute number and ages of children involved.[1]

Instructional Grouping

One way of dealing with individual differences that is probably used most often at the primary level is the practice of grouping children for instruction. The organization of a classroom into three reading groups, each representing a limited range of performance levels, is typical. The groups can be organized by the teacher on the basis of formal or informal tests and children may be moved from one group to another as the year progresses. The teacher can work with one group at a time, listening to children read, holding phonics lessons, or engaging the students in other tasks. While the teacher is working with one group, other children are generally engaged in prescribed seatwork activity. In the self-contained class as it most often exists, grouping for instruction usually carries with it the requirement that some children are engaged in activities requiring no teacher attention; thus constructive seatwork should be designed to keep the children busy. Using a team approach or individualizing instruction limits the amount of occupational seatwork needed, since more than one instructional group can be dealt with at one time.

Individualized Instruction

Another way of dealing with the range of differences found in a classroom is to provide a high degree of individualization within the

---

[1]For a discussion of differentiated staffing patterns see Bernard Spodek, "Staffing Patterns in Early Childhood Education," in *Early Childhood Education*, 71st Yearbook of the National Society for the Study of Education. Chicago: University of Chicago Press, 1972 (in press).

instructional tasks. This may be done by keeping the goals of education constant but allowing children to move through the same instructional tasks at different paces. The Individually Prescribed Instruction (IPI) program fits into this model. Work is broken down into small steps and children are given individual instructional tasks based on diagnostic tests. The children complete work sheets, are tested, and upon evidence of successful attainment move on to the next set of instructional tasks. All children move through the same series of tasks, but at their own pace. Opportunities are provided for children to skip over sets of instructional tasks if they evidence competence in the area.

IPI uses the model of programmed instruction in its attempt to individualize instruction. Only the pace of instruction is individualized. An activity-oriented class may individualize other aspects of instruction. Children are placed in a setting more like a workshop than a classroom and allowed to pursue different enterprises based upon the teacher's judgment as to the most productive activity for individuals. Goals are different for each child, as are the means used to attain the goals. Children can also be given greater opportunities to feed their interests into the classroom situation or to vary the ways in which they could achieve similar goals, thus changing the program planned by the teacher.

The Nongraded School

One way of dealing with individual differences in the classroom suggested by many educators is to do away with the age-grade organization of the school. Rather than limit the range of differences in any one classroom, this solution might increase it; this forces the teacher to look for new solutions to the problems. Teachers cannot possibly have the same expectations for all children when the children in a classroom vary greatly in age or developmental level. In addition, less formal methods of instruction are possible and higher degrees of individualization may be obtained. Children can help one another and teach one another as well. Age-grade expectations are lessened and the children's own performance capabilities become the basis for judgments about programs.

Nongrading (or developing inter-age groupings), like any other administrative-organizational scheme, only presents the possibility for increasing the individualization of instruction in the classroom, partially by breaking down barriers created by tradition. It is what teachers and administrators do with the potential provided by an organizational structure that becomes crucial for supporting children's learning. In some cases, nongrading has meant merely substituting one criterion for grouping (age), for another criterion (possibly reading achievement) with no real change in classroom practice. This is an unfortunate distortion of the principle.

In the nongraded approach, the range of individual differences in the classroom is viewed as an asset rather than a liability. If children are viewed as learning resources, then increasing the range of children in a school unit can increase the range of learning resources available to each child.

Although each of these methods of dealing with individual differences has been described independently, each can be combined with any number of others to improve the match of instruction to children. A nongraded framework can exist in which children are grouped for instruction, or in which there is an individualized instructional program. It can be organized in a self-contained classroom or can be part of a team teaching approach.

In order to achieve maximum effectiveness, each arrangement of groups requires a different way of thinking through the organization of the classroom. The layout of the physical facilities can enhance small group activities or it can thwart their operation. The availability of materials and equipment is also a concern. One does not need a full set of textbooks when teaching in an individualized program. On the other hand, a greater *variety* of materials and equipment must be available and the equipment must be such that it can be used independently by the children.

SCHEDULING   A daily schedule allocates time for activities each day. Children learn to anticipate future events because of a regularity of daily occurrences. In the nursery school and kindergarten, allotments are made for different activities. Classroom learning may be organized into subject lessons in the primary grades.

The following are typical schedules in early childhood classes. The schedule described for the nursery school and kindergarten is for mornings only, since these are typically half-day programs.

8:15–8:45 A.M.—Teacher planning and preparation.

8:45–9:00 A.M.—Arrival. The children may enter the classroom at various intervals during a prescribed arrival time, rather than be expected to arrive en masse on signal. Spaced entry allows the teacher to greet each child individually and provides the children with an opportunity to make the transition from home to school a gradual one. During the arrival period, they browse through books or work with manipulative materials. They might also be able to view displays the teacher has placed on the bulletin board or science table.

9:00–9:20 A.M.—Group time. The teacher may sit with the entire group to plan the day. She may describe the activities that will be available and take care of necessary routines such as attendance. Group time may also allow for discussions on a variety of topics. At the beginning of the year, a sharing or show-and-tell period might be appropriate if the children do not take the initiative in discussions. Once skills in group discussions are developed, the formal show-and-tell might be dispensed with.

9:20–10:10 A.M.—Activity period.   During this period, the children are given a choice of activities and may change activities at any time during the period. Many of the children may be working independent of the teacher, individually or in small groups. The teacher may work with a single child or a small group or she may supervise the entire room. Included in the activities offered may be an arts and crafts activity, some opportunity for dramatic play, and other activities planned by the teacher. Some children may be working with manipulative materials. Others might be working at a sand table or a water basin, or be involved in a planned science experience. The total range of activity will be under the guidance of the teacher even though she may not be directly supervising each child.

10:10–10:30 A.M.—Cleanup, snack, and rest.   After an activity period children need to clean their rooms and put away the materials they have been using. Often young children need an assigned time for going to the bathroom and washing up. Skills in this area may also have to be learned. Milk or fruit juice and crackers may be provided as a snack. Under the guidance of a competent teacher, this period can provide productive learning opportunities. Informal discussions can be stimulated, new food can be tasted, responsibilities and skills can be learned, and children can become aware of the characteristics and functions of the things used. A period of sedentary activity, such as listening to a story or record might be substituted for a formal rest period as more relaxing.

10:30–11:00 A.M.—Music and story time.   A period of time is usually set aside for activities involving the entire class. This might be group singing or rhythmic activities that allow the children to explore music as well as explore the use of their own body for creative expression. Teachers can read from picture books or tell stories. Children should also be encouraged to tell their own stories at this time.

11:00–11:20 A.M.—Outdoor activity time.   During this period children can be encouraged to climb, run, jump, and use wheel toys and large pieces of equipment. Sand and water play can also be included. The amount of time spent outdoors will probably vary with the climate and the opportunities children have to use the outdoors productively at home. When outdoor equipment is not available, teachers can plan games that involve some of the same physical activities.

11:20–11:40 A.M.—Preparation for dismissal and dismissal.   If possible, it is advisable to have children leave informally in the same manner they arrived. The children need time to get ready and collect their things before departing for home. If parents are expected to pick their children up, this time provides an excellent opportunity for mini-conferences and informal chats about the children.

11:40–noon—Teacher cleanup period.   At the end of the morning, the teacher needs time to reorder herself and her room and take care of records before preparing for the next group.

This schedule sketchily describes a typical day in a nursery school or kindergarten. Each day will vary from this schedule, of course, as teachers modify their programs to meet the learning needs of their class or to carry on special projects.

The large blocks of time in which activities are organized and the range of alternatives available for the children during the activity periods support a degree of individuality and allow for a variety of outcomes to be planned for different children.

Flexibility is necessary in any schedule that is developed by the teacher. It may happen that on one day conversations with children will stretch to forty-five minutes, while only twenty minutes have been scheduled. On other days, five minutes may seem too long. A teacher might wish to devote a whole day to a craft project and simply not include a story or music activity. Balance needs to be considered over a long time. There is no need to have children involved in every area of the school curriculum on every day.

A typical schedule in the primary grades may look like this:

8:40–9:00 A.M.—Opening exercises.   As the children arrive in the classroom, they will gather together for a range of total class activities including caretaking routines and other learning opportunities. At this time, attendance checks are often taken, lunch counts made, and the like. Discussions relating to the calendar and to current weather conditions may be held. Special events are noted and opportunities for discussion provided. Often the teacher will also use this time to review the plans for the day with the children.

9:00–10:15 A.M.—Reading instruction.   Children may be grouped by achievement criteria for reading instruction. The teacher may work directly with one group of children while the other groups are working independently on assigned tasks related to reading.

10:15–10:30 A.M.—Recess.   The children will be provided with a short period of free, supervised play in an outdoor area.

10:30–11:15 A.M.—Continuation of reading program as before.

11:15–11:45 A.M.—Arithmetic.   During this period, arithmetic instruction is provided. Grouping may not be practiced in primary grades for teaching arithmetic and the whole class may be involved in the lesson.

11:45–noon—Preparation for lunch.   Children will be given opportunities to clean up their room, go to the bathroom, and wash in preparation for lunch period. A teacher will often have available a core of short stories, poems, songs, and games that can be used to fill the time between the end of the learning activities and the sounding of the dismissal bell.

Noon–1:00 P.M.—Lunch.

1:00–1:30 P.M.—Language arts and writing.   This period of time may be devoted to lessons in penmanship, spelling, and the mechanics of writing, or may be used by children to write or read stories.

1:30–2:00 P.M.—Music and physical education.   Many subjects are not taught each day. Teachers often alternate subjects such as music and physical education, which may be taught by specialists who take over the class. Using specialists can free the classroom teacher during the day, providing her with time for preparation of materials, for planning, or for discretionary use. The provision of free time during the day through the use of auxiliary teachers is becoming more common today.

2:00–2:30 P.M.—Health and science.   Activities related to teaching of science or of proper health practices may be provided here.

2:30–3:00 P.M.—Social studies and art. This might also be an alter. period. On some days, social studies discussions or unit work might be scheduled while on other days the time could be devoted to work with an art media.

3:00–3:10 P.M.—Cleanup and preparation for dismissal. In many classes, the teacher has a culminating discussion at the end of the day that allows the children to review the day's work. In addition, cleanup is done, and announcements and materials to be taken home may be distributed at this time. Children may also be given an opportunity to plan for the next day, so that future activities can be anticipated.

Such a schedule is based upon certain assumptions, however, which may not be accepted by all educators. One assumption is that the content of the primary school is best taught when segregated into separate subjects. Another assumption is that all children should be involved in learning a subject at the same time. A third is that instruction ought to occur in a group setting.

An alternative to scheduling the day in the primary grades with periods reflecting separate school subjects would be to use some variation of the *integrated day* described earlier. If a teacher is concerned with individualizing instruction and developing autonomy in her children, she can plan so that many program strands are operating at the same time and children can move from one curriculum area to another at their own pace. Such an organization would limit the amount of waiting that children do in class, because they could make optimal use of their school time in individual learning opportunities. Such organization could also be an aid to integrating school subject matter, for artificial time barriers could be lessened considerably or done away with entirely.

Although teachers who have not organized their class into an integrated day might be concerned about providing children with so much unstructured time, much of the success of this type of scheduling rests on her preparing the children to function autonomously in the classroom. This often requires the planning of special activities to help children develop skills of independent learning. Some teachers may prefer to retain a structured portion of the day in addition to providing some time for independent activity in an unstructured block of time. Such a period might include opportunities for independent reading, project work, craft activities, and individual research, as well as opportunities to complete elective assignments in various interest areas. To insure the success of such a period, teachers should work with children in joint planning before the activities begin and in evaluation sessions at the end of the period.

ARRANGING THE ROOM   Classroom schedules are used to organize activities in time. Physical space also requires arrangement for optimal use of classroom facilities. If all children are expected to be involved in the same activity at the same time, there should be less concern about room arrangements than if individual and small group activities are to be nurtured in the classroom. These latter arrangements require a deployment of facilities so that the children's work is facilitated without constant teacher supervision and so that they do not interfere with each other's activities.

Organizing Physical Space

Space requirements for classroom use are often prescribed by law. Many states require a minimum of 35 square feet per child of classroom space in a nursery school. The same minimum figure is sometimes suggested for space in a primary classroom. Many experts, however, recommend that as much as 100 square feet per child be available. In addition, from 50 to 200 square feet per child of outdoor space should be provided for the program. The indoor space should be well lighted, well ventilated, and well heated. Ideally there should be easy access from the classroom to the outdoor play area and to toilet facilities. If the classroom has a door leading directly to a play yard or terrace, the program can flow easily between the indoors and outdoors.

Arranging the Primary Classroom

Not too many years ago, primary classrooms were characterized by neat rows of single or double desks securely bolted to the floor. While one seldom finds the desks bolted into classroom floors today, they might as well be in many classes. Not all teachers see the organization of furniture and equipment as an instructional tool that might need periodic modification.

While most classrooms provide more informal seating arrangements, this may not necessarily be advantageous to children. Unfortunately, as Jackson has pointed out, we may have made life harder for many children by placing them in informal situations.[2] The temptation to speak to a peer is lessened when only the back of his head is visible. Seating children face-to-face at tables or in informal semicircles while still denying them the opportunity for verbal interaction is a torture we should seldom inflict on anyone.

Many primary classrooms have chairs and desks or tables, arranged informally, grouped together in horizontal rows or in a semicircle. A small group of chairs may be set aside in a corner of the room for reading instruction. There may be an easel or a table for art work placed in the

[2]Philip Jackson, *Life in Classrooms* (New York: Holt, Rinehart & Winston, 1968), pp. 3–37.

back of the room. In addition, there should be shelves and closets for storage of books and materials and a display area for science or nature study.

This type of room arrangements fits well in a classroom in which the basic mode of instruction is verbal and in which children are expected to function in a total class learning situation or in a small group situation under the teacher's supervision. It may not support other kinds of learnings. Constructions for social studies and children's experiments require other kinds of space and other materials than are generally provided. A teacher who wishes to individualize instruction and provide a degree of self-pacing in the classroom will also find such an arrangement restrictive. Just as schedules reflect the kind of program a teacher wishes to develop, so does the arrangement of the room.

An activity-oriented primary classroom might benefit from a room arrangement closely resembling that of a nursery school or kindergarten. Interest centers could be developed to support the primary curriculum. As in the nursery school, some of these centers might be used for arts and crafts activities or for dramatic play. A library center would be a critical resource in the primary classroom. In addition, centers for activities in mathematics, science, social studies, and language arts could also be developed. Ideas for organizing such centers can be abstracted from the earlier chapters dealing with these academic areas.

Outdoor Area

The outdoor play area should have both some paved surface and some grassy area. The pavement allows children to use tricycles or other wheel toys. In addition, block-building is more satisfying on a flat surface. A covered terrace or patio is desirable as part of the outdoors area so that children can be outdoors even when it rains. Some shade is necessary under any circumstances. There ought to be some area for digging as well; a dirt area will suffice; a sand box or pit large enough for a group of children to play in is desirable. Such a sand pit can be built right into the ground, with provisions for drainage and a cover to keep the sand clean and usable. A garden should be set aside for the children's use. They can plant seeds, care for the flowers and vegetables, and reap the harvest at the appropriate season.

There should be provisions made for large-muscle activities and for dramatic play. Permanently installed equipment of steel, concrete, and fiberglass can be made available as well as portable equipment, such as packing crates, boards, and ladders. Very young children may be offered simple equipment. As they become more competent, more sophisticated and challenging equipment can be introduced.

Adequate storage space in the outdoor area, such as a shed in the play yard or a locker at the door leading to the play area allows play equipment to be used. Naturally the prevailing climate will determine what kinds of activities will be offered children outdoors and, in turn, how the outdoor play area should be designed. Other considerations include the possible problems of vandalism and the other uses that will be made of the outdoor area when school is not in session. The outdoor area should be considered an extension of the classroom, providing opportunity for exciting learning experiences.

The Classroom

Ideally, the indoor space should be designed to support flexible educational programs. This requires that surfaces be treated with acoustical materials wherever possible. Walls should be pleasantly but unobtrusively colored and there should be adequate display space, including bulletin boards and possibly a small chalkboard on the walls. Floors can be carpeted or covered with resilient tiles. Shades or blinds that both reduce glare and darken the room completely can be provided for windows. A water fountain to serve thirsty children and a sink to be used to provide water for activity and cleaning purposes can limit the number of trips the children make down the hallway. Bathrooms should be adjacent to the classroom or at least close by.

An adequate classroom would also have enough storage and locker facilities for children's coats, boots, extra clothing, and personal belongings. The teacher should have a similar facility available to her, but scaled to adult size. In addition, storage space should be provided for materials and equipment. The amount of storage space necessary may be considerable, for there are often more materials and equipment available for a classroom than the amount visible at any one time. Storage space needs to be varied. Large wheel toys, paper, and art supplies all need different kinds of storage facilities.

Interest Centers

Many nursery-kindergarten activities are organized into interest centers in the room. The classroom is divided into areas, each of which supports some portion of the program through the organization of space and the availability of materials and equipment. Though the centers can expand or contract with the needs of the program, most of them are available throughout the activity period.

These centers can include:

Arts and crafts center
Housekeeping center
Blockbuilding center
Manipulative materials center
Library center
Music center
Display center

as well as other centers teachers might wish to organize.

Equipment and Supplies

While much of the equipment needed in the activity centers is available from educational supply houses, some can be purchased locally. Hardware stores, supermarkets, and discount houses may have many of the materials and supplies the teacher wishes to include in her room. Purchases made locally are often less expensive, since there is no cost for packaging and shipping. If a teacher does her purchasing locally, she should be aware of school policy regarding purchases and the possibility of not paying a local sales tax. Local purchasing does take time, however, and the teacher must make a judgement about whether the hours spent in purchasing offsets the amount of money saved. Many schools maintain a petty cash fund to help the teacher make small purchases of materials for special occasions, such as buying cake mix for a cooking experience or nails for the woodwork area.

Some schools find that pieces of equipment they cannot afford, such as easels, lockers, climbing apparatus, or storage facilities, are often contributed by parents or members of the community. The parents may have power tools that they can bring to the project, or these might be rented locally. A local sewing center will often donate the use of sewing machines to allow mothers to make doll clothes, sheets for resting cots, or curtains to make the room more attractive. Bringing the parents together for project work has advantages other than saving money on equipment, for the parents can meet one another, and working together on a joint project will help knit them into a group. They will also feel they have an investment in the school, which might bring them closer in their relationship with school personnel. Care must be taken that parents do not feel exploited by such work sessions, however.

Many useful learning materials do not have to be bought. The teacher can salvage material that would otherwise be thrown away or even involve children and their parents in this process. Beans or pebbles can be used for counting as easily as can carefully designed mathematics material. Castoff clothes make excellent additions to a dramatic play area. The chassis of a discarded radio, a broken alarm clock, castoffs from repair shops, buttons, egg cartons, and other materials too numerous to mention can all find fitting use in an early childhood classroom.

Criteria for Selecting Materials and Equipment

In selecting materials teachers may use a number of criteria:

COST.   The amount of money one must spend for an object is an important consideration. Price alone, however, is often a false yardstick to use. Some less expensive items will not be as satisfactory for their intended purpose as would more expensive items. Often the more expensive item will last longer and in the final analysis cost less. In any event, the cost of an item has to be balanced with the benefits that the item can provide in the school program.

RELATIONSHIP TO THE SCHOOL PROGRAM.   Educational equipment illustrated in catalogues may often seem fascinating to the adult, sometimes more to the adult than to the child for whom it is being purchased. At other times, the item may be interesting but unrelated to the program. Teachers should select materials and equipment that will be interesting to children and will help further their educational goals.

QUALITY AND DURABILITY.   There are many elements to consider in judging the quality of a piece of equipment. Equipment adequate for home use is often inappropriate for inclusion in the school. The design of the equipment is an important consideration, but the way the design is executed is equally important. Judgements about the kind of materials used, the quality of the wood, metal, or plastic, the care with which the equipment is fabricated, the way pieces are joined, the type of finish applied, and so on, all go into determining quality. Often equally priced pieces of equipment are available from more than one supplier, but a careful look at the finished product will tell the watchful teacher that one is a better bargain than the other.

FLEXIBILITY OF USE.   Since both budget and space are limited in most programs for young children, teachers should consider equipment that can be used in a variety of ways and situations. Such equipment will need to be stored less often and may be used to replace highly specific equipment. In the dramatic play area, the equipment that has the fewest details can often be used most flexibly, for the child's imagination can turn a simple box into a rocket ship or a covered wagon. Much equipment, of course, is designed for specific purposes and teachers should not overlook these in making decisions.

Equipment and Materials

There are a number of educational supply houses throughout the United States that manufacture and/or sell equipment and supplies for early childhood educational programs. Some of the traditional textbook publishers have also started to develop kits containing materials as well as books.

Most teachers have difficulty in selecting appropriate materials and equipment and deciding which manufacturer offers the highest quality at the most moderate price. Unfortunately, there are no *Consumers Reports* for this kind of equipment. Some can be viewed at teachers' conferences or in other schools, and there are some catalogues available. It is helpful to ask the advice of teachers who have had some experience using specific equipment.

A number of guides for the selection of equipment for early childhood education are available. These include lists available in textbooks and pamphlets. Only the equipment listed in the ACEI pamphlet below is tested, and this list is rather limited in terms of the variety currently on the market. Some useful lists are found in the following material:

Association for Childhood Education International, *Equipment and Supplies, Tested and Approved for Preschool, School and Home*. Washington, D.C.: The Association for Childhood Education International, 1966.

Evans, Anne Marie, "How to Equip and Supply Your Prekindergarten Classrooms." In *Early Childhood Education Rediscovered*, ed. Joe L. Frost. New York: Holt, Rinehart & Winston, 1968, pp. 567–76.

Foster and Headley, *Education in the Kindergarten*, 3rd ed. New York: American Book Co., 1969, Chapter 7.

Heffernan and Todd, *The Kindergarten Teacher*. Boston: D.C. Heath, 1960, pp. 59–65.

Project Headstart, *Equipment and Supplies: Guidelines for Administrators and Teachers in Child Development Centers*. Washington, D.C.: Office of Economic Opportunity. n.d.

Although all classrooms present differing needs for materials and equipment, it is helpful to know generally what would best fit into the classroom.

Furniture

Furniture for an early childhood classroom should be movable and durable. It should be scaled to the children's size. Tables and chairs of varying heights might be included in a single classroom, because children in any one age group vary in size. Tables of different shapes might also be included, for they will be used for different purposes. Tables can be used for both art work and eating. Special tables might also be designated for use in the doll corner, the housekeeping area, the library area, and for display purposes. Trapezoidal tables are quite flexible in that they can be grouped and arranged in many different ways. Furniture should be lightweight yet sturdy to enable the children and teachers to move it easily. If chairs and tables are stackable, they can be stored in a corner of the room when not in use. This is important, for during most of the day there does not need to be a chair always available for each child.

A teacher might also wish to have some furniture for her own use. A desk, a couple of chairs, and a file cabinet are useful items. If she is provided with office space adjacent to her room (often part of a cloakroom will do) she will not have to sacrifice precious classroom space that the children might be able to use. Otherwise, she can probably find a relatively unobtrusive portion of the room to call her own. She may keep her planning material, records, personal supplies, and possibly a first-aid kit in this area.

In each area of the classroom, there should be adequate shelf and cabinet space to make materials readily available to children. Enough supplies should be provided, but clutter should be avoided. This requires that thought be given to the selection of cabinets and shelf units and to their use. It also requires that children learn how to use things properly and return them. Sometimes teachers have shelves built into their rooms under windows and around the walls of the classroom. These are exceedingly useful, but additional portable storage units should be provided. They can serve as room dividers as well as storage units. Each kind of material requires its own storage. Teachers should be aware of this and avoid the use of universal cabinets when they are not appropriate.

If young children stay in school a full day, they may need to have cots provided for rest. Lightweight aluminum cots with canvas or plastic covers that stack for easy storage can be purchased. These are not necessary for children in a half-day program. Children of nursery-school age may rest on mats or rugs stretched out on the floor. Although many kindergartens provide a rest period, some experts suggest that formal rest is unnecessary and that substituting an informal quiet activity is advantageous. Such a substitute not only improves the tempers of children and lowers the number of disciplinary problems encountered, but also does away with the need to provide storage space for mats or cots.

A teacher who wishes to support independent learning must provide a classroom that allows children to behave freely and reasonably. A physical setting with interest centers allows children to move into areas that support a particular activity in which they are involved rather than being constrained in a single chair or at a single desk for most of the day. It is important that teachers realize that the test of a good room arrangement is the degree to which it helps children achieve the goals of the program. Teachers should experiment with room settings and modify them regularly to make them fit supportively into a dynamic learning situation.

SUGGESTED READING

Bits and Pieces. Washington, D.C.: Association for Childhood Education, 1967.

Equipment and Supplies. Washington, D.C.: Association for Childhood Education, 1965.

Equipment and Supplies. Washington, D. C.: Office of Economic Opportunity, 1965.

12

Working With Children

One of the first concerns of a teacher is the need to induct the child into the ways of the school. For many children, entrance into the kindergarten or primary grades is just one of many school beginnings and, since schools are more alike than different, they have experience upon which to base their expectations. For other children, the first school day may be the first experience away from home and the teacher may represent the first authority figure other than the parents to whom the child has had to relate. In any event, the beginning of school is always fraught with some fear, for the new situation raises a set of questions for the child who does not yet know exactly what to expect. School beginnings, therefore, require special consideration.

BEGINNING SCHOOL: NURSERY-KINDERGARTEN LEVEL The child's introduction to school often begins many months prior to the first school day. Many schools provide time in the spring for a visit by children who will be entering that fall. They may be brought into the classroom individually or in small groups, either when the class is in session or after school. They become familiar with the physical layout of the school and the class and are allowed to explore the materials and equipment that are available in the class, much of which will be there when they return in September. Most of all, they have a chance to meet some of the school personnel with whom they will later interact. The teacher in charge of the class visited will probably be the child's teacher.

The parents are also given a chance in this orientation to find out about the school's expectations and routines. This allows them to prepare their child properly for his formal entrance to school, which may be months away.

Most children enter school in the fall. Our American tradition suggests that all children come to class at about the same time, and this mass arrival creates several problems for the teacher. For one thing, all the children entering the classroom are ignorant of the resources available to them and the procedures they are to follow. An additional problem stems from the fact that they all have highly individual reactions to this new experience. Some find the new school setting stimulating and exhilarating and, rising to the challenge of a new environment, immediately plunge into exploration, testing every facet of the new situation. Other children find the newness of the situation frightening and withdraw from contact with people or things.

In addition to the children's reactions to the new school situation, the teacher should be sensitive to the parents' reactions. Some parents wish to leave the child immediately, thus freeing him for independent pursuits. Some feel guilt at the sense of freedom and relief they may be experiencing. Others react hesitantly to "giving up" their children. The fact that their children can function independently of them is hard for many parents to take. At times, the child's attendance in school is also a sign of the parents' aging, a hard realization to face for many in our society.

If the child has recently moved to the community, an increasing occurrence in our society, there may be a compounding of problems because the child must deal with additional uncertainty. And the child who finds himself bussed from his neighborhood to a strange, possibly hostile one, has other problems.

This is the situation with which the teacher must deal in her first days. She may bring additional problems to the situation herself. A new teacher, unsure of herself and her school, finds the first day more anxiety-provoking than does the experienced teacher who is firmly entrenched in a familiar situation. But to all teachers, the sense of novelty and uncertainty about children and class may generate feelings that closely parallel those of the children.

Many teachers find that the transition is eased for them as well as for the children if the school term begins with some form of staggered enrollment, in which only a part of the group comes to school each day for the first week. Teachers often have only one-third of the class attend each day. The three groups may alternate attendance during the first few days, or the children may come cumulatively. The former plan creates a situation in which no one child has any more school days for attendance than another child. But children who come to school on the first day and then are kept out for the next two may feel strange when they return.

Starting the school year with a small group each day allows the teacher to give each child the attention he may need. It also lessens the shock for the child of having to work each day within a large group of other children. In addition, it allows the teacher to deal personally with the child, insuring his awareness of school procedures.

Many of the problems of induction are significantly lessened in a nongraded setting. With only a few children beginning a group each year, most of them do not require a formal induction, for they are already familiar with the teacher, room, and total school situation. In addition, the more experienced children can help in orienting the younger and newer ones, thus simplifying matters for the teacher. Since she knows many of her children from the previous year, she can plan better; relationships are already established and only need to be extended.

Children do not naturally know how to behave in school nor do they come to school aware of the rules and regulations established for them. The teacher must make a conscious effort to acquaint them with unfamiliar routines and procedures. It is helpful if she goes through a typical schedule, though perhaps in simplified form, during these first days. At each transition and before each set of new routines, she can talk to the group and tell them what to anticipate next. She can demonstrate new routines such as cleaning up after a work period or getting ready for dismissal. Nor will one demonstration suffice, for the children will need many repetitions before they master routines and feel comfortable with school expectations. Keeping a degree of constancy in the school schedule helps them learn an established routine and adds a degree of predictability to the school day. This predictability and constancy provides some security for the child; once established, it is a base from which to operate rather than a system to which one should slavishly adhere.

While teachers are giving attention to the children, they should not forget the parents. In some schools, the parents are expected to drop their children off outside the door on the first day and immediately leave. It is becoming a standard practice in many nursery schools to expect parents to bring the new children to school the first day and stay with them, thus providing a transition for the child from home to school routine. The child need not feel that he is being abandoned or that the school is entirely separate from his home life, for his parent provides a bridge to his new life situation. Although some parents cannot bring their children to school and stay with them, it is a highly desirable practice. The teacher may begin separation by having the parent leave for a short period of time to have a cup of coffee, provided in another part of the school. Usually the child can be weaned from his parent in a relatively short period of time. It may take longer to wean the parent.

BEGINNING SCHOOL: THE PRIMARY GRADES   The teacher in the primary grades may not have to deal with the problems of separation that concern the teacher of younger children. Generally, primary children have been to school before and have some idea of what to expect. The primary teacher has several similar concerns, however. As early as possible she should establish classroom routines and set ways of organizing school life. A daily schedule should be posted and adhered to as much as possible. She should also introduce certain procedures of group life. Ways of getting the teacher's attention, of using materials in the classroom, of moving from the room to the outdoor area, lunchroom, or other places in the school need to be presented, explained, discussed, and practiced. In addition, children need to learn what resources are available and how they can be used. Even though they may have had similar experiences in earlier years, each teacher has some procedures that are different from those of her colleagues. If operating procedures are clearly communicated to the children, there is a greater chance that they will be adhered to.

In addition to getting children acquainted with school procedure, the teacher must get to know the children and establish positive relations with each one. Teachers should also become familiar with the children's records, which tell about academic progress as well as other aspects of school experiences. The meaning of entries in this vital record must be interpreted, for not all teachers have the same expectations of children or the same interpretations of their behavior. A teacher who is aware of the expectations of the child's former teacher can make better use of records. In addition to analyzing these records, she should make other assessments of her students.

Academic work can be assessed in a variety of ways. Teachers probably should give informal inventories or tests in the area of reading and mathematics at the beginning of the school year. They may also wish to have some writing done in class so that writing skill and ability to communicate may be ascertained. Group discussions and short conferences allow the teacher to make judgments about the children's oral language abilities. In addition, informal contacts allow the teacher to gather information about social abilities, interests in school, ability to handle conflict and deal with frustration, and many other important things. At all times the teacher should be aware of the need to make only tentative judgments, for children do change in their relationships as they become familiar with new people and new surroundings. It would be unfortunate to set up a series of expectations based only upon the limited and not too reliable information the teacher can gather in the first few days of school.

During these early days of school, the teacher and the children often participate in a series of interactions that allows them to test each other and to establish a balanced relationship. Just as the teacher is testing the children in the first few days, the children are also testing the teacher. Each child soon finds his place in the classroom social structure, establishing his own identity in the classroom and his own set of relationships with the other children and the teacher. Although many friendships and animosities are carried over from earlier years, the fact that most children are in a new class with a new teacher each year means that a fresh set of balances must be created each fall.

ORGANIZING THE CHILDREN The classroom can be made to reflect the children by using their interests in the organization of the room and the displaying of their work. The children can assume much responsibility for their classroom.

Each child also needs to have some place he can call his own. The nursery-kindergarten child is usually provided with a cubby or locker, but may have no definite work space assigned. The primary child may also have a locker for his clothes or simply a hook in a cloakroom or closet. In most primary school classes, the child has a desk assigned for him at which he spends most of the day and does most of his work. In an activity program, individual desks may be eliminated and the child can work in many areas, moving around the room as he changes his activity. Though a personal desk becomes unnecessary, every child needs a place of his own for his treasures. A drawer in a cabinet may be adequate, or a part of a shelf might do. Even plastic stacking vegetable bins have been used to provide such space.

Children need to assume responsibility for caring for their space, seeing that things are neat and uncluttered. They can assume responsibility for caring for the rest of their room as well. Early in the year, the teacher should try to instill a sense of responsibility in each child. Every time a child uses an area or a piece of equipment, he can be made responsible for cleaning up and replacing the equipment so that others may find and use it.

The room must be properly designed to enable children to operate in this fashion. Each piece of equipment and set of materials should have its own designated spot so that the children know where to find things and where to replace them. It is helpful if shelf areas are clearly labeled with the names of things. If children cannot read, the teacher can substitute pictures or symbols on these labels. She should also see that shelves are uncluttered and that there is not too much equipment and material in the room.

Crayons and pencils can be placed in open-topped boxes; jars of paste can be put on shelves. Small objects like beads or pegs can be stored in containers with covers so that they do not easily fall out. There should be racks for drying paintings and a place where clay work can rest undisturbed until it is dried and ready for firing, painting, or taking home.

Finally, the teacher must make sure that the children know how to use the materials and care for them. If they are not taught to clean a paint brush or replace pieces of paper, they will not do these things. They may pick up proper habits from teachers or peers, but unless there is a conscious effort to teach a child, he may never learn some of the skills that provide individual responsibility.

In addition to these personal responsibilities, children can assume responsibilities for general care of the room. Not every child needs to do everything, but there can be a sharing of responsibility by all the group. Such tasks as setting tables and cleaning up after lunch and snacks, getting a room ready for rest, cleaning scraps of paper from the floor after the day, caring for animals, fish, or plants are all tasks that children may share. A teacher may assign these on a rotating basis, often by setting up a chart and changing jobs weekly. Actually, children enjoy this kind of work, because it allows them to show their developing competencies.

PREPARING FOR SPECIAL ACTIVITIES   It is important that the teacher begin to establish classroom routines early, but children should also feel that they are able to depart from routines when it is appropriate. A special visitor, the bringing of a pet to class, development of an activity that takes a long period of time, or a visit to an out-of-school place are all occasions for departing from routines for which teachers can prepare the children. This requires planning that may even involve the children.

Although most teachers give lip-service to pupil-teacher planning, there is really only a limited area in which such planning is actually legitimate. If a teacher uses a basal program to teach reading, there can be little effective involvement of the children in planning the procedures of the reading program. Similarly, many other areas of the program are outside the children's sphere of knowledge so that any decision making in which they would be involved would force them to make improper decisions based on ignorance, or to be manipulated by the teacher to make the decisions she would make anyway. The key to involvement in planning is the process of decision making.

There are legitimate areas for decision making open to young children and there are aspects of planning in which they can be involved. Whether the arithmetic lesson will be held in the morning or the afternoon is not a legitimate decision for the children to make, since the consequences are minor, but decisions about the distribution of resources or the preparation that needs to be made for special events can be legitimately made by children.

The visit of a resource person might be such a special event. Though the teacher might make the arrangements for the resource person to come and even extend the original invitation, the children can be involved in planning for the visit. Some of this group planning entails helping them to anticipate what may happen and to plan for contingencies.

In planning with the children, the teacher should talk about the purposes of the visit and how they can best use the resources brought to the classroom. If the visitor is coming to talk about his occupation, the children may wish to question him about the tasks he does, the equipment he uses, and whatever other aspects of the job might interest them. Asking appropriate questions requires that the children have a basis for judging the value of questions that might be asked, and this sometimes requires research prior to the visitor's arrival. Such preplanning and preparation allows the children to make optimal use of the visitor's time.

If the visitor is to perform for the children, the teacher may help them plan for appropriate room arrangement so that all the children can see. They might also wish to invite pupils from another class to share the experience. Although few of the problems raised in a preplanning session could be anticipated without the guidance of the teacher, involving the children helps them begin to anticipate future contingencies and makes use of their ideas in providing adequately for future events. Children cannot always be involved in these plans, and when involved they may not always make major contributions, but the act of planning and thinking about the future is important.

Children can also contribute ideas to planning for a field trip. Most of the arrangements will have to be made by the teacher, but the children should be involved in some of the planning so they will know what to anticipate as well as how to behave. In this manner, they are also involved in establishing the code of acceptable behavior for the class on trips.

Much of the planning for a field trip rests in the teacher's domain. She makes arrangements with the school, gets permission from the parents and from the place that will be visited, takes care of transportation, and sets a time schedule. Any field trip, of course, should be related to the school program. Pupil-teacher planning includes helping children anticipate what will be happening on the trip and what uses will be made of it, for a field trip is not simply an excursion out of the school building used to fill up time, but is rather a means of collecting primary source data to be used in school studies. Of course there are occasions when teachers do take children on pleasure excursions, but these are relatively few.

If the children are to make maximum use of the trip, they should be helped in focusing on significant things.

Prior knowledge about what the children will be seeing on a trip is helpful to them. More general knowledge about the area of concern is also useful. They may do research on the topic by themselves or the teacher may present information from informations books or films and filmstrips. Children can be helped to formulate questions that going on the field trip might answer.

It is important that children learn to behave properly on a field trip. Certain limitations on behavior need to be placed on them when they are traveling away from school in a group simply because the size of the group and the strangeness of the setting may compound the effects of behavior disorders. Children can be involved in developing an appropriate code of behavior for field trips under the guidance of the teacher. This is an important part of the planning for each trip.

What constitutes appropriate behavior on a field trip may vary, for what is appropriate in one setting may not be appropriate in another. Children walking through a business office or factory where people are working need to behave in quite a different way than children walking through a park or a field. Similarly, traveling on a school bus requires different kinds of behavior than walking through a city street or using public transportation systems. In setting codes of behavior, it is important for the teacher to communicate to the children not only the limits of acceptable behavior, but the reasons these limits are set. Within these limits, the children should be able to set their own behavior pattern.

DISCIPLINE

Setting rules for appropriate behavior is no different at school than it is at home. The school, as a specialized institution having a particular set of goals and a setting peculiar to itself, has to establish appropriate ways of behavior for children. In the old elementary school tradition in which children were to be "seen and not heard," the rules for behaving were quite simple and were understood by all concerned. Children were to speak and to move as little as possible, and then only with the express permission of the teacher. The less noise produced, the better the class.

Such an approach for establishing a code of appropriate behavior in the school is no longer desirable, for in the modern school, especially in classes for young children, movement, speaking, and a degree of noise is considered acceptable. In replacing the old code with new standards of acceptable behavior, though, teachers have often missed the ease with which the old code could be administered. Everyone knew the rules and under the old system any infraction of the rules was observable. Today, both teachers and children are often not quite sure of the rules; and what might be considered an infraction of rules by one teacher may not be considered so by another teacher in the same school. Relative standards, rather than absolute ones, abound.

Children entering school for the first time are not sure of what is considered appropriate behavior. In addition, the very young child has often not yet learned to control his own desires. If he wants a toy that he sees, he might simply take it, in spite of the fact that another child is using it. He also often reacts immediately and physically to hurt or frustration. An occasional tantrum by a nursery-age child is not necessarily a sign of emotional disturbance.

Proper behavior in school settings is learned gradually. It should be a goal to be achieved through extended experience rather than an expectation. Teachers should plan for teaching proper behavior as they teach other things. For such teaching to be effective, the teacher must first be aware of the goals she wishes to achieve. Does she wish to prepare children to be docile and conforming, and responsive only to authority? Does she wish to prepare children who have developed many modes and skills of self-expression, but whose concerns are with continually acting out their feelings and desires? Or does she wish to prepare children who are responsive to the needs of others as well as themselves, who are flexible enough to change their behavior in response to a situation, and who behave appropriately because they feel it is right rather than because they have been told to do so?

Each type of individual suggested above could be developed as a result of the form of discipline used in a particular school. If a teacher is continually setting limits and telling children to behave in certain ways because "I told you so," the children will become authority-oriented, learning from their experience that the reasons for behaving in particular ways have their roots in the commands of authority figures. On the other hand, children who are given no limits may well learn that their own inner desires ought to be responded to continually and that nothing else should be their concern. Ultimately, we wish to develop autonomous individuals who realize that there are reasons for order and that limits set by authority are legitimate. We want them to learn to be flexible in their behavior, responding to each situation differently. Such an approach to discipline also extends the child's intellectual capacity, for he finds that he can use his intellect in making sense of the social world as well as of the physical world and that patterns of behavior have regularity and reason that can ultimately be understood.

In attempting to develop an approach to discipline based upon reason the teacher may follow several steps:

1. *Behaviors expected of children should be known to them.* It is

important that the teacher tell the children what will be expected of them. All too often children's improper behavior is a result of ignorance, nor will telling children one time how to behave have the desired effect. Instructions will have to be repeated many times in many contexts before the children truly understand them.

2. *Children need to be told why rules are in effect.* Even if they cannot fully *understand* the reasons for behaving in certain ways, children need the reasons for rules. Questions asked by the children need to be responded to honestly. Most rules for school behavior are reasonable. Children can begin to see the reason for lining up at a slide that many wish to use, or limiting the amount of time a child can ride on a popular bicycle. Similarly, children can understand why they should behave differently in a crowded lunchroom than in their own room and why rules are promulgated for behaving certain ways in class, other ways in the hall, and still other ways on a school bus.

3. *Children should have opportunities to observe and practice proper behavior.* Simply telling a child how to behave may not be enough. Children need to view demonstrations at times and must also have opportunities to *practice* proper behavior. The result of practice ought to be feedback from the teacher as to whether certain behavior is appropriate or not.

4. *Proper behavior is a working goal.* Teachers should be aware of the fact that proper behavior is something to be achieved with practice. Children cannot be expected to know or obey all the rules the first time; they may have to go through a series of successive approximations before they learn proper behavior, just as they do in reading and every other area of curriculum.

5. *The behavior expected of children ought to be possible for them.* A developmental principle should be applied in this area of performance as in other areas. Expectations of children's behavior need to be attainable. Children are not miniature adults and should not be expected to behave like adults. Teachers instead should have as their goals reasonable child-like behavior.

6. *Children cannot always be expected to behave properly at all times.* Nobody is perfect, including adults. We do not expect adults to always be on their best behavior. As a matter of fact, we often feel that it is good for an adult to "let his hair down" on occasion. The same is true for children. They should not be expected to conform to standards of model behavior at all times any more than adults should.

7. *Teachers should behave with consistency.* The teacher's own be-

havior communicates a message to the children about what is acceptable and appropriate and what is not. If teachers vacillate in their desires or accept certain kinds of behaviors from children one time and reject or punish for the same behavior under similar circumstances another time, they confuse children and blur their goals. Though teachers cannot always behave consistently, this is a goal for which they should aim.

For many years educators have argued about whether or not to reward children for proper behavior. Some have felt that rewards constitute bribery, and since children should learn that proper behavior is its own reward, such bribery should be avoided. Some suggest that rewards constitute a form of feedback, telling the child he has performed well and so can repeat the behavior on other occasions. Others think that rewards should be given in order to shape the behavior of children—that they should be used to help children move toward appropriate modes of behavior. Once that point is reached, the proper behavior will maintain itself and become its own reward, but this is a goal to be achieved, and rewards are useful in the attainment of the goals. There are even long discussions in the literature about the kinds of rewards that are most effective and most appropriate. Rewards may be tangible. They may be given in the form of consumables, such as candies or raisins, or nonconsumables, such as balloons or toys. Symbolic rewards can be given, such as stars or stamps. Tokens may be given that could be traded for tangible rewards, or the teacher may use social reinforcement, making a show of approval the reinforcing agent.

Actually, all teachers use some reinforcement in working with children. The question needs to be raised more in terms of the *systematic* use of rewards as a way of controlling the behavior of children. The *behavior modification* approach suggests consistent systematic reinforcement of positive behavior as a way of getting children to perform properly. Punishment can be used on some occasions or inappropriate behavior ignored. Teachers using this approach may consciously practice systematic rewarding of desirable behavior and ignoring or punishing undesirable behavior in managing their class. Children who are behaving in an undesirable fashion may also be withdrawn from a personally rewarding situation. The children's behaviors are defined as observable events which may be managed by the teacher.

Reinforcement is one technique the teacher can use in dealing with immediate behavior problems manifested by children. There are other important methods that should be a part of the teacher's repertoire as well, *redirection* being one of them. The basic ploy in this case is to take the child's attention from the situation creating the difficulty and move him into a situation that will provide immediate satisfactions. A child who is fighting with another over a fire truck, for example, might be steered to the woodworking area so that the conflict is done away with and the child is immediately involved in the pursuit of satisfying activity. For redirection to be possible, the teacher needs to know her children and to know which activities have high appeal for each of them. She must also have alternatives available.

Although redirection is a means to avoid conflict, the suggestion that it be used does not indicate either that conflicts can be completely avoided or that conflict is necessarily bad. There are always some situations that will lead to conflict in any classroom. The opposition of individual needs or the clash of strong personalities may cause it. Teachers should help children develop acceptable means of dealing with conflict. These would include the use of compromise as well as the use of verbal skills in influencing persons, as opposed to forms of physical coercion. Teachers continually have to step in to resolve conflicts among children. Unfortunately, they may have to use some forms of arbitrary coercion and even physical restraint in classes. This should not mean, however, the use of physical punishment. Ultimately, any system of discipline should move from having the child's behavior controlled by the teacher to having the child become autonomous. The success of a teacher's discipline can be judged by the degree of autonomy found in the class.

All classrooms have some children who do not behave appropriately at all times. Teachers also find that they are not as effective with some children as with others. Too often, teachers foolishly feel that their ability to control a class at all times is crucial to their ability to teach, and that any failure in dealing with a child or a group on an occasion means failure as a teacher. Teachers need to realize that they are not infallible, and that they, as all professionals, need the help of others. Sometimes they can call on other teachers. A principal can often provide an additional resource. In some schools, teachers have access to school counselors, psychologists, and social workers. Appropriate use should be made of all these resources.

SUGGESTED READING

BECKER, WESLEY C., DON R. THOMAS, AND DOUGLAS CARNINE, *Reducing Behavior Problems: An Operant Conditioning Guide for Teachers*. Urbana, Ill.: ERIC Clearinghouse on Early Childhood Education, 1969.

HYMES, JAMES L., *The Child Under Six*. Englewood Cliffs, N.J.: Prentice-Hall, Inc., 1963.

SHEVIAKOV, GEORGE V., AND FRITZ REDL, *Discipline for Today's Children and Youth*. Washington, D.C.: Association for Supervision and Curriculum Development, 1956.

13

Working With Parents

The close relationship between the education of young children and parent programming has been evident throughout the history of early childhood education. This relationship may have grown out of an understanding of the close bond between parent and young child, a bond causing the parent to become the prime influencer of the young child's learning and development. Because this bond may have a greater impact on the life of the child than any educational programs, educators have learned to use it to extend their programs.

The writings of Comenius and Pestalozzi, educators who predated the creation of kindergartens and nursery schools and who were concerned with young children, expressed the belief in the importance of the mother's role in the education of the young. Friederich Froebel, pioneer of the kindergarten, also expressed his belief in the importance of educating mothers for child rearing as well as in the significance of the harmonious education of children in school and at home. - wording

As kindergartens were established in the United States, classes were formed for the mothers of the children as a means of carrying out Froebel's philosophy. In some cases in which kindergartens were organized as philanthropic agencies, the mothers' clubs were concerned with the acculturation of the family, helping to "Americanize" as well as teaching about child-rearing practices. Classes for all kindergarten parents were concerned with teaching about child study and about the theory and practice of kindergarten education.

It is interesting to note that the importance that early kindergarten educators placed upon involving mothers significantly affected the total American education scene. The National Congress of Mothers grew out of a convocation of women connected with these kindergarten mothers' classes. This group eventually became the National Congress of Parents and Teachers, an organization well-known in school circles today.

As nursery schools developed, they became thought of as an important influence in augmenting and improving healthy parent-child relationships. The McMillan sisters' emphasis on placing nursery schools close to children's homes, of allowing parents to observe nursery-school practices, and of establishing a good working relationship between parent and teacher all were meant to support close cooperation between the home and the school. The hope of the pioneers of nursery education was that the parents themselves would ultimately become responsible for the education of their young children.

As the nursery school was transplanted in the United States, this concern for a close relationship between family and school in the early years continued. One of the first nursery schools established in the United States was a parent-cooperative nursery school started by a group of twelve faculty wives at the University of Chicago in 1916. These parents wanted to secure "social education for their children, parent education for themselves and a little free time for Red Cross work."[1]

The nursery school and kindergarten were often the creation of the parents they were designed to serve. Nursery schools are still organized by groups of parents and concerned community members and even today, one may still find kindergartens sponsored by elementary school parent-teacher associations. Parents who create a school feel a sense of belonging to that school in a way that few parents of established schools can experience.

The relationships between schools and parents at the early childhood level are as diverse as the kinds of schools that exist and the populations of parents they serve. The day-care center operates quite differently in its relationship to the families it serves than does the parent-cooperative nursery school. Similarly, the primary grades of an elementary public school may also support a different relationship between home and school than does a private nursery school.

Recently concerns about parent programs have shifted from viewing the parent only as a client of educational institutions to viewing him as a policy maker for those institutions as well. The concern for community control of schools and the demand of the parents to have a voice in educational policy making at all levels must be understood as an extension of the responsibility of the parent for the education of his child.

To some extent, this right to determine policy is considered part of every relationship that a client has with a professional, for, in all but a few encounters with professionals, a parent may select the professional

[1]Katherine Whiteside Taylor, *Parents and Children Learn Together* (New York: Teachers College Press, 1968), p. 294.

that best characterizes his concept of treatment. In the area of education, however, neither the client nor the professional has the freedom of selection that characterizes most other client-professional relationships. Public educational institutions hold such a real monopoly over educational services that usually choice of school or teacher is not available to the parent, nor can most teachers determine which children will be included in their class. This lack of choice is one constraint that molds the relationship between parent and teacher.

WHO OWNS THE CHILD?   In our culture we believe that parents have the right to rear their children in any way they see fit. Actually, however, this right of the parent is significantly abridged as a result of our concern for the safety of the child. No parent has the right to inflict bodily harm on his child. Although the publicity given to the existence of "battered children" in our communities might make this seem a recent concern, Humane Societies have been established for many years for the protection of animals and *children.*

The imposition of society on the rights of parents goes far beyond stopping dangerous parental practices, for the states also legislate compulsory education. Every parent *must* send his child to school for a certain period of the child's life and is held responsible for the child's attendance in school. This requirement grows as much from the cultural need to maintain the social order as from the personal needs of children and their parents.

As schools begin to offer educational opportunities for the very young, the matter of compulsory school attendance becomes even more critical. Schools for the young concern themselves with teaching basic attitudes and concepts that go beyond traditional instruction in the three R's. Although parents are free today to keep a child out of school until age six or seven, it may well be that in the years to come the compulsory school attendance laws will include requirements for children age five, four, or even younger. This may present no problem for a family whose parents are in complete agreement with school authorities as to the goals of education and the appropriate means for achieving these goals, but serious problems may develop when the school authorities and the parents disagree about either goals or means of education. At this point, the responsiveness of schools to the needs, wishes, and demands of parents may be crucial.

Who does own the child? It becomes evident that the "ownership" of children by parents is far from unencumbered by our society. In many schools, however, teachers feel that they "own" the child, at least for those hours in which the child is in attendance in the classroom. During this period, many teachers feel that their right to determine what experiences will be provided to children is inviolable. It is a "right" delegated to them by society by virtue of their special knowledge and the preparation they have had in becoming teachers, a "right" authorized in the issuance of a teacher's certificate and evidenced by the signing of a contract with a school board.

Just as there are restraints placed upon what parents can do to children, there are restraints placed upon teachers. The curriculum set by the school board, the regulations set by administration, and the laws of the state relating to education all create some restraints. In addition to these, there are professional restraints imposed implicitly by the teachers and informally communicated by the colleagues in a school.

One of the larger issues confronting education today relates to the extent to which parents' wishes and demands should also constitute a legitimate set of restraints upon the actions of teachers. Parents have traditionally been kept out of decision-making roles in school except at the broadest level, as in school board membership. Aside from this arena, however, teachers have not considered parents an important source of constraint. Parents who came to school to meet with teachers were to be informed, listened to, placated, and counseled. Seldom did the teacher see the parent as a source of decision making about classroom procedure. The limited knowledge of parents about schooling was considered adequate reason to deny their legitimate involvement in the decision-making process, and even when they were considered knowledgeable, such matters were thought to be outside their sphere.

The establishment of policy advisory committees including large numbers of parents in Head Start programs and the demands of black, Indian, and Mexican-American parents for community control of schools suggests that the relationship between parent and teacher may be changing in many communities. This change is moving toward more involvement of parents and other community members, as extensions of parents, in important areas of decision making relating to school policy and classroom practice. The teacher in the elementary school of a ghetto area may soon find her relationship to the parents of the children in her class similar to that of the teacher in the parent cooperative nursery school. Although the parents are the clients of the teacher, they also hire her and constitute the governing board of the school concerned with making decisions about school policy and its implementation.

If this change does come about, teachers will need to view their role in relationship to schools and children in a somewhat different light and will need to develop new skills in working with parents and new perceptions of what constitutes a viable parent-teacher relationship.

Such a relationship is further compounded by the demands that teachers are making, through their organizations, for increased decision-making power. Teachers today are demanding a voice in deciding policy and administrative issues as well as asking for improved salaries and working conditions in their contracts. On occasion, parent and teacher groups have clashed in their independent demands for a greater voice in educational policy. In some cases, however, parents and teachers have joined together in the common pursuit of educational opportunity for all children through shared decision making.

Traditionally the boundary of teacher-parent-community power has been determined by the kinds of decisions that need to be made. Parent and/or community agents have been responsible for policy decisions, and teachers and administrators have been responsible for decisions relating to the implementation of policy. These lines, however, are often blurred, for implementation can affect policies considerably and policy decisions often require professional knowledge relating to the consequences of policy.

RELATIONSHIPS   Working with parents requires that the teacher establish a new set of professional relationships. In working with children, teachers have a great deal of power, whether they use it or not. Children have little recourse to outsiders in the classroom, so the teacher's decisions have a great degree of finality to them. The teacher has much less power in the relationship she establishes with parents, however. In age, size, and role, the parent differs from the child. There is much more parity in the relationship, although the teacher still maintains a degree of status that may allow her to control situations. This parity requires that teachers work differently with parents and have different sets of expectations. There can be few demands upon parents, although there can be many requests. Coercion is at a minimum and the teacher must learn to influence parents' behavior. Because of this parity, however, there can also be a greater degree of mutual respect and a higher form of affection shown by both parties as they establish a satisfying relationship.

The teacher and parent are both constrained in their relationship by roles and role expectations. Teachers can and must behave in specific ways, as must parents in this relationship. Certain behavior patterns are expected and make for the smooth establishment of rapport.

Both parents and teachers, however, come into the situation with experiences that can distort these expectations. Each has had a history of prior relationships with others in similar roles that may color their present relationships with one another. Each parent has had many teachers himself, just as each teacher has his own parents. The residue of these relationships exists for all, and must be taken into consideration in working with one another. Each parent, upon entering an elementary school building for the first time after many years, has memories of his own school experiences awakened within him. These memories may make the surrounding walls seem intimidating, or they may bring back feelings of happiness. In any event, they recall a time of immaturity. If teachers or other school personnel behave in a way that intimidates parents in their initial contacts with the school, making them feel less than mature individuals, then it becomes difficult to establish a relationship built upon mutual trust and respect.

Similarly, many teachers may feel intimidated by their need to work directly with parents feeling much more comfortable in the classroom setting where their dominion is not open to question. They, too, may feel intimidated by parents who, at times, can be overbearing or even hostile. Teachers need to feel secure in their relationships with their school and in their professional roles in order to overcome these feelings. The professional role of the teacher, however, requires that she work with parents, and this is especially important when teaching young children. Teachers who are unsure of themselves in relationship to parents may wish to begin a parent program slowly, organizing first those activities in which the highest degree of success can be expected, then venturing to try other elements of parent programming. Teachers should also be able to call upon other school personnel to help them develop effective techniques of working with parents.

DIFFERING ROLES IN WORKING WITH PARENTS   The content of a parent-teacher relationship varies greatly with the parent population and with the particular institutional setting of the educational program. Teachers should be sensitive to the needs of parents and provide a range of programming possibilities. Generally, the teacher's role may consist of communicating pupil progress to parents, sharing information, jointly solving problems, organizing parent meetings, developing parent education programs, supervising classroom participation, and providing professional consultation to policy-making groups. Each element of parent programs is different from the others and requires different skills and techniques on the part of the teacher. Although teachers are not prepared as parent counselors and often lack the preparation to be parent educators, their position provides them with an opportunity to serve the parent population in a unique way. Within the limitations of skills and roles, teachers should accept the challenge in each area, although some areas might provide more satisfactions for individual teachers than others.

Reporting Pupil Progress

One of the results of evaluation is the report to parents of the child's progress in school. Report cards, letters, and individual conferences are discussed more fully in Chapter 15. It is important in reporting to be sure that the goals of the program are understood by the parents, that the criteria for making judgments are public, and that the parents have a clear understanding of their child's progress in school. Avoiding adverse reporting can be dangerous; parents should be informed regularly and frankly.

Sharing Information

Reporting pupil progress is usually one-way communication, with the only feedback relating to whether or not the message has been received. Parents and teachers both have information about the child that would be useful to exchange—information that may not necessarily be related to pupil progress. Teachers often elicit information about children through the applications that many nursery schools and kindergartens require to be filled out prior to the child's admission. Data on the child's health and developmental background is required in this form, and can provide useful knowledge to the teacher.

Such forms may be supplemented by individual conferences at the beginning of school or during a preschool orientation session. Holding such conferences a few weeks after the child's entrance to school allows the teacher time to collect information about the child's initial reaction to school and his developing behavior patterns. She may then be able to ask specific questions relating to important areas of behavior. What is significant for one child may be irrelevant to the teacher's understanding of another child.

Such a sharing conference held at any time of the year is useful particularly if the teacher finds that she has problems with a child. The information provided by a parent often helps explain a child's change in behavior. Similarly, parents may wish to have information from the teacher that will help them deal with the child at home. If the teacher and parent are both concerned primarily with the welfare of the child, information-sharing conferences may provide the beginning of a beneficial mutual relationship in support of the child. Such conferences can easily lead to joint problem solving sessions.

Joint Problem Solving

The child's entrance in school often leads to a new awareness on the part of the parents. In many families, the child may have had few contacts with other children his age up to this time, and sometimes the parents will have made few demands of the child, nor have they had the opportunity to compare him with other children at a similar developmental stage. If, in addition, the family has had few contacts with a pediatrician, the parents may suddenly see problems or abnormalities that have existed but have not been evident to them.

The entrance into school, with its new demands on the child, may suddenly bring forth a series of behavior problems. Hearing losses, poor vision, or other problems may also appear as new pressures are placed upon the child. At times, a change in the family situation—divorce, the arrival of a new baby, or moving to a new community—may also cause problems to occur in class. The teacher may be able to handle these problems without outside help, but it is sometimes necessary for her to work out the solutions with the parents. The sharing of information, the pooling of ideas for dealing with the problems, and the development of a consistent way of handling the child both at home and at school may go a long way in providing solutions to difficult problems. The teacher may play a crucial role in helping parents deal with these problems, for too often the teacher is the only professional with whom the parents have regular contact.

The teacher may suddenly find herself in a role for which she is poorly trained, because she has not been prepared as a psychologist, social worker, or guidance counselor and may be considered a child development specialist in only the broadest sense. Yet within her responsibility as teacher she must find ways to help the parent become aware of problems and deal with them. Sometimes this requires a friendly conversation over a cup of coffee, and other times it may require a series of conferences leading to referral to an appropriate agency. The teacher must be careful not to overstep the bounds of her role. Often it is best to refer a problem to someone else better qualified to deal with the problem. She should become familiar with the agencies that service children and their families in her community and with the procedures used to seek the help of each agency. Many schools have ancillary personnel— guidance workers or family coordinators—that can help the parent and teacher deal with problems.

Although referral is a significant contribution that teachers can make to parents with problems, the importance of the personal support a teacher can provide should not be underestimated.

Home Visits

Parent conferences generally take place in the school, the domain of the teacher, and a place where she feels comfortable. However, this may be a place in which parents feel less than comfortable. It is possible to move some parent activities out of the school and into the home.

A home visit has many advantages, among them, the familiarity and comfort to the parent. A conference in the home may allow the parent to talk more freely than he would at school, where he faces the teacher across a desk. In addition, the teacher can learn about the environment in which the child functions during most of his waking hours. Knowing this environment may help the teacher understand the child better. Home visits may also be more convenient for the parents who might not be able to come to the child's classroom during school hours; often, fathers as well as mothers can be reached by the teacher through home visits.

If a home visit is to be effective, the parents should feel that they are inviting the teacher into their home. Forcing a visit on an unwilling family may cause hostility. A number of dates and times might be proposed by the teacher so that the visit can take place at a mutually convenient time. A teacher who visits a child in the home without warning is acting unfairly. Such an action can be disastrous from the point of view of establishing a working relationship.

The purpose of a home visit is similar to that of a conference: sharing information and working on problems. The teacher should be careful that these purposes are achieved while friendly social relations are established.

Informal Contacts

Many of the individual contacts a teacher has with parents are informal in nature. The child's arrival or departure from school, the meetings of the parents' association, the invitation to a parent to accompany the class on a field trip, all provide opportunity for informal contacts. The teacher should use these opportunities to convey a feeling of friendliness and mutual concern for the children in these sessions. Holding parents at a distance or talking down to them on these occasions can destroy the relationship that the rest of the parent program is attempting to build.

These occasions also allow the teacher to hold mini-conferences— short informal sessions in which minor problems can be dealt with or information elicited easily. Such conferences can be extremely fruitful for the amount of time and energy expended. Teachers should encourage these contacts, being careful that they do not become too involved with the parents when they need to be working with children.

Parent Meetings

There are many occasions when the teacher must deal with parents in groups as well as individually. She may be called upon to plan and direct parent meetings, or looked upon as a resource for meetings planned and executed by the parents themselves.

The first meeting for which the teacher has responsibility is often the orientation meeting that takes place either before the children enter school or near their time of entry. This orientation meeting provides an opportunity to communicate to the parent what school will be like for them and for their child. If parents have never had a child in school before, this type of information is an important part of the meeting. They may be full of questions and may feel uncertain about the school. Honest responses to questions and the acceptance of parental anxiety can help build a good relationship. Such a meeting may also be used to provide parents with information about the school's expectations of them and their children.

Although orientation meetings usually require the transmission of a great deal of information, the teacher should be careful to communicate to parents the fact that the school is a friendly place and one that welcomes parents as well as children (assuming that this is true). Teachers should provide time in these meetings for informal chatter and opportunities for parents to become acquainted with one another. If information can be printed in a simple brochure or leaflet, more of the meeting time can be devoted to establishing relationships and less to lecturing. It is a waste of meeting time to read materials that parents could easily read themselves.

During the school year, the teacher may want to call other meetings, for the purpose of providing the opportunity for the teacher to talk about her program, to show some of the children's work, and to answer whatever questions parents might have about what their children are doing. Because such meetings deal directly with their children, parents are usually happy to attend them. Care must be taken to schedule meetings at times when there can be maximum attendance. It may be necessary to provide an informal baby-sitting arrangement for the children of invited parents, or to allow the children to come to the meetings in order to insure attendance. In some communities, however, parents can make their own arrangements and caring for children presents no problem.

Most schools have a formal parent association or parent-teacher association that attempts to organize all the parents in the school. Such an association plans regular meetings and social events throughout the school year. Though the responsibility for such meetings is often in the hands of the parent officers of the association, teachers may be asked to serve on programs or to act as resource persons.

The attendance of teachers at these meetings is important in building close ties with families. A brief word to a parent on such an occasion can frequently do more in establishing good relationships than a lengthy conference.

Parent Education Programs

In many schools, formal or informal parent education programs are organized in conjunction with educational programs for young children.

These vary from highly organized courses that teach about child growth and development, child-rearing practices, and homemaking skills, to informal club activities whose content is determined by the parents themselves. Still other programs may focus on group process and parent interaction rather than on any substantive content. In some cases, the responsibility for parent education will lie outside the domain of the classroom teacher and a parent educator or group worker may be assigned to it. In other situations, the classroom teacher is responsible for parent education.

Many parent-cooperative nursery schools require that parents enroll in a parent education program as a prerequisite for the child's enrollment in the program. Nursery schools in settlement houses, parent-child centers, and Head Start programs often include a strong parent education component in their total service program. In some cases, parents are required to spend many hours in classes. Sometimes the maintenance of a parent library is a strong addition to a child's program.

More recently, many parent education programs have been concerned with teaching specific parental skills that will support intellectual and language learning in the school. A typical program may portray model parental behavior such as including children in discussions, conveying to children the meanings of parental action, reading simple stories aloud, and providing instructional activities and material in the home. The specific techniques needed in these activities are often taught directly to parents, who have opportunities to practice these skills under supervision. Sometimes kits of materials are loaned to parents for their use with their children at home. In these programs, working with babies may be stressed as much as working with preschoolers. The hope is that ultimately all the children in a family will be affected by what the parent learns.

Supervising Parent Participation

Parent participation in classroom activities is an integral part of the organization of cooperative nursery schools and Head Start programs. Parents can be invited into classes to read stories to children, to provide tutoring services for needy children, to help with instructional groups, to help with classroom routines, and to serve as resource persons. They can often participate as teaching assistants as well.

Careful supervision should be provided when parents are invited to participate in the teaching program. Holding a series of orientation meetings with participating parents can help lessen possible confusion. Parents need to know about the program, including the daily schedule of activities and the rules and patterns of behavior expected of children in different areas of the classroom and the school. Finally, they need to be told their specific responsibilities. The development of a parent manual containing this information is helpful if a number of parents are used in the program.

Teachers should supervise parents who participate in the program, keeping track of their behavior and possibly making notes to be used in evaluative conferences later. At the end of the day, it is useful for these parents and the teacher to meet to review the work that both have done. Praise and support should be amply given, as should criticism and advice for improving practice. As parents continue their work with the teacher, the area of responsibility and the amount of freedom allowed can often increase.

Working with Parent Policy Boards

The most difficult part of the teacher's relationship with parents is often working with them in developing educational and administrative policy for schools. Sometimes the difficulty stems from the teacher's feeling that she is better prepared to make decisions than are the parents because she has a greater amount of specialized knowledge upon which to base a decision. In addition, the teacher has a vested interest in the decisions the parents might make about school practices. Teachers have their own ideological biases as well, which can limit what they consider proper school policy.

Both parents and teachers may come to board meetings with their own particular difficulties. Minority group members and lower-class parents may view teachers with a certain amount of distrust. Previous experience as victims of discrimination or differences in values and behavior patterns may lead to a feeling of suspicion on the part of the parents. Teachers, on the other hand, may have difficulty in communicating with persons who do not share their personal and professional vocabulary.

The effectiveness of a teacher's relationship with a board is a function of the feeling of trust shared by all involved. This takes time, energy, and effort and grows out of a series of encounters in which the teacher demonstrates that she can be trusted; it is facilitated by a show of competence and an honest concern for the children in the program. Keeping lines of communication open, listening to parents, and keeping the sources of decisions public also helps in the achievement of trust.

Ultimately, the role of the teacher working with a policy board is to help the parents make their decisions. The decisions made by parents may be different from those the teacher might make herself, but this must be accepted. This does not mean the teacher abrogates her professional responsibility, but rather that there must be a redefinition of that responsibility. The teacher should use her role in policy board sessions to educate the parents, seeing that they have appropriate information upon which to base their decisions. Further, she must help them anticipate the consequences of the decisions they make upon the program and upon the people involved. A teacher who can allow parents to move independently beyond her shows a great deal of professional maturity.

DEVELOPING
TECHNIQUES FOR
WORKING WITH PARENTS

Working with parents, like working with children, requires the development of long-range plans, interview and guidance skills and the ability to work with small and large groups. Teachers must also develop skills in evaluating and recording the results of encounters with parents.

Planning

A teacher must be clear about the purposes of parent contacts, knowledgeable about the availability and use of resources, and able to think through the consequences of parent activities. Most important is the need to match the parent activity to the specific purposes of parent work.

If a teacher wishes to refer a parent for help to a social agency, she must be able to communicate that need to the parent without becoming too threatening. She ought to have available the names and addresses of social agencies and know how to make application to them. If she wishes to enlist parents in helping with the problem of a child's behavior in class, she should have observational records of the child's behavior available so that she can be as concrete in her descriptions of the problem as possible.

A total parent program should be planned on a full-year basis. Such planning allows the teacher to create a balance of different kinds of parent contacts during the year. Meetings can be spaced so that they occur with a degree of frequency without interfering with school operations or family traditions. In addition, teachers can anticipate the needs of the parent programs and prepare for them. If conferences are to be held, the teacher must collect examples of the children's work or behavior as well as assemble records relating to school performance.

In planning meetings with groups of parents, a teacher should think through the proposed content of the program well in advance, make arrangements for speakers or films if they are to be used, and assign responsibility for specific tasks such as hostessing or cleaning up in order to insure a smooth running meeting.

She should also plan to have appropriate space available for the particular kind of parent activity. A large meeting may require the use of a school auditorium or multipurpose room. A class mothers' meeting might be held in the classroom after school but may require rearrangement of the furniture. A conference with individual parents might best be held in a special room or in the classroom if it will be quiet and free of interruptions. A parents' work session, using woodwork tools or sewing machines, requires special facilities and adequate space for equipment and material.

Interviewing

Interviewing techniques include both the means of gathering information from and providing information to parents. A teacher should learn how to put a parent at ease in a conference; sometimes providing coffee will help; at other times, speaking first about general school matters of interest to the parent is also useful. Such simple steps can help the teacher establish rapport in the conference. It is important not to spend too much time in preliminaries, however, for if the parent feels the teacher is "beating around the bush," he can become defensive, thereby creating rather than solving a problem.

Teachers often find it useful to use an interview schedule or outline to make sure they elicit the information they want in a conference. Such a schedule lists the kinds of information needed from the parent and outlines the points she wishes to cover. An interview schedule should always be flexible, however. Questions should not be read directly from the form, because it is only a guide to be used to insure that the purposes of the conference are met no matter what sequence or degree of formality is used.

Counseling techniques are also useful for the teacher. It is vital to learn how to *listen* to parents. This requires that she know something about the parents and is sensitive to their feelings as well as to the information being communicated. It is important to listen responsively, reacting to the parents' messages when appropriate and helping them work toward realistic solutions of problems regarding the children.

Although it is sometimes easy to give advice, within a parent-teacher context the counseling must be particularly meaningful and relevant to each specific situation. If a child should be read to at home, the teacher should help the parent find the source of books, or make books available. She should also help the parent learn some of the techniques of reading that will eventually benefit the child.

Working with Groups

Large groups are not as useful as small ones for the development of discussions and the support of interaction processes. Small group sessions require the teacher to use group leadership techniques. As the leader, she must convene the group and chair the discussion; she must be sensitive to the needs of the group and allow the members to become responsible for its actions. She cannot impose her will on the group unless she wishes discussion to cease and parent involvement to lessen, but neither can she allow the group discussion to move aimlessly for long periods of time. She must become a democratic leader, responsive and flexible while maintaining her authority, if she wishes to make best use of the group process.

Large group meetings are practical for expository purposes—the same speakers or films used for these meetings can be used for small groups as well.

A group convened by a teacher frequently develops its own independent life. Projects undertaken by parents may develop for the education of the group's members or as a service to the school. Changes in the nature of the group sometimes require more time than a teacher can possibly give if she wishes to remain the group leader; in this event, she may help find another leader, either someone from the group itself or from outside. She may then continue working with the parent group as an adviser, helping the parent group as the need arises. Teachers can feel legitimate pride when groups they have started become autonomous as a result of the leadership they have provided.

The group process can be a powerful force. Groups can be helpful and supportive, or aggressive and oppressive. It is important to use the group process carefully, ever cautious of any limitations in skills involving working with groups.

Evaluating Parent Work

Just as children's programs are evaluated in school, so are parent programs. Goals need to be defined and judgments made with the achievement of these goals in mind. The kind of relationships the school wishes to establish with the home and the purposes of the parent program should be carefully thought through. Parent programs take much less time than do the children's programs, and schools should be willing to expend ample time and resources for continuing and evaluating constructive parent programs.

Informal checks on parent programs can include simply counting the attendance at parent meetings or conferences. This is a broad gauge and needs to be interpreted carefully—some portions of our society will have high attendance at parent functions no matter how useful or well implemented they are. Teachers can often intuitively gauge the relationship they have with the parents of children in their class, but this also needs to be cautiously interpreted. Teachers have been known to delude themselves and parents can, in being polite, act more responsively than they really feel. A school crisis often shows the quality of the relationship established between home and school. No matter how difficult, attempts should be made to evaluate the quality of any parent program, and each teacher ought to be responsible for maintaining at least a narrative record of parent activities.

USING PUBLIC RELATIONS TECHNIQUES   Most of the ways of working with parents discussed here have dealt with face-to-face relations with parents, but other types of relationships with family and community should also be established. A good school should have a strong, though not necessarily polished program of public relations. Because the school belongs to the parents and the community, it must be responsive to them and communicate to them what happens in school.

A good public relations program includes maintaining a rapport with the community so that parents and others feel welcome in visiting the school. This should go beyond the annual "Open School Week" that has become an American tradition.

Displays, both in and out of school, are also helpful in telling the community what children are doing. Art work, the results of projects, tapes of children's songs and stories, and so forth can be tastefully organized and used to tell parents about the children's school experiences. Local merchants are often quite helpful in making space available for such displays and in other kinds of support. The local news media can be helpful in telling the school's story to the public; news coverage of important or interesting school events is of value to both school and community. Field trips, holiday celebrations, and other special events are often considered newsworthy by local news media.

Teachers can carry on their own public relations activities through newsletters, notes sent home, and invitations to parents to participate in special events. All of these need to be considered in a good public relations program.

WORKING WITH PARENTS: A TWO-WAY STREET   Too often teachers feel that a parent program is an opportunity for them to do something *to* the parents—to somehow change them. In reality, a good parent program works differently, for the parents should also have an opportunity to influence teachers and possibly change the school. A strong parent program can open up new avenues of communication both ways. When there is no information, there can be little criticism, but as parents become more knowledgeable about the school, there will be more—hopefully constructive to a large degree.

Actually, the judgments of parents can be considered another source of information about the effectiveness of the program. Parent grievances should be considered as well as other data in making school decisions, and teachers should always be receptive to parents' ideas and criticisms. Changes should not be instituted merely as a way of placating parents, however—teachers should feel strong enough in their professional role to be able to justify their acts in school and to stand by programs they believe constitute sound professional practices.

SUGGESTED READING

AUERBACH, ALINE B., AND CHILD STUDY ASSOCIATION, *Parents Learn Through Discussion: Principles and Practices of Parent-Group Education.* New York: John Wiley and Sons, 1968.

BAILARD, VIRGINIA, AND RUTH STRANG, *Parent-Teacher Conferences.* New York: McGraw-Hill, 1964.

BEYER, EVELYN, *Sharing—A New Level in Teacher-Parent Relationship.* Washington, D.C.: National Association for the Education of Young Children, 1968.

National Conference on Social Welfare, *Helping the Family in Urban Society.* New York: Columbia University Press, 1963.

CHILMAN, CATHERINE S., *Growing Up Poor.* Washington, D.C.: U.S. Department of Health, Education, and Welfare, 1966.

D'EVELYN, KATHERINE E., *Individual Parent-Teacher Conferences.* New York: Teachers College Press, 1952.

GINOTT, HAIM G., *Between Parent and Child.* New York: Macmillan, 1965.

HEFFERNAN, HELEN, AND VIVIAN E. TODD, *Elementary Teacher's Guide to Working with Parents.* West Nyack, New York: Parker Publishing Company, 1969.

HYMES, J. L., *Effective Home-School Relations.* Englewood Cliffs, N.J.: Prentice-Hall, Inc., 1963.

LANGDON, GRACE, AND I. W. STOUT, *Parent-Teacher Interviews.* Englewood Cliffs, N.J.: Prentice-Hall, Inc., 1954.

LEONARD, EDITH M., DOROTHY D. VANDEMAN, AND LILLIAN E. MILES, *Counselling with Parents in Early Childhood Education.* New York: Macmillan, 1954.

MEDINNUS, GENE R., *Readings in the Psychology of Parent-Child Relations.* New York: John Wiley and Sons, 1967.

OSBORN, ERNEST, *The Parent-Teacher Partnership.* New York: Teachers College Press, 1959.

PROJECT HEAD START, *Parents Are Needed.* Washington, D.C.: Office of Economic Opportunity, n.d.

Working with Parents. Washington, D.C.: National School Public Relations Association, 1968.

14

Programs for Young
Disadvantaged Children

The field of early childhood education, in particular, has been greatly affected by the recent concern for the education of disadvantaged children. Beginning with small research and demonstration projects and continuing through larger mass-service programs, a wide range of proposals for program organization and content have brought this field of education to life. While it may take years to assess the full impact of the new programs on the development of disadvantaged children, teachers are now beginning to see the positive implications and incorporating some of them into their classroom programs.

Attempting to sort out the many projects related to the education of disadvantaged children is no simple matter. Some programs suggest that the problem of developing educational curricula is primarily one of determining the goals we wish children to achieve and then logically programming backwards to insure the acquisition of prerequisite skills leading to these goals. Such a process tends to oversimplify curriculum development, however. At present there is no total agreement on the legitimate goals of education for the disadvantaged, nor can one ignore the relationship between public policy and educational programs. To judge the problem adequately, one must appreciate the context in which the concern for disadvantaged children has recently developed, the theories about disadvantaged cultures and child-rearing practices that have been promulgated, the relationship between education and behavior that exists, and the constraints that school organization places upon education in order to develop a truly useful program for children and parents.

WHO ARE THE "DISADVANTAGED"?

Over the years, a number of terms have been used to label the group we call "disadvantaged"—"culturally deprived," "economically depressed," and "children of the inner city" are but a few of them. All the terms relate to poor persons for whom the school's traditional program does not seem to be effective.

Sometimes economic guidelines are used to identify the disadvantaged group. Children in families with yearly incomes below $3,000 for example, might be considered disadvantaged. These guidelines, however, do not adequately differentiate the many groups of people having little money. There are differences in what money can buy in different sections of the country—differences in the amount of money needed to maintain families. There are also concerns other than monetary that are related to being disadvantaged.

The disadvantaged are sometimes identified as being persons from minority groups, or persons with identifiable subcultural backgrounds. Southern Appalachian whites, residents of urban black ghettoes, Mexican-Americans, Puerto Ricans, and American Indians have all been identified as "disadvantaged." Actually, while each of these groups contributes more than its share to the disadvantaged population, obviously not *all* members of these groups can be considered disadvantaged.

Although formal definitions of "disadvantaged" may be of little use to teachers, it is helpful to note that we identify in this group children reared in poverty, whether in rural or urban circumstances, and that a large proportion of the persons identified as disadvantaged are from subcultural groups which have traditionally experienced discrimination, and which have been isolated from the majority culture.

FACTORS AFFECTING CONCERN FOR THE DISADVANTAGED

Major changes in educational policy usually have their roots in changes in society and are continued only as they remain responsive to social needs. The factors that have led to the concern for the education of disadvantaged children are multiple. Among the social factors are the emerging civil rights movement and the politically voiced concern over the existence of poverty in an affluent country. In addition, changes in psychological theory, especially as related to the development of intelligence discussed earlier, support newer hypotheses about the effects of educational treatment on children. Also, there has been increased concern about the intellectual content offered to children in schools.

Civil Rights and Poverty

The famous 1954 Supreme Court decision, which held that separate educational facilities for Negro children could not provide equal education opportunity, was to herald a long battle to bring about integration and equality in the schools. Many different ways of attempting to achieve this goal have been tried in the decade and a half following this decision. The first tactic was to attempt to do away with legal barriers of segregation and to desegregate schools throughout the country. This has been a difficult task and is still incomplete. In addition to the legal barriers to desegregation, the segregated housing patterns in most communities necessitated the use of elaborate changes in organization and transportation in schools aiming to desegregate their facilities. At times these plans have been opposed by parents whose children would be inconvenienced by them. Some school systems have become almost all-black, as large cities experienced the mass movements of white middle-class families escaping to all-white suburbs. In addition, the areas in which disadvantaged and minority groups live are the oldest sections in many cities, and hence contain the oldest school buildings, often extremely overcrowded. Teachers with the least amount of experience and expertise are often assigned to these inner-city schools.

When minority-group children began to be grouped for instruction with "advantaged" students, it was often found that they were behind in academic work. Some attributed the failure to the inadequate schooling previously available, and others suggested that the homes and communities in which these children were reared provided inadequate background for school learning. This gap in academic achievement broadened as the children continued in school. Programs of compensatory education, designed to make up for early environmental inadequacies, were developed, sometimes as an aid to integrating the schools, other times as an alternative to integration.

More recently, local control of area schools has been demanded by members of minority groups in the hope that increased responsiveness of schools to the community and the diminution of feelings of powerlessness in disadvantaged communities might accomplish what integration and compensatory education have so far failed to achieve—true equality of educational opportunity for all children.

Unfortunately, neither integration (or the more limited concept of desegregation), compensatory education, or community control of schools has been tried in enough areas or for an adequate period of time to enable assessment of the impact of each on the academic achievement of disadvantaged children.

Changes in Psychological Theory

Since the beginning of the scientific study of human development, arguments have raged about the modifiability of human development as a result of environmental manipulations. Arguments suggesting that large subgroups of populations were disadvantaged because of genetic endowments have been countered over the years by research and theory demonstrating the effect of environment on intelligence. These have led to the concept of compensatory education, wherein school experiences attempt to make up for environmental deficits.

The issue of modifiability of human intelligence has not been resolved by any means. A recent article by Jensen seriously questions the notion that one can make significant changes in a human being's intellectual development as a result of environmental manipulations. Jensen continues to theorize that the impact of the environment is slight when considered along with the individual's genetic makeup. He goes on to postulate that certain subgroups in our society may have gene "pools" that cause them to have lower ability to pursue certain intellectual tasks in spite of the kinds of environmental backgrounds or educational programs that might be offered to them.[1]

In spite of the fact that this argument has been countered by many psychologists, it is noted here to show that the controversy still rages at this writing and will probably continue for some time to come. Teachers, as professional environmentalists, must act as if what they do can have profound effects on their charges in spite of the fact that the last word on the argument is not yet in.

Too often teachers have used intelligence tests and other sources of information about children to determine placement of children in different kinds of educational programs. Intelligence tests are actually tests of general achievement which assume that people have equal access to the learnings sampled in test items. When such an assumption is not valid, as happens with many minority groups, one may be testing differences in learning *opportunity* rather than in learning *ability*. To use such a test to continue to limit the learning opportunities of children is to create a self-fulfilling prophesy. In addition, tests administered in groups or to very young children may not adequately reflect the disadvantaged child's true ability. Teachers should instead be concerned with extending the learning capacity of all children, regardless of background.

[1] Arthur R. Jensen, "How Much Can We Boost IQ and Scholastic Achievement?" *Harvard Educational Review*, Vol. 39, No. 1 (Winter 1969), 1–123.

Changes in the Role of the School

The third factor that serves as background to new programs for the disadvantaged is the recent change in the concept of the role of the school, especially relating to the early years of schooling. During earlier periods of history, schools for young children were concerned primarily with socio-emotional development or with character training. As long as schools were not concerned with intellectual learning there was little concern for using them as a means of increasing intellectual development in children.

Beginning with the new curriculum development movement of the late 1950s and early 1960s, however, the early childhood years were seen as providing increased opportunities for nurturing intellectual development. New curricula for teaching the sciences, social science, mathematics, and languages were developed for lower grade levels. Changes in human developmental theories added support to the arguments of new curricula developers; the ideas of Piaget were often invoked in support of the new curriculum proposals.

These social and intellectual movements converged slowly. Early attempts to improve the education of disadvantaged children focused primarily on older children. Programs affecting school dropouts or enriching the experience of secondary school children, as in the Higher Horizons program of the New York City Schools, gave way slowly to programs focusing on the early years. Pioneer programs for young children included those of the Institute for Developmental Studies in New York City, as well as the Early Admission Program of Baltimore. Each of these supported generally enriched preschool education for disadvantaged children as well as specifically designed learning opportunities to alleviate learning deficits.

In 1965, *Operation Head Start*, under the auspices of the Office of Economic Opportunity, provided the first mass preschool program for disadvantaged children. Parallel to this development, numbers of experimentally designed programs were established in many places in the United States, most of them implemented on a limited scale. As it became evident that a single year or a few months of education prior to the child's entrance to school was inadequate to meet the needs of disadvantaged children, Project *Follow Through* was conceived by the federal government to extend programs of compensatory education through the primary grades. As it exists now, *Follow Through* utilizes a number of models of compensatory education presently being promulgated in the hope that some comparative judgment can result from their comparative evaluation.

Although it is still too soon to make evaluative judgments, it is helpful to analyze the approaches used in many of these programs and the possible effects they may have. Approaches to compensatory education stem from a number of assumptions about the nature and needs of disadvantaged children. Some of these assumptions are discussed in the following section.

CHARACTERISTICS OF THE DISADVANTAGED   In order to provide adequately for the education of disadvantaged young children we must do two things. First we must identify his educational problems, including the background and personal attributes that affect or are affected by education. Second, we need to make some decisions about the goals of education for disadvantaged children—whether we wish to educate them for a separate niche in the nation's social structure, or whether we wish to provide differentiated goals for differentiated elements of our total population.

It was stated earlier that the disadvantaged population does not constitute a single group in our society but is made up of members of many subcultures. These subcultures do share certain characteristics, which include a higher degree of poverty than is found in the general population and a sharing of the effects of discriminatory practices in employment, housing, education, and other areas of life.

The problem of the education of the disadvantaged must also be analyzed in the context of an increasingly technical urban society. In the past years, there has been a lessening of employment opportunities for poorly educated and unskilled persons. Many jobs previously handled by unskilled workers have been eliminated through the use of machines, and new jobs being created in our society generally require a high degree of training.

Although in the past, many unskilled and uneducated persons were able to find employment on farms, this area of employment is also shrinking, with fewer workers able to produce increasing yields because of the application of new technology and the use of complex machinery. The move to northern cities from southern rural areas by the poor has also been precipitated by the promise of better welfare payments. This does not suggest that there is no problem in educating disadvantaged children in rural areas but rather that, because of economic and population shifts, the problems of educating disadvantaged children is seen by many as primarily an urban problem, with rural problems often not receiving as great attention.

Any generalized description of a population as diverse as that labeled *disadvantaged* must be presented with a word of caution. First it must again be stressed that there is no single population group that can be identified as disadvantaged. In addition, any group description must necessarily obliterate individual differences within the group. This does not deny the existence of such differences, but the qualifications of group description would only confuse any discussion. Many statements made here are not equally applicable to *all* persons in the group labeled as disadvantaged. Indeed, many persons in this group do not fit these descriptions at all. The fact that over the years many individuals who were brought up in poor circumstances have been able to achieve success in our society does not negate the usefulness of descriptions of group trends among the disadvantaged but rather highlights the importance of individual difference in any group.

For a teacher working with a particular group of children, any discussion of disadvantaged children and educational programs designed for them must stand as a statement of working hypotheses that are to be tested in the reality of the classroom. To the degree that her charges differ from the global descriptions provided or do not seem to benefit from suggested educational treatments, such hypotheses must be modified or discarded. This, by the way, is as true of statements made about working with advantaged children.

Physical Characteristics of Disadvantaged Children

As a result of the circumstances of poverty, certain physical characteristics can often be noted in disadvantaged children. On the whole, they are less healthy than advantaged children, suffering from more physical problems and being more susceptible to illness. This results from the lack of available medical services in areas in which they live, as well as from the difficulty in using what services are available.

Generally speaking, there are fewer doctors and hospitals in slum areas than in middle-class areas. Where clinics exist, they often require great expenditures in time and energy for people to make use of them. There are long lines requiring tedious waiting; in addition, the impersonal treatment in clinics and the inability of patients to establish a continuing relationship with a doctor often discourages the poor from seeking medical attention for minor problems.

As a result, a person usually feels the impact of being disadvantaged from birth—indeed sooner, for the percentage of stillbirths, premature births, and obstetrical complications is higher for disadvantaged persons than for the general population, as is the rate of infant mortality. As the child matures, his chances of being ill are greater than average and he may also suffer from nutritional problems brought about by the lack of food or an improperly balanced diet. Though to some extent this is some-times the result of the absence of dietary knowledge, it is also a direct result of simply being too poor to buy needed foods. Research also sug-gests that poor persons must often pay more for food in slum areas or are offered inferior goods at the same prices that are charged in middle-class areas. These price differentials may be the result of both the higher costs of doing business in slum areas and differentiated shopping patterns of slum dwellers (such as buying in smaller quantities), but the slum culture also provides opportunities for unethical practices by merchants. In addition, the relative high costs of other necessities, (rent, furniture, and so forth) leave a smaller percentage of the income available to poor families.[2]

Social Characteristics of Disadvantaged Children

A large proportion of disadvantaged children are reared in homes from which the father is absent; this may be in part a result of policies relating to the administration of welfare and the Aid to Dependent Chil-dren programs. Generally, such aid has not been available in homes in which the father is present, often leading to the separation of parents in order to qualify for aid. Families may, in addition, have larger numbers of children. Living accommodations are generally poorer and more crowded for disadvantaged children, and there are distinct differences in child-rearing patterns.

Many children in the disadvantaged population, especially in heavily urban areas, suffer from a high degree of isolation. The mobility of fam-ilies and the dangers of living in the area, including possibilities of per-sonal attacks and theft, create a living pattern in which children may spend inordinate amounts of time in the home and have contact with relatively few persons outside their immediate family.

Whiteman and Deutsch have postulated a deprivation index to identify disadvantaged children which includes the following:

1. Housing dilapidation index for the block on which he resides, and assigned to him, computed from census data.
2. The educational aspirational level of the parent for the child.
3. The number of children under 18 in the home.
4. Dinner conversation.
5. Total number of cultural experiences anticipated by child for the coming weekend, i.e. visiting relatives, family, museums, library, zoo, travel out-side [the] city, school or lesson work.
6. Attendance of child in kindergarten.[3]

[2]David Caplowitz, *The Poor Pay More* (New York: The Free Press, 1963).
[3]Martin Whiteman and Martin Deutsch, "Social Disadvantage as Related to Intellective and Language Development," in Martin Deutsch, Irwin Katz, and Arthur A. Jensen, *Social Class, Race, and Psychological Development* (New York: Holt, Rinehart & Winston, 1968), p. 100.

While this index was designed specifically for a New York population, it can easily be modified for use in other areas.

Wolf concurs with the idea that environment affects intelligence more as a set of forces than as a set of particular characteristics. The forces that he studied that correlated with a child's intellectual development were:

Press for achievement motivation

Nature of intellectual expectations of child
Nature of intellectual aspirations for child
Amount of information about child's intellectual development
Nature of reward for intellectual development

Press for language development

Emphasis on use of language in a variety of situations
Opportunities for enlarging vocabulary
Emphasis on correctness of usage
Quality of language models available

Provision for general learning

Opportunities provided for learning at home
Opportunities provided for learning outside the home
Availability of learning supplies
Availability and encouragement of use of books, periodicals, and library facilities
Nature and amount of assistance provided to facilitate learning in a variety of situations[4]

While such indices might need modification to increase their applicability to different communities, their use can help identify the level of disadvantage in a child's background.

Psychological Characteristics of Disadvantaged Children

The major concern of most teachers in dealing with the disadvantaged is with their psychological characteristics, especially those related to performance in school. Of course these characteristics may have their antecedents in physical or social phenomena, but they are primarily manifest in the relationship to the school, the learning situation, and the teacher.

The most apparent psychological characteristic of many disadvantaged children is their inability to cope with the academic studies of the school. They frequently manifest a lower ability to perform on verbal

---

[4]Richard M. Wolf, *Identification and Measurement of Environmental Process Variables Related to Intelligence* (Unpublished Ph.D. Thesis, University of Chicago, 1964), p. 48.

tasks than on nonverbal tasks, and because many of the tasks of school learning become increasingly verbal in nature, the problems created by poor linguistic ability are heightened as they continue through school.

Some educators have also identified differences in the intellectual style of disadvantaged and advantaged children. Reissman has named elements of style in the disadvantaged child's mode of behavior that cause difficulties in traditional classroom settings. Whether these appear in the early years or are manifest only later is open to question.[5]

Among the intellectual differences between disadvantaged and non-disadvantaged children are those related to the ability to learn conceptually or associatively. Jensen has stated that disadvantaged children lack the ability to learn conceptual material—that is, material taught through understanding. He contends, however, that there is no lack of ability on the part of disadvantaged children to learn material associatively, through memorization. He goes on to suggest that schools might do better by teaching disadvantaged children primarily through associative means.[6] Although some researchers have found associative learning patterns useful for the education of disadvantaged children, many programs have successfully demonstrated the ability of disadvantaged children to learn conceptually.

Much has been written about the disadvantaged child's language deficits. Probably the most basic description of the differences—one accepted by most psychologists—is that postulated by Bernstein, who suggests that the key differences between the language of disadvantaged and advantaged children lies in the area of syntax or linguistic structure. He has theorized that disadvantaged children use a *restricted* linguistic code, whereas advantaged children used an *elaborated* code. The *restricted* code is characterized by short, grammatically simple sentences. It is limited and condensed, containing symbols of a low order of generality. It is a language of implicit meaning, useful for reinforcing a sense of identity, but not as adequate for communicating information. The *elaborated* code is more accurate and grammatically correct. It is precise and can express a wide range of thought.[7]

The language of the school and the language of most formal discourse is of an elaborated nature. Children lacking the ability to use this code have a receptive and expressive disadvantage in the school, for their

[5]Frank Reissman, *The Culturally Deprived Child* (New York: Harper & Row, 1962), pp. 63–73.

[6]Jensen, "How Much Can We Boost IQ and Scholastic Achievement?" pp. 111–17.

[7]Basil Bernstein, "Social Structure, Language and Learning," in A. Harry Passow, Miriam Goldberg, and Abraham J. Tannenbaum, eds., *Education of the Disadvantaged* (New York: Holt, Rinehart & Winston, 1967), pp. 225–44.

discourse is useless in communicating with teachers or the various educational media which are the extensions of the teacher.

Intellectual and language skills are taught to children from the moment of birth. Child-rearing practices and the nature of parent-child interactions constitute what has been called a "hidden curriculum" aimed at teaching children skills which they are assumed to have upon entry to school. The absence of such a curriculum in the homes of disadvantaged children has been suggested as one of the major causes of their difficulty. Parents in disadvantaged homes have different strategies for teaching proper behavior to their children—they have less time to spend with each child, and they achieve their personal satisfactions in somewhat different ways than do middle-class parents. It is easy to see how the physical, social, and psychological aspects of development are interrelated in a pattern that leads to the child being disadvantaged in school.

Although the picture drawn here suggests that the problems of the disadvantaged are problems they bring to school, it is not suggested that the school bears no responsibility for creating educational problems. Insensitivity to the needs of the disadvantaged leads, in many cases, to turning the schools into custodial agencies, or in other instances, into agencies that have extended patterns of discrimination. It is beyond the limits of this discussion to describe how these conditions have come about and what can be done to eliminate them. The problems of the disadvantaged go far beyond the schools and, contrary to the beliefs held by some, improved education will not eradicate them. There are many things, however, that the school can do to improve the lot of the disadvantaged and to create better educational opportunities for them.

DEVELOPING INTERVENTION TECHNIQUES

One of the major changes that have taken place in our thinking about poverty and discrimination is the general feeling that they are not normal and natural. It is now felt that we may not only be able to alleviate the plight of the poor but eventually we might do away with poverty entirely. The key to this process is the identification of the *causes* of poverty, which tend to operate in a cyclical fashion, supporting and recreating one another in a continuing cause-effect relationship, and intervention in such a way that the cycle can be broken. One area of intervention has been identified as education.

There are two basic strategies for intervention in education that can be attempted. One identifies the formal and informal educational opportunities provided to advantaged children from birth and suggests replicating these opportunities for disadvantaged children. The other identifies those elements of disadvantagement considered to be most crucial and creates increased opportunities to alleviate these particular problems only. The first strategy suggests a program of general enrichment; the second leads to the establishment of a narrower program of compensatory education which is significantly different from the education provided to middle-class children. Each of these strategies has been tried, although most programs of compensatory education attempt to find a middle position.

STRATEGIES IN WORKING WITH THE DISADVANTAGED

There are several general approaches and sets of basic assumptions that are common to a number of different projects providing teachers with useful information applicable in teaching disadvantaged children. These approaches include providing for the "out-of-classroom" needs of the child, changing the community structure, educating parents, working with infants, making schools more responsive to the needs of the children, providing general enrichment, teaching specific readiness skills to children, improving their intellectual functioning, developing language facility, and increasing the motivation for learning.

Providing for the "Out-of-Classroom"
Needs of Children

Because the problems of disadvantaged children range far beyond their difficulty with school work, many of the programs for them put great emphasis on the provision of noneducational services. A good example of the kinds of services that may be offered is evidenced in most *Head Start* programs.

The concept of the Child Development Center used in *Head Start* grows out of the assumption that to alleviate their difficulties, one must deal with all the developmental problems of disadvantaged children and not simply with their academic problems. The Head Start program becomes more than a program of preschool education; attention is given to the physical, social, and medical problems of the children enrolled. The nutritional portion of the program provides them with a well-balanced lunch in addition to nutritious snacks and sometimes breakfast. Attention is given to the nature of the food served, the way it is served, and the children's eating habits. In a good center, a conscious effort is made to extend children's experiences with food while taking into consideration individual likes and dislikes as well as cultural food preferences.

A health services program is a part of each Child Development

Center. Children are given medical and dental examinations, and may receive needed immunizations. After they go through the various evaluation and examination procedures, correctable physical and dental problems lead to a program of treatment. The center is expected to help devise a plan for follow-up treatment using available public or private health resources. The health program often goes beyond the provision of service in conferring with parents about health problems and providing increased education and consultation about health practices at home.

Social services are also a part of the Child Development Center's program. Trained social workers or community workers may be members of the staff, providing such services as helping the parent deal with the problems of raising children as well as with personal problems that arise in the family. In some instances, counseling can be offered the parent directly.

The services required are sometimes beyond those the center can perform, and in this case the parent may be referred to a community agency for help. Ideally, the center develops close working relations with community agencies so that referrals are not simply perfunctory. The community worker may act as liaison between parent and agency, interpreting when necessary and helping to see that the proper aid is given.

Although teachers are seldom involved in providing such services directly to parents, they may be given the responsibility for coordinating the administration of services and seeing that families receive those services that are needed. The teacher should be informed about what is happening to a child's family, even when others are responsible for the provision of these services. Changes in family status may be mirrored in changes in the child's behavior in school. A knowledge of what is happening to the child outside the school is helpful in interpreting the child's in-school behavior and in making the school setting more relevant to the child at particular times.

Changing the Community Structure

Most schools are considered to be extensions of the community, reflecting its structure and values. The teacher, as an agent of the school, is expected to be responsive to the community, possibly even bending to its will as necessary. Seldom is the school considered as an instrument for changing the community. In some instances, however, the way educational services for disadvantaged children are provided can have a significant impact on the community structure.

In the operation of the Child Development Group of Mississippi, the organization of preschools grew out of the need to cope with the reality of providing a service to Negro children in isolated Mississippi communities, often without the cooperation of the local school systems or other governmental agencies. The organization also grew out of the belief that the preschool program should reflect the cultural heritage and values of the Negro population the program served. In each community, CDGM committees were established to develop and support the preschools. These committees first had to find adequate physical facilities to house the program; the buildings that were found often had to be repaired and altered to be made usable. In the absence of trained teachers to work with the children, it was possible for a teacher to be elected from the committee, irrespective of formal educational background. Consultative services were provided by resource persons so that novice teachers were trained on the job and helped to deal with the problems of providing an educational program for the children. The materials for learning often grew out of the experiences of the children in their particular environment.

The experience of CDGM, though shortlived, led to a concept of early childhood education closely related to community development. In organizing to establish a preschool center, committee members developed skills and strategies that could be used in other areas of community concern. Levin has summed up the basic concepts of this community approach to educating young children.

Preconceived concepts of child development cannot be imposed upon communities of the poor. The program content must develop as a dynamic of the growth of community understanding.

Any community program will be experienced as an agent of an external power unless it is run by the communities of the poor themselves. The strengths and talents of the poor must be fully utilized in the planning and execution of a significant Head Start program.

Putting up cupboards and wiping up juice cannot be the major contribution of the parents and members of the communities of the poor. This concept of the use of the nonprofessional perpetuates a second-class vocational citizenship and encourages relating to the poor as second class human beings. The nonprofessional community aides must be afforded fully dignified work and full and realistic educational opportunities to achieve professional status.

Head Start must be an instrument for social change. Preschool education for communities of the poor which prepares the child for a better life without mobilizing the community toward social change is an educational and sociological "fraud." New approaches to the solution of the problems of poverty are growing out of the increased awareness of self-power developing within the poverty communities. Professionals must be prepared to reject traditional donor-donee relationships which perpetuate loss of self-worth and consequent resignation to powerlessness.[8]

[8]Tom Levin, "Preschool Education and the Communities of the Poor," in Jerome Hellmuth, ed., *The Disadvantaged Child*, Vol. 1 (Seattle: Special Child Publications, 1967), p. 398.

Underlying these concepts is the assumption that the education of the children of a community cannot be understood or dealt with outside the context of the community structure in which the children are reared. Adequate education for disadvantaged children must go beyond simply providing reading readiness skills, for when parents are alienated from a community or are powerless in having the larger community provide for legitimate needs, education cannot take hold in their children.

Working with Parents

One of the most valuable ways of enhancing the effect of the child development center is to involve the parents actively in the program. Such involvement promotes a closer, more continuous relationship between young children and their parents.[9]

This statement, included in one of the handbooks of the Head Start program, typifies the general concern for involving parents in programs for disadvantaged children. Although the kind and degree of parent involvement found in different programs varies, parent involvement is generally considered an essential part of each one. One of the major contributions of this type of program to concepts of parent programming has been the involvement of poor, often uneducated parents in the decision-making process of the school. The degree of parent involvement in these programs is what sets them off from earlier philanthropic attempts at early education for the disadvantaged. The change in the decision-making process that such involvement creates often has significant effects both in the classrooms of the preschool center and in the communities in which the center operates.

Another significant addition to work with parents is that of providing them with specific teaching skills they might use with their children. In effect, these programs consciously incorporate elements of the teacher's role into the behavior of parents, much as middle-class parents might realize in an unconscious fashion.

Gordon, at the University of Florida, has developed procedures whereby women from the disadvantaged community work with parents of infants in the same community. The parents are taught specific parent-child interactions during weekly visits to the homes, and are then expected to use these procedures in playing with their children on a regular basis each day.[10]

[9]*Parents Are Needed* (Washington, D.C.: Office of Economic Opportunity, n.d.), p. 8.
[10]Ira Gordon, "Stimulation via Parent Education," *Children*, Vol. 16, No. 2 (March–April 1969), 57–58.

The Early Training Program directed by Susan Gray includes an education-oriented parent program that is carried on by a professional educator. This program is concerned with helping parents develop a feeling that they can cope with their environment, as well as providing specific techniques to use with their children.[11]

The Karnes program at the University of Illinois and the Nurseries in Cross-Cultural Education (NICE) directed by Mary Lane at San Francisco State College also developed specific home tasks for parents to use with their children weekly. In the NICE Project, materials such as books, toys, or games were made available to the parents, as well as instructions for their use.[12] In the Karnes program parents met weekly, and in the two-hour seminars mothers made educational materials such as puppets, flannel boards, matching and lotto games, and materials for sorting and classifying activities. They were also taught songs and finger-plays. They were expected to use the games and songs as well as the material they made with their children throughout the week. Ways to use these materials, and weekly successes and failures were discussed with the parents.[13]

Specific techniques for working with parents may vary, but there are some central considerations that remain constant in all these projects. First, it is assumed that there is a need to go beyond the experience of the classroom if meaningful results with disadvantaged children are to accrue. In addition, the parents are seen as lacking in specific skills needed for educating their child effectively, but able to learn these skills with some outside help. Finally, there is a concern for improving the relationship between parent and child as a result of a program rather than alienating the child from the parent by offering the child alone access to a different cultural milieu.

Working with Infants

With the realization that the process of education begins at birth and continues in the home long before there is any thought of sending them to formal schools, new programs are attempting to focus on this earliest educational period. Some of them work through the parent as illustrated above, and others attempt to develop institutional structures to meet the needs of the very young. The Parent-Child Center and pro-

[11]Susan B. Gray, Rupert A. Klaus, James O. Miller, and Bettye J. Forrester, *Before First Grade: The Early Training Project for Culturally Disadvantaged Children* (New York: Teachers College Press, 1966).

[12]Mary B. Lane, "Nurseries in Cross-Cultural Education," *Childhood Education*, Vol. 45, No. 6 (February 1969), 333–35.

[13]Merle B. Karnes, W. S. Studley, W. R. Wright, and A. S. Hodkins, "An Approach for Working with Mothers of Disadvantaged Preschool Children," *Merrill-Palmer Quarterly of Behavior and Development*, Vol. 14 (April 1968), 174–84.

posed 4–C programs are illustrations of these attempts. These projects see the family as an integral unit and attempt to evolve new patterns of service for families rather than simply for children.[14]

There are many ways early development can be stimulated; some involve introducing interesting apparatus into the child's environment, others involve the improvement of the parent-child relationships, with possible restructuring of the interactions that take place between the nurturing adult and the child. Approaches to improving the education of infants are being developed that build upon the child's existing home environment without changing in any way the basic structure of that environment.

In the past, the attitudes of child development specialists toward institutional settings for young children has been negative. These attitudes are changing as a result of the realization that institutions do not have to be cold, impersonal environments. New day-care settings for the very young, adequately designed and adequately staffed to meet the needs of parents and children, are changing this attitude in our country and abroad. In addition, the experience of group child rearing in the Israeli *kibbutz* is being studied.

In the kibbutz, children are reared in groups away from their natural parents beginning a few weeks after birth. Although parents visit their children daily, the prime responsibility for rearing the child is given to a *metapelet*, a trained child-care worker. Studies of these institutions and of children reared in them show little or no negative effects from such child rearing. Though the results of kibbutz child rearing may be different from its non-kibbutz counterpart, the results vary in the direction of the value structure of the entire kibbutz culture and may be a function of the culture rather than of specific child-rearing procedures.[15]

Making Schools More Responsive to the Needs of Children

A number of books have been published in recent years illustrating the negative educational effects that are a result of practices in some

---

[14]Alice V. Keliher, "Parent and Child Centers—What are They? Where Are They Going?" and Jule M. Sugarman, "The 4–C Program," *Children*, Vol. 16, No. 2 (March–April 1969), 63–66, 76–77.

[15]Those interested in learning more about kibbutz education and child-rearing practices can refer to the following books:

Bruno Bettelheim, *The Children of the Dream* (New York: Macmillan, 1969).

Peter B. Neubauer, ed., *Children in Collectives: Child-Rearing Aims and Practices in the Kibbutz* (Springfield, Ill.: Charles E. Thomas, Publishers, 1965).

A. S. Rabin, *Growing up in the Kibbutz* (New York: Springer Publishing, 1965).

M. E. Spiro, *Children of the Kibbutz* (Cambridge: Harvard University Press, 1958).

slum schools. It would be difficult for the children attending such schools not to become educationally disadvantaged, no matter how enriched their preschool experience. In many cities, members of disadvantaged communities are suggesting that no change in school programs or procedures can really make a change in the children's education because of the deep schism between school and community. They suggest that in order to effect change, the schools themselves need to be restructured, and that this can only take place when the schools become responsive to the local community. This calls for community control.

Such demands may be a response to an existing problem and may represent a necessary phase in improving the education of disadvantaged children. Until the disadvantaged community can shed the reality as well as the feeling of powerlessness, the creating of responsive schools will serve a legitimate social purpose. True school integration cannot take place without community integration, which in essence is the sharing of power by all groups in our society.

EDUCATIONAL PROGRAMS FOR YOUNG DISADVANTAGED CHILDREN

The admonition to provide preschool programs for disadvantaged children has led to a variety of responses. Children have sometimes been placed in previously existing programs or in new programs without any concern for the *kind* of educational experience provided or the *quality* of instruction in the program. In some cases, though, careful consideration has been given to program content and teaching methodology. Program may be determined by readiness requirements for academic skills or by identified learning and environmental deficits. Different ideologies relating to how children learn, how they think, and how they develop also have led to different approaches to program content and teaching methodology. Although most program innovations can be credited with making some difference in children's behavior or performance, whether these differences are lasting or whether one program is actually superior in all respects to all others is open to question. Many programs are actually eclectic in nature, using ideas from many theories.

Placing Children in Preschool Programs

Too often children from disadvantaged environments are placed in preschool settings without too much concern for the content of the experience offered. This may be due to the conflicting reasons for placing children in a preschool setting or it may be due to ignorance of what makes for a fruitful early learning experience. In some communities, for example, children are placed in preschool settings primarily to furnish them with custodial care. The parents may have to work or may be participating in an educational experience that forces them to leave their children. When there are inadequate facilities for good day care, program sponsors may feel the need to offer less than an ideal situation for the children in order to benefit the parents. Sometimes they may even feel that any day-care program is better than having the children spend their days in dilapidated or deteriorated homes. Too often program sponsors fail to realize that in offering only custodial care, they may be harming rather than benefiting children; even though a substandard house may be physically poor, it still may contain rich personal interactions that nurture a child intellectually and socially, and these kinds of interactions may be missing in an inadequate institutional setting.

In some instances, preschool programs for disadvantaged children are viewed primarily as opportunities for employment for persons from disadvantaged communities. Members of the community may be hired to the exclusion of well-prepared qualified staff. Though there are many advantages to using community persons in programs for the disadvantaged, all staff persons who work with children need to be carefully selected and supported in their working roles. Many new career opportunities are becoming available in disadvantaged areas, as schools at all levels are learning to use paraprofessionals in education. The paraprofessional, a person without professional preparation in education, needs to be specifically prepared for his job. Many junior colleges, school systems, and community agencies have developed programs to prepare such personnel for school work, with preparation often taking the form of a work-studies program.

To the extent that paraprofessionals are used to staff a program, there needs to be adequate supervision and in-service training provided. Until the paraprofessional can make decisions based upon knowledge and begin to anticipate the consequences of these decisions, he will need guidance and supervision. As personnel become trained and demonstrate competence, they can be given a higher degree of autonomy and authority.

On occasion, one will find programs that attempt to educate children without providing adequate facilities, materials, or equipment. Because programs for young children are activity-oriented, equipment and materials become necessary instructional tools at this level just as books and writing implements are essential at higher levels of education. Inadequate equipment too often stifles learning in young children. The physical setting, the program, and the instructional staff all need to be carefully selected if adequate educational opportunities are to be provided.

Teaching for Academic Readiness

The most obvious shortcoming of disadvantaged children in schools is their lack of academic achievement. The problem is often diagnosed as a need to improve general intellectual and language abilities of young children. Such a diagnosis usually leads to a program of intellectual stimulation and to activities that require children to use various information-processing skills as well as a number of techniques to extend language facility. Other programs deal more directly with the problem of academic achievement. Some use reading and mathematics readiness workbooks, having the children work out exercises that have been identified as helping them achieve success in later instruction.

The program representing this approach that has received the most attention has been the academically oriented preschool program developed by Carl Bereiter and Siegfried Engelmann. Their program is extensively described in the book *Teaching Disadvantaged Children in the Preschool* (Englewood Cliffs, N.J.: Prentice-Hall, Inc., 1966). The Bereiter-Engelmann program of preschool education is built around three daily twenty-minute sessions of direct instruction in the areas of reading, language learning, and arithmetic. Small groups of children work intensively with a teacher in a carefully controlled situation, primarily using fast-paced units of work requiring continual verbal responses. Demands are placed upon the children, who are regularly reminded of their competence. The instruction is ordered into small increments of learning, with each unit providing continual feedback of success to both teacher and child. The work is often departmentalized, with one teacher having responsibility for teaching reading, another arithmetic, and a third assigned to the language area. The twenty-minute sessions are alternated with free sessions in which art activities, music, or snacks can be provided.

The program of the Bereiter-Engelmann preschool teaches children a limited range of learnings by way of a strategy that relies heavily on associative thinking. Patterning of responses and memorization through exact repetition of adult-invoked models represent the primary instructional strategy. While the authors and others report favorable results from their program, a number of criticisms have been raised about it. Some of this relates to the content of the program, while others relate to what is absent from the content.

A number of linguists suggest that the Bereiter-Engelmann program has faulty assumptions about language acquisition and language differences in minority groups and thus may actually do more harm than good. Children do not learn their language by repeating patterns they hear but rather by developing ways of generating new phrases as a result of the vast array of language forms heard. All children come to school with a great deal of linguistic competence, although often the competence is in a different language form than that used in the school. It is unfortunate that a program designed to build language in children ignores the language competencies they have when they enter school.

Bereiter and Engelmann assume that disadvantaged children cannot think cognitively and so their program is built on associative thinking processes. Nor does the program contain within it opportunities to shift from associative to cognitive thought processes—that is, from memorization to learning through understanding. The authors of the program share their view with psychologists such as Jensen, cited earlier, who feel that one must begin with associative thinking processes to be successful in teaching disadvantaged children. Whether or not these associative processes will lead to cognitive skills is open to question. Kamii and Derman report testing children (not disadvantaged) who had been taught Piagetian constructs of conservation, specific gravity, and judgment of speed by Engelmann. Though they were able to apply their rules verbally, inconsistencies and limited understanding were evident in their conception of the phenomena.[16]

Moskovitz's criticisms of the assumptions of this program reflect much of the reaction in the field and are summarized as follows:

> He [Bereiter] has come up with a well-planned, firm methodology, but one which may indeed rest on faulty assumptions with respect to (1) language acquisition, (2) language and thought, (3) non-standard language forms in the Negro community, (4) the environment of learning, and (5) learner motivation.[17]

In spite of the criticisms, there are some positive aspects of the program. Most important, the teachers are expected to teach in an enthusiastic manner and the children are told in no uncertain terms that they can learn and that they will be expected to succeed in difficult tasks.

The Bereiter-Engelmann Program has shown positive results for its clients on achievement tests. As in other programs, it is still too soon to tell whether or not these results will hold up over time. The program has been a popular one in various circles in spite of the fact that it has probably received more criticism than any other preschool program for disadvantaged children. One of the reasons for its popularity might rest in the fact that the authors have successfully caricatured traditional primary education in form and in emphasis. The press for language, reading, and arithmetic instruction is just what concerns most primary teachers. The model also provides children with skills in responding properly to teachers' queries and to the social scheme of the school.

[16]Constance Kamii and Louise Derman, *The Engelmann Approach to Teaching Logical Thinking: Findings from the Administrations of Some Piagetian Tasks,* Mimeographed (Ypsilanti, Michigan: Ypsilanti Public Schools, February 1969), pp. 16–22.

[17]Sarah Traister Moskovitz, "Some Assumptions Underlying the Bereiter Approach," *Young Children,* Vol. 24, No. 1 (October 1968), 31.

Teaching for Intellectual Development

A number of programs for the disadvantaged are designed to generally enhance the intellectual development of children. This is probably at least a partial goal of almost all programs of compensatory education. The Institute for Developmental Studies of New York University, one of the oldest programs in existence, is working toward that aim. While there is evidence that this program shows some positive results when compared to control groups, there have been no results as spectacular as those reported for the Bereiter-Engelmann program noted above. The curriculum developed by this organization is concerned with stimulating development along parameters identified as areas of deficit for the disadvantaged child. The environment for such stimulation development includes:

> ... sensorimotor stimulation, opportunities for making perceptual discriminations, interacting with a verbally adequate adult, receiving some individual attention, linking words with objects and meaningfully relating them in stories or to varying experiential contexts, being assisted in experiencing positive self-identifications, being encouraged toward task perseverance, and being helped to receive both tangible and verbal rewards for relatively competent performances. Such an environment includes stimulation which would be demanding of responses consistent with achieved developmental capabilities and which would have sufficient and continual feedback from adults.[18]

The program of the Institute builds upon the curriculum of the traditional nursery school. The specific learning needs of children are diagnosed and new activities or materials are developed to meet those needs. The Alphabet Form Board developed by the Institute, as well as the Gotkin Language Lotto, are examples of materials developed in response to curriculum needs. Listening Centers, using tape recorders and headsets mounted in booths that effectively isolate the child, represent attempts to deal with the problem of distractability in auditory discrimination learning. The careful use of the environment and the resources available to the teacher are as important as any innovative materials in creating the curriculum of the Institute.[19]

Additional strategies for teaching intellectual skills have been developed in the Early Training Program of George Peabody College. Gray and her associates report using picture puzzles, picture sorting activities,

[18]Cynthia P. and Martin Deutsch, "Brief Reflections on the Theory of Early Childhood Enrichment Programs," in Martin Deutsch and associates, *The Disadvantaged Child* (New York: Basic Books, 1967), pp. 382–83.

[19]Fred Powledge, *To Change a Child* (Chicago: Quadrangle Books, 1967).

and other materials normally found in classrooms for young children to stimulate intellectual development. Very specific ways of using pegboards, beads and strings, parquetry blocks, and colored wooden cubes were also developed. Children were given models of designs to copy in order to learn spatial orientation, visual discrimination, and positional concepts, as well as to develop persistence and fine motor control.[20]

The work of Jean Piaget is often invoked by early childhood educators to support their ideas of education for young children. Several projects aimed at enhancing intellectual development in children have used the Piaget model of intellectual development as the basis for creating specific curricula for disadvantaged children. Lavatelli reports on a project aimed at developing a number of intellectual schema in children, including one-to-one correspondence, classification, and seriation. In the area of one-to-one correspondence, activities were planned that involved matching sets of objects that varied in color, size, shape, and number. Other activities established correspondence between groups of objects and then teachers asked the children about the equality of the groups when the physical correspondence was destroyed. Additional activities involved children in conservation of quantities.

In the classification activities, care was taken that classifications were not based solely on visual or tactile perception.[21]

Sonquist and Kamii have described a Piaget-based curriculum for disadvantaged children that was developed in Ypsilanti, Michigan, under the direction of David P. Weikart. This program uses the traditional activities and materials of the nursery school, but "in different ways and for different purposes." Using a Piagetian scheme of analysis, activities are designed to move children through levels of representation—from the index level to the symbol level to the sign level. Relationships among objects are also taught, including grouping and ordering as well as relating objects and events in time and space. Although a number of games and specific interactions are used, traditional activities such as dramatic play provide important sources of diagnoses and teaching.

Reflecting on their program in relation to other programs, Sonquist and Kamii state, "In conclusion, there appears little doubt that the traditional nursery school program, which is effective with middle-class children, can be adapted to the needs of disadvantaged children if there is continuous awareness that the program must begin at the sensorimotor level and move slowly into symbolization and the teaching of relation-

[20]Gray, Klaus, Miller, and Forrester, *Before First Grade: The Early Training Project for Culturally Disadvantaged Children*, pp. 31–77.

[21]Celia Stendler Lavatelli, "A Piaget-Derived Model for Compensatory Preschool Education," Joe L. Frost, ed., *Early Childhood Education Rediscovered* (New York: Holt, Rinehart & Winston, 1968), pp. 530–44.

ships. As each new step is mastered, the child will have a firmer foundation on which to build future learnings."[22]

Although Smilansky did not use a Piagetian framework, it is interesting to note in this context that she reports increases in IQ scores in disadvantaged children as a result of the use of specific techniques, similar to those used by Sonquist and Kamii, to improve the quality and content of their dramatic play.[23]

Feigenbaum has also described activities that nursery school teachers can use to teach conservation which, though not specifically designed for disadvantaged children, could probably be used with them. The activities suggested include games using musical chairs and instruments, animal name-cards, dolls, and carriages, as well as activities similar to traditional Piaget tasks, for example pouring liquids into differently shaped containers and comparing the weight of differently shaped lumps of playdough.[24]

Teaching Language Skills

It is difficult to separate the teaching of language skills from the teaching of intellectual skills, for in symbolizing ideas and in developing intellectual operations, language is used extensively. A number of strategies used to teach language skills to disadvantaged children were discussed in Chapter IV; they include the "academically-oriented" preschool of Bereiter and Engelmann, which teaches language through patterned drill; Cazden's teaching of language through expatiation; and Blank's description of an expansive one-to-one tutorial program. The programs of both the Institute for Developmental Studies and the Early Training Program discussed above also include language learning using traditional activities such as reading and telling stories to children and holding discussions as well as by using audiovisual aids, including tape recorders and Language Masters.

Developing Motivation for Learning

Cognitive skills and language development are not enough to alleviate the educational problems of disadvantaged children. Most educators

[22]Hanna D. Sonquist and Constance K. Kamii, "Applying Some Piagetian Concepts in the Classroom for the Disadvantaged," *Young Children*, Vol. 22, No. 4 (March 1967), 231–40.

[23]Sara Smilansky, *The Effects of Sociodramatic Play on Preschool Children* (New York: John Wiley and Sons, 1968).

[24]Kenneth Feigenbaum, "Activities to Teach the Concept of Conservation," *Young Children*, Vol. 24, No. 3 (January 1969), 151–53.

feel that the motivation of disadvantaged children must also be improved. Some programs do this by developing specific techniques of behavior modification. In the Early Training Program, positive reinforcement is used. Children may be given raisins or candy upon completion of a task, and these are later replaced by tokens, which can be accumulated and traded for toys or crayons. Still later, teachers use praise and social reinforcement instead of tangible rewards. Finally, it is hoped that the positive achievements of the children will become reinforcements themselves. Similar development of rewards to teach motivation are a part of other programs.

Although motivation training is considered a part of most programs, there are some who suggest that many of the gains of intelligence test scores resulting from programs of compensatory education result mainly from changes in children's motivation. Zigler and Butterfield have demonstrated that results can be improved without any intervention techniques other than changing motivation.

> The findings indicate that the deprived child suffers from an emotional and motivational deficit which decreases his usual intellectual performance to a lower level than we would expect from his intellectual potential as measured in an optimating test situation. ... It would appear that such institutions (as Head Start) should be assessed in terms of their success in fostering general competence among deprived children rather than their success in developing particular cognitive abilities alone.[25]

A child's motivation to perform academic tasks is closely related to the response he receives from his environment. If he is not expected to perform well, chances are he will not be motivated to perform well in that situation. Some educators and psychologists suggest that the school problems of the disadvantaged stem at least in part from the teachers' low expectations of them, thus creating a self-fulfilling prophecy. All programs of compensatory education expect children to perform better than they normally would, and the children generally do, no matter what the specific content of the program.

A recent study by Rosenthal and Jacobsen attempted to assess the impact of teacher expectancy on school performance and intelligence test scores. Children who were identified as "intellectual spurters" by the researchers were shown to spurt ahead academically even though they were surreptitiously so identified by random selection. The results seemed to be higher for the young children in school than for the older ones.[26]

25Edward Zigler and Earl C. Butterfield, "Motivational Aspects of Changes in IQ Test Performance of Culturally Deprived Nursery-School Children," *Child Development*, Vol. 39, No. 1 (March 1968), 12.

26Robert Rosenthal and Lenore Jacobsen, *Pygmalion in the Classroom* (New York: Holt, Rinehart & Winston, 1968).

This study raises some interesting issues both about the results of experimental intervention procedures with disadvantaged children and about the nature of the academic deficit of these children in school.

It is quite possible, for example, that the positive results of many of the experimental compensatory educational programs stem from a change in the beliefs relating to the educability of the children rather than to the power of any particular intervention strategy. The programs may work because the teachers believe they *will* work with these children.

The poor performance of a disadvantaged child in school may be a function of a negative expectation phenomenon that creates self-perpetuating school failure throughout his academic career. As he enters school he is seen as lacking in the skills needed for school success. The manifestations are evident, and some of them are real. The teacher then reflects back a lack of belief in the child's ability, causing him to refrain from attempting to achieve, thus reinforcing the teacher's original belief. This can continue to happen through the grades, with the child's records and reputation supporting the process through the years.

At present we can demonstrate that the phenomenon exists, although we do not know the process by which the self-fulfilling prophecy is communicated to children. In spite of the limitations in present knowledge we must still consider the possibility that the key to the improved academic performance of disadvantaged children is not the amelioration of learning deficits, but rather the improvement of their images in the minds of teachers who will then expect higher levels of academic performance from them.

SELECTING A PROGRAM FOR DISADVANTAGED CHILDREN

The number of available models of preschool programs for disadvantaged children has only been lightly sampled here. Many other alternatives exist. The question that must come to the mind of the practitioner is: Which program should I choose? All programs demonstrate some improvement in intellectual and language functioning on the part of children enrolled in them, although some programs report greater results than others.

One suggestion would be to subject available programs to the type of analysis suggested in the final chapter of this book. The identification of *assumptions, goals, curriculum, method, style, organization, effectiveness,* and *practicality* would help teachers develop the information necessary for a decision of whether or not to adopt a program. Teachers might also wish to combine aspects of different programs or adopt portions of innovative programs for inclusion into their existing program—for example, they may adopt a parent program or increase the number of intellectually oriented activities available to children. This may be a reasonable approach if innovative elements are compatible with the existing program. Teachers might also wish to look at aspects of programs that seem to have promise and attempt to modify their own programs along similar lines.

Language programs for disadvantaged children generally operate best on an individual tutorial or small group basis. Teachers might wish to change the organization of the class to allow this to happen. For such an approach to be effective, the organization has to change as well as the nature of the teacher-child interactions. This would require that the teacher learn both more about language development and how to behave differently toward the children. It is easier, unfortunately, to change the schedule of a class than to change the nature of teaching behavior.

Few programs as yet have had extensive replications, so one must always question the influence on reported results of both a "Hawthorne Effect" (an effect that results simply from the application of innovative practice) and experimenter bias, no matter how unconscious it may be. A number of recent studies only complicate the problem of selection for a teacher.

In an attempt to compare the results of divergent approaches to compensatory education for young disadvantaged children, Weikart organized a study in which he implemented three different approaches in parallel. One approach, identified as the *language development approach,* consisted of the "Bereiter-Engelmann curriculum." A second approach was a moderately structured program based upon developing cognitive skills similar to that reported by Sonquist and Kamii. A third approach was based upon traditional kindergarten practice and labeled a *unit-based* program. At the end of one year, children in all three programs manifested significant gains in IQ test scores when compared to children in a non-preschool group. There were no significant differences in average gains in IQ test scores or in language test scores among the groups, however.[27] These findings might suggest that as programs became public, the *type* of preschool intervention program provided to the children may not be significant as long as *some* systematic approach to instruction is used.

A study by Katz attempts to compare the results of "traditional" and "experimental" approaches to preschool education. Classroom observation indicated that the experimental teachers failed to fully apply their approach in the classroom. This suggests that a classroom situation labeled as a particular approach to early childhood education may be

[27]David P. Weikart, *A Comparative Study of Three Preschool Curricula* (Paper presented at the Biennial Meeting of the Society for Research in Child Development) Santa Monica, California, March 1969.

related less to the curriculum model that is being followed, and more to teachers' prior habits of classroom behavior.[28]

A study reported by Seifert comparing verbal interaction in a moderately structured and a highly structured preschool curriculum also suggests that these programs differ less in verbal interaction than one would expect.[29] If one postulates that the results of an educational experience is more a function of the human interactions that take place in the classroom than of any other element of the program, a position held by many practitioners in early childhood education, then it is possible that decisions about curricula might make less of a difference than is generally supposed. Since every curriculum and instructional method may be modified by any individual teacher's style, this might suggest that more attention ought to be given to the individual teacher's modification of programs in her classroom and her style of teaching than to the concerns about curriculum models and methods of instruction.

AFTER PRESCHOOL
INTERVENTION—WHAT?

Many preschool programs of compensatory education demonstrate gains in intellectual functioning at the termination of the program. Too often, any difference between children enrolled in such programs and those not enrolled tends to fade after a period of years. Some educators suggest that this fading phenomenon means that preschool programs make no basic difference and that test results showing immediate gains stem either from conscious or unconscious promoting for the test or increases in test scores that often occur naturally upon admission to school. Others suggest that the fading is a result of what happens or does not happen once the child enters the elementary grades. If the teachers of these children make no use of the new competencies derived from preschool programs, or if the elementary educational experience is a poor one, then no amount of preschool education can overcome its effects.

It has been suggested that any program of compensatory education must continue beyond the preschool years and into the primary grades, if not beyond. A number of programs have realized the need for continuity of educational experience through the primary grades. The Institute for Developmental Studies, for example, which began its work in preschool intervention originally, has continued the process of curriculum development through the primary grades. The National Laboratory in Early Childhood Education unit, located at the University of Arizona,

[28]Lilian G. Katz, "Children and Teachers in Two Types of Headstart Classes," *Young Children*, Vol. 24, No. 6 (September 1969), 242–49.

[29]Kelvin Seifert, "Comparison of Verbal Interaction in Two Preschool Programs," *Young Children*, Vol. 24, No. 6 (September 1969), 350–55.

begins its program of compensatory education in the primary grades, since it is located in a geographic area in which children seldom attend either a preschool or a kindergarten. In these programs, the curriculum of the primary grades has been modified to meet the needs of the children, with teaching methodology developed to build upon their strengths and improve the areas of deficit.

The federal government has also realized that Head Start programs alone are inadequate to meet the needs of disadvantaged children. Extending the ideas of Head Start into the kindergarten and primary grades, through the Follow-Through program, educators are seeking ways of maintaining intellectual and academic gains through the elementary school. As it is presently operating, Follow-Through is attempting to use a range of models of compensatory education, including both highly structured and highly flexible approaches. Many of the approaches are extensions of those used in preschool programs, such as the Becker-Engelmann model, the Community Development model of Levins, and the Parent Education model of Gordon. Primary programs such as the English Infant School and the Early Childhood Laboratory at the University of Arizona program have also been included.

It is hoped that growing out of the comparative evaluations of the effects of different programs, greater understanding of the educational problems of the disadvantaged and the ways in which these problems can be alleviated can be discovered. Follow Through, like Head Start, retains the concept of community involvement so that in each model the education problems of the children are not treated in isolation.

Although a great deal of research, basic and applied, has been done on the educational problems of the disadvantaged, there are still more questions than answers that prevail in the field. We are far from solving the educational problem of this important segment of the population, nor are we sure that we are even asking all the right questions. The need to alleviate the problems of the children and adults in the communities of the disadvantaged requires that programs be implemented based upon still inadequate information. Though the problems are so great that we must take chances on some of the innovations presently being applied, we must also be cautious in what we do as educators, for we are dealing with human beings in our research and service programs. The same cautions that apply in all human research must apply in our work with the disadvantaged.

The concept of *compensatory education* as well as the concept of *disadvantagement* upon which it is built is based upon the view that the differences in the behavior of poor and minority group children are pathological in nature; that the problem lies within the nature of the child. Cultural inferiority has often supplanted the idea of genetic inferiority in separating populations of children in school. Many educators are rejecting these concepts, accepting differences in values, social structure, and behavior that may exist without evaluating one culture as being "better" than the other.

If these differences are conceived of as cultural rather than pathological, then the problems lie not in the nature of the child but in the nature of the school that fails to educate the child, and the methods of instruction used by those schools. Although it may be difficult for professionals to admit that the best efforts of conventional educational methods might fail because of weaknesses inherent in the method, rather than because of the nature of the difficulty inherent in the client, such a possibility cannot be denied by those concerned with providing equal educational opportunities for all children.

SUGGESTED READING

BEREITER, CARL, AND SIEGFRIED ENGELMANN, *Teaching Disadvantaged Children in the Preschool.* Englewood Cliffs, N.J.: Prentice-Hall, Inc., 1966.

CHEYNEY, ARNOLD B., *Teaching the Culturally Disadvantaged in the Elementary School.* Columbus, Ohio: Charles E. Merrill Books, 1967.

CORBIN, RICHARD, AND MURIEL CROSBY, *Language Programs for the Disadvantaged.* Champaign, Ill.: National Council of Teachers of English, 1965.

COWLES, MILLY, *Perspectives in the Education of Disadvantaged Children.* Cleveland: World Publishing Company, 1967.

DEUTSCH, MARTIN, AND ASSOCIATES, *The Disadvantaged Child.* New York: Basic Books, 1967.

————, IRVIN KATZ, AND ARTHUR R. JENSEN, *Social Class, Race and Psychological Development.* New York: Holt, Rinehart & Winston, 1967.

FANTINI, MARIO D., AND GERALD WEINSTEIN, *The Disadvantaged: Challenge to Education.* New York: Harper and Row, 1968.

FEDDER, RUTH, AND JAQUELINE GABALDEN, *No Longer Deprived.* New York: Teachers College Press, 1970.

FROST, JOE L., AND GLENN R. HAWKES, *The Disadvantaged Child: Issues and Innovations,* 2nd ed. Boston: Houghton Mifflin Company, 1970.

GORDON, EDMUND W., AND DOXEY A. WILKERSON, *Compensatory Education for the Disadvantaged Programs and Practices: Preschool Through College.* New York: College Entrance Examination, 1966.

GRAY, SUSAN W., RUPERT A. KLAUS, JANIS O. MILLER, AND BETTYE J. FORRESTER, *Before First Grade: The Early Training Project for Culturally Disadvantaged Children.* New York: Teachers College Press, 1966.

HALSEY, A. H., JEAN FLOUD, AND C. ARNOLD ANDERSON, *Education, Economy, and Society—A Reader in the Sociology of Education.* New York: The Free Press, 1961.

HECHINGER, FRED M., ed., *Preschool Education Today*. Garden City, New York: Doubleday and Company, 1966.

HESS, ROBERT D., AND ROBERTA MEGER BEAR, *Early Education: Current Theory, Research and Action*. Chicago: Aldine Publishing Company, 1968.

KOZOL, JONATHAN, *Death at an Early Age*. Boston: Houghton Mifflin Company, 1967.

PASSOW, A. HARRY, MIRIAM GOLDBERG, AND ABRAHAM J. TANNENBAUM, *Education of the Disadvantaged: A Book of Readings*. New York: Holt, Rinehart & Winston, 1967.

PEARL, ARTHUR, AND FRANK RIESSMAN, *New Careers for the Poor—The Nonprofessional in Human Service*. New York: The Free Press, 1965.

POWLEDGE, FRED, *To Change a Child: A Report on the Institute for Developmental Studies*. Chicago: Quadrangle Books, 1967.

RIESSMAN, FRANK, *The Culturally Deprived Child*. New York: Harper & Row, 1962.

ROSENTHAL, ROBERT, AND LENORE JACOBSON, *Pygmalion in the Classroom*. New York: Holt, Rinehart & Winston, 1965.

SMILANSKY, SARA, *The Effects of Sociodramatic Play in Disadvantaged Preschool Children*. New York: John Wiley and Sons, 1968.

purport to improve the education of children are often disseminated in the field. These new curricula have goals established for them. Ideally, the teacher, in adopting a new curriculum or in maintaining an older one when alternatives are available, should evaluate all available programs in terms of the viability of the alternative goals as well as of the effectiveness of the program in helping children attain these goals. One mathematics program may have the development of computational skills as its prime goal, while another may stress an understanding of basic concepts over skill development. The teacher must determine which set of goals and in turn which program is more worthy.

EVALUATING PROGRAMS   Even at the nursery-school level, different programs exist. Some programs stress academic achievement, some social relations, and others combinations of goals. Judging a curriculum is a difficult task; the teacher may have neither the background of experience nor the competence to make judgments about a program. Sometimes evaluation is a joint effort involving teachers, administrators, and specialists in evaluation. Ideally, the teacher should participate in the evaluative process even when she does not have final responsibility for accepting or rejecting programs. She is the one who implements the programs and her judgment may be based upon sound practical considerations as well as theoretical background. Her intuitive knowledge of what children can use in a classroom is one source of information that can be brought to the evaluative process which may be lacking in the others involved.

Unfortunately, teachers often lack the information upon which to base decisions about programs for children. There are many programs available in early childhood education today, some of them encompassing the entire range of curricula, others concerned with but a single curriculum area. Although it is possible to wade through lengthy descriptions of all these programs and the materials used in them to cull the necessary information upon which to base decisions, few teachers are able to complete this cumbersome and time-consuming task. However, too often and curriculum committees are swayed by book salesmen or popular press, adopting programs without comparing alternatives because they familiar or have been endorsed by someone.

few attempts have been made to develop organized descriptions of available programs and program elements, and some of these descriptions contain evaluative statements as well. In most instances a single evaluative framework is used to compare many programs in relation to attributes. Chall, in her book, *Learning to Read: The Great Debate* discussed earlier, analyzes several reading programs in relation to

15

Evaluating Education in the Early Years

In the first three chapters of this book, the bases for early childhood education programs were stated. The chapters following have been an elaboration of ideas about how these goals might be achieved. Curriculum, classroom organization, materials, and equipment can all be marshalled by the teacher in developing her educational program. Each area of responsibility requires that significant decisions be made.

Teachers are often asked to select programs or program elements. They are also asked to make judgments about the ability of children to profit from educational programs. Assessments of the effects of educational programs are also expected. Each of these decisions requires that the teacher be involved in the process of evaluation and concerned with ways of recording and communicating the results of these evaluations.

The process of evaluation needs to be considered separately from the process of instruction, although the two are certainly related. Evaluation includes both the description and judgment of school programs and children's attainment. Central to the process of evaluation is a consideration of the goals of education and a determination of whether these goals are achieved.

Some programs have as their goals "supporting the optimal development of the individual," or "developing the ability to live effectively as a contributing member of society." While such goals are worthy, they are often exceedingly difficult, if not impossible, to assess at any but the most subjective or inferential level. The achievement of such a goal as "living effectively as a contributing member of society" cannot be manifested in school. Nor can the optimal development of the individual ever be judged during the duration of an early childhood program, if ever.

The ultimate goals of early childhood education cannot be achieved in any short-term program; they are only identifiable later in life. Few educational programs are assessed in any way approximating the *Eight-Year Study*, for example, which looked at the products of progressive high school education upon completion of college. Most teachers are asked to make judgements about their program and the achievement of children in their class at the end of an academic year or even at the completion of a unit of work which may have taken only a few days.

Long-range assessment is expensive, and at the same time has limited value for a teacher. To some extent, therefore, all education is based upon a faith that the goals of the program will ultimately be achieved. Neither taxpayers, nor parents, nor the academic community are willing to base their continued support of the schools on faith alone. In addition to faith, teachers can use logical analysis, determining whether or not the content of a program is consistent with its goals. They can also derive short-range objectives from long-range goals and use empirical analyses to determine the achievement of these goals. The social sciences have been able to provide useful tools that have been adapted to the evaluation of educational programs. They can be used to improve the observation and description portion of the evaluative process. The other portion of evaluation, that of making judgments, goes beyond the descriptive phase, although few good judgments can be made based upon poor or inadequate information.

Many programs state goals in specific behavioral terms that are immediately identifiable during the program's operation. Indeed, some psychologists feel that the identification of behavioral objectives based upon the requirements of later schooling are the only legitimate goals of education in the early years. The ability to make a specific judgment, categorizing an object by a visible attribute, or the ability to manifest a particular skill, such as reading a prescribed set of words, might constitute such a goal. Behavioral goals are attractive to those concerned with educational evaluation because their attainment is easily judged. Often a criteria level of attainment is also stated, thus defining even more clearly the judgments made. Information about attainment, which can be immediately supplied to the teacher, can be used to modify the program and improve its effectiveness. The availability of evaluation results is an extremely attractive aspect of the use of behavioral goals.

Behavioral goals are often not significant in themselves; they achieve their significance because of their relationship to broader goals of education, often neither behavioral nor observable in nature. The relationship between these observable goals and the more significant nonbehavioral

ones may be slight or great. Ultimately, this relationship is inferential in nature. The difference between using behavioral and nonbehavioral goals may, in the final analysis, be based upon the consciousness with which one uses inference and belief.

The exclusive use of predetermined behavioral objectives to judge educational achievement also tends to narrow education, for those activities that do not terminate in stated behavioral objectives may be considered to be unimportant or may even constitute interference with the achievement of stated objectives. Certain kinds of educational activities may also terminate in a range of behaviors rather than single behavioral patterns, some of which cannot be predetermined by the teacher. Children manifesting these divergent behaviors rather than those predetermined by the evaluators may be incorrectly judged as nonattainers. A distortion of an educational activity by narrowly defined behavioral goals might be seen in an activity organized to elicit divergent thinking the children in a class, but whose acceptable responses have been sta previously by the teacher. Another danger in the use of behavioral is in the possibility of having the teacher focus on behaviors which, overtly relating to the goals of the program may, in essence, be im only to a particular teacher's classroom organization. Although children to learn to attend to verbal and visual stimuli in the translating this into an objective such as "the ability to sit still to a story-reading session for a period of ten minutes" may serve to develop conforming behaviors. Young children can out sitting still. Legitimate criteria for attending would be gained from the story-reading situation rather than how li ment was manifest.

Teachers, nevertheless, need to state goals in such information about the effectiveness of their program The goals of a program should be attainable during program, whether this be a day or an academic ye ioral objectives can certainly improve the eval Though behavioral objectives may not be appr the program, there should be some degree of sp of goals so that the teacher can determine attain

In determining the objectives of a prog judgments about the acceptability of each ment level. She should be concerned wit performance in the program, but the eff as well as the effectiveness of its separa

[1]Teachers interested in improving th terms might refer to Robert F. Mager, *Prep* California: Fearon Publishers, 1962).

a number of significant attributes. Unfortunately, the evaluation includes only a sample of the reading programs available at that time, and many popular current reading programs are not included.[2]

A system for analyzing social science curricula has been developed by the Social Science Education Consortium. This system describes program attributes using the following categories:

1. *Descriptive characteristics*—The "nuts and bolts" of the curriculum.
2. *Rationale and objectives*—Why the program was created and what the anticipated outcomes are.
3. *Antecedent conditions*—The particular conditions under which the program might be successful.
4. *Content*—The specific changes intended in the knowledge, attitudes, and behavior of the students.
5. *Instructional theory and teaching strategies*—The underlying learning theory and teaching strategies and their relationship in the program.
6. *Overall judgments*—Evaluative judgments about the materials.

These broad categories are further broken down into subcategories for analysis. The category of *antecedent conditions*, for example, includes subcategories relating to pupil characteristics, teaching capabilities, and community requirements, school requirements, and the articulation of requirements.[3]

A number of social science curricula, including some designed for young children, have been analyzed using this framework. The analyses are available for a modest price from the Consortium.[4]

Another source of information about educational programs and program components is the Education Products Information Exchange (EPIE). The Exchange publishes a journal, the *EPIE Forum*, which contains information about the evaluation of programs and educational products as well as information about particular products.[5]

Information about educational programs can also be requested from the Educational Resources Information Centers. These ERIC Centers, supported by the U.S. Office of Education, collect information about educational programs in a particular area of education. Although the information available might not be as systematically developed as the ones provided by SSEC, they still can be a useful resource. Current ERIC clearinghouses are listed below.

[2]Jean Chall, *Learning to Read: The Great Debate* (New York: McGraw-Hill, 1967), pp. 336–55.

[3]W. William Stevens and William Fetsko, "A Curriculum Analysis System," *Social Science Education Consortium Newsletter*, No. 4 (February 1968), pp. 1–4.

[4]Social Science Education Consortium, 1424 15th Street, Boulder, Colorado, 80302.

[5]EPIE, P. O. Box 2379, Grand Central Station, New York, New York, 10017.

Adult Education
Syracuse University
107 Roney Lane
Syracuse, New York 13210

Counseling and Personnel Services
611 Church Street
Ann Arbor, Michigan 48104

The Disadvantaged
Teachers College, Box 40
Columbia University
New York, New York 10027

Early Childhood Education
University of Illinois
805 West Pennsylvania Avenue
Urbana, Illinois 61801

Educational Administration
Hendricks Hall
University of Oregon
Eugene, Oregon 97403

Educational Facilities
University of Wisconsin
606 State Street, Room 314
Madison, Wisconsin 53703

Educational Media and Technology
Institute for Communication Research
Stanford University
Stanford, California 94305

Exceptional Children
The Council for Exceptional Children
1499 Jefferson Davis Highway
Arlington, Virginia 22202

Higher Education
George Washington University
1 Dupont Circle
Suite 630
Washington, D.C. 20036

Junior Colleges
University of California at Los Angeles
405 Hilgard Avenue
Los Angeles, California 90024

Library and Information Sciences
University of Minnesota
2122 Riverside Avenue
Minneapolis, Minnesota 55404

Linguistics
Center for Applied Linguistics
1717 Massachusetts Avenue, N.W.
Washington, D.C. 20036

Reading
200 Pine Hall
School of Education
Indiana University
Bloomington, Indiana 47401

Rural Education and Small Schools
New Mexico State University
Box 3AP, University Park Branch
Las Cruces, New Mexico 88001

Science Education
Ohio State University
1460 West Lane Avenue
Columbus, Ohio 43221

Teacher Education
1 Dupont Circle
Suite 616
Washington, D.C. 20036

Teaching of English
National Council of Teachers of English
508 South Sixth Street
Champaign, Illinois 61820

Teaching of Foreign Languages
Modern Language Association of America
62 Fifth Avenue
New York, New York 10011

Vocational and Technical Education
Ohio State University
1900 Kenney Road
Columbus, Ohio 43212

Teachers might also wish to communicate directly with schools and agencies developing innovative programs as well as with the Head Start and Follow-Through programs. Many of these are reported in various education journals and at educational conferences.

Much of the information received from these sources will be difficult to compare. Teachers can develop their own framework for analysis of programs, which can improve their abilities to gather adequate program

15

Evaluating Education in the
Early Years

In the first three chapters of this book, the bases for early childhood education programs were stated. The chapters following have been an elaboration of ideas about how these goals might be achieved. Curriculum, classroom organization, materials, and equipment can all be marshalled by the teacher in developing her educational program. Each area of responsibility requires that significant decisions be made.

Teachers are often asked to select programs or program elements. They are also asked to make judgments about the ability of children to profit from educational programs. Assessments of the effects of educational programs are also expected. Each of these decisions requires that the teacher be involved in the process of evaluation and concerned with ways of recording and communicating the results of these evaluations.

The process of evaluation needs to be considered separately from the process of instruction, although the two are certainly related. Evaluation includes both the description and judgment of school programs and children's attainment. Central to the process of evaluation is a consideration of the goals of education and a determination of whether these goals are achieved.

Some programs have as their goals "supporting the optimal development of the individual," or "developing the ability to live effectively as a contributing member of society." While such goals are worthy, they are often exceedingly difficult, if not impossible, to assess at any but the most subjective or inferential level. The achievement of such a goal as "living effectively as a contributing member of society" cannot be manifested in school. Nor can the optimal development of the individual ever be judged during the duration of an early childhood program, if ever.

The ultimate goals of early childhood education cannot be achieved in any short-term program; they are only identifiable later in life. Few educational programs are assessed in any way approximating the *Eight-Year Study*, for example, which looked at the products of progressive high school education upon completion of college. Most teachers are asked to make judgements about their program and the achievement of children in their class at the end of an academic year or even at the completion of a unit of work which may have taken only a few days.

Long-range assessment is expensive, and at the same time has limited value for a teacher. To some extent, therefore, all education is based upon a faith that the goals of the program will ultimately be achieved. Neither taxpayers, nor parents, nor the academic community are willing to base their continued support of the schools on faith alone. In addition to faith, teachers can use logical analysis, determining whether or not the content of a program is consistent with its goals. They can also derive short-range objectives from long-range goals and use empirical analyses to determine the achievement of these goals. The social sciences have been able to provide useful tools that have been adapted to the evaluation of educational programs. They can be used to improve the observation and description portion of the evaluative process. The other portion of evaluation, that of making judgments, goes beyond the descriptive phase, although few good judgments can be made based upon poor or inadequate information.

Many programs state goals in specific behavioral terms that are immediately identifiable during the program's operation. Indeed, some psychologists feel that the identification of behavioral objectives based upon the requirements of later schooling are the only legitimate goals of education in the early years. The ability to make a specific judgment, categorizing an object by a visible attribute, or the ability to manifest a particular skill, such as reading a prescribed set of words, might constitute such a goal. Behavioral goals are attractive to those concerned with educational evaluation because their attainment is easily judged. Often a criteria level of attainment is also stated, thus defining even more clearly the judgments made. Information about attainment, which can be immediately supplied to the teacher, can be used to modify the program and improve its effectiveness. The availability of evaluation results is an extremely attractive aspect of the use of behavioral goals.

Behavioral goals are often not significant in themselves; they achieve their significance because of their relationship to broader goals of education, often neither behavioral nor observable in nature. The relationship between these observable goals and the more significant nonbehavioral ones may be slight or great. Ultimately, this relationship is inferential in nature. The difference between using behavioral and nonbehavioral goals may, in the final analysis, be based upon the consciousness with which one uses inference and belief.

The exclusive use of predetermined behavioral objectives to judge educational achievement also tends to narrow education, for those activities that do not terminate in stated behavioral objectives may be considered to be unimportant or may even constitute interference with the achievement of stated objectives. Certain kinds of educational activities may also terminate in a range of behaviors rather than single behavioral patterns, some of which cannot be predetermined by the teacher. Children manifesting these divergent behaviors rather than those predetermined by the evaluators may be incorrectly judged as nonattainers. A distortion of an educational activity by narrowly defined behavioral goals might be seen in an activity organized to elicit divergent thinking by the children in a class, but whose acceptable responses have been stated previously by the teacher. Another danger in the use of behavioral goals is in the possibility of having the teacher focus on behaviors which, while overtly relating to the goals of the program may, in essence, be important only to a particular teacher's classroom organization. Although we wish children to learn to attend to verbal and visual stimuli in the classroom, translating this into an objective such as "the ability to sit still and attend to a story-reading session for a period of ten minutes" may really only serve to develop conforming behaviors. Young children can attend without sitting still. Legitimate criteria for attending would be what the child gained from the story-reading situation rather than how little overt movement was manifest.

Teachers, nevertheless, need to state goals in such a way that some information about the effectiveness of their programs can be collected. The goals of a program should be attainable during the duration of the program, whether this be a day or an academic year. The use of behavioral objectives can certainly improve the evaluation of a program. Though behavioral objectives may not be appropriate for all areas of the program, there should be some degree of specificity in any statement of goals so that the teacher can determine attainment.[1]

In determining the objectives of a program, the teacher must make judgments about the acceptability of each child's performance or attainment level. She should be concerned with judging not just the child's performance in the program, but the effectiveness of the program itself as well as the effectiveness of its separate elements. New curricula that

---

[1]Teachers interested in improving the statement of objectives in behavioral terms might refer to Robert F. Mager, *Preparing Instructional Objectives* (Palo Alto, California: Fearon Publishers, 1962).

purport to improve the education of children are often disseminated in the field. These new curricula have goals established for them. Ideally, the teacher, in adopting a new curriculum or in maintaining an older one when alternatives are available, should evaluate all available programs in terms of the viability of the alternative goals as well as of the effectiveness of the program in helping children attain these goals. One mathematics program may have the development of computational skills as its prime goal, while another may stress an understanding of basic concepts over skill development. The teacher must determine which set of goals and in turn which program is more worthy.

EVALUATING PROGRAMS   Even at the nursery-school level, different programs exist. Some programs stress academic achievement, some social relations, and others combinations of goals. Judging a curriculum is a difficult task; the teacher may have neither the background of experience nor the competence to make judgments about a program. Sometimes evaluation is a joint effort involving teachers, administrators, and specialists in evaluation. Ideally, the teacher should participate in the evaluative process even when she does not have final responsibility for accepting or rejecting programs. She is the one who implements the programs and her judgment may be based upon sound practical considerations as well as theoretical background. Her intuitive knowledge of what children can use in a classroom is one source of information that can be brought to the evaluative process which may be lacking in the others involved.

Unfortunately, teachers often lack the information upon which to base decisions about programs for children. There are many programs available in early childhood education today, some of them encompassing the entire range of curricula, others concerned with but a single curriculum area. Although it is possible to wade through lengthy descriptions of all these programs and the materials used in them to cull the necessary information upon which to base decisions, few teachers are able to complete this cumbersome and time-consuming task. However, too often they and curriculum committees are swayed by book salesmen or popular articles, adopting programs without comparing alternatives because they are familiar or have been endorsed by someone.

A few attempts have been made to develop organized descriptions of available programs and program elements, and some of these descriptions contain evaluative statements as well. In most instances a single descriptive framework is used to compare many programs in relation to specific attributes. Chall, in her book, *Learning to Read: The Great Debate*, discussed earlier, analyzes several reading programs in relation to a number of significant attributes. Unfortunately, the evaluation includes only a sample of the reading programs available at that time, and many popular current reading programs are not included.[2]

A system for analyzing social science curricula has been developed by the Social Science Education Consortium. This system describes program attributes using the following categories:

1. *Descriptive characteristics*—The "nuts and bolts" of the curriculum.
2. *Rationale and objectives*—Why the program was created and what the anticipated outcomes are.
3. *Antecedent conditions*—The particular conditions under which the program might be successful.
4. *Content*—The specific changes intended in the knowledge, attitudes, and behavior of the students.
5. *Instructional theory and teaching strategies*—The underlying learning theory and teaching strategies and their relationship in the program.
6. *Overall judgments*—Evaluative judgments about the materials.

These broad categories are further broken down into subcategories for analysis. The category of *antecedent conditions,* for example, includes subcategories relating to pupil characteristics, teaching capabilities, and community requirements, school requirements, and the articulation of requirements.[3]

A number of social science curricula, including some designed for young children, have been analyzed using this framework. The analyses are available for a modest price from the Consortium.[4]

Another source of information about educational programs and program components is the Education Products Information Exchange (EPIE). The Exchange publishes a journal, the *EPIE Forum*, which contains information about the evaluation of programs and educational products as well as information about particular products.[5]

Information about educational programs can also be requested from the Educational Resources Information Centers. These ERIC Centers, supported by the U.S. Office of Education, collect information about educational programs in a particular area of education. Although the information available might not be as systematically developed as the ones provided by SSEC, they still can be a useful resource. Current ERIC clearinghouses are listed below.

[2]Jean Chall, *Learning to Read: The Great Debate* (New York: McGraw-Hill, 1967), pp. 336–55.

[3]W. William Stevens and William Fetsko, "A Curriculum Analysis System," *Social Science Education Consortium Newsletter*, No. 4 (February 1968), pp. 1–4.

[4]Social Science Education Consortium, 1424 15th Street, Boulder, Colorado, 80302.

[5]EPIE, P. O. Box 2379, Grand Central Station, New York, New York, 10017.

Adult Education
Syracuse University
107 Roney Lane
Syracuse, New York 13210

Counseling and Personnel Services
611 Church Street
Ann Arbor, Michigan 48104

The Disadvantaged
Teachers College, Box 40
Columbia University
New York, New York 10027

Early Childhood Education
University of Illinois
805 West Pennsylvania Avenue
Urbana, Illinois 61801

Educational Administration
Hendricks Hall
University of Oregon
Eugene, Oregon 97403

Educational Facilities
University of Wisconsin
606 State Street, Room 314
Madison, Wisconsin 53703

Educational Media and Technology
Institute for Communication Research
Stanford University
Stanford, California 94305

Exceptional Children
The Council for Exceptional Children
1499 Jefferson Davis Highway
Arlington, Virginia 22202

Higher Education
George Washington University
1 Dupont Circle
Suite 630
Washington, D.C. 20036

Junior Colleges
University of California at Los Angeles
405 Hilgard Avenue
Los Angeles, California 90024

Library and Information Sciences
University of Minnesota
2122 Riverside Avenue
Minneapolis, Minnesota 55404

Linguistics
Center for Applied Linguistics
1717 Massachusetts Avenue, N.W.
Washington, D.C. 20036

Reading
200 Pine Hall
School of Education
Indiana University
Bloomington, Indiana 47401

Rural Education and Small Schools
New Mexico State University
Box 3AP, University Park Branch
Las Cruces, New Mexico 88001

Science Education
Ohio State University
1460 West Lane Avenue
Columbus, Ohio 43221

Teacher Education
1 Dupont Circle
Suite 616
Washington, D.C. 20036

Teaching of English
National Council of Teachers of English
508 South Sixth Street
Champaign, Illinois 61820

Teaching of Foreign Languages
Modern Language Association of America
62 Fifth Avenue
New York, New York 10011

Vocational and Technical Education
Ohio State University
1900 Kenney Road
Columbus, Ohio 43212

Teachers might also wish to communicate directly with schools and agencies developing innovative programs as well as with the Head Start and Follow-Through programs. Many of these are reported in various education journals and at educational conferences.

Much of the information received from these sources will be difficult to compare. Teachers can develop their own framework for analysis of programs, which can improve their abilities to gather adequate program descriptions and make cross-program comparisons. The following framework, an elaboration of one developed earlier by the author, should prove helpful:

1.0 *Assumptions*—The basic "givens" of a program.
    1.1 *Assumptions about the client.* How does the program conceive of the child and of childhood? Are parents considered clients as well?
    1.2 *Assumptions about the educative process.* Are there specific theories of learning or of instruction underlying the program? Are they related?
    1.3 *Assumptions about the school.* Is the school conceived as a broad social agency or narrowly concerned with limited learnings?
    1.4 *Assumptions about the teacher.* Is the teacher considered as an instrument of the program or is she a major decision maker?

2.0 *Goals of the program*—The purposes of the program.
    2.1 *Long-range goals.* What long-range objectives are to be achieved?
    2.2 *Short-term objectives.* Are immediate objectives stated?
    2.3 *Relationship between the two.* Is there consistency between long- and short-range goals?
    2.4 *Degree of specificity of objectives.* Are objectives stated as observable behavior? Are objectives stated in other ways?

3.0 *Curriculum*—The content of the program.
    3.1 *Range of content of the program.* Is the program broadly conceived?
    3.2 *Sequence of learnings or experiences.* Is a specific sequence prescribed?

4.0 *Method*—The teaching strategies used.
    4.1 *Child-child transactions.* What is the nature of the child and child transaction behavior?
    4.2 *Child-teacher transactions.* What is the nature of the child and teacher transaction behavior?
    4.3 *Child-materials transactions.* What is the nature of the child and material transaction behavior?
    4.4 *Explicitness of prescriptions.* How explicitly are these transactions prescribed?

5.0 *Style*—The degree of personalization allowed in teaching the program.

6.0 *Organization*—The way in which elements are put together.
    6.1 *Scheduling.* How is time used?
    6.2 *Spatial organization.* How are resources deployed?
    6.3 *Grouping of children.* Are children grouped in some specific manner in the program?
    6.4 *Use of staff.* What kinds of staffing patterns are suggested?

7.0 *Effectiveness*
    7.1 *Achievement of goals.* Is there information about the degree to which the program can achieve its goals?
    7.2 *Comparisons with other programs.* How does the program compare with the available programs?

8.0 *Practicality*

    8.1 *Cost of program.* How much does the program cost to implement?

    8.2 *Staff requirements.* How many staff members are needed? What sorts of qualifications are required?

    8.3 *Space requirements.* How much space is needed?

    8.4 *Materials requirements.* What kinds of materials must be used in the program? How many?

    8.5 *Availability of supportive resources.* Are the necessary materials available? Are resource materials and persons available to support the program?

EVALUATING CHILDREN   In addition to the evaluation of programs, the teacher has prime responsibility for the evaluation of children. In this evaluation, two basic concerns can be identified: (1) the *ability* of children to benefit from instructional experiences and (2) the *degree* to which they benefit. The former leads to a judgment about readiness for learning; the latter to a judgment about school achievement. In either case the teacher usually has to make a judgment based upon observations of each child's behavior. If we want to judge what children can do, the best way is to observe everything they do. Observational data-gathering expeditions are possible and can yield a great amount of information, but they are cumbersome, time-consuming and expensive.[6] The amount of time and energy necessary to conduct such observations would completely remove the teacher from any teaching.

Instead, a teacher can sample the behavior and products of children and generalize about readiness and achievement from the sample selected. This sampling procedure resembles that used by researchers and public opinion poll takers and, if properly conducted, can provide information in which the teacher can place a high degree of confidence. In order to achieve this level of confidence, she must be sure that the sample she selects is representative of the total population of possible products and behaviors; in order to insure representativeness, a systematic procedure must be adopted.

One systematic way of collecting samples of behavior is to administer a test which contains a select number of items to which a child can respond. These items are a sample drawn from a larger number of possible items. The teacher should select broadly from all possible learnings to assure representativeness. Administration of tests is useful because the same behaviors are sampled in all the children, and this not only provides information about what each child has learned, but also allows the teacher to make comparisons among all the children tested.

[6]See Roger B. Barker and Herbert F. Wright, *One Boy's Day* (New York: Harper & Row, 1951).

Although one often thinks of classroom tests as written examinations, they are not necessarily administered in writing. A teacher might administer a test to a group of nursery-school children by taking each child aside and asking him a set of standard questions. She can also make use of standardized tests, developed and refined through application to a large population of children.

Other ways of sampling behavior do not collect comparable samples from each child. Observations of classroom behavior is one way of collecting information, as is the collection of samples of children's products. The teacher must be careful that the techniques used are appropriate for the kind of information gathered about the children and that it is truly representative. This requires that the techniques have a degree of reliability—that is, the instruments, whether tests or observations, should collect essentially similar data when used on different occasions and when used by different persons. Techniques used must also be valid; they should collect the kind of information that the teacher purports they collect.

Finally, the methods the teacher uses to collect information about the children should be practical. It is of no use for her to develop methods of studying children that are too cumbersome to use in the classroom or that require equipment not generally available to her. Simple techniques that do not require the expenditure of a large amount of time and effort are best. The teacher's role is a varied one and she is called upon to do much more than evaluate children and programs during the day.

Too often teachers think of evaluation as the administration of tests at the end of the school year or at the end of a unit of work. The results of such tests may clearly summarize what children have learned during the period prior to their administration, and provide an important source of information to pass on to the next year's teachers. Other means of gathering evaluative information need to be used by the teacher as an aid to her instruction.

Primary classroom teachers often use informal inventory techniques to assess a child's ability to read or to perform computational skills; such inventories provide them with a baseline from which to begin instruction. Some teachers also administer readiness or developmental tests at the beginning of kindergarten or first grade to provide a similar baseline for planning.

Evans has identified a number of tests that have been used frequently in early childhood education research. These include:

Basic Concept Inventory. Chicago: Follett, 1968.

Cincinnati Autonomy Test Battery. Cincinnati, Ohio: Cincinnati University, Department of Psychology, 1966.

Illinois Test of Psycholinguistic Processes, rev. ed. Urbana, Ill.: University of Illinois Press, 1970.

Metropolitan Readiness Tests. New York: Harcourt, 1965.

Peabody Picture Vocabulary Test. Minneapolis: American Guidance Service, 1959.

Preschool Inventory. Princeton, N.J.: Educational Testing Service, 1967.

Stanford-Binet Intelligence Scale. New York: Houghton Mifflin, 1960.

Torrance Tests of Creative Thinking. Princeton, N.J.: Personnel Press, 1966.[7]

Some of these tests can be administered by classroom teachers as part of their evaluation procedures. A number of other tests are also available.

Administration of tests early in a child's career has certain inherent pitfalls. Many young children are unfamiliar with testing procedures and do not know appropriate response behavior, thus making test results invalid. It may be well to postpone administering tests to young children until they have been in school long enough to have been acculturated to the ways of the school.

A teacher may use ongoing assessment procedures as an aid to planning; she may assess her program at the end of each day in order to plan activities for the following day.

Most often, the assessment is made on a "gut level," the teacher evaluating on the basis of whether or not the day went well or poorly for her. The most outstanding incidents may be recalled and recorded, whether representative or not. Improvement of evaluation techniques and planning are implemented by the use of systematic means of collecting and recording information.

The teacher needs a broad repertoire of techniques for evaluation. She should understand the uses of each and apply the appropriate ones for each occasion and need. Both standardized and nonstandardized tools should be available to her.

A number of fine standardized tests are available to teachers for use in the primary grades. Some are designed to be administered to a group of children at one time, others require individual administration.

These tests are usually standardized by being administered to a sample population of children representative of the total population of children in the United States. Judgments can then be made about how a child's score compares to those of the standardizing group. This fact should be taken into consideration in the interpretation of a test as well as in making a decision about whether or not to use a test. If the children in a particular class are significantly different from the standardized population, the results of the test need to be carefully interpreted to provide useful information to the teacher.

The tests available for use in the early years of schooling can gen-

[7]Ellis D. Evans, *Contemporary Influences in Early Childhood Education* (New York: Holt, Rinehart & Winston, 1971), pp. 337–41.

erally be categorized into developmental tests, intelligence tests, readiness tests, and achievement tests. Although these three are related to one another, there are differences in the tests themselves as well as in the purposes for which they are administered. Developmental tests are most often given to young children. Intelligence tests are usually used to determine the level of general intellectual behavior. Readiness tests are specific to one or more areas of learning for which predictions are made, and items on these tests may be more sensitive to specific instruction. The term readiness, often used glibly by teachers in early childhood education, is generally conceived as the state in which a child can benefit from instruction. Such a determination is usually based upon his maturational state, his achievement of prior learnings, and his motivation for learning. Most tests used to determine readiness assess both maturation and prior learning. The assessment of motivation is most often made informally by the teacher.

Developmental Tests

Developmental tests are used to determine the degree of maturation. Observation of a child's physical characteristics, such as body proportions or development of the wrist bone, can be used to assess maturation. Most tests, however, consist of items that require children's actual performance. Ilg and Ames' book, *School Readiness* (New York: Harper and Row, 1965), contains a series of tasks for children to perform. From an analysis of a child's performance on these tasks a teacher might determine if he is mature enough to profit from school instruction. The tasks described in many of Piaget's reports may also be considered a series of developmental tests. These tests have been used primarily to determine level of intellectual development.

The information from developmental tests is useful in deciding whether a child is ready for a particular school experience or whether he can handle the content of a particular set of instructional tasks. However, teachers should be careful not to exclude children from formal educational experiences because of lack of maturation. Human development is highly plastic and a child's experiences tend to modify his development. Rather than exclusion, what may be needed are differentiated educational opportunities.

Intelligence Tests

Intelligence tests contain sets of tasks that require using learned skills for adequate performance at specific levels. The assumption underlying them is that if all children have equal opportunities to learn skills, the differences in levels of performance are the result of differences in inherent ability. Though it is evident that all children do not have the same inherent ability, it is equally evident that many do not have the same opportunities to learn the skills sampled in intelligence tests. These tests generally seem to favor the children of white, middle-class background and less adequately sample the inherent abilities of disadvantaged and minority-group children.

Intelligence tests were originally designed to provide a way of predicting the academic achievement of children. Most intelligence tests can predict academic performance well when there is no significant change in the child's educational circumstances. Evidence suggests that when these circumstances are varied, predictive ability does not hold up as well. Moving children with low IQ levels from an educationally dull environment to one that is educationally stimulating may not only increase educational performance but may also lead to increases in scores on intelligence tests.

Significant decisions about a child's education are often based upon the results of the intelligence tests administered when he is young. For this reason, great care needs to be taken in interpreting and using the results of these tests. It is unfortunate for children to be penalized for not being able to score well on these tests because they have been denied the opportunity to learn those things sampled in the test. Although intelligence tests do not create discrimination, their careless use can perpetuate unequal educational practices in schools. Improper use of intelligence tests can lead to the creation of a cycle of educational disadvantagement from which a child cannot escape, for the opportunity that would allow him to excel in later tests are denied *because* he does not excel in the test.

Readiness Tests

Readiness tests are used to assess the child's ability to profit from instruction. The most prevalently used readiness tests are in the area of reading. Since readiness is conceived not merely as a maturational state but as a state in which a child has achieved some prerequisite learnings, these tests are actually early achievement tests. They can be used for diagnostic purposes as well as a basis for making decisions about beginning instruction.

In addition to using tests, teachers can also use a range of informal techniques for determining the appropriateness of planned learning experiences for children. Observations of children in class, such as those described later, can produce information about readiness as well as about achievement. Since these two concepts are so related, any information about a child's achievement also provides information about his pre-disposition for further learning.

ASSESSING ACHIEVEMENT In making judgments about what a child has learned, the teacher uses many techniques and instruments, which include the "formal" procedures of testing as well as the less formal procedures of observing behavior and collecting products.

Achievement Tests

Standardized achievement tests are used to assess a child's or class's achievement in the areas of academic learning. Such tests are designed for administration at the primary grades or beyond. A number of achievement tests are available for different curricular areas, and teachers may select a full battery of tests or administer only a single subtest.

In interpreting achievement tests, teachers should be aware that they do not sample the total curriculum offerings of the school but generally limit themselves to academic skills. Other areas of the school learning, of equal importance, may not be sampled. Teachers need to insure that inappropriate use of test results does not distort the program offerings.

In interpreting tests, teachers must know the meaning of the concept of *grade level* used in these tests. The achievement test, like the intelligence test, is generally standardized by being administered to a sample group of children representing the total range of children at each level nationally. This population includes children from rural and urban areas, from advantaged and disadvantaged homes, and from all geographic areas. All the scores are averaged together to create a grade level norm. Since this is an average, half the tests scores fall above the grade norm and half fall below. Within the standardizing population, one can often find differences in average test scores of subgroups identifiable by geographic area, degree of urbanization, socioeconomic status, and ethnic group.

Grade-level norms are only useful to the degree that the population tested reflects the standardized population. To the degree that any class of children differs from that population, the norms become less meaningful as a standard. Schools often find that it is useful to establish their own norms rather than use standardized norms.

It is also important to note that norms are descriptive of a population at a particular time. They need not set expectation. It is possible for every group to exceed the norms on almost every achievement test under optimal learning conditions, assuming this achievement is the teacher's goal.

Although standardized tests have much to commend them as a method of gathering data, there are times when nonstandardized means are more appropriate. Teachers should develop many formal and informal techniques to systematically sample children's learning. Standardized tests may provide a way of assessing learning and of comparing a single class or child to a large population of children, but nonstandardized methods of assessment can provide process data that can be used to improve instruction. If evaluation is used as a diagnostic tool in planning, this type of data collection becomes invaluable. Nonstandardized means of data collection include teacher-developed tests, observational techniques, checklists, rating scales, sociometric techniques, and collections of children's products.

Teacher-developed Tests

Teachers can create their own tests when they wish to collect a comparable sample of behavior from all the children in the class. Careful construction of the test is necessary to insure that the desired behavior is being elicited. The teacher also needs to make sure that the items on the test are representative of those she wishes to evaluate. Although she may not formally determine the validity and reliability of each test she develops, she should keep these attributes of a good test in mind.

A test may be a paper-and-pencil device administered to all children at one time or a set of oral questions administered individually. A teacher who wishes to evaluate a field trip may develop a list of questions to ask each child independently. Using the same questions will draw a comparable sample of knowledge from each child. Pictures of objects may be used as stimuli to elicit responses.

Although similar questions might be asked of all the children in a group discussion situation, the teacher would not be sure if the response elicited was the result of the trip experience or of hearing other children's responses in the discussion. Informal test situations allow her to know about all of the children, not just the ones that continually volunteer verbal responses.

Observational Techniques

Teachers may take time at the end of a day to record the significant occurrences of the school session. They can note what happened to individual children or individual problems that arose. Such anecdotal records are helpful in thinking through a school day and in planning for future activities, but relying on such records alone can be dangerous. Human minds tend to be forgetful, and memory is selective. It is the extraordinary, rather than the normal, that is etched upon teacher's memories, and an unrepresentative picture of a child's behavior may result. The use of running records—on-the-spot observations of occurrences—is far superior in recreating a true picture of the day. It is helpful for the teacher to learn techniques for taking running records.[8]

Direct observations of children's behavior has the advantage of giving teachers clues about the process of children's learning. A careful recording of the interactions that take place between a child and other children or between a child and a set of instructional materials can provide the basis for judgments made about how a child is thinking or feeling. The results of such observations can be compared over time to judge changes in behavior for individual children.

Observing and recording children's actions is time-consuming. Teachers are busy enough working with children without being expected to record their behavior, yet this sort of record provides an important source of information upon which to build and evaluate programs. Teachers should develop ways that are practical, take up little time, and still provide an adequate picture of children's behavior.

One way to do this is to systematically sample behavior. Selecting children in some order and keeping a running record of each child for just a few minutes a day, observing possibly two or three children on any one day, will lead to a large file of behavior records over a semester. These records should be descriptive in nature. After recording the descriptions, the teacher may note interpretations and comments on behavior separately. In this way she will always be able to return to the source of her judgments, for she may want to reinterpret a child's behavior as she becomes more familiar with him.

The key to the successful collection of running records is in the regular, systematic sampling of all the children and in the careful reporting of behavior in descriptive rather than judgmental terms.

Observational Scales and Checklists

When teachers are concerned about specific behaviors, less descriptive forms of observation can be used. A teacher who wishes to study aggressive behavior in her classroom may simply use a frequency tally, recording a mark every time an aggressive act is observed. If these are identified by the actual time they occurred or by the activity with which

[8]See Dorothy H. Cohen and Virginia Stern, *Observing and Recording the Behavior of Young Children* (New York: Teachers College Press, 1956).

they were related, the teacher may be able to judge not only the amount of aggressive behavior occurring in the class, but also at what time and during which activities most aggression takes place. A similar checklist could be used to determine the frequency of other kinds of behavior, such as helping behavior or creative activity.

Teachers might wish to determine the kinds of materials used and the frequency with which children become involved in particular learning centers during an activity period in the school. Creating a code that includes a symbol for each activity and systematically observing the classroom and recording the placement and activity of each child at intervals (for example, five minutes after the period is underway, halfway through the period, and five minutes before the period ends) will yield information about the involvement of particular children in classroom activities.

The children can assume responsibility for some of the recording, too. If a checklist is available for each activity, listing the children's names and leaving space for them to enter a mark each time they participate, they can provide the teacher with a great deal of information about their own activities.

A range of simple scales and checklists can be devised by the teacher, depending upon what kind of information she wishes to observe and what uses she has for the information. Such information becomes invaluable in planning programs, in making decisions about the children, and in reporting a child's school experiences to his parent.

Sociometric Techniques

Although teachers are concerned with children's academic achievement, they should also be concerned with social behavior, for social goals are important in education as well. In order to assess this, teachers can make use of sociometric techniques to provide such information.

A simple way of determining the social structure of the class is to ask each child a set of questions to elicit his choice of friends. Such questions as "Whom would you like to play with outside?" "Whom would you like to have sit near you at snack time?" or "Whom would you like to invite home after school?" might be used at the nursery or kindergarten level. Appropriate questions for older children can be developed as well.

The children's responses to the questions asked can be plotted on a chart, which will eventually determine the most popular and least popular children and what groupings of friendships exist in the class.

Children's social relationships are not as stable as those of adults. Sociometric techniques, therefore, provide less reliable information about children. Although children may be able to respond to questions about activity mates, best friends can easily change from day to day. Observations of interactions in classroom situations where children are free to select playmates results in information that can be charted into a sociogram, but teachers need to be careful to collect a number of such observations over a period of time, looking for evidence of stable relationships and shifts that might occur as a result of program changes.

Collecting Pupil Products

Another way of sampling the children's learning in the classroom is to systematically collect the products of their work. Children's drawings and paintings, their stories and mathematics work, as well as the reports that they have prepared, may be collected and stored for later study. Such a cumulative collection allows the teacher to review progress as well as to make judgments about students' work at any point in time. The collection of children's products must be systematic; the great temptation is to allow the child to carry each product home, leaving the teacher without an important data source. A painting or a story can be periodically selected to keep in school, and if children are told why materials are being collected, they will usually not resist the acquisition. Selecting a child's picture each week or two and labeling it as to producer, date, and circumstance of production helps, and if the teacher provides a portfolio for each child, storage problems are minimized.

Some products are hard to collect. A clay bowl will not store easily in a portfolio, and a child's block construction cannot be saved. A verbal production disappears immediately. Productions of this kind can be collected on tape or film, however, and saved as evidence of what the child has done in addition to collected products.

JUDGING CHILDREN   The collection of evaluative data is only one step in the process of evaluation. The data must be interpreted by the teacher and judgments made about them. Finally, plans for action may result from these interpretations.

Teachers use evaluation data to make decisions about children's programs. If the children have achieved the goals of a unit of study, the teacher can confidently move on to new work. If they have not, she may wish to plan some special activities or repeat activities. If there is a degree of involvement in the range of activities she provides, she can comfortably continue. If children are not involved in using materials provided, then she may need to modify her program. The constant feedback from the information collected tells her how successful her planning has been and provides clues for the introduction of new program elements.

The information collected on each child can also provide the basis for differentiated educational activities. As the teacher becomes aware of each child's skills and abilities as well as his interests and behavior patterns, she can plan with this specific knowledge in mind. Programming becomes more meaningful and closer to the needs of the particular children in a class. Pacing is one dimension of differential programming that can grow out of continued evaluation. Other forms of program differentiation can also accrue.

The results of evaluation are often shared with a number of persons. The teacher may be asked to communicate these results to future teachers of the children in her class, to ancillary personnel in the school, to the school principal, and to the children's parents. The need for communication and for later reference requires that the teacher use some record-keeping system. Many schools maintain cumulative record folders on children, and teachers may supplement these with their own records. A good record-keeping system is one in which significant information may be found easily.

Cumulative Record Folders

Schools often prepare a record folder for a child at the time he enters that will remain with him throughout his career in that school system. The information from this folder may also be passed on when the child moves to another school. A cumulative record folder generally contains significant information about the child and his family, as well as information about his school achievement. Personal information may include such data as date and place of birth, names of parents and siblings, and addresses at which the child has lived. Health data including height and weight, collected regularly, dates of immunizations, and the results of medical and dental examinations might also be recorded. If there is a referral to an outside agency, there will be a place to note this also.

These record folders also contain space in which each teacher may record significant information about the child during each school year. Information about academic achievement and the results of standardized tests are recorded. The teacher is usually able to write descriptive comments about the child's school behavior and attitudes as well. In some schools, test results are also recorded in these folders. Sometimes there is space provided for recording the results of parent-teacher conferences as well.

Cumulative record folders may also contain test score sheets, letters from parents, and samples of teachers' observations. Care must be taken that the teacher includes only those things that are judged to be of lasting importance in understanding the child, otherwise the folders can become quickly filled with trivia that cloud rather than clarify the understanding of the child.

It is important that the teachers include the sources of judgments about children as well as the results of these judgments. Teachers vary in their interpretations of children's behavior and the judgments they make about children's acts. It is helpful if they communicate the sources of interpretations so that future teachers may judge as well.

Maintaining Classroom Records

In addition to the cumulative record folder, teachers keep a variety of records on the children that may not necessarily follow the child on to later classes. Records of daily attendance are generally required, allowing the teacher to keep track of absences and the reasons for them. The form of attendance record used varies among schools. New teachers should become quickly familiar with the procedures used in their schools —some schools require that all absences be accounted for, or children may have to submit a release from a physician before entering school after certain illnesses. Even when a child is not seriously ill, it is wise for a teacher to contact the family if the child is absent even for a short period of time. Such absences may signal family crisis. At times, families may even move from a community without notifying the school. Brief contact with the family helps the teacher understand the reasons for absence and may provide clues to help her or the child.

Teachers often have the children tally their participation in specific activities. A check next to a child's name each time he uses the easel or reads a book is a record of his activity, and such a tally can provide significant information about his use of room resources and can provide the basis for changing activities or suggesting new activities. While teacher and child may both be involved in tallying, the teacher may wish to transfer the results of the tally to a more compact form than one that a child might comfortably use.

The results of teacher's observations are also an important record of the child's activities. A file of 5″ × 8″ cards can often be used for such purposes; most observations are short and can easily fit on one or two such cards. Organizing these in a card file allows the teacher to leaf through quickly to review her understanding of the child.

The regular recording of the results of evaluation will insure that the teacher has the information available that she will later need. How records are kept is determined by their later use. A review of records may show that a teacher has not attended closely to a child or a group of children for a period of time. Knowing this, she can focus on these children, thus insuring a continued familiarity with all of the children over the year. Careful record-keeping also allows the teacher to find information easily that she will need at a later date. With a teacher's life so full during the day, it is too easy to misplace important documents, or to forget significant observations that have been made.

Records are important not only for the teacher's decision making but also as a way of justifying the decisions she has made to others. Because teaching is a public trust, teachers are being called upon more and more to justify their professional acts. Demands may come from supervisors or from the parents and the community the school serves. Although they may feel a need to guard their professional roles, teachers, as all other professionals, are accountable. The ability to document the sources of decisions and judgments is a requirement that the public can make on the professional, and teachers must be prepared to meet this requirement.

REPORTING TO PARENTS   Parents are interested in the progress of their children in school, in varying degrees. These contacts represent only one part of the teacher's relationship with parents, but they are important and require the utmost in care and honesty.

An ideal report to a parent should be easy to devise, requiring a minimum of time and effort to administer, and yet be comprehensive in its content. It should communicate clearly and unequivocally the child's behavior and learning in school without being burdensome to read or requiring the parent's comprehension of professional language.

These requirements are easier to state than to put into practice; it is difficult to communicate clearly when the teacher and the parent may have different referents for the same words. It is also difficult to be fully descriptive when it is necessary to report on thirty or more children several times during the year. And it is difficult to pinpoint progress without seeming unnecessarily judgmental.

Most reporting systems in practice are the result of compromise. They are systems which are not too difficult to administer and which can communicate clearly. Teachers seem unsatisfied with almost all reporting systems, however. Perhaps there is no ideal system. Most schools tend to use report cards, descriptive letters to parents, or parent conferences as ways of reporting; often these are used in some combination.

Report Cards

Many primary classes and kindergartens use report cards as one way of reporting. These cards are relatively simple to complete and communicate fairly well to parents. A report card may contain lines representing various areas of pupil achievement, including reading, writing, and other subject matter areas. Schools might also sometimes include certain behavior characteristics or study habits in their areas for reporting.

Symbols are often used to report a child's achievement, such as letter grades A to D or E, or *U* for unsatisfactory and S for satisfactory achievement. Additional symbols for improvement or high achievement can also be used.

Though it is simple to assign a letter grade, it is often difficult to determine exactly what a letter grade or symbol communicates. If there are grade-level standards of performance expected of every child in the school, then performance level is fairly well communicated by the report card. It is difficult to know, however, if a child is operating at his expected capacity, above it, or below it. If children are graded according to the teacher's estimate of their capability, then the letter or symbol will mean something different for each child and the common base in communication breaks down.

Despite the limitations of report cards, both parents and teachers often report that they like to use them, possibly a result of the security built by years of tradition, but schools frequently find that they must augment this type of communication.

Descriptive Letters

A report card can communicate a child's level of performance; it cannot communicate the qualitative aspects of school work, however. Teachers may use descriptive letters to tell parents more about the quality and content of the child's work. A letter can often provide a fuller picture for the parent. It might contain information about the child's learning style, about the books he has read, the materials he has used, or the nature of the interactions he has had with others. It can also communicate to the parent the nature of the experiences the child has undergone in school, something that the parents of uncommunicative children may not know. Teachers may write individual letters about each child. Too often they run out of descriptive phrases for each child, however, and these letters can become stereotyped in their descriptions. Sometimes teachers duplicate a single letter communicating to the parents what the class as a whole has done during the year, supplementing this with individual reports through report cards or conferences.

Parent Conferences

The most communicative (but also the most time-consuming) means of reporting is the parent conference. In a conference, parent and teacher can sit face-to-face and discuss mutual concerns about the child. Any misunderstandings can be instantly corrected, and the teacher has immediate feedback as to the quality of the communication.

Parents conferences are often used in the nursery and kindergarten level because of the lack of grade-level standards upon which to base a grade symbol. This requires that descriptive reporting take place.

Reporting is really only one consequence of a system of evaluation. The major impact of the teacher's evaluation is in the improvement of the educational experience of each child. By knowing her children and the results of classroom activities of each individual, the teacher can return to her planning, continuing activities that have proved successful, replacing unsuccessful ones with new activities, and continuing to extend the learning opportunities of the children in her class. A realistic picture of classroom activities and their consequences can help her provide continually richer educational opportunities to children during their early years in school.

SUGGESTED READING

ALMY, MILLIE, *Ways of Studying Children*. New York: Columbia University Press, 1959.

BUROS, OSCAR K., *Tests in Print*. Highland Park, N.J.: Gryphon Press, 1961.

COHEN, DOROTHY AND VIRGINIA STERN, *Observing and Recording the Behavior of Young Children*. New York: Teachers College Press, 1969.

GAGE, N. L., ed., *Handbook of Research on Teaching*. Chicago: Rand-McNally, 1963.

MAGER, ROBERT F., *Preparing Instructional Objectives*. Palo Alto, Calif.: Fearon Publishers, 1962.

McDONALD, FREDERICK J., *Educational Psychology*, 2nd ed. Belmont, Calif: Wadsworth Publishing Co., 1965.

MUSSEN, P. H., ed., *Handbook of Research Methods in Child Psychology*. New York: Wiley Publishers, 1960.

STAKE, ROBERT E., "The Countenance of Educational Evaluation," *Teachers College Record*, Vol. 68, No. 4 (April 1967), 523–40.

SUCHMAN, J. R., *Observation and Analysis in Child Development: A Laboratory Manual*. New York: Harcourt Brace and World, 1959.

Index

Disadvantaged children:
  absent fathers, 280
  academic readiness, teaching for,
    291–93
  associate vs. cognitive teaching
    approach, 282, 292–93
  changes in role of school, effects
    of, 277–78
  characteristics of, 84–89
  civil rights movement and, 275
  community structure, changing of,
    291–93
  cultural inferiority concept, 307–8
  custodial care programs, 290–91
  definition of, 274, 278–79, 281,
    301–302
  educational programs for, 290–300
  health of, 285–86
  increasing responsiveness of
    schools to, 289–90
  infants, working with, 288–89
  integration of schools, 275
  intellectual development, teaching
    for, 294–96
  intelligence of, 276, 282–83
  intelligence tests and, 315–16
  intervention techniques, develop-
    ment of, 283–84
  language, teaching of, 63–65, 296,
    299
  linguistic code of, 282
  motivation, development of, 296–98
  "out-of-classroom needs," providing
    for, 284–85
  parents, working with, 287–88
  parents' rearing practices, 283
  physical characteristics of, 279–80
  preschool programs:
    need for follow-through, 300–301
    placing children in, 290–91
  psychological characteristics of,
    281–83
  psychological theories regarding,
    276
  social characteristics of, 280–81
  strategies in working with, 284–90
  unemployment of parents, 278
  (see also) Head Start, Operation
Discipline
  behavior modification, approach to,
    251
  goals of, 249

Discipline (*cont.*)
  lack of consistent standards, 248–49
  noise, 248
  recommended procedure, 249–51
  redirection, 249–50
  reinforcement, 249
  rewards for good behavior, 251
Discussion sessions, 68–70
Dramatic play, 66–68, 166–67,
    206–208, 212
Dramatics, creative, 70–71

E

Early Training Program (George
    Peabody College), 288, 294–95
Education Products Information
    Exchange (EPIE), 309
Educational Research Council of
    Greater Cleveland, 161n.
Educational Resources Information
    Centers (ERIC), 309–10
Eight-Year Study of Progressive High
    Schools, 49–50, 306
Elaborated linguistic code, 62
Elementary Science Study, 125–27
Engelmann, Siegfried, 49, 64, 292–94,
    296, 299, 301
EPIE (Education Products Information
    Exchange), 309
Equipment and supplies, 235–38
  criteria for selecting, 236
  obtaining, 235–36
ERIC (Educational Resources Infor-
    mation Centers), 309–10
Erickson, Frederick, 62
Erikson, Erik H., 51
Etch-a-Sketch boards, 106
Evaluation:
  of academic level, 248
  of children, 312–17
    developmental tests, 315
    intelligence tests, 315–16
    readiness tests, 316–17
  classroom records, maintaining,
    323–24
  cumulative record folders, 322–23
  of goals, 305–308
  and judging of children, 321–24
  nature of process, 305
  parents, reporting to, 324–26